Shopping Centers and Other Retail Properties

Investment, Development, Financing, and Management

Edited by

JOHN R. WHITE

AND

KEVIN D. GRAY

*in Association with the
Urban Land Institute*

John Wiley & Sons, Inc.
New York • Chichester • Brisbane • Toronto • Singapore

Library of Congress Cataloging-in-Publication Data:

ISBN 0-471-04002-9

Printed in the United States of America

10 9 8 7 6 5 4 3 2 1

Printed and bound by Malloy Lithographing, Inc.

Contributors

Roger D. Blackwell is a professor of marketing at the Ohio State University and president of Roger Blackwell Associates, Inc., a consulting firm in Columbus, Ohio. Considered to be one of the founding fathers of consumer behavior, Blackwell is co-author of one of the leading books in this field entitled *Consumer Behavior*. He has also written 21 other books on marketing strategy and research. Blackwell received his BS and MS degrees from The University of Missouri and his PhD from Northwestern University.

Martin Bucksbaum, prior to his death, was chairman and chief executive officer of General Growth Properties, Inc., an equity real estate investment trust listed on the New York Stock Exchange. The trust currently owns enclosed interests in 67 shopping centers located in 26 states. Mr. Bucksbaum was a pioneer in the shopping center industry having developed his first shopping center project in 1956; he continued to develop and manage shopping centers during his career. He was a trustee of the Urban Land Institute and the International Council of Shopping Centers.

Matthew Bucksbaum is chairman and chief executive officer of General Growth Properties, Inc. To date his companies presently manage 120 major shopping centers throughout the United States. He is a trustee of the International Council of Shopping Centers having previously served as its chairman, and is a member of the Urban Land Institute. He holds a BA degree in economics from the University of Iowa.

Harold J. Carlson, MAI, CSM, CPM, CRE, is president of DK/Carlson Associates, Inc., a shopping center management and consulting firm in Rosemont, Illinois, and president of the Retail Properties Group of Draper and Kramer, Incorporated. He is the president and publisher of the *Carlson Report*, a subscription newsletter for shopping center managers, and has served as an author, contributing author, and editorial consultant for several trade publications and associations in connection with various articles and books on real estate-related topics.

Howard C. Gelbtuch, MAI, CRE, is a founder and principal of Greenwich Realty Advisors, Incorporated, a real estate appraisal and counseling firm in New York City. He has primarily provided advice on valuation related issues. Previously, he was in charge of all valuation activities for Jones Lang Wootton and headed the real estate valuation practice at Coopers & Lybrand. He has authored numerous articles on retailing, and authored the valuation chapter in *The Office Building: From Concept to Investment Reality,* published in 1993.

Alfred J. Gobar, PhD, CRE, is president and chairman of Alfred Gobar Associates. The firm has pioneered the development of mathematically-based models for retail site selection. Gobar early in his career was an applications engineer, sales engineer, marketing manager, and financial analyst. He also served as a venture capital specialist consulting in finance and marketing for several small electronics and computer manufacturers. He has published more than 150 journal articles, trade magazine reports, and academic papers. Gobar holds BA and MA degrees from Whittier College, and a PhD from the University of Southern California.

Kevin D. Gray, CRE, is a senior vice president at Landauer Associates in New York with 17 years of experience in investment consulting, retail planning, and architecture. He specializes in strategy consulting and research for foreign and domestic pension funds, institutions, investment banks, and developers. His experience includes most market and property types, with an emphasis on retail property. From Yale School of Management, Gray holds a MA degree in finance and from the University of Pennsylvania a BA and a MA degree in architecture.

Charles Grossman is a managing director of Jones Lang Wootton Realty Advisors, an investment advisory firm responsible for $2.0 billion in real estate assets under management. He has been in real estate acquisition, development, and management for over 25 years and has been involved in the acquisition and operation of centers containing total leasable area of approximately 25,000,000 square feet. He is a member of the International Council of Shopping Centers, the Pension Real Estate Association, the Urban Land Institute, and the Real Estate Board of New York.

Richard B. Jennings is president of Realty Capital International, Inc., a real estate investment banking firm, specializing in raising debt and equity for REITs and other real estate owners, securitized debt financing, and sales of real estate portfolios. Since 1991, Realty Capital has closed over $3 billion of such transactions as advisor or investment banker. Jennings holds a BA in economics from Yale University and an MBA from Harvard Business School.

Lance K. Josal, AIA, is vice president and managing director of RTKL Associates' Dallas office. He leads a team of experienced designers and project managers on all phases of design and construction for a wide variety of domestic and international projects. His project experience includes Canal Place, retail/hotel/parking mixed-use complex, New Orleans, LA; and Galleria at South Bay, a new retail center, Redondo Beach, CA. Josal holds a BA in architecture and art from North Dakota State University. He is a member of the American Institute of Architects, Construction Specifications Institute, the International Council of Shopping Centers, and the Urban Land Institute.

Richard Kateley is executive vice president and director of Investment Research at Heitman Financial Ltd. He is also a member of the investment committee of Heitman Advisory Corporation, one of the nation's largest real estate money managers and pension fund advisors. He has authored the industry forecast, *Emerging Trends in Real Estate,* and more than 20 articles in professional and trade journals. He has a BA from the University of Texas, an MA from the University of Chicago, and was a Fulbright Fellow.

Peter F. Korpacz, MAI, is president of Peter F. Korpacz & Associates, Inc., a national, real estate appraisal and counseling firm specializing in investment-grade shopping centers, office buildings, industrial properties, apartment complexes, hotels, and resorts. Korpacz currently serves on the board of directors of the National Council of Real Estate Investment Fiduciaries. He is a widely published author, former editor-in-chief of *The Appraisal Journal,* and is the publisher and editor-in-chief of the *Korpacz Real Estate Investor Survey,* a quarterly publication on real estate investment market conditions.

David A. Lapins is a partner at the Chicago office of the law firm of Sonnenschein Nath & Rosenthal. His extensive real estate practice encompasses all aspects of complex real estate acquisitions, sales, and financings. Lapins' transactional experience also includes the construction, acquisition, and permanent financing of hotels, regional shopping malls, community shopping centers, and other types of commercial properties. He graduated from Northwestern University School of Law with a JD. He also holds a BA degree in political science from the University of Illinois.

Weldon "Joe" Larsen, SCSM, SCMD, is chief operating officer and executive vice president of The Hahn Company, a regional mall development company in San Diego. Prior to this position, he was executive vice president in charge of Asset Management, for Homart, the real estate development and management arm of Sears, Roebuck and Co., responsible for all operations including leasing, marketing, and retail tenant coordination of Homart's regional shopping centers nationwide. Formerly president of General Growth Management, Inc., he has been involved in the shopping center industry since 1970. Larsen received his BA degree in advertising and public relations from Brigham Young University.

John J. Lawlor is a partner at the Chicago office of the law firm of Sonnenschein Nath & Rosenthal. His wide-ranging experience includes representing institutions, developers, and national retailers in master planning efforts respecting their real estate needs, large-scale property acquisitions, drafting and negotiating office leases, purchase and sale agreements, options, ground leases, shopping center reciprocal easement agreements, space leases, construction contracts, and architects' agreements. He holds a BA from Northwestern University and a JD from Northwestern University School of Law.

Richard W. Lowe is a partner in the audit and business advisory practice of Arthur Andersen LLP and is a member of its real estate services group. He specializes in providing services to the real estate industry and works extensively with mortgage lenders, syndicators, developers, managers, and owner/operators of both commercial and residential properties. He has served as a consultant in structuring real estate transactions, financings and leases. Lowe is a graduate of Hofstra University and is a member of the American Institute of Certified Public Accountants and the New York State Society of Certified Public Accountants in which he has served on its real estate accounting committee for many years.

Richard Marchitelli, CRE, MAI, is president of Marchitelli Barnes & Company, Inc., a New York City real estate counseling and valuation firm. He is engaged in a national practice regarding the development of marketing strategies, representation of clients in the sale or lease of real estate assets, valuation of real property, arbitration, site selection, and litigation support. He is a frequent contributor to professional publications and is former editor-in-chief of *The Appraisal Journal (1989–1994).* He lectures at New York University where he is an adjunct assistant professor of real estate.

Hans C. Mautner is chairman and chief executive officer of Corporate Property Investors, a large privately held owner/developer of 26 major regional shopping centers across the United States. Mautner has been associated with CPI since 1971. Prior to that, he was a general partner of the investment banking firm of Lazard Freres & Co. Mautner is a graduate of Princeton University and the Harvard Graduate School of Business Administration. He is a member of the Urban Land Institute and a trustee of the International Council of Shopping Centers.

Mr. Mautner acknowledges the contribution of Ms. Veronica Volk, a graduate of Moscow State and Alaska Southeast Universities.

John C. Melaniphy, CRE, founder of Melaniphy & Associates, Inc., has been a market analyst, site selection specialist, and real estate counselor for over 35 years. His firm has assisted hundreds of shopping center developers and owners throughout the world. He is a graduate of the University of Illinois and attended the University of Chicago. Melaniphy's affiliations include: the Counselors of Real Estate, the International Council of Shopping Centers, the National Retail Federation, and the National Restaurant Association.

Diane Melish, principal of The Development Consortium, Ltd., specializes in retail development consulting, from initial feasibility analysis to operating properties management. She served as project coordinator for the development of South Street Seaport and senior research analyst. Ms. Melish holds a BA degree in history of art and architecture from Wellesley College and a MCP degree from Harvard University's Graduate School of Design. Her memberships include the International Council of Shopping Centers, the Urban Land Institute, and the National Trust for Historic Preservation.

Marc J. Munaretto, CSM, is the executive vice president of Mark IV Realty Group, Inc., a Chicago developer. His extensive national experience includes development, leasing, management, finance, acquisition, and disposition of retail, office, and industrial real estate. As a principal and executive vice president of asset management for Hiffman Shaffer Associates, Inc., he was responsible for developing new management business from the institutional investment sector and for developing and executing real estate value enhancement strategies.

Mr. Munaretto acknowledges Martin Becker, Esq. of Becker & Gurian, Highland Park, IL, as having authored the retail lease form.

Harry Newman, Jr., is chairman of Newman Properties based in Long Beach, California, and Newman Properties Northwest in Seattle, Washington. Newman's group has developed nine million square feet of neighborhood, community, and regional shopping centers in California, Washington, Iowa, and Texas over the past 31 years. He was national trustee of the International Council of Shopping Centers and its first West Coast president. Newman is currently president of the ICSC Educational Foundation, and a committee member of the Urban Land Institute. He is a graduate of Harvard College, Harvard Business School, and Cambridge University, England.

Cynthia T. Ray is director, area research for Federated Department Stores, Inc. Federated, with its 1994 acquisition of R. H. Macy & Co., became the nation's largest traditional department store company with annual sales of $14 million. Ray is responsible for evaluating new store locations, existing store renovations, expansions and relocations, and various strategic corporate issues. Previously Ray was vice president with JMB Retail Properties Co., responsible for site and consumer research for new development projects and the management portfolio of 55 regional malls. She is a former chair of the International Council of Shopping Centers' Research Advisory Task Force. Ray holds a degree from Stanford University and did graduate studies at the University of Wisconsin and the University of Chicago.

Glenn J. Rufrano is chief operating officer, chief financial officer, and director of J. W. O'Connor Co., Inc. In addition, he is a director of Trizec Holdings, Inc. He holds a BA degree from Rutgers University and a MSM degree from Florida International University. His professional affiliations include the Appraisal Institute and the Counselors of Real Estate. Mr. Rufrano is also an adjunct professor at New York University's Real Estate Institute.

Joseph J. Scalabrin, FAIA, RIBA, vice president of operations for The Limited with responsibility for all store planning, design and construction. Formerly executive vice president and director of RTKL's Dallas office, he participated in the design and management of major projects, including corporate and commercial office buildings, retail and mixed-use developments, hotels, and resorts. Scalabrin holds BA and MA degrees in architecture from Montana State University and Columbia University, respectively. He is a fellow of the American Institute of Architects, and holds memberships in the International Council of Shopping Centers, the Institute for Urban Design, and the Urban Land Institute.

Ron Sher, PhD, is the managing partner of Terranomics Northwest, which develops shopping centers, and owns and manages 15 centers. He is the president and a partner in Terranomics International Investors, a real estate lending company which makes participating loans in retail shopping centers. Sher is a partner in Terranomics Retail Services, a brokerage, development, and management company headquartered in San Francisco. He is a graduate of Colorado College, and holds a MA in finance from Columbia University, and a PhD in agricultural economics from Washington State University.

Merritt Sher, as chairman of Terranomics, has been at the forefront of the retail development industry for nearly 20 years. His focus in retail real estate ranges from marketing and merchandising strategies to site planning, financing, and building design. Sher also created Terranomics International Investors, a company formed for the purpose of lending on quality retail properties. He has been a part of the development of several retail companies, and also served as a real estate consultant for many retailers. Sher holds a JD from Hasting College of Law.

Melvin Simon is chairman of the Simon Property Group, Inc., Indianapolis, which began public trading in December 1993 as the largest Real Estate Investment Trust (REIT) in the United States. Simon served as chairman of the board of Melvin Simon & Associates, Inc. until the formation of the REIT, the nation's largest developer and manager of shopping centers. Simon is a trustee of the Urban Land Institute and the International Council of Shopping Centers. From City College of New York, he holds a BS in accounting and an MBA with emphasis on real estate.

Jane Snoddy Smith is a real estate partner at the St. Louis office of the law firm of Sonnenschein Nath & Rosenthal. Smith concentrates in commercial real estate, representing developers, lenders, owners, purchasers, and sellers. She has extensive experience in shopping center development having worked on transactions involving more than 130 regional, million-plus square foot shopping centers. She is active in the American Bar Association (ABA) Real Property, Probate and Trust Law Section; Commercial and Industrial Leasing Committee; and the International Council of Shopping Centers.

A. Joseph Traum is senior vice president of Nomura Real Estate U.S.A., Inc. responsible for managing the company's retail and office investments. The company's retail projects include regional mall and community centers, and office projects include downtown and suburban high-rise buildings. Traum has been involved in real estate since 1971, and was formerly an asset manager for Eastdil Realty, Inc. He holds a BBA from City College of New York and was the winner of the Haskins & Sells gold medal for the 1958 CPA examination.

Glenn E. Whitmore is managing director for CB Commercial Real Estate Group, Inc., Investment Properties Division, in New York. He has specialized in real estate investment banking involving over $2.5 billion of investment sales, primarily for institutional clients. He is a member of the Urban Land Institute, Pension Real Estate Association, and the International Council of Shopping Centers. Whitmore holds a BA from Brown University and postgraduate degrees from Harvard University (MA) and Columbia University (MPA/MBA).

Acknowledgments

This book is dedicated to the memory of John Robert White, whose death in March 1995 was a great loss for the real estate industry. This book represents one of John's last accomplishments in a career filled with special achievements. Even as John's health was failing, his incredible energy and intensity were unfailing. Special thanks are due to Mary H. Rasmussen, editorial assistant, whose diligence was extraordinary in seeing this book through to completion after John's death. Thanks are also due to our colleagues at Landauer, where John served for many years as chairman, for their support and encouragement, especially James C. Kafes, Jonathan C. Sorkenn, and my assistant Carol Saenz.

At John Wiley & Sons, thanks to Michael Hamilton, our editor, Nicole Nowitz, his assistant; Mary Daniello, production, and Jean Morely, cover design. At Publications Development Company of Texas, thanks to Nancy Marcus Land for her expert guidance through the production process. At RTKL Architects/Dallas, thanks to Lance Josal, AIA, and Christopher Hornbaker for the jacket design.

At the Urban Land Institute, Frank H. Spink, Jr., vice president/publisher, provided invaluable assistance at every stage of a lengthy production process. Also thanks to Ruben A. Roca and the professionals who reviewed individual chapters on behalf of ULI, including Dougal M. Casey, Stanley L. Eichelbaum, Eric Kuhne, Arthur Margon, Vincent W. McBrien, Lat Purser III, Stephen A. Quintin, Mark A. Randol, James P. Regan, and Marilyn Kramer Weitzman.

At the International Council of Shopping Centers, thanks to John T. Riordan, president and CEO, and Bena Green, editorial director, for their enthusiastic support and advice. At the Counselors of Real Estate, thanks to James E. Gibbons, our consulting editor, who reviewed many of the chapters for us. Special thanks to Jody Hotchkiss at Sterling Lord for his sound business advice.

Thanks above all to the thirty contributing authors of this book, who gave freely and generously of their time and expertise. Each of these authors is a true and dedicated professional. Every one of them approached this project with a real spirit of excellence.

Lastly, my gratitude to the White family, especially to John's wife, Gloria, who was a model of support, and to my wife Joellyn, and to our four sons, for their eternal patience.

KEVIN D. GRAY

Contents

Foreword

The shopping center represents one of the most socially influential forms of real estate. While there were a few forerunners, the shopping center really became a firmly established part of the American scene in the late 1950s and 1960s. In a relatively short time, the industry has changed national and international retail distribution systems, shopping habits the world over, and the character and growth of the communities and neighborhoods in which they are located.

While the shopping center format is international, it definitely is an American phenomenon. The return of the veterans from World War II and the subsequent government low-interest loans for home building began a population shift that resulted in a significant expansion of the suburbs, the creation of a national highway system, and the preference for personal versus a mass transportation mode, all of which gave the shopping center industry a huge jump start.

Like blue jeans and jazz, shopping centers have made the leap to other parts of the world. Most shopping center development abroad took place in the 1970s, and increasingly in the 1980s and 1990s. Study groups from other parts of the world regularly make trips to the United States and study our newest developments so that their newest efforts will reflect the latest models in the United States. For example, the entertainment element as illustrated in the Forum Shops and Mall of America is being replicated with cultural twists in South America and the Far East.

Most of the U.S. shopping center industry is suburban-based, while population is still city-centered in much of the rest of the world, with street retailing still dominant. The most successful developments abroad adapted our concepts to meet their cultural needs. Many city-center historic buildings have been conscientiously and meticulously reworked to house shopping centers. Stores are often smaller, reflecting tighter spaces and the tenant mix varies with the culture. National and international chains are not as dominant in foreign centers, though this may change as many American companies begin to explore their options for growth.

The shopping center industry is worthy of study for many reasons. While the shopping center may be most often thought of as a form of real estate, it is also the most powerful distribution system for retail goods the world has ever known. The growth and development of regional and national chain and department stores can be directly traced to the proliferation of shopping centers. Consequently, fads and fashion trends can be nearly simultaneously introduced across the breadth of the country. One may debate the desirability of the homogeneous nature of American goods and services, but not the shopping center's role in helping deliver them. Today, over 50% of all non-automotive retail sales in the United States are made in shopping centers.

Shopping centers are also worthy of study because of their catalytic effect on property values and the additional development they spawn as well as their role in shaping the lifestyle patterns of the citizens in those communities. They are major employers; one out of every nine non-agricultural jobs in the United States is located in a shopping center.

In addition to retail goods, shopping centers now house many of the services and entertainment that are such a large part of American life. Every day thousands of Americans go to their local shopping centers for reasons other than to purchase retail goods—community activities, fashion shows, or educational displays. Like so many other American institutions, we have come to take shopping centers for granted. However, in many cases, removing the shopping center from a community would have devastating effects.

Shopping centers hold a unique place in the real estate arena that necessitates a broader base of understanding of market conditions and trends and a more intense management system. Unlike office buildings that are primarily inhabited by people who work in them, or warehouses that are primarily concerned about the receiving, storing, and delivery of goods, or hotels whose cliental are transient, shopping centers have thousands of repeat customers who tend to have an emotional attachment. It is *their* shopping center, *their* place to hang out, the place where *their* child first visited Santa, where they take *their* friends when they come to visit from out of town. It is a part of *their* lives. It is all those things as long as the shopping center management lives up to its end of the bargain and provides a clean, safe, exciting place to shop, filled with the range of merchandise that is appropriate for that particular market.

As you will see in the pages that follow, the shopping center is not just another piece of real estate. It is a form of retailing estate, an investment vehicle, a source of employment, a shaper of community patterns and character. And in its broadest definition, a social force.

No body of information about shopping centers can be considered definitive because shopping centers continue to evolve with the neighborhoods, communities, and regions they serve. However, this book deals with the industry in a scholarly and professional manner. Most of the authors are personal friends and colleagues whose opinions I value and whose insights are well-respected in the shopping center community as well as on the national scene.

View this book as an excellent way to significantly enrich your knowledge about the shopping center industry and its place in American retailing. Then visit this country's wide range of shopping centers with a new understanding of the complexities of their development and management. Envision what selection, competitive pricing, and convenience would be missing from your life without them.

REBECCA MACCARDINI

Prologue

Harry Newman, Jr.

I urge you to read the chapters that follow carefully and absorb as much of the information as possible, but be forewarned! Even if you memorize this entire book, that is not enough. There are many unplanned, ill-timed circumstances that surface unexpectedly and can undermine your success in any development project. No book can cover all these special situations, which characterize most projects, nor can a book substitute completely for practical experience. However, it can provide an essential foundation for on-the-job learning. After all, the next best thing to knowing is knowing how!

DECISIVE ROLE OF DEPARTMENT STORES

In one of the fastest growing western suburbs in the nation, three department stores committed to become anchor tenants in a proposed regional mall. Even though their sales performances in an older, established adjacent community were disappointing, they committed to the center solely to keep a major new competitor out of the market. The newly incorporated city, desperate for sales tax revenue, made this move more palatable by offering a $27 million subsidy. The center has proved to be a major disappointment. Sales are far below

1

expectations. In short, the mall was premature and too high-priced for the limited blue-collar income market it served.

In the past, if developers were able to attract two or more department stores to a site, they would develop a regional mall. The department store commitments on new locations were critical to making this type of center possible; hence the usual give-away terms and other subsidies they were able to exact from developer-suitors. Despite the current trend to "big box," value-oriented anchors, the department store remains the decisive factor and key element in new or existing centers.

Another example of this special role department stores play in determining a center's future occurred in a regional mall in a rapidly expanding suburban area on the East Coast. The center had three middle-line anchors, although it was adjacent to very affluent residential neighborhoods. After many efforts, the developer secured a commitment from Nordstrom for a new store to be erected in a two-story addition to the existing 12-year-old, one-level structure. Based on Nordstrom's anticipated occupancy, two other upscale department stores agreed to join the center. All necessary approvals had been obtained with the exception of one of the three existing majors, who had the right in the Reciprocal Easement Agreement to approve or reject any proposed change in the layout of the center. The executive in charge rejected the plan, which would have required the mall to go through his store's ground floor to connect the existing center with the two-level addition. His refusal was based on his concern that "all those people in my store, think of what it will do to shrinkage (theft)." Despite the property owners' providing overwhelming evidence from three other department store chains that they had experienced dramatic sales increases under identical circumstances, he was adamant. Presumably, he did not want the competition. As a result, all three upscale chains anchored a new mall, which was built less than five miles away, and his store suffered, as did the entire center.

VALUE OF 20-20 HINDSIGHT

The major anchors in almost all regional centers have the right to approve or reject any proposed change in the layout of the center. In view of the disapproval of the proposed expansion, what could the owners of this older mall have done, considering that they were flanked on both sides by newer and dominant enclosed malls?

Using 20-20 hindsight, they could have sold the mall at the height of the booming 1980s market and made a significant profit. However, they waited too long and were then faced with declining sales and the daunting prospect of remerchandising the mall and converting it into a center with value-oriented, large-space users, who pay half the rent per square foot of the original tenants. Timing is a key ingredient in decision making.

INTERPRETING MARKET STUDY RESULTS

One of the most challenging developer/investor responsibilities is to obtain, and even more important, to evaluate market studies and demographics of a proposed site, whether it is a convenience, neighborhood, community, regional center, or super-regional enclosed mall. There are many examples of the disastrous effects of the failure to assess market surveys critically. It is equally important to continue to monitor demographic and psychographic data in each market area on a regular basis, so that the tenant mix, merchandise, and promotional efforts can be adjusted to reflect these changes.

One national developer, for example, agreed to develop a mall in the center of a well-established midwestern city of 500,000 population. He was influenced by the size of the city's subsidy of the project through its redevelopment agency and so did not object when the site was switched from the concentration of the new high-rise office buildings and hotels to a location in the older, more blighted downtown area. Many national chains were induced to take space in this mall in return for obtaining leases in stronger, more profitable centers also controlled by the developer. Three years after completion, with three majors in place, the developer sold the center to a syndicator at a modest price with a penalty payment in the event the center did not perform to a certain agreed level. It did not and continued to decline, with almost 50% of the tenant leases expiring at the end of their 10-year terms. There were several serious problems. Office workers and residents from the more affluent residential areas avoided the mall because of its reputation for attracting many undesirable elements. The center was offered for sale at $100 million, a 4% capitalization rate, at the height of the market. The price was reduced several times, as sales declined and vacancies were increased with the same result—no sale. Subsequently, a survey disclosed that the median income in a three-mile radius was $17,000 and the residents consisted primarily of ethnic minorities and impecunious elderly. This critically important statistic might have saved millions of dollars, if it had been analyzed before the center was built.

LOCATION, LOCATION, LOCATION?

This example illustrates not only the importance of market research, but also the vital issue of selecting an appropriate location. There are many elements in the development process which seem obvious, but may not be. For example, in a major eastern city, a regional mall was developed adjacent to a busy freeway between two interchanges. However, the interchanges were five miles apart. This proved confusing to potential shoppers, who passed one interchange and recognized their error when they roared past the mall. Leasing agents for this project advertised, "How would you like to enjoy 250,000 shoppers passing your front door each day." The operative word here was "passing." Access must be convenient and readily identifiable.

In addition to access, visibility is another key ingredient for an effective location. For example, an enclosed three-level mall containing more than a million square feet, anchored by Dillard's, Neiman-Marcus, Marshall Field, and J.C. Penney, opened in 1983 in a southwestern metropolitan area. Despite these strong anchors, the center's performance has been a major disappointment because of poor visibility. Other factors, such as strong competition and inadequately sized quality majors for that specific trade area, also contributed to the center's lackluster sales.

ZONING CONSIDERATIONS

At a midwestern site, the zoning process was complicated by competition between the city and county for the sales and property taxes to be generated by a proposed regional mall on a private airport site one-third of a mile outside the city limits. Because of the serious financial problems facing many cities and counties during the current recession and, in part, from state and federal grant cutbacks, many cities and counties are competing for sales and property tax revenues, often resulting in decisions to proceed with an unsound development. Before the controversy was resolved, there were lawsuits and countersuits, drafting of the first county zoning code for shopping centers, and a delay in development because the environmental impact report concluded that such a large project could adversely affect the breeding habits of field mice. The cost of such delays in land-carrying charges, legal fees, loss of potential anchors, and so on, can be crippling.

Our company was involved in two rezoning problems in northern California, which were resolved in dramatically opposite ways. Our partners agreed to handle the rezoning in Marin County, an affluent suburban area of San Francisco. We were to tackle rezoning in Berkeley. In Marin County, it took our partners 14 years and three new city councils, a change in the Corps of Engineers' leadership, the donation of a lake for migrating ducks, plus the gift of some open space to avoid threatening the field mice that inhabited the adjacent swampy area to secure appropriate zoning for an open-mall regional. The low parking ratio (3.5 cars per 1,000 square feet of GLA) which the environmentalist demanded to discourage traffic led to congestion and back-ups on the adjacent freeway and off-ramp.

In short, be aware in advance of the possible political hurdles that might be encountered. Even if you are advised that forthcoming local elections will not hinder your zoning, check and double-check independently. In our efforts in Berkeley, California, we were advised by the city attorney that a radical council had been elected. Needless to say, the rezoning of a bordering site for a regional became a political football and was denied after openly expressed opposition by members of the planning commission at a public zoning hearing. "Let's grant them the delay they request," said a member of the commission to the chairman, "so we can organize the opposition."

As you will see in the case of the Vermont-Slauson Center in the heart of the Watts riot area, community support is an essential component of a successful project. A vocal, well-organized minority can often obstruct the entitlement procedure and scuttle a worthwhile center at this initial political stage. Sensitivity to environmental and community issues is essential.

In one of our centers in an extremely environmentally sensitive area of the Pacific Northwest, we canvassed every resident within a half-mile radius of the proposed development site, to acquaint them with detailed plans for replanting stands of trees that had to be removed to make way for the improvements. In the final zoning hearing before the county board of commissioners, only one person objected and he had been away during the door-to-door survey. The head of the regional environmental/activist group, Southwestern Washington Environmental Action Team (with the appropriate acronym SWEAT) said, "I regret that I cannot find anything objectionable in the EIR or the proposed development and re-landscaping plan." The zoning was approved unanimously.

ASSESSING THE RISK FACTOR

Perhaps one of the best examples of the crucial role a developer's visceral reaction can play in deciding to tackle a high-risk project is the Vermont-Slauson community shopping center in South Central Los Angeles. In light of the basic facts, a location three miles from the heart of the Watts riot, a crime-ridden area, a rapidly declining number of mom-and-pop stores, a closed obsolete Sears store and supermarket, a lack of security, and the low-end demographics of the immediate surrounding residents, this would seem to be the least desirable site imaginable for developing a community center.

Despite active efforts by the long-time mayor to recruit a developer for the project, only one was willing to tackle the monumental risks involved in this development. An innovative and creative developer of neighborhood centers, he had no experience with inner-city projects. However, he sensed the potential for a secure retail center to serve the needs of an area almost devoid of retail facilities. But how would he provide adequate security, attract anchor tenants, secure financing, and organize community support?

This is where the developer's intuition, long-standing relationships with key tenants, fortuitous timing, and creativity paid off. The developer put his personal credit on-the-line, and successfully solicited federal grants to acquire the nine-plus acres for the center. He arranged for a decorative metal fence with landscaping around the property, installed his own security force, plus a police substation, and built an architecturally attractive shopping center. He offered open-end, percentage-only rents with escape clauses to a supermarket, drugstore, and discount chain. By 1983, two years after opening, the center was fully tenanted with minimum-against-percentage clauses in every lease. The developer set up a community development partnership, deeded the property to it, and took back a 90+ year ground lease. After a 20% cash-on-cash return to him, the community was to receive 60% of the profits with 40% for developer. Finally, he discovered that the Community Reinvestment Act of 1977 enabled him to convert his personal loan to a real estate loan from a local bank at 10% for a term of ten years at a time when interest rates were above 20%. Within seven years, he had paid off the loan completely and was realizing an infinite annual return on his original investment.

Another developer's experience with an apparently low-risk remodeling of an older open-mall regional center was dramatically different. Located adjacent to one of the most affluent African-

American areas in the United States with two strong department store anchors, this project seemed a sure-fire success, particularly with a $21 million contribution from the city's Community Redevelopment Agency and proceeds of $30 million from industrial development bonds. The developer was required to front any losses in this public/private partnership without recapture.

Four factors, difficult to foresee, created financial problems for the project. First was the reluctance of the two department stores, despite the fact that they were the least productive units in their chains, to upgrade their merchandise to fit the potential customers. They also insisted on a third major. It cost the developer $46 million to acquire and develop a Sears store. The automatic refusal of major national retail chains to consider opening stores in a predominantly African-American community, however affluent, was a second factor. The third problem was created by the unwillingness of the prospective female customers to patronize a local mall, which, despite a handsome interior, Nordstrom-like piano music, and white-gloved doormen, did not have any prestigious fashion stores. Instead, the ladies shopped elsewhere at more fashionable, upscale department stores. Finally, there was not the local community support and financial participation, which contributed so much to the success of the Vermont-Slauson center.

After more than seven years of planning and 12 months of construction in a $120 million renovation, the center opened for business in time for Christmas shoppers in 1988. Despite significant annual operating losses, the mall was sold five years later as part of a package with the developer's other more profitable centers.

AN ESSENTIAL SKILL—KNOWLEDGE OF RETAIL

It is not enough to learn about the various stages of development. For a successful career as a shopping center developer, you must understand retailing, be able to evaluate every category of tenant, and recognize new trends at an early enough stage to react in a productive manner. You must also be aware of changing retail formats, such as warehouse clubs, power centers, factory outlet centers, and the large-scale (over one million square feet) discount centers. If you are a mall developer, for example, you may not have the appropriate tenant relationships to enable you to become a power center or outlet center developer. If you have tied up a piece of land suitable for such use, you might consider a joint venture with a specialist in that particular field or hire leasing agents with the appropriate track record and contacts. Alternatively, you can broaden your scope to include this type of development.

Before becoming committed to any project, you must investigate the financial strength of every major tenant. Out of 20 warehouse club chains that operated in 1986, only three have prospered. It would be interesting and enlightening to learn what happened to the 100-plus empty warehouse club buildings after these chains closed their doors.

With the spate of mergers, acquisitions, and bankruptcies in department stores, supermarkets, and many of the chains that fill mall shop space, it has become critically important for the developer to work with a high percentage of financially strong tenants, whether majors, national, or regional chains.

CREATIVE APPROACH TO FINANCING

Real estate investment trusts, mortgage-backed securities, or private placements for individual properties are just a few of the securitization financing techniques that have emerged as lenders and institutional as well as individual investors have become more comfortable with the field of real estate. Investment bankers, Wall Street brokerage companies, major accounting firms, and syndicators are all active and well-versed in the various securitization techniques that have proved effective.

Another important source of financing is the local redevelopment agency. Cities are desperately seeking additional income from sources like sales tax at a time when other forms of government grants and tax revenue have declined significantly. In a repositioning and expansion of a mall, for example, redevelopment agencies frequently participate by issuing bonds to cover the cost of building additional parking decks to service the expanded retail area.

Another important trend indicator is the lending policy of financial institutions. Lenders are becoming more cautious about financing power centers because of their concern about re-leasing any of the large "boxes," if the tenant goes broke or uses Chapter 11 as a basis for vacating the space without further liability.

The entire field of financing deserves constant scrutiny and creative thinking. For example, if you are planning to develop a neighborhood or community center, you might consider a joint venture with the landowner, which would reduce or possibly eliminate the need for any equity investment on your part. Alternatively, you might presell the center to a Real Estate Investment Trust (REIT) or pension fund, based on your major supermarket and drugstore chain lease commitments. This would enable you to get construction financing with a minimum of personal liability.

Recourse loans, which require the personal guarantee of the developer in case of default, should be avoided. If you have a strong financial statement, find an equity partner, take a smaller share of the pie, and avoid personal liability. Nonrecourse loans are now rarely available, unless there is a sizeable equity investment and precommitments from a majority of the tenants.

PROBLEMS OF OVERBUILDING

In the 15 years between 1976 and 1991, the number of shopping centers increased from 17,523 to 37,975. Gross leasable area grew from 2.3 to 4.9 billion square feet, and sales more than tripled from $211.5 to $716.9 billion. However, construction starts for new centers dropped dramatically and only a handful of super-regionals over 800,000 square feet has been built since 1990.

In short, there is a very serious overbuilding problem. Between 1986 and 1991, retail footage increased 23%, while the population increased only 5%. Having tenants and financing are available does not insure success. You must be conscious of the ability of the trade area to absorb another center.

NEW TECHNOLOGIES IN RETAILING

While Nordstrom has been the role model for customer service, other role models have existed for inventory position, private label, and chainwide buying, and, most important, for state-of-the-art information systems. These enable retailers to react quickly to the trends in fads and fashion, to avoid out-of-stock by reordering in time from vendors, and to minimize dead merchandise and mark-downs. This is an American copy of the Japanese just-in-time system.

Dillard's has been the prototype for this new technology. Its sophisticated point-of-sale terminals have produced enough profits to raise the funds to buy underperforming divisions from Associated Dry Goods, Dayton Hudson, Macy, and Allied, and turn them into moneymakers. In ten years, Dillard's has grown from a relatively small retailer with $331 million in sales and 41 units into a formidable $2.2 billion, 138-store empire, and is now selectively trading up.

REACTIONS TO RECESSION

Since there is little demand and little financing available for new malls, the major trend has been remodeling and expansion of existing ones. Many malls have added a second story and one or two new anchor tenants. A current trend on a smaller scale to produce additional income is the development of mobile cart programs within many regionals. Custom-designed for the display and sale of specialized merchandise and services, they have become a year-round feature of most enclosed regional malls. Ranging in number from four to 20, these carts supplement the variety of goods and services offered by in-line shops and kiosks, as well as contributing to common-area costs. That is why they have been accepted by existing tenants. In addition, they offer mall owners an important new source of income to offset increasing operating costs as well as a testing ground for potential new in-line mall shop tenants.

PERCENTAGITIS—THE KEY TO FAILURE

Mervin Morris, founder of Mervyn's promotional department stores (now a division of Dayton Hudson), recalls the demise of many traditional department stores and the rise of category killers and discounters this way. "Many chains suffer from percentagitis. They buy 1,000 items in a month at $30.00 each and apply the usual keystone markup, to $60.00. Mervyn's approach was to buy the same item for $30.00 and sell it for $49.95. Instead of selling 1,000, we would sell 4,000 and realize 80,000 in gross-margin dollars instead of $30,000, in short more than twice the gross margin as well as net profit, since our overhead, rent, and labor costs are the same as the other department stores." "The formula for retail success," he says, "is to have your own strategy and game plan and do it!"

CUSTOMER SERVICE—NOT LIP SERVICE

Ease of access and parking, efficient center layout, and fully stocked stores are basic requirements. So is customer service. Quality of service stems from the corporate culture. Nordstrom, for example, promotes from within and offers higher wages than its competitors, plus bonuses based on performance. The top five executives answer their own phones, have an open-door policy of availability, and personally respond to suggestions, complaints, and the numerous letters of congratulations. The company also has a policy of recognizing the leading salespeople in every store. That is why Nordstrom is famous for the quality of its service.

In the San Francisco Center development, Nordstrom occupies 336,000 square feet on the fourth to the eighth floor of a vertical shopping center. Because it was the first Nordstrom without a direct street entrance and limited off-street parking, many in the development field expected it to be a failure. Instead, their reputation for service preceded them and they set a new record for their opening-day sales—$1.7 million.

There is a 6,000-pound rock outside Stew Leonard's famous supermarket in Norwalk, Connecticut. It took two weeks to carve these rules on it.

Rule #1 The customer is always right.

Rule #2 If the customer is wrong, go back and read Rule #1.

Leonard has a colossal suggestion box with a large picture of himself next to it. He takes customer complaints seriously. By 10 A.M., all managers have received a typed list of any complaints and are taking actions to correct them. For example, someone suggested that the strawberries should not be sold in little boxes. A customer said, "You put the huge strawberries on top, the small on the bottom, and the rotten ones in the middle." So Leonard displayed the strawberries in huge barrels, so the customers could pick the ones they wanted. Employees worried that the customers would eat them. Instead, the number of strawberries sold increased tenfold!

Mervin Morris, when he was running Mervyn's, had the same philosophy. Every morning, he would review customers' comments and criticisms collected from the suggestion boxes the night before and take appropriate corrective action.

PIONEERING CUSTOMER SERVICE

My own company responds in writing to all customer complaints and/or suggestions. It is time-consuming, but well worth the effort.

Complaints often highlight serious problems with some of the tenants, which require mall management's corrective advice or action. We pioneered customer service centers in our malls. The service desk personnel provided complimentary strollers, wheelchairs, free parcel checking, large shopping bags for consolidating purchases, package carry-out service, escort service to the parking area, car-start (battery jump) and opening-locked-cars service, information on all merchants and merchandise, senior citizen Dial-a-Ride service, taxi calls, ice cream treat fund for lost children, and change for phone calls. If we can solve the liability insurance problem, we plan to add child care and pet sitting. We also provided free gift wrapping on six special occasions. In addition, the Customer Service Center handles the sale of gift certificates, gift wrapping, lottery/lotto, UPS, postal service, security lockers, and bus passes.

Unfortunately, most of today's service is not customer service, but lip service—and that is not too surprising, since the turnover of mall store managers, according to surveys conducted by Newman Properties, was 115% a year. The turnover among sales staff was between 300% and 500% a year, depending on whether part-time help was included. Apart from the importance of customer service, having items in stock which shoppers want is even more crucial, requiring technology for inventory control and "just-in-time" delivery. Customers in each trade area have different characteristics, which are reflected in their choice of merchandise. Micromarketing is necessary to satisfy these varying preferences. For example, Target, which micromarkets 30% of its goods, supplies different brands of potato chips in Chicago, Atlanta, and elsewhere to suit varying tastes.

UPGRADING CENTER CONVENIENCE

As a developer owner, you also must be aware of changes that could make your center more convenient. These include:

1. Automatic doors at the main entrances.
2. New directories with larger type for the elderly and interactive video and audio to answer shoppers' questions.
3. Directional signs, legible and facing the correct way.
4. Color-coded parking lot signage consistent with interior graphics.

5. Women's restrooms twice as large as men's restrooms, with diaper-changing boards in both and even more important— *clean* restrooms.

6. Better vertical transportation, if you have a multilevel mall.

7. Periodic color and lighting changes to create a fresh new look.

8. Full-line customer service center.

9. Increased lighting and brighter colors in parking lots and structures to improve perception of safety for shoppers.

MANAGEMENT AND MARKETING— A FRESH VIEW

As owners/developers, you must also keep an eye on the changes that are occurring in management and marketing. You should:

1. Monitor tenant sales and delinquencies regularly in order to identify trends and weak tenants ripe for replacement.

2. Get monthly reports from the manager, summarizing the action items and noting the tenants with the greatest sales increases or decreases, with explanations for their performance.

3. Inspect the project with the manager at regular intervals to bring a fresh viewpoint on existing problems and potential improvements.

4. Have your marketing director emphasize community-related promotions in place of the traditional "dog-and-pony show," in order to differentiate your center from competing projects.

5. At the outset, identify your trade area and determine how it is defined. Next, determine any changes in competitive centers. Then, at least once a year, review the demographic changes in your trade area and note any significant ethnic, age, occupational, or income changes, which could affect your advertising efforts to target these market segments.

6. Where there is a heavy concentration of an ethnic group, such as Hispanic, have someone at the customer service center who can speak Spanish or other appropriate languages and encourage each store manager to do the same.

7. Regularly monitor trade area penetration by zip, census tract, and so on. If penetration decreases in a part of the trade area,

figure out why and then use targeted mailers and geographically related promotions.

DEMOGRAPHICS—IMPACT ON MERCHANDISE AND TENANT MIX

Demographics help to explain the changing face of retailing and
shopping centers. The 1990–1991 recession, changing lifestyles, and
the 57 million women in the workforce have changed basic shopping
habits dramatically. There is no time for browsing. Most customers
visit an average of two shops after going to a department store and
now spend four hours a month in shopping centers compared to ten
hours in 1985.

There are two other major demographic changes that will increasingly affect retailing and shopping centers—senior citizens and
ethnic minorities. Their tastes and shopping patterns are already having a significant effect on retailing, but you will have to work closely
with your tenants to help them decide how to change their merchandise mix and how to target these "new" categories of customers.

How will you interpret the fact that the 55-and-over category represents 22% of all Americans and is growing three times faster than
the rest of the population? This age group has 55% of all the discretionary income, 42% of all after-tax income, and 77% of all financial
holdings. Their households account for 45% of all consumers. Are
your tenants catering to this older customer? How do their tastes and
buying habits differ from the teenagers who represent a significant
and growing market in the 1990s?

A recent report showed that teens spent $71 billion annually on
themselves and their families. Unlike their parents, teens are not intimidated by high technology and a reported 44% of teens own their
own VCR. Shopping center management needs to make them feel
more welcome, while discouraging the undesirable rowdy elements.

ETHNIC MINORITY SHOPPING PATTERNS

Ethnic minorities also have a significant impact on retail and shopping centers. In the 1980s, the African-American population increased
13% from 26.5 to 30 million. During the same period, the Hispanic
population grew from 14.6 to 22.4 million, a 53% increase, and continues to expand six times faster than the rest of the U.S. population.

Hispanics spent over $171 billion in 1990 on goods and services. They are displacing African-Americans in many urban areas. The Asian population nearly doubled to 7 million in the 1980s. Their median household income in 1990 was $42,245, the highest for any ethnic group in the country. Their income will double by the year 2000. Currently, they spend $38 billion annually on retail. By 2000, demographers predict population increases of 4.1 million for African Americans, 7.9 million for Hispanics, and 4.7 million for Asians.

These figures are a reminder that you must focus on ethnic statistics center by center. In addition, you must be able to differentiate and identify the various subsections of each ethnic minority in every center's specific trade area. For example, in evaluating methods for targeting these special ethnic groups, you must analyze countries of origin, languages spoken, knowledge of English, length of stay in the United States, immigrant status, citizenship, numbers of second generation, degree of assimilation. Only then can you propose an effective advertising and marketing plan to attract those ethnic customers. National statistics alone may mislead you. For example, the Hispanic category includes Mexicans, Central Americans, and South Americans. Asian encompasses Koreans, Chinese, Japanese, Vietnamese, Cambodians, Taiwanese, and so on. One final dramatic fact! The primary language of a growing number of public school students in this country is not English. For example, the primary languages of 34.6% of the students in the Long Beach Unified School District in California are Hispanic (66.5%) and Asian (26.1%) and European, Samoan, and so on. (7.4%). These figures are typical of many urban areas.

Think of the impact these statistics should have on location, services, product assortment, store hours, signage, decor, sales training, and so on.

DANGERS OF EMOTIONAL ATTACHMENT

Keep in mind another caveat. Do not become emotionally attached to the shopping center. Based on new competition, the state of the economy, current capitalization rates, and possibly decreasing sales trends, you should be willing to sell the center and trade liquidity for a declining asset.

No other specialized form of real estate involves such a complexity of interrelated elements as retail development. On a new center, for example, you have zoning and other entitlements, architecture and design, construction, tenant mix, financing, market research, leasing, management, promotion and marketing decisions to make. Any one of these can destroy the viability of a project, if you misinterpret the information.

Add to that complexity the incredible growth and the rapid changes in retailing, in types of centers, in demographics and psychographics, in the economy, and in financing. You can begin to see why it is so important for you to apply to each problem area all the disciplines you are about to study and to develop and apply critical, situational thinking, because each center is unique. The problems may be the same, but the circumstances and personalities creating them are different in every case.

SITUATIONAL THINKING ON THE INDUSTRY'S #1 PROBLEM

With the recession, overbuilding, and competitive value-oriented development like power centers, outlet centers, and warehouse clubs, the owners of 70% to 80% of regional malls face a challenging situation. First and foremost, they are overshadowed and their very existence is threatened by the dominant, so-called Class A malls, who boast the strongest majors, national chains, and impressive growth in sales per square foot of mall shop tenants. Conversely, Class B and C malls are faced with declining sales, chain and independent tenant lease terminations, constant requests for rent relief, and a mounting number of bankruptcies or abrupt departures before lease terminations.

If you, as the owner, decide to create a discount image for your center, you will be faced with substantial remodeling costs, because value-oriented tenants usually require much larger spaces than were originally designed and occupied. Further, the rents paid by discounters are substantially below the levels previously paid. Many chains also insist on low-limits to Common Area Maintenance (CAM) costs, reducing the center's total income by 30 to 50%. Rents may average $6.00 to $10.00 net, compared to the original rental income of $18.00 to $30.00 net per square foot. Thus, net operating income may prove to be inadequate even to service existing debt.

You can readily see that the solution requires an in-depth knowledge of retailing, an understanding of marketing techniques and public relations, a clear grasp of redevelopment and local politics, and an innovative approach to design and financing. And do not forget psychology, sociology, human relations, and a clear, strong management philosophy. In short, it needs *situational thinking*—a marriage of theory and practice, as applied to each particular center and its unique characteristics and trade area.

Because it is a relatively new facet of real estate, the study and research into subjects affecting shopping centers and retail have been neglected. Most universities do not teach anything industry-specific, but concentrate instead on theories, functions, and procedure—subjects like finance, marketing, accounting and control, business policy, management practice, and so on.

We must apply these academic disciplines to complex problems, which require exercising a major element of judgment and relating the appropriate specialized academic knowledge to a complex real-life situation. Then we will have consummated the marriage of theory and practice and given birth to that all-important new generation—situational thinkers—and that is what I feel confident all of you will become, especially after absorbing what you are about to read.

One

Retailing in the Twenty-First Century

Roger D. Blackwell

R etailing in the twenty-first century promises both challenges and rewards. The twentieth century began with a retailing environment dominated by department stores depending on service and luxury and is ending dominated by discount stores and micro-marketers offering convenience and economy.

A study by retail consultants Kurt Salmon & Associates indicates that adult American shopping dropped from 12 hours a month in the 1980s to 4 hours a month in the 1990s. When consumers do shop, they increasingly favor nearby strip shopping centers and factory outlets to malls. Shoppers visit about half the stores they used to—4 stores per trip as opposed to seven. Retailing space increases from 8 square feet per capita in the early 1970s to more than 18 square feet by the 1990s. While store space was more than doubling and inventory expanding, retail sales dropped from about $190 to $160 per square foot. Overbuilding, a flattening population growth rate, and decreasing disposable income have resulted in an intensely competitive environment.

A STRUGGLE FOR DISTRIBUTION

An intense power struggle is occurring in channels of distribution—the manufacturers, wholesalers, and retailers. The development of strategies to create "customers for life" rather than discrete sales transactions in the flow of goods from manufacturer to consumer is called relationship marketing. Conflict often arises as manufacturers and retailers compete to be the primary partner in this relationship with consumers. Increasingly, retailers are winning the struggle.

The struggle for channel power is not new. Only the winner is new. The emergence of large-scale mass merchants with high volume and turnover put retailers in the driver's seat. When power retailers such as Wal-Mart or Home Depot speak, manufacturers and distributors listen. Buyers at such firms know their customers well and buy in such volume that when they tell suppliers, "change it" the suppliers do!

Internal power is also becoming more concentrated at the best retailers, as they seek more efficient infrastructures. In the past, only large department stores were highly decentralized buying cooperatives. Today, centralized buying, national promotions, and sophisticated database and logistics systems are common, forcing manufacturers to conform to retailer requirements in order to achieve low costs and rapid response. Vendors may have their national brands stores, but the orders are probably entered and controlled through RetailLink, Wal-Mart's EDI and MIS system, or other systems. Retailers such as The Gap and The Limited control nearly every aspect of what manufacturers do from design through physical distribution, ending in advertising, merchandising, and in-store selling under the control of power retailers.

MARKET SEGMENTATION

In the next century, marketing and retailing will be dominated by *market segmentation,* the process of understanding demand and developing marketing programs that will have special appeal to defined segments of the total market. The goal is to measure consumer behavior and place each person into a group (segment) that will minimize the variance in behavior between each member of the segment and maximize the variance between segments.

The ability exists now to measure and identify groups within the broader market that are sufficiently similar in characteristics and responses to warrant separate treatment in marketing programs. Intense competition between global firms makes such ability a necessity for survival.

Market segmentation can be implemented through concentrated (single-segment) marketing, or differentiated (multisegment) marketing.

In *concentrated* or *niche marketing*, the primary focus is on a single segment. Clothing firms such as Laura Ashley concentrate on a specific market target with fashions that appeal to some women but not others.

The goal in concentrated marketing is to dominate a segment. The late Jerry Garcia of the Grateful Dead defined what is necessary to succeed when he said, "You do not merely want to be considered just the best of the best. You want to be considered the only one who does what you do."

An alternative approach is to focus on two or more segments, offering a *differentiated marketing mix* for each. There is a distinct trend toward multiple product offerings targeted at different segments. Differentiated or multiple segment strategies was the key to growth at The Limited. In the 1970s and 1980s, The Limited concentrated on young, moderately affluent, fashion-oriented women. As this market segment matured, so did The Limited with more sophistication, higher price points, and slightly larger sizes. To continue growth of the corporation, a differentiated or multiple segment strategy evolved as Limited Express (now Express) was developed to reach the same segment The Limited originally reached. Lane Bryant, Lerner, Henri Bendel, Victoria's Secret, and other chains were acquired to reach different market targets with a differentiated appeal. Male segments also became target markets with Structure and Abercrombie & Fitch.

The zenith in segmentation may be found in direct marketing. Multichannel retailers are turning to direct marketing with impressive results. Through database management and sophisticated computer software, it may be nearly possible to reach the goal of a "segment of one." Using complete information on customer characteristics and preferences, highly tailored, personalized appeals can be made to buyers who otherwise are indifferent to retail advertising.

Effective marketing strategy requires that every element of the marketing mix fits together to deliver a coordinated and integrated appeal to the target customer group.

THE CHANGING STRUCTURE OF CONSUMER MARKETS

Finding growth segments involves analysis of geographical growth areas, enlarging age groups, intercultural changes, new sources of income, global opportunities to replace declining domestic markets, and other trends. Consumer trend analysis also includes reaching growth segments sooner or more effectively than competitors.

Consumer markets have four major components: (1) People and their needs, (2) ability to buy, (3) willingness to buy, and (4) authority to buy. Much of the developed world is characterized by slow population growth. But if a firm can concentrate on growing segments or take share from competitors, a firm can grow even when the total market is slowing in growth or declining.

Ethnic Segmentation in Retailing

Market segmentation by successful retailers in the twenty-first century will increasingly be influenced by ethnic trends. About three-quarters of the population was non-Hispanic White in 1992, but this segment is expected to contribute only 30% of the total population growth between 1992 and 2000 and nothing to population growth after 2030, since the segment will be declining in size. The African-American population is projected to almost double from 32 million in 1992 to 62 million in 2050. After about 2005, more African-Americans than non-Hispanic Whites will be added to the population each year. The Hispanic population will increase from 24 million in 1992 to 81 million in 2050, contributing 33% of the nation's growth from 1992 to 2000 but 57% of the growth from 2030 to 2050. The Asian and Pacific Islander population is expected to continue to be the fastest growing group, increasing from 9 million in 1992 to 13 million in 2000 and 41 million in 2050.

Changing Demographics

A changing age distribution will profoundly affect retailing. Retailers will face markets characterized by the following trends:

1. Fewer children in numbers but exerting more influence.
2. Declining numbers of young adults but increasing attention to them because of their need for consumer products already owned by older consumers.

3. Dominance of the baby boomers.
4. Rise of the mature and young again markets.

The most important key to understanding the twenty-first century may occur in 1996 when baby boomers hit age 50. Baby boomers are the large cohort of people born following World War II. Those 74 million births continued to impact markets and all other aspects of society for decades. Baby boomers know what they want—quality products that are aesthetically pleasing; personally satisfying; natural; and, if possible, noncaloric. Products and services for baby boomers must be available in convenient and value-oriented distribution channels, such as off-price but quality retailers, often in factory outlet or "value" malls. They are also the major users of catalogues because of the time convenience and high information content. By the twenty-first century, most baby boomers will be empty nesters—families whose children have not only left home but have also left the university. The result will be small families at the height of their earning power with low or no mortgages and generally reduced family responsibilities.

Marketers more recently focused on Yuppies—young urban professionals—because of their discretionary income and their influence on market trends. In the future, Yuppies will become Muppies—middle-aged, urban professionals creating even more profitable markets.

The key to understanding the empty-nesters is freedom, since they already have an adequate inventory of housing, cars, clothing, and such products. They not only have the freedom to spend on what they want; they have the freedom to withhold until they receive precisely what they want.

The Young-Again Market

Another rapid growth segment in the twenty-first century is the young-again market: consumers who have accumulated lots of chronological age but who feel, think, and buy young.

Older families have more to spend, but they need to spend less. They are thrifty and careful with the money they spend. They have experience with shopping and the ability to wait to find good value. They respond more to coupons and are willing to shift their buying to off-peak times if given an adequate incentive to do so. Nevertheless, with home mortgages paid off or nearly so, no more college educations to finance, and an ample inventory of basic appliances and furnishings, mature families are especially good prospects for luxury goods, travel-related goods and services, health care, and a wide range of financial services. On per capita after-tax basis, consumers aged 65 to 69 have high levels of discretionary income. Young-again markets are "experience" markets rather than "things" markets because they have the maturity to not associate things with happiness.

They are less willing to take risks, whether they be physical, social, or financial. Thus, need for security is higher than with other markets. Convenience is also a price for which the mature market will reward marketers. They want a computer that is easy to understand. They want to go to stores where they are sure they will find what they expect in a secure environment.

RELATIONSHIP MARKETING

Relationship retailing offers a key to understanding the next century. The best real estate and shopping center firms in the future will join with retailers and their suppliers to become process partners in establishing a strong relationship with consumers. Four requirements for a quality relationship between process partners are (a) trust, (b) frequency of communication, (c) quality of communication, and (d) norms of relationship. Effectiveness in relationship marketing is similar in structure and function to a good marriage. Values must be shared for relationships to be effective and continuing. Trust is a core variable in effective relationships.

Changing Demand

The search for growing segments in a slow growth society almost always leads to specific geographic areas. Where people live and earn their money influences consumer demand: geodemography. Projections are based on the components of change: births, deaths, and net migration. California, Texas, and Florida accounted for more than half of national population growth in the past decade. Almost half of the migrants to California are from another country. Cities are the most important unit of analysis in most marketing plans. Because of the amount of income in metropolitan areas, the New York-Newark-Jersey City CMSA is a market larger than Canada. Suburbs have grown rapidly, but today the fastest growth is occurring in "exurbs," nonmetropolitan or rural counties, adjacent to suburban or metropolitan areas.

Cities are especially important for ethnic marketing. Over half of all Americans lived in the 50 largest metro areas in 1990, but more than 70% of Asians and Hispanics lived in those areas. Most new immigrants settle in urban areas. New York is the most popular destination, but 37 other metropolitan areas in the United States receive at least 2,000 immigrants a year. Specific cities often attract immigrants from some countries more than others and retailing in the next century will increasingly take into consideration specialty stores or adaptations among retailers who recognize the specialized product preferences, languages, values, and buying patterns of geodemographic segments related to ethnic consumer groups.

Multichannel Retailing Formats

Attracting consumers to buy more from a particular supply-chain partnership (a retailer and its vendors) increasingly involves process partners and multichannel retailing formats. Specialty stores, mass merchants, and factory-direct stores dominate the in-store part of the retailing revolution. Out-of-store formats are growing in importance and need to be described as a separate trend.

Two opposing trends are especially important among retailing formats in recent years and will dominate in-store retailing formats: specialty stores and mass merchants.

Limited-line specialty stores feature narrow product lines but wide assortments, meeting the service needs of customers on a personalized basis.

Mass merchandisers provide strong price appeal based on economies associated with self-service and operational efficiencies based on cost reductions in the infrastructure. They may also offer wide assortments to consumers closely related to consumer lifestyles. Caught in the middle between these two extremes, independent and small conventional retailers of apparel, hardware, grocery, and other lines are decreasing rapidly.

Successful retailing firms will build portfolios of retailing chains which may include many formats, each positioned to specific lifestyle segments, such as Dayton-Hudson, Melville Co., Woolworth, and The Limited.

Mass merchants include Wal-Mart, one of the most successful retailers in the world with a portfolio of Wal-Mart, Sam's Club, and superstores that include groceries. Some stores include McDonald's and other retailers to provide a portfolio of formats within Wal-Mart stores that help appeal to changing lifestyles.

Superstores will become even more important participants in the retailing revolution. Home Depot, Circuit City, and Incredible Universe concentrate on specific product lines in ways that make them commodity supermarkets or category killers. They meet consumer needs in much the way that Kroger, Publix, and others do for food products.

Another form of multichannel retailing likely to dominate the next century is the factory-outlet stores. Two forms predominate. One form is factory-outlet stores in which the emphasis is on name brand merchandise at discount prices—Liz Claiborne, Mikasa, Anne Klein, and Dansk. Often they are clustered in factory outlet or "value malls" containing so many of these stores that customers are attracted from a wide area. Outlet stores provide the greatest competitive challenge to department stores because of name brands and prices. For the manufacturers, the net profit margin is often larger because they are selling in their own stores.

Other outlet stores operated by manufacturers are exemplars of customer service and selection rather than discount prices, for example Nike Town and Sony. Nike Town provides more selection than would be found at other retailers, expert salespeople backed up by computerized databases throughout the store, and merchandising excitement.

Nonstore Retailing

Dominant forms of *nonstore retailing* include direct selling, direct marketing, and electronic retailing. In-store retailing will increasingly compete with out-of-store retailing. As nonstore retailing grows, shopping centers should capture a reduced share of total retail sales. The size of nonstore retailing's market share is unknown.

In-home retailing has some advantages. Security is a concern which is expected to increase substantially in the future. Traffic congestion and increasing time pressure are other concerns enhancing in-home retail markets. Compared with the general population, in-home shoppers will differ in some important ways:

- Somewhat younger.
- Somewhat above average in education and income.
- More likely to live in a smaller town or rural area.

- Most are active retail shoppers who shop at home for reasons other than deliberate avoidance of the store or shopping mall.

Direct Selling

Direct selling includes methods of directly selling goods and services to consumers by means of personal selling, often in consumers' homes. Examples include Avon, World Book, Amway, Tupperware, and many others. Many of these firms are members of the Direct Selling Association and subscribe to a set of ethical standards designed to protect consumers and sales representatives of the firms. Longaberger baskets, as an example, failed to sell baskets effectively through retailers, but after developing a direct sales program, the firm skyrocketed in sales of handmade baskets direct to consumers through a channel employing over 25,000 representatives selling in the homes of consumers.

Direct Marketing

Direct marketing involves direct contact with consumers other than by salespersons. Direct selling is considered part of direct marketing, but usually a distinction is made between them. Direct marketing normally involves direct response to media such as advertisements, catalogues, and direct mail. Direct marketing offers the possibility of selecting specific target markets through the use of specialized mailing lists, databases or media, permitting customized appeals and creative strategy based on lifestyles and needs. Direct marketers are heavy users of predictive modeling, mailing list enhancement, lifetime value analysis, advanced forms of cross-selling or up-selling, controlled testing, and experimentation.

Electronic Retailing

Electronic retailing is a special form of direct marketing using electronic media to sell to customers. There are many forms of this rapidly growing way of reaching consumers and it is difficult to determine which one of the many competitors will be the big winners in the next century. In the past, home shoppers had an image as junk jewelry buyers with overextended credit cards, but new studies indicate that most shoppers are women in their peak earning years, socially active, married, working outside the home, and generally

better educated than the average store shopper. Shoppers on Com-
puServe and Prodigy typically are males, who are well-educated and
have a relatively high family income.

Survival of Retail Stores

Can in-store retailing survive the challenge provided by electronic
retailing and other forms of nonstore or direct marketing? It appears
that electronic marketing is about 5% of total retail sales now and
some industry analysts project about 15% sometime after the year
2000. Leading retailers will probably use the new media selectively in
combination with their store formats.

Retail Consolidation

Retail consolidation can be expected to increase. When retailers
move toward portfolio strategies, they do so by acquiring smaller retailers and infusing them with management and capital. They sometimes acquire large but slow growing retailers and "right size" their
management and capital. Also a factor is the centralization of key
retailing functions, such as logistics, management information systems (MIS), credit, distribution, finance, and product and brand
design.

Consolidation activities of the future will be based on understanding the *shiftability of functions* to their most efficient level
within and among retailers. Marketing functions include design,
storage, buying, selling, finance, promotion, and market information. Functional shiftability will also be the determinant of success
for institutions other than retailers—the wholesalers, financing institutions, and real estate developers and managers. To the degree
that these other institutions evolve programs or activities to facilitate
the efficient accomplishment of retail functions, the consolidation
movement could be more of a contractual or administrative vertical
consolidation among separate companies rather than consolidation
within a single entity. Retailers who fail to understand functional
shiftability will fail or be acquired by those who do.

With little opportunity for large retailers to open new stores,
growth will be by acquisition. Increasingly, shopping center developers and other real estate firms will be dealing with fewer retailers
at the national level who control an increasing proportion of total retail space. Complicating the problem for independent real estate

firms will be the trend for major retailers and major developers to combine strength to develop jointly the remaining few regional malls or other real estate projects that will be needed.

From Merchandising to Marketing

An evolution is occurring in retail management from merchandising to marketing. Major retail firms traditionally put great emphasis on merchandising—buying the right merchandise, displaying and stocking it correctly, pricing and taking markdowns at the right time. The career path to the top of major department and specialty stores was always as a "merchant." Today retailers are starting to put more emphasis on marketing activities that communicate with consumers outside the store environment, in an effort to create changed perceptions of the store.

The new role of advertising for retailers is for *positioning* in contrast to the traditional role of advertising for *communicating price.* An example is the use of TV advertising by Home Depot, one of America's most successful retailers, featuring an associate who is asked to define his job at Home Depot. He replies, "To help customers make their dreams come true." Wal-Mart uses advertising to position itself with "Every Day Low Prices" rather than price advertising. Sears Roebuck recently undertook a major marketing campaign to introduce the "softer side of Sears."

Marketing, rather than merchandising, requires the highest level of management to define what the retailer should be. In the past, a grocery store, department store, or apparel store was a defined type and top management attention focused on what merchandise should be inside the store. Today, and increasingly in the future, management attention will be defining the position of a retailer in the marketplace even when they have no well-defined position.

Superstores feature excellent quality, prices, and service on every imaginable item ranging from clothing to groceries. What, then, is the role of other retailers? What is the role for malls that formerly housed a variety of retailers who must now compete with superstores that duplicate merchandise lines found in the mall?

Retail Globalization

Successful retailers in the United States in the next century will also participate in retail globalization. Some firms are well established as global retailers—the Body Shop (U.K.), Benetton (Italy), and Escada

(Germany). McDonald's has circled the world, with its largest restaurants in Moscow and Beijing. Swedish retailer IKEA operates enormous home furnishings stores from New Jersey to Hong Kong.

Many retailers have been good at global sourcing for decades but retailers preparing for the next century recognize the need for global selling. Manufacturers who are successful in selling to global retailers are reorganizing their sales and marketing activities to follow global retailers around the world. The most successful real estate developers and managers will need to do the same in the twenty-first century.

STRATEGIES OF WINNING RETAILERS IN THE TWENTY-FIRST CENTURY

Only the best retailers can be expected to survive and thrive in the twenty-first century. Those that do will be those who understand the changing nature of consumer decisions as well as retailing trends that increasingly dominate the management of retailing. Store locations and understanding how consumers choose individual stores are essential to the strategy.

Location, Location, Location

Location strategies of retailers will remain critical. More consumers buy fast food from McDonald's than any other organization, partially because McDonald's has two or three times more stores than its closest competitors. Attitude research may indicate consumers prefer Wendy's or taste tests may indicate consumers prefer Burger King's Whopper, but McDonald's, with over 12,000 stores, sells twice as much as the combined sales of both of its rivals. It is difficult to find a place where consumers are not close to a McDonald's.

Cognitive maps or consumer perceptions of store locations and shopping areas are more important than actual location. Cognitive maps refer both to distances and traveling times. Consumers generally overestimate both functional (actual) distance and functional time. Variations between cognitive and functional distance are related to factors such as ease of parking in the area, quality of merchandise offered by area stores, display and presentation of merchandise by stores, and ease of driving to an area. Other factors affecting the cognitive maps of consumers include price of merchandise and helpfulness of salespeople.

The Store-Choice Decision

The process of choosing a specific store is a function of consumer characteristics and store characteristics. Consumers in each market segment form images of various stores based on their perceptions of the attributes they consider important. Consumers sort out or compare perceived characteristics of stores with evaluative criteria of the core customers. Store choice is thus a function of four variables shown in Figure 1.1, evaluative criteria, perceived characteristics of stores, comparison process, and acceptable and unacceptable stores.

Determinants of store choice decision vary by market segment and by product class. Salient or determinant attributes usually fall into the following categories: (1) location, (2) nature and quality of assortment, (3) price, (4) advertising and promotion, (5) sales personnel, (6) services offered, (7) physical store attributes, (8) nature of store clientele, (9) store atmosphere, and (10) post-transaction service and satisfaction. Location, as we have already seen, may be

FIGURE 1.1

Store Choice Process Is a Function of Salient Variables

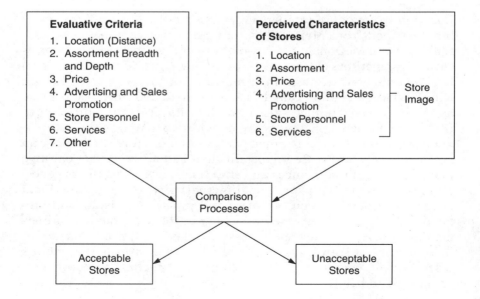

perceived by consumers in terms of time and hassle as well as actual distance.

Sales Personnel

Knowledgeable and helpful salespeople were rated as an important consideration in choice of a shopping center by more than three-quarters of those interviewed in five major metropolitan areas. Retailer performance, unfortunately, does not always match consumer expectations.

Consumer confidence in retail salespeople is often low. Home Depot has become the most successful do-it-yourself, home improvement store. Part of its success is its policy of four weeks or more training for people walking the floors to help consumers—a rarity among most retailers. Before salespeople start, they must learn about every item in their aisle and in two aisles adjacent. Salespeople, often recruited from the ranks of carpenters and electricians, are encouraged to spend time with customers, even if it takes hours.

Many people believe that no retailer can match the customer service offered by Nordstrom's. Most likely a halo effect has developed around the company's outstanding service. But service is provided by highly trained and motivated sales personnel enmeshed in a culture that defines success as personal service to customers.

What are the keys that will open doors for retailers prepared to survive the future? Three concepts will dominate the industry in the future: Retailers are (1) building a market intelligence culture, (2) developing a rapid response organization, and (3) creating a low-cost infrastructure.

Retailing provides the ultimate test of marketing strategy. Manufacturers may develop excellent products, advertise them well, and produce them with quality at a reasonable cost, but the entire process will be wasted unless it meets the ultimate test: Will retailers stock, price, service, and sell a manufacturer's product effectively? The best designed, produced, and advertised product is worthless unless retailers make it available to consumers in a rapid response format and at a cost that satisfies them.

Two

Real Estate Product Response to Retail Demand

A Community View of Retail Development

Alfred Julian Gobar

T he composition of consumer mix and the technology of retailing
have dictated changes in real estate product to respond to changing consumer needs and wants. The current evolution in retailing
focuses on value. This has stimulated innovation in real estate product—power centers, discount centers, off-price centers, factory outlet malls, and freestanding specialty retailing buildings—redefining
trade area concepts. Lack of a clearly accepted set of definitions for
new real estate products has created ambiguity. An arbitrary set of
working definitions of retail facilities that has evolved in response
to changing technology and changing consumers is as follows:

- *Convenience retailing* often takes the form of small freestanding
  merchants or strip centers that are microcosmic versions of

the pre-World War II downtown retail environment or central business district that characterized much retail real estate product before the emergence of supermarkets and shopping centers.

- *Neighborhood shopping centers* became a dominant element in real estate development for retail use beginning in about 1950. These shopping centers are designed to serve a consumer population of approximately 10,000 to 15,000 persons, generally in a trade area extending no more than two miles from the site. They assume access by private automobile. General characteristics of neighborhood shopping centers defined on this basis have changed in recent years as supermarkets have become larger and embraced more nonfood merchandise under the umbrella of the "anchor store."

- *Community shopping centers* represent a hybrid anchored by combinations of supermarkets and selected types of general merchandise stores—elements of both neighborhood and regional centers. Historically, community centers have not been competitively efficient. Their role has been to provide shopper goods to a trade area which is too small to support a full-scale regional shopping center.

- *Power centers* are typically anchored by major general merchandise stores of a type not found in regional shopping centers and specialized merchants with a discount or promotional orientation—chains such as Oshman's, Sportmart, PetsMart, Marshalls, Ross, and Circuit City. Tenant mix in power centers is still evolving.

- *Discount centers* (off-price centers, factory outlets, etc.) are in some cases anchored by a major discounter or warehouse store such as Sam's Club or Price Club. Factory outlets are a specialized type of discount center. Their locations were initially subject to "trade sensitivity" conventions, remote from major shopping facilities (regional centers) distributing the factory outlets' merchandise lines at retail prices. This constraint is being eroded, as factory outlet centers are being developed close to established conventional retail centers.

- *Regional shopping centers* are anchored by general merchandise stores (in most cases conventional department stores such as Macy's, Sears, Nordstrom, etc.). Typically, their mall shops provide a broad range of apparel merchandise. In mature markets, regional shopping centers capture about 11% to 15% of retail purchases in their trade areas. Support base for a typical regional center is defined at a ratio of approximately five to six square feet of regional center gross leasable area per capita population within the trade area (i.e., a one-million-square-foot regional center requires a trade area population of approximately 200,000 consumers).

- *Traditional central business district and main street retailers* are in large measure obsolete. Competition from power centers is hastening the demise of traditional CBD retailing. However, in the east and elsewhere, Main Street retail has survived, as in Greenwich, Connecticut, where parking is adequate, where regional centers are not particularly convenient, and where disposable personal income in the trade area is high. Some Main Streets have been invaded by chains anxious to establish deeper market penetration, contributing in some instances to a stabilization, if not a renaissance, of Main Street retailing.

- *Specialized non-anchored shopping facilities* are another emerging concept. Jewelry Marts—an unorganized assemblage of jewelry-related retailers, manufacturers, and service providers in a central place—develop a substantial cumulative anchor effect drawing support from a trade area extending 20 to 30 miles or more. Informal accumulations of furniture stores (in some cases surrounding a major anchor store) have evolved in some areas. Retailers comprehend the advantage of offering shopper goods in an environment with enough critical mass to act as an anchor, drawing support from a larger-than-typical trade area and providing greater breadth of merchandise.

- *Festival markets* have sometimes been a successful vehicle for revitalizing downtowns. Much of the gross leasable retail floor area in festival markets is devoted to product that is a repetitive purchase—principally restaurants. Relatively little space is devoted to specialty merchants. Festival markets provide extensive ongoing entertainment to enhance their draw. Festival markets usually require a large concentration of daytime population whose restaurant expenditures—a significant proportion of most consumer budgets—generate the ongoing sales volume to sustain the center. These types of shopping facilities also benefit from a large visitor population, an important component for traditional specialty shopping center merchants—with merchandise lines that represent only a small proportion of each consumer's budget.

- *True specialty shopping centers* (which embody many of the elements of a festival market) have not been a universal success. This concept usually involves some sort of unique architectural design within the facility—often in direct violation of many of the basic design rules for conventional shopping centers. Historically, specialty shopping centers have had problems defining appropriate tenants. Specialty tenants require a huge number of consumer exposures to generate significant sales volume. If, for example, average per capita expenditure in supermarkets is $1,800 a year and average per capita expenditure for crystal is $20, a crystal shop would have to be exposed to 90 times the number of consumers per square foot of gross leasable area as would a supermarket to generate a comparable sales volume. In order to achieve this exposure, successful specialty shopping centers are often located in heavy tourist traffic areas.

- *Auto plazas* have evolved in the past ten years partly because of their economic benefits to cities, as auto sales are a substantial component of retail sales. In some jurisdictions, cities share in sales taxes on new car sales. A typical relationship between consumer population and new car dealerships is on the order of 10,000 consumers per dealership. An isolated population of 20,000 persons will not necessarily support two dealerships, because not all 20,000 potential consumers prefer either a Chevrolet or a Ford. As a result, auto merchandising has a major component of "shopper good" orientation. Synergism resulting from proximity of several automobile dealerships to one another tends to benefit most of the dealerships in these plazas. Typically, car dealerships in auto plazas experience average sales volume per dealership that is two to three times the average volume per dealership for all dealerships (those in auto plazas and freestanding auto dealerships) operating in the same market areas. Ultimately, when most or all new automobile dealerships are in auto plazas, average sales volume per dealership will either revert to the mean (i.e., one-half to one-third the sales volumes of initial plaza tenants) or there will be fewer dealerships in the market area.

The evolution of new technologies in retailing and the corresponding emergence of new real estate product have frequently had a devastating impact on conventional downtown and central business district retailing and other land uses. Active local governments (motivated in some cases by chambers of commerce and real estate investors observing decreasing values for downtown real estate assets) have attempted to impede the tide of market-driven "creative destruction" by treating the symptoms of technological obsolescence. New retail development in downtowns is often subsidized or otherwise encouraged by nonmarket techniques. Most of these efforts have been unproductive because of a failure to address the principal basis for selecting a retail location—accessibility of the site to the consumers from whom the retailers will draw their support.

Effect of the Zero Sum Game

Consumer expenditure for retail purchases has been a more or less constant percentage of disposable personal income for decades. If it is assumed that a finite expenditure pool is available (albeit growing by increased real income per capita and the increased number of consumers), consumer dollars spent in one place are dollars no longer available to be spent at another place. The most prominent concepts of new real estate technology from the retail revolution typically involve stores with incredible sales volume per square foot. Dollars capture by these "Black Hole" merchants are not available to be spent in conventional retail floor space. Specific examples include the following:

- The Price Club stores (part of the Costco/Price Club organization) frequently achieve annual sales of $1,200 per square foot or more. The level of annual expenditure per one square foot of gross leasable area in a Price Club operation is enough to support eight square feet of conventional retail floor space with an average sales volume of $150 per square foot. This volume of sales would support nearly three square feet of conventional supermarket gross leasable area at average sales of $450 per square foot.

- Silo, Circuit City, Adrays, Good Guys, Frys, and so on, have emerged as high-volume consumer electronics merchants. In some areas, they capture sales of as much as $1,500 per square foot in an industry where sales in mom and pop stores are more typically less than $200 per square foot. The displacement ratio in this sector is probably three-to-one on an average basis. West Coast consumer electronics chains such as Federated, Leo's, Roger's, Sound Lab, and so on have disappeared from the scene. Even among the high-volume merchants, competition is causing reallocation of floor space in competitive markets by chains restricting the distribution of their stores.

- Home Depot, the giant in the building materials sector, frequently achieves sales volumes of as much as $350 per square foot or more at key locations. Typical independent hardware store sales has typically been less than $150 per square foot. The square footage displacement ratio of Home Depot, therefore, is at least two-to-one.

· The inevitable result of concentration of more consumer expenditure in facilities with high sales per square foot is reduced economic support for conventional retail floor space and eventually a reduction in the ratio of required gross leasable area per capita consumer.

This projection of a movement toward efficiency has resulted in some interesting anomalies: Home Depot has recently become a tenant in a large conventional regional shopping center. Two decades ago, few would have considered Home Depot and conventional regional shopping center anchor tenants as complementary to one another. Circuit City recently became a tenant in a fashion-oriented regional shopping center which is also tenanted by Neiman Marcus. This also is a strange juxtaposition of merchants in a nontraditional manner, reflecting inroads of the new concept merchandising into established venues of conventional tenant mix concepts.

Developers have a sudden, intense interest in recreation facilities as potential tenants to fill vacant space and, perhaps, infuse excitement into older centers.

Changing Community Attitudes

An increasingly adversarial environment is observed in many aspects of society, including real estate development for the retail sector. Local communities and their representatives have become concerned with the nature and type of real estate development occurring within the community for all types of land uses. This interest has been manifest in unusual ways: (1) Interminable discussions occur regarding signage (height, size, size of letters, color, positioning, etc.). (2) Parking ratios and landscape requirements have become the subject of city council and planning commission hearings as well as the delegated responsibility of ad hoc citizens' groups created to protect elected officials and staff from political pressure. (3) Developers of potentially competitive retail shopping centers have mounted local campaigns to stimulate public resistance to new retail facilities under the environmental issues.

Pressure from voter constituencies has caused elected bodies to impede development of new retail facilities that in a different political environment would have been welcome because of their fiscal benefits. Illustrative of the limited logic of some initiatives to restrict development of new and more efficient retail facilities was a proposal in a large city in southern California to impose a traffic impact fee on new supermarkets under the mistaken belief that new supermarkets increase traffic. The essence of locational strategy for supermarkets implies that the market opportunity to support a new supermarket is predicated on convenience. Therefore, the aggregate number of trip miles in a community after development of a new supermarket should be less than the prior condition if the site selection is based on sound economic reasons. If a new supermarket is not more convenient than its competitors, there is no need for it. If it is more convenient, presumably it will generate less traffic than the before condition.

Mercantilism (protection of local business from foreign competition) has now emerged at the local level. In some areas, campaigns against new Wal-Mart stores are a reaction to the perceived potential adverse competitive impact of this merchandiser on local independent merchants. The logic is analogous to defending high tariffs to protect domestic manufacturers from foreign competition at the expense of consumers. The impact of both types of policies is not good for consumers but has a certain emotional appeal.

It is increasingly incumbent on developers to demonstrate to elected officials as well as to the general public (by means of extensive public relations and educational efforts) the relationship between new retail facilities and the consumers they will serve. This requires ever more sophisticated analyses of the profile of the consumer population base pertinent to various types of merchants and communicating these relationships to political decision-making entities who become involved in this process.

Site planning has become a crucial element for achieving entitlement to develop new retail centers. Site plans seek to overcome opponents' resistance to new facilities by mitigating traffic impacts and visual impacts (through line of sight planning and landscape planning), concern over streetscape, sensitivity to parking lot lighting and its impact on surrounding residential areas, screening of truck entry and unloading dock areas from nearby residences, selection of building materials compatible with community themes (tile, brick, roof treatments, etc.), selection of compatible colors, landscaping, parking lot design, circulation, and designing for pedestrian access that may seldom be used.

Design parameters have been influenced by public resistance to merchandisers' trademarks. Some chains have been required to modify trademarks, logo, and signage in order to enter specific markets in which a particular theme is not perceived as compatible with local aesthetics. Concern over trash and paper litter associated with drive-through windows at fast-food restaurants has been responsible for imposition of design constraints that purport to control this impact.

These issues require substantial documentation of all aspects of a proposed development. For example, plans to revitalize an existing regional shopping center required the developer's expenditure of large sums on traffic studies, environmental impact reports, detailed site plans, renderings, models, public relations efforts, economic impact analyses, and a host of other documentation, all of which was subject to review by three different elected and appointed boards as well as several ad hoc citizen committees. Public hearings lasted for over a year. The number of consultants in attendance at public hearings implied consulting fees for one evening's public hearing in excess of $30,000, costs which eventually must be recovered from consumers.

While visible evidence highlights some negative public attitudes to new retail developments, less publicized public behavior is silent testimony to the good favor in which the public holds the new retail concepts. New power centers and big box discounters experience instant sales success when they open. The State Highway Patrol was called in to control traffic at the opening of a new IKEA store in California. The actions of the general public speak volumes.

The Problem and the Opportunity

Changing aspects of consumer support for retail facilities and innovative responses to changing needs devised by the retail industry have created special needs that increasingly dictate broad participation by government and the public in the development process for new shopping centers.

The new concepts of retailing generally require large sites to accommodate large anchors in order to compete in a broad trade area and offer a range of specialized goods and services. The requirement for exposure to a broad trade area population implies a special premium for sites near the centers of population groupings—a distinct change from the previous wave of evolution of shopping facilities from downtown locations to sites on the edge of town. It is virtually impossible in many cases for a developer to assemble an adequately sized site near the center of a trade area population base without the power of eminent domain that resides in the public sector. Even if a site in a central location could be assembled by a private entity, its cost may be prohibitive in terms of the time involved and the cost of purchasing developed real estate that must be demolished in order to make way for a new shopping center.

The understandable incentive for cooperation between cities and community redevelopment agencies and the developers of the new concept shopping centers is influenced by a number of factors.

Although cities may have the power of eminent domain which is crucial to assembling sites in some areas, they may not have the financial resources to acquire a site for an overall price that permits development of new retail shopping centers in a financially feasible manner. This problem implies the need to capture part of the increased cash flow benefits derivative of a new shopping center in a vehicle to permit the public agency to employ these resources to assemble a site.

Sites in the center of population nodes are frequently associated with highway transportation networks that are old and with inadequate capacity to accommodate increased traffic associated with the high volumes achieved in the new concept centers. This poses yet another financial obstacle to be overcome by the successful cooperation of public and private entities.

One essential element common to a number of the key new concepts of retailing is thin profit margins. New retail concepts are based on value retailing at one end of the value/service spectrum and service at the other. Value-oriented centers are the heart of the new wave. A private sector developer, therefore, represents only a limited source of funds to overcome the financial obstacles to this process.

These constraints are exacerbated in many areas by increasing community involvement in land use decisions motivated by environmental concerns and also by generalized mistrust of government initiatives, especially those that involve cooperation with developers who in turn are the object of distrust by the general public.

Despite these obstacles, each entity involved in collective effort to respond to a changing market environment has incentives to achieve the objective. City management and city staff view commercial development as a device for enhancing the fiscal strength of the city. Major commercial developments also provide a vehicle for achieving desirable land use and circulation goals with regard to blighted areas, improving infrastructure, providing better highway access, and a variety of other planning goals. Within the past 20 years, city management has taken an increasingly activist role in land use planning of all types, especially in relationship to retail development.

Developers of shopping centers respond to a profit incentive that requires key locations in the center of a large consumer population base at an affordable land price in order to accommodate the new types of retailing that are making several types of conventional retailing technologically obsolete.

The general public also benefits from the introduction of new retail concepts into the trade areas in which they reside in terms of exposure to a broader selection of merchandise at convenient locations, price competition, enhanced service levels—all the elements that combine to make a shopping center development feasible in the traditional sense of feasibility dictated by market support.

The key challenge to embracing the objectives of entities interested in and affected by the development process is to define procedures that are an effective tradeoff between the objectives and constraints perceived by each entity—multiple vectors in a multidimensional problem.

The market in its infinite creativity has been trying with uncertain success (in terms of the marginally effective efforts historically to revitalize central business districts, for example) to find techniques to balance these positive goals and the negative byproducts for each entity in an equitable and efficient way. The case studies that follow illustrate how competing objectives have been balanced against one another to result in effective resolution.

CASE STUDY 1: THE DILEMMA CONFRONTING FOUNTAIN VALLEY, CALIFORNIA

Problem

In 1987, the City of Fountain Valley, California, represented 2.51% of Orange County's population base but accounted for only 1.67% of its taxable retail sales. Essentially, a third of the taxable retail expenditures of the city's population base benefited retail sectors in other cities. As a practical matter, residents of Fountain Valley were subsidizing surrounding cities in an amount equivalent to $1,262,640 a year—the city's share of California sales tax collections lost because of poor market capture. Opportunities to ameliorate this outflow of potential tax revenue were tactically limited. A regional shopping center which would effectively reverse these flows was a practical impossibility. Fountain Valley is located between two major regional shopping centers immediately adjacent to it both east and west.

Development of an auto plaza in Fountain Valley (the City) was restricted by the limited availability of a suitable site with freeway visibility and access, and more importantly by the competitive impact of existing concentrations of new car dealerships located both to the east and the west of the City along the major east/west freeway that passes through the City.

Outflows of consumer support were concentrated in merchandise lines associated with regional centers—apparel stores, general merchandise, and the "other" category—and in auto sales. These four categories accounted for $160,350,000 a year outflow of consumer expenditure—more than the net outflow overall. Some elements in the City's retail sector were being supported in part by shoppers residing in neighboring cities. Convenience-type retailing, as well as some specialized categories of retailing within the City, generated minor inflows of consumer support in 1987.

Limited practical ability to capture the major outflows through development of either a regional shopping center or a new car auto plaza implied the need to focus attention on a potential solution from the new concepts of retailing related to big box superstores with high sales volume per square foot. In this competitive market area, these types of tenants or land users were being aggressively wooed by other cities. As a result, the merchants representing the best solution to the City's fiscal problem had little or no incentive to pay high prices for even excellent sites in Fountain Valley.

Because of a long-term landbanking investment philosophy of one major landowner in the City, a large, vacant site of about 120 acres on a major highway was available, without the need for parcel assemblage or demolition of improvements, in order to create a site for development of a big box retail operation. The landowner, however, had for more than 20 years maintained a high reservation price for the land and was reluctant to consider sale at a price compatible with the merchandiser's financial parameters. In addition, off-site highway and drainage infrastructure would be required to facilitate development of the approximate 120 acres for this or any other use.

The merchandiser, although unwilling to pay a premium price for the land, had extensive financial resources and was convinced that the available site was an excellent location.

Solution

A financial arrangement that addressed each of the objectives and limitations of the three parties involved—the merchant, the City/Redevelopment Agency, and the landowner—included the following components:

1. The merchant agreed to lend the City/Redevelopment Agency the funds to provide for installation of necessary highway and roadway infrastructure, drainage, and other infrastructure elements, as well as to write the purchase price of the land down to an acceptable level.

2. The City/Redevelopment Agency agreed to rebate a defined percentage of the incremental sales tax that would be generated by the project back to the merchant as a repayment of the loan. The periodic payment (defined in terms of a share of the incremental sales tax generated) was not specified in an absolute dollar amount. The key element in the financial negotiations was the term (maturity) of the loan and the interest rate. The terms of the agreement specified the share of sales taxes rebated (a variable cost to the public agency), the life of the loan (a fixed period of years or until fully paid off), and the interest rate (tied to prime). The City received about half the incremental sales tax for the life of the loan and all of it at the end of the loan, even if the loan were never to be fully retired within the specified time limit.

3. The landowner agreed to make the site available for a purchase price consisting of the amount that the merchant would willingly pay plus pay a subsidy from the City/Redevelopment Agency. In addition, the balance of the landowner's parcel would become more immediately developable as a result of the installation of new highways and streets, drainage facilities, and so on.

The general structure of this arrangement resulted in several benefits. The City's tax revenue from sales tax was increased. The net increase was only a portion of the gross incremental sales tax derivative of the new retailer's contribution to total sales tax collections in the City. This was tax revenue, however, that would not otherwise be generated. The public agency also had funds available to facilitate the project and to accelerate development of the balance of the large

parcel for other tax-generating uses. The merchant acquired a key location at a price consistent with its objectives, generated tax-exempt
interest income plus repayment of the initial cash advance over a period of somewhat less than 20 years, and acquired a site large
enough to accommodate complementary retail uses. The landowner
received payment for the site provided for the shopping center at a
price consistent with the landowner's objectives and benefited from
the increased developability of the balance of the site due to installation of off-site and on-site infrastructure at no cost to the
landowner.

Reactions

However, concerned residents of the area surrounding the site generated vociferous opposition to the project, employing many arguments relative to environmental impact, traffic, and general distrust
of an activist program on the part of the City administration. This
issue required that the transaction be exposed to a public election,
which in turn involved aggressive public relations and education
campaigns throughout the community—on both sides.

Results

In 1992, total taxable sales in the City (on a constant 1992 dollar
basis) were $209 million a year more than in 1988 when the negoti-
ations were initiated. Based on the applicable tax rate, sales tax revenues to the City in 1992 (on a current dollar basis) were $2.7 million
more than in 1987. The City was 2.14% of the County's population
and 3.12% of Countywide sales tax collection, in contrast with its
being 2.51% of the County's population and only 1.67% of its sales
tax generation in 1987. Part of this increment of sales taxes, however
(less than half), was diverted to amortize the merchant's initial loan
to the public sector. If the sales tax revenues are extraordinarily high,
the loan will be paid off prior to the defined time limit and diversion
cease. As a worst case situation for the City/Redevelopment Agency,
the loan will not be fully paid off at its expiration date, at which time
loan payments will cease in any case and the full sales tax increment
flow to the City. The City generates a net fiscal benefit out of the incremental revenues that, by terms of the agreement, was unambiguous and involved virtually no downside financial risk to the City's
position.

CASE STUDY 2: ATTEMPTS TO INCREASE SALES TAX REVENUE IN BREA, CALIFORNIA

Problem

A market research report commissioned by Brea (the City) in 1985 identified additional developmental potential within the City for a large neighborhood shopping center (±200,000 square feet). This type center would not cannibalize sales tax collections from existing retail developments in the City since it would respond to outleakage of consumer support. As a result of a previous shopping center development initiative, the City/Redevelopment Agency was in strong financial position from property tax increment and sales tax flow from a regional shopping center that had been in operation for approximately ten years. In 1985, the most significant outflow of consumer retail expenditure from the City was concentrated in convenience-type retailing as drugstores, food stores and liquor stores, and so on and hard goods as building materials, furniture and appliances, plus the auto sector. Sales at the regional shopping center generated total sales tax revenues in the City (despite these outflows) well in excess of the level consistent with consumer expenditures of City residents. This extraordinary financial position provided the City/Redevelopment Agency with the financial resources to attempt to fine-tune its retail sector through encouraging development of either an auto plaza (requiring freeway frontage) or a large neighborhood center, a component of which would be a building materials outlet.

The opportunity to assemble a freeway-oriented site for developing an auto plaza was constrained not only by a lack of effective land availability, but also by competitive factors. Although large contiguous parcels adjacent to the freeway were potentially available, they were committed to uses that implied some difficulty and time to assemble a site. New auto plazas had recently been developed along the freeway that serves this community at locations less than five miles away. Several other cities in the surrounding area had also recently initiated efforts to assemble auto plazas, creating the risk of an unproductive bidding war.

The key location in this city for the development of a large neighborhood shopping center (the 100% old downtown intersection) was characterized by old commercial development (more than 60 years old), and old and substandard single family units, much of which had become rental housing for low-income Hispanic families.

In addition, the City's long-term traffic plan required widening of both of the major streets that create the intersection that defines the key location for this type of center within the community.

The City Council was initially constrained by a self-imposed commitment not to employ eminent domain to acquire residential property—a large component of the land use at the site most ideally suited for the target type of retail development. Condemnation of the commercial land along the two major highways, although permissible under City policy, would result in the demolition of the old downtown commercial element of the City. Much of this commercial development was substandard and typified by low rents attracting relatively marginal uses such as auto body shops, low-rent restaurants, bars, churches, obsolete movie theaters, hobby shops, upholsterers, hardware stores—all very low-rent uses.

Policy Alternatives

The least-intensive policy to achieve the necessary highway improvements and removal of the blighted commercial facilities from the City's old downtown core would have been a program to acquire the commercial properties by threat of condemnation for purposes of street widening. The City/Redevelopment Agency's financial resources were more than adequate to achieve this limited solution. Its achievement, however, would leave unaddressed the large amount of blighted residential development remaining in the area. In fact, it would have visually exposed this land use element to traffic on the improved highways after the highway redevelopment process had been completed.

A more aggressive alternative was to embark on a program to assemble a site suitable for the type of shopping center for which there was at that time an apparent market opportunity. In order to implement this solution, however, it would be necessary for the City to reverse its self-imposed restriction on use of eminent domain in order to acquire residential property. The second policy option was selected as being most appropriate in terms of all of the objectives of the City's policymakers—a decision which generated a number of ancillary problems contributing to a good deal of political turmoil and lawsuits.

One obstacle to implementing the second alternative was locating and securing cooperation of a strong developer with the patience to accommodate the long time required to assemble the site. As the process evolved, the multiple landowners in the site area developed an intense stake in the outcome. This concern eventually stimulated a number of lawsuits and generated acrimonious debate in the City over a period extending from 1985 through 1994. Some landowners opposed the use of eminent domain to acquire residential properties in the study area—probably from a misunderstanding of the tax and financial benefits of selling property under threat of condemnation (proceeds of sale of property under threat of condemnation are not subject to capital gains tax if a replacement property of similar or greater value is acquired within three years of the date of the sale of the property to the public agency).

Tenants in the older commercial portions of the study area became increasingly sensitive to the risk of being dislocated from cost-effective facilities and not being able to acquire facilities with comparable traffic exposure at similarly low rents. Additional opposition was based on the historical implications of parts of the established central business district—potential demolition of buildings which had given character to the City for more than 70 years. These demolitions would have occurred under the first policy option in any case—a factor that became lost in the debate. Another constituency involved in the process was the low-income renters in the substandard residential elements of the site area, the vast majority of which were low-income Hispanic families, occasioning some discussion of ethnic discrimination.

Solution

Despite the wide range of potential opposition to the project inherent in the noncongruent objectives of the various affected parties, the City/Redevelopment Agency implemented an orderly process which included the following elements:

1.   Financially strong shopping center developers were solicited to identify a developer with whom an exclusive negotiation could be undertaken. Developers were encouraged to include local landowners as part of the development partnership—a procedure that confers priority on those developers who successfully achieve this type of partnership.

2.   On the basis of the powers of eminent domain available for street widening purposes, tenants along the frontage of both the major streets were relocated and properties acquired in order to facilitate the street widening process prior to development of the shopping center.

3. In order to acquire the interior portions of the study area, the City's policy against use of eminent domain to acquire residential property was reversed. This achievement occasioned controversy, some of which was resolved in the negotiation of particularly favorable purchase prices for specific sites, land swaps, and a variety of other tactical devices.

4. Many relocated and potential relocated tenants in the older commercial portions of the area became vocal opponents in the process because of dissatisfaction with the substitute locations at which relocated businesses eventually found themselves.

The historical constituency's concerns were addressed in terms of design concepts for the new center, physical relocation of some historical buildings, donations of artifacts and architectural features to the local historical museum, and so on. Other public relations initiatives included walking tours of the project area, eliciting resident input to design concepts, provisions for parks, paseos, and other qualitative features in the design, and so on. Nonetheless, this procedure stimulated tremendous civic dispute resulting in changes in the structure of the City Council, addition of staff members with special talents in related fields, and public relations campaigns on both sides of the issue.

Results

Eventually, nine years after the original policy discussions, the site had been assembled, the structures had been demolished, the highway widening process was nearing completion.

The City/Redevelopment Agency's financial contribution to the success of the project has been extraordinary and probably exceeds the present value of the combined financial benefits of the shopping center development both in terms of property tax increment (which is limited because of the high price at which the sites were acquired) and the net sales tax that will be generated as a result of the project's completion and occupancy.

Over the protracted time period required to implement this program, two new neighborhood centers were developed in areas either within the subject site's trade area or close enough to it to exercise a competitive influence on the new center. In addition, a nearby preexisting Gemco store was converted to a large Lucky supermarket, further eroding the underexploited market opportunity defined in

1985. During this interval, development of new retail facilities in the region had resulted in a gradual reduction in supportable land values which in turn caused a reduction in the value of the site to the developer and stimulated renegotiation of the land price and terms. These circumstances implied uncertain financial results in terms of the City/Redevelopment Agency's commitment of capital relative to the projected financial benefits of the City/Redevelopment Agency. There were, however, several clearly unambiguous benefits, many of which are still in the process of being realized.

The street widening and improvement process that would have been mandatory in any case has been virtually fully achieved with excellent results. The City's most blighted area has been razed and is being redeveloped with new facilities, which architecturally capture many attributes of the pre-existing central business district. Citizens of the community will have greater access to retail shopping opportunities. Parts of the site have been dedicated to high-density, moderate-priced housing, replacing the low-density, old, moderate-priced housing that was demolished to make way for the development, improving land use efficiency of residential elements of the project area. The developer acquired a site at well below market price which should confer on the project the potential for financial success. Some relocated businesses are prospering in new locations. Some of the affected landowners were able to liquidate investments in California real estate at a time when values were declining and to reinvest in properties that are significantly more financially efficient than the properties that were sold to make way for the project. Not all of the participants in this process, however, wound up being net beneficiaries.

CASE STUDY 3: REDEVELOPMENT OF A REGIONAL SHOPPING CENTER IN RIVERSIDE, CALIFORNIA

Problem

In the mid-1980s, owners of the Tyler Mall in Riverside (the City) announced plans to expand and modernize this fifteen-year-old regional shopping center, capitalizing on its excellent location by expansion through intensive development. This regional shopping center was first opened in 1970. Sited on 65-acres, the Tyler Mall consisted of slightly over 800,000 square feet of gross leasable area in 1985. Plans for its revitalization included addition of Nordstrom as an anchor, modernization of the facility, and expanding it to slightly over 1.1 million square feet to become the Galleria at Tyler. The two-level enclosed Galleria with 1.1 million square feet on 64 acres required development of parking structures. Anticipated increase in traffic dictated street and road improvements.

The City was prepared to assist the development of either a new regional shopping center or a rehabilitated Tyler Mall within the City in order to capture increased sales tax revenues. The City's general commitment to any developer of a regional shopping center consisted essentially of a rebate of one-half the incremental sales tax generated.

The financial structure to facilitate more intense use of the 65-acre Tyler Mall site included a complex arrangement for providing structural parking. Steps in this process were as follows:

1. The Mall entity and one of its anchors leased three parcels of land to the City.
2. The City leased these parcels to a municipal improvement corporation.
3. The municipal improvement corporation (employing the shopping center management group) developed a parking structure on the three parcels of leased ground.
4. The completed parking structure was leased to the City which in turn leased the facility to the shopping center for parking.

Financing for development of the parking structure was facilitated through a general obligation of the City secured by a series of revenue sources arranged in decreasing order of seniority as follows:

- The City pledged up to 50% of the incremental sales tax revenue to the City derivative of the expansion of Tyler Mall and its conversion into the Galleria at Tyler to debt service on $7.9 million of bonds. The sales tax rebate pledge was limited to 20 years which in turn limited the life of the bonds.
- Shopping center owners were committed (by the lease) to cover any shortfall in revenues from sales tax rebates required to service the debt on the parking structure. This guarantee allowed for no subsequent recapture at the time that sales tax revenue became adequate to service the debt if in fact this became an issue.

- The full faith and credit of the City of Riverside provided the third level of support for the bonds.

Even in this case, it was difficult to secure insurance on the $7.9 million bond issue. The bonds, although basically a public sector financing vehicle, are not tax exempt. Taxable bonds are increasingly being used to finance economic development involving public/private partnership.

Construction of required traffic improvements was financed by an $8.0 million bond issue supported by an assessment district. The taxpayer support for the assessment district is the tenant base in the renamed Galleria at Tyler.

Assessment districts are a common means of financing infrastructure in California on the presumption that landowners in the assessment district area benefit from the infrastructure improvements and, therefore, are able to retire the debt.

Opposition to the project was in large measure driven by developers of a potentially competitive shopping center located in another part of the community—about ten miles from the Tyler Mall location. This entity financed a strong campaign in opposition to the Galleria at Tyler, attacking the project on the basis of traffic, crime, visual pollution, air pollution, destruction of citrus groves (through pollution), inadequate market support, and unrealistic financial projections. Any element in the entitlement package that appeared vulnerable to challenge was attacked—often by qualified professionals retained by the opposing shopping center developers.

The opposition enlisted enthusiastic cooperation from a range of environmentalists seeking to stem urbanization in this once semirural area on all fronts. Top financial experts were brought to public hearings in Riverside from as far away as New York City in order to contest the economic and financial projections on which the Galleria at Tyler restructuring was based. The opposition's presentations were managed by a skillful local attorney.

The process became almost siege-like, costing the centers' owners between $2 and $3 million. Managers of the entitlement process for the shopping center owner became active in local civic and charitable groups, enlisting active support from local business and political leaders. Public relations campaigns on both sides created a flurry of news articles, "studies," quotes from civic leaders, and visits to the community by top management of the major chains that would tenant the Galleria at Tyler.

Results

The grand re-opening of the Galleria at Tyler occurred in October 1991, just at the beginning of southern California's most severe economic downturn since the depression. Nonetheless, achieved sales at the Galleria at Tyler fell only slightly below projections. The project is performing much as anticipated.

Another major regional shopping center was developed at a location outside the City near the site of the center proposed by the opponents of the Galleria at Tyler. Various components of the opposition development entity have filed for bankruptcy. Local shoppers generally reflect enthusiastic support for this shopping center, which utilized a site that had been incubated by a small conventional regional shopping center for nearly twenty years as market demand in the surrounding area matured to a level to support a full-scale 1.1-million-square-foot, well-anchored, super-regional shopping center.

CONCLUSION

Retail development attracts public scrutiny out of all proportion to retail land use as a share of all developed urban land. Typically, retail land use represents considerably less than 5% of all developed land in a balanced urban area—actually closer to 3.6%.

An important aspect of the political interest in retail land use is the implication that retail developers and their tenants represent an unlimited source of financial resources available to achieve community goals—infrastructure, fees, and tax revenues. A retail center becomes a vehicle to impose additional taxes on the consumer support base to the extent that the cost of development of the retail center is increased because of onerous regulations and controls. These costs are passed along to consumers (voters) in a way that is obscure to most. The incidence of the increased cost is masked. The impact is reflected in higher cost of goods in the shopping center in order to compensate for higher rents. New centers, therefore, are a politically effective vehicle to extract resources from consumers under the guise of "protecting" them from negative environmental factors and the implication that these costs will be borne by "outside developers."

The broad definition of environmental concerns embraces diverse elements—traffic, visual impact, privacy, potential for increased crime, negative fiscal consequences, negative competitive impact on established local merchants, air quality concerns, employment opportunities (and the quality of new jobs), and noise pollution. Some of these issues are germane. Often overlooked is the likelihood that a new center will succeed only if it gives consumers something better than they have now. Convenience, price, service, and the retail site itself are market factors which if efficiently exploited will tend to reduce environmental impacts of traffic, noise, and air pollution. The general perception, however, is that while the ambient level of these impacts will be reduced by development of more conveniently located and consumer friendly retail facilities, the impact of the facility on the immediate neighborhood is not a good trade off for the general benefit.

General beneficiaries of a new project are usually not motivated actively to support it. The constituency that perceives a risk of being damaged by geographic redistribution of environmental impacts is more likely to oppose actively a new project. This imbalance between general benefits and costs and localized benefits and costs has contributed to a need for stronger efforts to communicate both the advantages and disadvantages of alternate forms of retail land use. This communication should occur in a dispassionate—even academic—format, not in an adversarial hearing at which the issues are being discussed in relationship to a specific project.

Three

The Investment Structure and Investors in Retail Real Estate

Hans C. Mautner

Approximately 40,000 shopping centers exist currently in the United States. This is the estimate of the International Council of Shopping Centers (ICSC) and the National Research Bureau (NRB), the authoritative sources in this industry. Even the ICSC and NRB are limited to highly educated estimates rather than an exact census because the definition of what is a shopping center is quite loose and the construction/development of shopping centers, however defined, goes on even during periods of economic downturns. Table 3.1 shows one possible categorization and inventory of shopping centers.

The ICSC defines the various categories of shopping centers as:

Neighborhood Center

- Probably anchored by a supermarket.
- GLA square footage: 30,000–100,000.
- Total area: 3–10 acres.
- Total stores: 15–20.
- Population: 2,500–40,000 living within 1.5 miles.
- Drive time: 10 minutes or less.

Community Center

- Probably anchored by a junior department store, a variety store, or a discount store in addition to a supermarket.
- GLA square footage: 100,000–300,000.
- Total area: 10–30 acres.
- Total stores: 40.
- Population: 40,000–150,000 living within 3–5 miles.
- Drive time: 15 minutes or less.

Regional Center

- Probably anchored by one or two department stores.
- GLA square footage: 400,000–800,000.
- Total area: 30–50 acres.

TABLE 3.1

U.S. Shopping Centers as of December 31, 1994

Center Type	Number of Centers	Aggregate Gross Leasable Area (Millions of Sq. Ft.)
Neighborhood	25,450	1,239
Community	13,035	2,198
Regional	1,210	675
Super Regional	673	749
Total	40,368	4,861

Source: National Research Bureau.

- Total stores: 100.
- Population: 150,000 living within 8 miles.
- Drive time: 20 minutes or less.

Super-Regional Center

- Probably anchored by three or more department stores.
- GLA square footage: 800,000–1.5 million.
- Total area: 50–125 acres.
- Total stores: 200–225.
- Population: 300,000 living within 12 miles.
- Drive time: 30 minutes or less.

These are the shopping center categories that have dominated the industry for the past 3 to 4 decades. Not everyone would make the same distinctions. There is overlap, but these categories are useful for getting some idea of the composition of the universe of shopping centers.

There have been some relatively recent additions to product-type that may fall outside of these categories and which are of increasing significance, but which do not necessarily fit into any convenient size or definitional matrix. These include power centers and outlet centers.

Power centers are a more recent phenomenon, having come into existence less than a decade ago. The ICSC defines a power center as a center "dominated by several large anchors, including discount department stores, off-price retailers, warehouse clubs, or category killers." Retail facilities known as category killers get their name from their focus on vast selection of goods and expertise at low prices. Power centers can consist of several free-standing anchors; typically there are few specialty-store tenants. Power center characteristics are:

- Probably anchored by three or more "category killers," home improvement, discount department, warehouse club, and/or off price stores.
- GLA square footage: 250,000–800,000.
- Total area: 25–80 acres.
- Primary trade area: 5–10 miles.

Outlet centers consist of sizable accumulations of discount and manufacturers' outlet stores. They range from the almost haphazard accumulation of retail facilities that has occurred in tourist centers (such as Freeport, Maine, the home of L.L. Bean) and older mill towns like New Bedford, Massachusetts, to specifically designed and created off-price centers like the various "Mills"-designated properties developed by Western Development Co. The size of these collections of retail outlets ranges from 100,000 sq. ft. to 2 million sq. ft.

Shopping centers have been in a state of continuing evolution. Table 3.2 documents how aggregate square footage of shopping centers, each by our arbitrarily selected categories, has evolved.

Notice the enormous growth in shopping center space of all kinds. The aggregate gross leasable area of all centers is about 20 sq. ft. of shopping center space for every man, woman, and child in the United States. At 20 feet per capita, the United States has almost 50% more shopping center square footage than the most heavily retailed countries in Western Europe, and certainly more than seems necessary here—a fact which would seem laden with portent for the future.

A second development of some interest is the recent, rapid, and significant emergence of the power and off-price center categories. These are categories that did not exist until the early 1980s and now represent reasonably significant numbers—particularly in the power

TABLE 3.2

Aggregate Gross Leasable Area
(Millions of Sq. Ft.)

	Center Type				
Year	Neighborhood	Community	Regional	Super-Regional	Total
1974[a]	549	748	319	259	1,875
1980[a]	798	1,127	487	541	2,953
1990[b]	1,132	1,931	618	716	4,397
1993[b]	1,214	2,146	666	744	4,770
1994[b]	1,239	2,198	675	749	4,861
Increase 1974–1994	226	294	212	289	259

[a] *Source:* Shopping Center World Magazine.
[b] *Source:* National Research Bureau.

center category. Power center space—much of which has been developed in conjunction with the expansion of Wal-Mart, surely *the* retailing phenomenon of the last decade or two—now represents approximately 2% of all shopping center space.

A third observation is the increasing impact of regional and super-regional centers. Table 3.2 suggests that as a percentage of total retail square footage the regional and super-regional center categories have maintained a generally constant percentage. Super-regional centers generate a disproportionate percentage of retail sales, however. They are truly the heavyweight shopping facilities—and as such they and regional centers will be the focal point of the balance of this chapter.

THE INDUSTRY'S STRUCTURE

The retail industry is sufficiently diffuse so that single definitions do not suffice. With that reservation noted, the sectors which make up the industry's fundamental constituency are:

1. Retailers.
2. Financing sources.
3. Developers.

Participants from the three sectors are common, at least generically, to shopping centers of all kinds—although different combinations of retailers, financing sources, and developers will be found in the different center types.

Retailers

The universe of retailers is substantial, diverse, and almost always in the process of change. Retailers who appear in shopping centers range from titans such as Wal-Mart, Sears, and The Limited to a local laundry or barbershop. Neighborhood and community centers have a greater representation of neighborhood tenants, for example, service-oriented stores and/or shops with a local flavor, while the larger regional centers are primarily home to retailers having regional or national presences. The high rents and long operating hours required by regional centers have led to the virtual disappearance of local tenants in malls.

The presence of viable anchor tenants—department stores and/or mass merchants—is still critical to a successful mall. The business arrangement with a mall's anchors is characteristically financially burdensome to the center's developer/owner. As the number of viable anchor tenants continues to contract, the bargaining leverage of these anchor tenants has increased. The difficulty and expense of negotiating arrangements with them has increased correspondingly.

There has been a concurrent and significant contraction in the number of retailers who are viable mall tenants. If it is the anchor tenants who are essential for the development of the shopping center, the mall tenants are most important from the developer's point of view. It is the revenue from the mall tenants that provides the lion's share of the financial return to the regional shopping center owner. Furthermore, it is the mix of tenancy achieved by the owner, that is, what stores appear in the mall and where, that is a material factor in determining the appeal and ultimate success of a particular shopping center. A reduction in the number of viable, attractive mall retailers is bad news for the industry, particularly for shopping center owners/developers. Not only is there a reduction of potential offerings to customers—the increasing sameness of shopping centers is a recurring and increasing complaint—but also the increasing concentration of mall retailing amongst a few companies of significance has greatly increased the negotiating leverage of those tenants. Additionally, the economic consequences to a center of the bankruptcy of such a larger tenant(s) are obviously much more severe.

Some indication of the degree of concentration in mall retailing that has occurred over the past few years is suggested in Table 3.3. Department store anchor tenants are not considered in either the numerator or denominator in establishing the percentages which appear in Table 3.3.

Financing Sources

Except in rare cases, one or more third-party sources of short- and long-term finance are an integral part of the creation and/or ownership of a shopping center. As such, financing sources have been and are a critical part of the shopping center industry. In fact, the health of the shopping center industry at any given time is probably directly related to the corresponding level of participation of financial institutions in the business.

The sources of capital for this industry are broad and have changed over time, as have the ways in which those sources have

TABLE 3.3

Retailer Concentration[a]
**Percentage of Mall Space Occupied by Largest Space
Users (as Percent of Total Mall GLA)**

Mall Area Occupied By	1986	1990	1994
Five largest users[b]	19.39%	23.67%	29.21%
Eight largest users[b]	24.70%	29.59%	35.09%

[a] Based on average of three specific major regional shopping centers.
[b] Includes all tenants owned by a single corporate parent. The top five and eight users were not necessarily the same throughout the period covered.
Source: Corporate Property Investors.

participated. A listing of major capital sources—both presently active and some no longer so—includes:

- Commercial banks (U.S. and foreign).
- Insurance companies (U.S. and foreign).
- Pension funds (U.S. and foreign).
- Savings and Loan organizations.
- Mutual funds.
- Private equity from:
  Property developers (private and corporate).
  Tax-motivated investors.
  REIT investors.
  Wall Street sources.

Developers

Shopping center developers come in all shapes and sizes. Neighborhood and community centers have been developed by all manner of individuals and organizations, often as an adjunct to the developer's principal activity. For example, countless small centers have been developed by home builders as an amenity to a housing development that represented his or her principal developmental undertaking. Some centers been developed by a local entrepreneur with little or no specific experience in the business except local knowledge, good commercial instincts, access to capital—either third party or his own—and the ability to persevere (a high tolerance for frustration is a required characteristic in the development process). At the other end of the spectrum, some highly professional development organizations have undertaken neighborhood and community center creation on a regional or national basis. Representative organizations include:

Developers Diversified
Federal Realty
Leo Eisenberg & Co.
Konover & Associates, Inc.
Melvin Simon & Associates, Inc.
Lat Purser & Associates
Riley-Pearlman
Terranomics
Weingarten Realty Investors
George D. Zamias Co.

The business of regional mall creation has involved a much smaller group of more specialized and powerful developmental organizations. The complexity, cost, and huge time commitment involved in regional mall creation cannot safely be treated as an adjunct to another business, but requires the full effort of a multidisciplined and specialized organization.

Mall development has essentially been the purview of two types of organizations: (1) family companies that have evolved into specialists in this particular field and (2) corporate subsidiaries of major retailers who saw mall creation as a way to be proactive in the expansion of their retailing business.

Among the more significant participants in the former category have been:

The Cafaro Co.
Crown America Corp.
The Edward J. De Bartolo Corp.
General Growth Properties
The Hahn Co.
Kravco
The Richard and David Jacobs Group
Melvin Simon & Associates, Inc.
The Taubman Co., Inc.

The category of retailer subsidiaries included, at one time or another, subsidiaries of:

Allied Stores Corp.
Dayton Hudson Corp.
Federated Department Stores
The May Company
Sears (Homart Development Company)

There are significant exceptions to the generalization that regional mall developers come from these two basic categories. A number of developments representing some of this country's greatest shopping centers, such as South Coast Plaza in Costa Mesa, California, Bellevue Square in Washington, DC, and Lenox Square in Atlanta, Georgia. These were projects conceived and initially implemented by individuals for whom this was their only shopping center project—although Lenox Square did subsequently become owned, expanded, and developed by an institutional owner.

There has been substantial evolution in the developer universe. Many of the family-dominated organizations have become corporate and/or made more institutional (the recent transformation into public REIT form being merely the most recent iteration). A number of the retailer-owned developmental organizations have been divested, some finding their way into (and then out of) large financial institutions, such as Equitable Co. and Prudential Insurance Co.

Further evolution is certain. For one thing, far less development is likely in the future. The United States already seems to have more square footage of retail space in place than it can use for some time. It is not all of the right type nor is it all in the right place, so additional development will occur. The periodic confluence of overanxious and/or overabundant capital, congenitally optimistic developers with existing organizations looking for something to do, and retailers who, no matter how competitive the environment, are convinced that their new store(s) will be the winner, will cause new centers to be built, whether they are needed or not. But the high watermark of the developmental part of the industry seems to be past.

The consolidation of retailers has caused many of the great names of retailing to fall victim to the forces of change. A similar consolidation of developers is surely coming—a cheerless prospect for that industry.

THE DEVELOPMENT PROCESS: FINANCE AND STRUCTURE

The development of a shopping center is fundamentally a joint undertaking among retailers, a developer, and one or more capital sources—which may include the retailers and the developer. The principal retailer participants in the financial structure are the anchor tenants, although the mall tenants are ultimately the basic source of the project's economics. The way in which the principal participants interrelate varies by circumstance and over time.

The changes in relationship have been neither steady nor linear. Rather, they have reflected differing economic conditions that have prevailed during the period from 1950 to the present. The strength at any given time of the retailing environment—and of particular retailers—has also had an effect on the respective roles of the participants.

Even though no consistently identifiable or uninterrupted trend is evident as one looks at the history of mall development, one or two major tendencies seem discernible, particularly in these last few years. They are (1) the increasing power of the surviving retailers; and (2) the ascendancy of capital.

If two of the three prime players are increasing in relative strength, it is likely at the expense of the third, the developer.

The Way It Was

The first regional enclosed shopping center, Southdale in Minneapolis, Minnesota, was completed in 1956. Others soon followed and an industry was born. The most prolific periods of regional mall creation were the 1970s and 1980s.

Certainly not all the shopping centers created during this era were financed in the same fashion. The very early ones probably paid some premium due to lender wariness and conservativism based on the newness of the concept. Lenox Square, for example, completed in 1959, was funded initially by the personal resources of the developer and his extended family. It was only when the property was expanded for the first time, some 5 to 6 years later, that third-party financing was obtained.

As the anchored regional shopping center became more familiar, however, lenders lost much of their reticence. This ushered in a period of liberal financing that most developers remember with fondness. Essentially, a well-conceived and well-executed regional shopping center development could be brought onstream without any capital investment of consequence by the developer.

At the risk of over-simplification, the important elements in the development process were:

1. Selecting and controlling the prospective site, likely through purchase of an option.

2. Negotiating and executing a reciprocal easement and/or operating agreement pursuant to which the two or more major retailers would commit to locate a significant store at the center and agree to operate such a store there for a period of 10 to 20 years.

3. Obtaining some level of commitment from creditworthy retailers to lease space in the mall upon its completion.

4. Armed with commitments manifest in the agreements described previously, and with the necessary permits to build, obtaining a financial commitment for long-term, fixed-rate mortgage financing in a stipulated amount.

5. With the long-term financing commitment, obtaining from a provider of shorter-term finance—probably a commercial bank—a construction loan commitment in an amount up to the size of the long-term financing commitment, which hopefully was an amount sufficient to buy the land and build the project.

When these projects worked out well, they were ventures to delight the prime players. The anchor tenants obtained new, presumably well-located sites on bases that were economically attractive and served to further the various companies' growth. The interim or short-term lender was able to deploy funds on a reasonably secure basis but at interest rates that were probably 200 to 300 basis points over a prime lending rate, an attractive premium over a prime rate that remained in single digits during most of that period. The long-term lender was able to create a mortgage loan providing for an attractive rate of interest and comfortable asset value and earnings coverages. And the developer would own, without any cash investment, the equity in a project that provided the prospect for increasing levels of annual cash income over time. In many cases, the long-term financing proceeds would be sufficient not only to recover all the costs of acquiring the land and building the center, but also to enable the developer to pocket an additional 10% or 20% of the project cost tax-free through over-financing.

There were instances when the formula did not work so well for all of the participants; when the relationship between rents—and therefore project income—and cost was less favorable, a lesser quantity of financing was justified and therefore developer equity may have been necessary. Similar results occurred during high interest rate periods when an increasing portion of the rental stream needed to be pledged to service higher rates. This meant that less could be borrowed. Developers, in these and other instances, had the alternative of making an equity investment or finding a third- party who would. Developers also found ways to devise financing alternatives to maximize the third party financing available.

"The Way It Was" era was highly favorable to the developer of major regional shopping malls. Regional malls were new, had a degree of uniqueness to them, and when measured against the then extant competitive facilities, were state of the art. Mall tenants were in an expansive mood, anxious to have locations in many or most of the malls being created, and willing to do so without subsidy or contribution from landlords. Real estate investment in general became more interesting to financial institutions. Historically active participants, like commercial banks and insurance companies, were joined by a flood of capital from pension funds, both domestic and foreign, pursuing property investment in the interests of diversification and inflation hedging. All of these factors conspired to produce an era in which developers of large shopping malls prospered.

Prosperity rarely lasts indefinitely. "The Way It Was" has become "The Way It Is"—a more challenging and difficult time for the industry, particularly for developers.

The Way It Is

The industry is currently beset by major change. The three prime players remain generally the same, but forces are at work that are changing the dynamic of their relationship.

Concentration continues to result in a lessened number of retailers with which to deal, but those that survive are generally stronger and more demanding. Further consolidation seems likely and can be expected to intensify. A concurrent development is the increasing strength of the discount or value-oriented sector. This includes Wal-Mart, and other conventional discounters such as Kmart and Target—although some troubles from over expansion lie ahead. It includes, as well, the warehouse stores such as Sam's Club and Price-Costco where over-expansion is also prevalent. The so-called "category killer" stores are also part of this phenomenon providing significant competition to conventional mall retailing.

All of these developments are taking place in an environment where there is already an excess of retail space and probably a lessened emphasis on the accumulation of "things," reflecting a shift away, at least temporarily, from the consumerism of the 1980s, and more stringent economic circumstances affecting much of the U.S. population. As a result, mall-oriented retailers are more careful, generally less expansive, and more difficult and/or expensive for landlords to deal with.

Significant change also continues in the capital-providing sector of the industry. The late 1980s and early 1990s were painful for many of the capital sources active in retail real estate. Financial institutions that had experienced almost uninterrupted success as participants in the regional shopping mall field—either as lender or equity owner—discovered that the forces of gravity are operative in this field as well. This discovery has made such institutions more wary. Exacerbating market difficulties has been the imposition, on both commercial banks and insurance companies, of risk-based capital rules that penalize the extension of credit to and/or equity investment in real estate projects of many kinds. Such rules made it easier for those sources of capital to find reasons to deny financing requests and have resulted in a substantial contraction in capital availability for shopping center projects in the early 1990s. This situation was, in retrospect, fortuitous since it prevented the initiation of developments that would have added to an already oversupplied inventory of retail space.

As of early 1995, capital for retail development is once again becoming plentiful, a somewhat surprising phenomenon given the severity of the recent unhappy experiences of many financial institutions. The capital that is available for retail real estate seems—for the time being at least—a bit more disciplined and more likely to emphasize security, coverage, and downside protection rather than the pursuit of heroic future returns. More emphasis is surely being placed on the reality of current return rather than on the wishful thinking of future appreciation. Whether those disciplines will erode as a result of an improved future economic environment or because of competitive pressures remains to be seen. One hopes not. For the time being, at any rate, capital for the shopping center industry is increasingly available but a bit more demanding vis-à-vis the owner/developer.

The development segment of the shopping center industry has also changed somewhat with more dramatic changes likely on the way. The same names still dominate in the development/ownership of regional shopping centers. The 15 largest owners of regional shopping centers follow, a list that would not have looked dramatically different 10 or 15 years ago (*Shopping Center World*, January 1994):

Equitable Real Estate
Simon Property Group
The Rouse Co.
Edward J. De Bartolo Corp.
The Richard and David Jacobs Corp.
The Cafaro Co.
The Hahn Co.
Corporate Property Investors
JMB Realty Corp.
The O'Connor Group
The Taubman Co.
Crown American Realty Trust
The Pyramid Cos.
Homart Development Company (Sears)
The Yarmouth Group

Many of the owning entities are now publicly owned, which was not previously the case. Many family or privately owned developers became public companies—fundamentally in REIT form—during the past 2 to 3 years. Although each case was different, the principal motivation in going public was to raise equity capital in an environment where it was not otherwise available on any reasonable basis. Although most who have become public entities extol the virtues of having done so, it remains to be seen how it will affect the ability to run the shopping center business. It may prove troublesome to make the difficult operating/investment decisions that have a long-term positive impact on the operation or asset, but which extract a near-term cost. A company whose stock trades publicly may find its shareholders unsympathetic to that type of tradeoff.

Another change is the lack of new development being undertaken by the developers on the previous list. Five new major regional malls were opened in 1993; four opened in 1994. Fourteen to fifteen are scheduled for each of the next two years, although how many of those materialize remains to be seen. The rate of development is a far cry from what it was in the 1970s and 1980s.

Capital for development is reasonably scarce for new projects. It is expensive in the sense that a fair amount of equity is required. Furthermore, the number of attractive sites where a new major mall is necessary and/or economically interesting is limited. The increasing economic demands of the strong retailers for subsidized rents and/or tenant allowances, and the more rigorous demands of capital sources have made development less appealing. The increasing difficulty in overcoming environmental and social resistance has not helped either. Most developers have turned their activity to the redevelopment and/or expansion of existing assets.

Many older malls have been in substantial need of improvement for competitive reasons; major regional malls no longer succeed in spite of themselves. Expansion of existing malls has also been a fertile area for developers as a number of anchor retailers have developed aspirations to expand nationally. The aggregate of these expansions is adding a fair amount to the nation's inventory of shopping center space thereby exacerbating oversupply. Expansion at the right center has the prospect of a successful economic outcome. However, not all of the expansions that dominate the current environment will be successful.

Redevelopment/expansion activity has been the major focus for developers during the past 3 to 4 years and promises to continue to be so for the foreseeable future. It is unlikely, however, that this activity alone can sustain the many developmental organizations that exist. Unless new mall development returns to prior levels of activity—which seems both unlikely and unwarranted—some significant consolidation is probable in the next several years.

CURRENT FINANCIAL PARTICIPANTS

Historically, the principal financiers of major shopping centers have been commercial banks, insurance companies, and pension funds, which is still largely the case. Banks have been construction lenders and that continues to be their principal interest. Their degree of activity is substantially lessened because the degree of construction has abated substantially except for expansion and renovation. Commercial banks have also been providers of medium-term mortgage financing, although a substantial portion of that was the involuntary conversion of construction loans into something slightly more permanent in the absence of long-term take-out financing. It is likely now that commercial banks will not put themselves in similar positions; rather, they will require long-term takeouts and/or highly reliable guarantors of on-time repayment. The medium-term mortgages that are available from banks require ample cash flow and asset coverage.

Insurance companies have been providers of long-term mortgage financing for regional malls. As market circumstances changed periodically, some developers were disposed to trade equity interests in projects for increased funding proceeds, principally from insurance companies and pension funds who supplied the long-term capital.

Emboldened by the success of these transactions during times when shopping center performance continued to improve, insurance companies and pension funds were induced to make more aggressive investments, trading security and prudence for the pursuit of higher returns. The experience of the recent real estate collapse has, at least for the time being, altered the investment outlook of such institutions, particularly insurance companies, and they are once again principally in the business of conventional mortgage lending.

Pension funds were the principal financial engine driving the great growth of regional shopping centers in the 1970s and 1980s. This period of rapid development in numbers of large regional shopping centers coincided with a time in which pension funds, particularly those of large corporations, aggressively pursued real estate investment as a desirable element of diversification and as a means of inflation hedging. Pension funds pursued investment in shopping centers, both debt and equity, in a number of ways through insurance company-sponsored co-mingled funds, through separate accounts managed by largely the same group of insurance companies; through specific shopping center pools created and managed by advisors and/or industry practitioners of one form or another; and also through the direct ownership of individual shopping center properties. The chronology of such investments by pension funds was generally comparable to the order suggested in the preceding sentence and reflected an increasing level of comfort—and perhaps some naivete regarding the operating complexity—with shopping center investment. Pension fund investment in regional shopping centers came to a spectacular halt in the collapsed market of the early 1990s, but is showing signs of a renaissance. Although reliable data are not available, pension funds have undoubtedly been the largest financial participants in the ownership of major regional shopping centers. Of all institutional real estate equity investments, major regional shopping centers have consistently performed better on a relative basis than any other segment. It is thus reasonable to expect that pension funds will continue to be significant investors in this area, particularly given the increasing interest of the public sector of the pension fund universe.

Financing through the REIT

A recent phenomenon in the evolution of financing for major regional shopping centers is an increasing reliance on public markets as a source of capital. The most visible manifestation—although probably not the most noteworthy—is the flurry of flotations in 1993–1994 of REITs. These initial public offerings have transformed into public companies a number of companies heretofore privately owned—principally private-family dominated shopping center developers. The public disclosure of financial data on an industry about which not much had been known probably generated interest somewhat out of proportion to the actual amount of capital raised. Many believe that public ownership of real estate, including major retail facilities, is the wave of the future and that in a reasonably short period of time, public ownership will be the norm in the shopping center industry. That is not necessarily the ordained outcome.

Another recent phenomenon, and one of greater consequence, is that involving the securitization of interests in real properties, particularly indebtedness. The volume of securitization to date would overwhelm the aggregate amount of initial public offerings of REIT equities.

A principal virtue of this type of financing is that it has expanded the universe of potential participants in shopping center finance, since it enables institutions—and individuals—to find a security that matches their risk tolerance and/or return requirements at a particular time. This has led to the emergence of new capital sources. Some of these more recent participants in shopping center financing, via securitization, are mutual funds, bond departments of financial institutions, such as insurance companies, and the public.

An expanded market for property finance is obviously good news for developers, perhaps less in terms of supporting new development—of which not much is needed near term—but more in making possible the orderly recapitalization of the property industry generally. Approximately $150 *billion* in term mortgages will be coming due *annually* in the next 2 to 3 years. The refinancing of that amount of debt is a daunting task that requires a broad market and the ingenuity to penetrate it. That refinancing burden does not fall too heavily on the owners of major regional centers since most are owned by strong holders and many are held clear of debt. Even so, an expanding and receptive capital market is an asset for owners/developers of major shopping centers, but chances that the market will become forthcoming enough to support a return to "The Way It Was" are remote if not nonexistent.

To the extent that additional shopping centers are created and/or existing ones are expanded and/or recapitalized, it seems unlikely that private developers will be disposed to invest the equity necessary to control ownership. It seems more likely that the ownership of these assets will gravitate further into the hands of pension funds and/or those investors who represent the principal market for public securities of real estate companies.

WHAT'S NEXT?

Notwithstanding the notion that the age of the large shopping malls is past, the regional mall will continue to be a significant factor in the retail landscape. At the same time, however, it will certainly exist in an increasingly dynamic environment, and owners of malls will have to be nimble, innovative, and well-capitalized to prosper. Not all of the existing regional malls will survive in their current form nor will all of the current participants in the industry.

The major forces within the retailing sector are: (1) the increasing concentration of strength in the hands of fewer retailers; (2) the expansion of value retailing, although there are some signs that this may have begun to peak, and (3) the increasing proliferation of retailing formats, are likely to be joined in time by (4) an increasing presence for interactive video-based shopping. This will be taking place in an environment probably marked by an aging population, increasing polarization of incomes, a perceived scarcity of leisure time (or at least a resistance to spending much of it shopping), increasing value consciousness, a temporary reaction against consumerism, and a sense of ennui vis-à-vis shopping as it currently exists at a large percentage of existing centers. The impact of these things need not in all cases be negative, but rather may be put to positive use by creative owners.

There are currently too many shopping centers and their number is likely to decrease. It seems logical to expect that the number of shopping center owners/developers will also decrease. The substantial abatement in the rate of shopping center creation in the last few years has already taxed the staying power of a number of developers. The organizations that seem best suited to survive this environment are those that own superior assets, are conservatively capitalized and therefore have continuing access to capital, and have the insight to see the business as it is or promises to be. Clearly, not all developers fulfill those requirements.

Depending on the operating performance of shopping centers, capital will continue to be available for this industry—subject to intermittent periods when real estate falls out of favor. On balance, capital will be increasingly sophisticated and discriminating and will seek out assets and owner/developers that have demonstrated the capacity to survive in difficult economic conditions.

The role of Wall Street will continue to be important in channeling funds into the shopping center industry. The role of pension funds, both domestic and foreign, will continue to be a significant one as regards the ownership and financing of major shopping malls.

Major regional shopping centers have, over the last 30 years, been the best real estate investment that pension funds have made and, thus, they should remain in favor. However, investment in shopping centers shares with all other real estate investment its site specificity. Sophisticated capital will need to be increasingly conscious of site specifics, particularly the competitive strength and potential of each individual shopping mall, or be certain that they invest with practitioners who are conscious of and expert in those things and who have their own capital at risk. If financing sources, particularly pension funds, are rigorous in their selection process—of assets, partners, and advisors—investing in retail real estate should continue to be rewarding.

Four

Legal Considerations Confronting the Shopping Center Industry

John J. Lawlor, David A. Lapins, and Jane Snoddy Smith

A lthough every form of real estate development—whether commercial or residential—is fast-paced, the very nature of retailing *guarantees* that shopping center development moves *very* quickly, since merchants' goals are defined in terms of opening at a given location by a specific selling season such as Christmas, Easter, "back-to-school," and so on.

Nonetheless, shopping center development is hampered by two formidable types of regulation. One is *governmental*, taking the form of land use and environmental laws and ordinances. The second type of regulation is imposed by the *private sector*, in the form of self-imposed 50- to 100-page documents typically referred to as Reciprocal Easement Agreements (REAs) or as Construction, Operation, and Reciprocal Easement Agreements (COREAs).

Land use and environmental regulations reflect the public's need to scrutinize major developments that can have a significant impact upon aesthetics, utility infrastructure, and traffic circulation. The development community can become very frustrated with the need to appear before various levels of informal and formal advisory committees, and to face the possibility of repeated continuances, even before appearing before the elected officials whose responsibility it is to review zoning applications. This multitiered development approval process, which can apply not only to initial construction but also to shopping center renovation, has become entrenched in the United States. Prudent developers no longer challenge the basis of what zoning pioneer Richard F. Babcock once referred to as "the zoning game"; instead, they assemble skilled teams of legal, civil engineering, architectural, traffic, and environmental consultants to lobby development applications through to completion.

What is a bit paradoxical is that the development community imposes an even greater degree of self-regulation upon *itself* through the imposition of REAs and COREAs within shopping centers. While planned development ordinances impose certain conditions upon the degree to which a site can be developed for retail development, a typical COREA and REA will go into far greater detail about not only what could be built, but also what *precisely* it can be used for, how continuously it must be used, and how, if ever, the development scheme can be altered.

Tensions arise when market forces dictate the need to renovate or expand an existing shopping center. Everything in the original REA or COREA can suddenly be targeted for renegotiation. Each party to the REA or COREA will study its own "wish list" and carefully assess its own bargaining power before agreeing to amendments. The process of amending these documents can take a long time indeed!

For the sake of simplicity, this chapter will describe how the retail development community overcomes the hurdles of acquiring land, obtaining zoning and related development approvals, and negotiating an REA. The techniques utilized to keep a property "under control" during the zoning approval process are discussed in the second part of this Chapter. The next part of the chapter contains an extensive description of the governmental approvals that are typically pursued by a developer during the "due diligence" contingency period afforded under a contract to purchase or an option agreement. Next we briefly describe additional due diligence that should occur prior to closing. Last is a description of the key provisions that must be negotiated in a typical REA or COREA, given the need to create retail synergy and to maintain and control common areas.

"GETTING CONTROL" OF THE PROPERTY

How do developers legally "tie up" potential sites when substantial zoning and infrastructure hurdles must be worked out? The two classic vehicles are the negotiation of either a contingent purchase contract or an option to purchase. The choice between these two vehicles will depend, in large part, on the amount of time needed by the developer to resolve the development puzzle and by the seller's impatience.

In urban centers and inner-ring suburbs, one does not ordinarily encounter significant problems with the adequacy of utilities or the need to annex property into a municipality. As a result, the development approval process may be relatively straightforward. In these instances, it may be possible to successfully negotiate a contingent purchase contract, stating that the developer is not obligated to purchase the property until it has an opportunity—say, within a six-month contingency period—to obtain a rezoning of the property from a manufacturing classification to that of retail planned development, and also to satisfy itself that the property does not contain subsurface environmental contaminants. The seller of an obsolete manufacturing site typically will be content to take the property off the market for six months in order to facilitate rezoning from an outmoded classification to one that reflects the gentrification of the urban core.

In a suburban context, however, the development challenges can take far longer to resolve. As described later, development in suburban areas in remote "collar counties" can involve not only zoning obstacles, but also the need to provide basic utility infrastructure. Where zoning, annexation, wetlands remediation, and public financing assistance are required, it would not be unusual for a developer to require an 18-month development contingency as a condition precedent to the obligation to close. Many sellers not only will be impatient with this prospect for delay, but also will be very suspicious about what it means to "satisfy" a development contingency. Would the municipality's approval of a 300,000 sq. ft. shopping center be "satisfactory" when the developer had applied initially for 400,000 sq. ft.? Should the developer be entitled to "walk" from the contract when it can obtain only 75% of the floor area initially sought? Should the developer be entitled to "walk" because it is unhappy with the degree of wetlands remediation required by the federal government? As a practical matter, it is probably impossible for the parties to negotiate, in advance, what the "satisfaction" of such zoning and environmental contingencies actually means. In these instances, the parties frequently will prefer to enter into an option to purchase agreement requiring the developer to pay the property owner for the right to keep the property off the market during the ensuing due diligence period. If the developer is unhappy with the conditions imposed by government upon any of the approvals sought or for any reason whatsoever, it can simply refuse to exercise the option. The seller should be content since it is receiving consideration in the form of regular option payments, which typically are geared toward addressing either the seller's need to pay real estate taxes and debt service on its mortgage during the option period, or the rental value of the property.

An attorney knowledgeable about local government can play a key role during the contract negotiation. The developer client will rely heavily on the attorney's knowledge of the local development approval process in negotiating contract rights. If, for example, the attorney is not familiar with the period of time required to obtain zoning approvals, the developer may fail to negotiate for a sufficient zoning contingency period or option period. Similarly, the developer needs to know how many different governmental applications must be filed, so that it reasonably can estimate how long it will take engineering and environmental consultants to obtain approvals. In short, the well-rounded development attorney is expected to have both keen legal skills and practical knowledge of the local political and regulatory environment.

PURSUING GOVERNMENTAL APPROVALS DURING THE DUE DILIGENCE PERIOD

Once the contingent sale contract or option agreement is signed, the developer and its consultants will be in hot pursuit of the approvals necessary to proceed with the retail project. The pressure can be unbelievable. The developer is eager to obtain approvals before it "loses control" under the agreement with the property owner. The developer also is mindful of the need to procure these approvals while market interest rates are low, so that it can "lock in" borrowing costs through a mortgage loan commitment. Simultaneously, the developer will hear daily complaints from prospective tenants about the need to get "in the ground" so that a particular "selling season" can be seized upon for the grand opening.

The developer will pursue these approvals by means of a development team consisting of an attorney, architect, civil engineer, traffic engineer, and environmental consultant. During the negotiation of the contract with the seller, the attorney will need to predict which governmental approvals will be necessary. Once the contract is signed, the duty of keeping the project applications on "the critical path" often falls upon the attorney, who is essentially "quarterbacking" the efforts of the developers' consultants. These duties include timely filing of the necessary paperwork and public notices, and responding to interim requests from governmental representatives, preparing for public hearings, and negotiating governmental ordinances and agreements. The attorney is often the key spokesperson for the developer, partly because the developer's attention, even at this early stage, is fragmented among the need to (1) obtain governmental approvals, (2) negotiate the terms of sale agreements, leases, and REAs with prospective shopping center occupants, and (3) obtain mortgage loan financing agreements from willing lenders.

The following is a brief summary of the governmental approvals that must be pursued during the contract contingency period. Each of these frequently apply to the renovation or expansion of existing shopping centers, with the same impact upon the progress of the redevelopment effort.

Zoning

In the majority of communities, the development of multitenant shopping centers requires not only that the subject property be located in a zoning district classified as "commercial" or "business," but also has duly legislated planned development approval. The planned development approval process typically involves the filing of a detailed planned development application, followed by the subsequent review of the application by a planning commission, possibly a zoning board, and, finally, by the elected aldermen, board of trustees, village council, and so on.

This process can be very time consuming. Amendments to existing planned developments to accommodate redevelopment can also be very time consuming, because the approval process is much the same. Planned developments are highly regulated because they are viewed as having a significant impact upon the community. Municipalities usually require detailed site plans, landscape plans, utility plans, storm water drainage plans, parking layouts, and even sign plans be filed as a condition precedent to appearing at the first duly noticed public hearing. In most communities, the first public hearing will not occur until either the developer or the municipality publishes at least 15 days' advance newspaper notice of the pendency of the hearing, usually accompanied by certified mail notices to taxpayers of record within approximately 250 feet of the subject property. In many communities, there is also an informal step which is essential before the first duly noticed public hearing—that is, to meet with local community groups (usually identified by the mayor or village trustee) having a vested interest in matters affecting land in the vicinity. The developer must understand that the community has legitimate concerns about the introduction of new uses into the area and their impact upon traffic circulation. What the community must understand is that not every change is deleterious to the quality of life, and that one rationally can study a proposed development and accurately predict its effect on local traffic circulation. Developers frequently fail to take advantage of these informal meetings as a means to defuse irrational opposition to a development proposal. If the emotions spill over at the first duly noticed public hearing, the usual reaction of a Planning Commission or Zoning Board chairperson is to continue the matter until the process is "worked out" through the negotiation of modifications in the development application.

The Rational Basis Test for Re-Zoning

The zoning application process is essentially a political process, and it is important for a developer to understand it as such. For example, in Illinois it is entirely within the discretion of a municipality whether it chooses to elect to annex property in order to include a parcel within its boundaries. The judiciary will not upset a municipality's decision unless it was motivated by an intention to violate civil rights laws.[1] Whenever municipal zoning decisions are challenged in court by either developers or by neighboring property owners, rezonings from one classification to another tend to be scrutinized by the judiciary in reliance upon a "rational basis" test, variously articulated. The legal analysis in Illinois is supplied by the Illinois Supreme Court's decision in *LaSalle National Bank* v. *County of Cook* and its progeny, which serve as Illinois' judicial guidelines for determining if the municipality's actions are arbitrary and capricious, and thus in violation of substantive due process.[2] The factors considered by Illinois courts are as follows:

1. The existing uses of nearby property;
2. The extent to which property values are diminished by the particular zoning restrictions;

3. The extent to which the destruction of property values promotes the health, safety or general welfare of the public;

4. The relative gain to the public as compared to the hardship imposed on the individual property owner;

5. The suitability of the property for the zoned purposes;

6. The length of time the property has been vacant as zoned, considered in the context of land development in the area in the vicinity of the subject property;

7. Community need for the proposed use; and

8. The care with which the community has undertaken to plan for the use of land.

The standards for zoning *variances* (as distinguished from map amendments) are stated with more precision in the text of most zoning ordinances. Variation provisions typically contain standards that are very difficult for a developer to satisfy, that is, standards that require that there must be a unique hardship, that the applicant for the variance has not contributed to the creation of the hardship, and that the motivation for seeking the variance is not solely the desire to add value to the property.

A developer may choose to litigate denial of the zoning applications, but in most jurisdictions it is impracticable to obtain an injunction, and the resulting declaratory judgment process can take years to argue through appeals. Few sellers will "stick" with the developer under a contingent contract to purchase, or even an option, for this period of time. In short, the development process in a participatory democracy is a detailed, highly sophisticated negotiation in which both the developer and neighboring community must agree upon a "win-win" solution for anything much to happen within a reasonable time frame.

Subdivision Approval

A subdivision is a division in the ownership of a tract of land by means of the creation of a new boundary. Where a proposed sale involves a subdivision, local subdivision ordinances require that a formal plat of subdivision showing the boundaries of the new parcels be formally approved by the Plan Commission and the local government body and executed by local government officials. Some state subdivision laws and local government subdivision ordinances create "exemptions" from these requirements for certain lot "splits," especially where the division of land does not involve new streets or easements of access.

A developer and its attorney must be alert to applicable subdivision requirements because, under the terms of many subdivision ordinances, the failure to obtain municipal subdivision plat approval can result in the denial of subsequent building permit applications. In addition, failure to abide by platting requirements is dangerous because sophisticated lenders and subsequent purchasers may object to the prior owner's failure to adhere to platting requirements, especially when the title insurer raises the issue as an exception in a title report or policy. Subdivision issues can arise in conjunction with the renovation of existing shopping centers if portions of the existing center, typically property along its periphery, are to be sold off to retailers entering the center for the first time.

Unfortunately, the subdivision approval process involves preparing a detailed subdivision plat, engineering drawings for required public infrastructure—such as streets, sewer, and water facilities—and appearances before the local planning commission and/or the local government body. This effort can be expensive and time consuming, although there are typically fewer "hot" issues with a subdivision than there are with respect to a rezoning. Provided that minimum lot area and street frontage dimension requirements contained in the Zoning Ordinance are satisfied, there should be little debate about an owner's legal ability to create new parcel configurations. However, if the subdivision entails the construction of public infrastructure, a site improvement agreement *requiring* the developer to proceed with their installation, and to post an adequate performance bond, usually must be negotiated.

Fortunately, subdivision applications usually can be processed simultaneously with planned development applications. It is, therefore, in the developer's best interest to identify in advance of filing for zoning relief whether a subdivision is needed, so that subdivision approval can be obtained simultaneously through the planned development process.

Traffic Approvals

The developer's traffic consultant faces the all-important task of predicting whether local transportation and highway authorities will issue necessary permits for traffic signalization, curb cuts, and median breaks or consider new or improved highway exchanges. The consultant's role is the same with respect to both initial development and later expansion or renovation of the center.

The traffic consultant must first ascertain which authorities have jurisdiction over which streets. For example, a shopping center may be bounded by three major arteries, one of which is regulated by the state, another by the county, and a third by the municipality, in which case the developer and its consultants must deal with three different traffic authorities. Each of these authorities may have its own vision of the region's traffic improvement needs which must be taken into account.

Usually, the developer will incur the costs involved in providing shopping center signalization. If the developer is the "pioneer" at a particular intersection in a rural area, they may be able to negotiate for a recapture agreement requiring the municipality to recoup traffic signalization installation costs from other property owners on behalf of the original developer as the area gets "build-out." On the other hand, developers occasionally reap the benefit of signalization already in place through federally funded programs. In either event, the traffic consultant is called upon to negotiate for left turn signals, where appropriate, and proper sequencing with nearby signals.

The availability of curb cut rights and median breaks is extremely important. In order to market the shopping center to potential tenants, the developer will be required to represent where these curb cuts will exist. Retailers may also ask about the availability of median breaks, realizing that a nonmountable traffic median will severely impede left-hand turning movements.

Unfortunately, in most jurisdictions the government's authority over curb cuts and median breaks is viewed by the judiciary as an exercise of the police power, giving the government great leeway in controlling the curb cuts and median break approval process as well as in modifying existing roadway features, if necessary, to protect the public health, safety, and welfare. Many shopping center outlot or peripheral parcel users, such as fast-food restaurants, have been negatively impacted by a state highway authority's belated decision to transform a mountable median strip into a nonmountable median strip, particularly in conjunction with intersection improvements which create lengthy dual lefthand turning lanes. As long as the courts view this activity as an exercise of the police power, the retail industry has little leverage "at law or equity" to control these highway design changes.

Development Incentives

In the past 15 years, local government has stimulated retail development in various ways. The major forms of local incentives described next are tax increment financing, tax abatement programs, and special service areas.

In a tax increment financing (TIF) district, the municipality in essence creates a special district which authorizes the diversion of the tax increment generated by ad valorem and sales taxes from a new or newly renovated shopping center into a special fund. The incremental revenue thus deposited in this special fund is not shared by existing tax levying districts, but rather is pledged entirely to finance or subsidize qualified development costs, which typically include land assembly costs, street construction, utility construction, traffic signalization, and certain financing costs.

Before a site will qualify for TIF, however, it is typically necessary for the site to be designated as a "blighted" or "conservation" area by local authorities. The issue of TIF district designation usually is heard preliminarily by an advisory economic development commission, and then finally approved by the elected local government council. Both new development in blighted areas and the renovation of outdated shopping centers in the urban core and "inner ring" suburbs are frequently recipients of TIF financing. Since the tax levies of not only the municipality, but also other local taxing districts, usually are affected, there is often a divergence of views among governmental authorities respecting the wisdom of TIF. Local school districts, for example, may tend to take a dim view of TIF proposals, primarily because school districts frequently are worried about the short-term impact upon their income stream. Properly understood, however, the TIF designation does not deprive the school districts of funds, if the municipality has properly determined that the project would not move forward *but for* TIF assistance—and TIF statutes typically require a municipality to make such a "but for" finding as a condition precedent to creating the district. Assuming the "but for" test is satisfied, the school district's remaining concern will be the anticipated duration of TIF treatment, the goal being to shorten the period of time which the TIF "increment" is diverted from unrestricted use by local taxing bodies. In some jurisdictions, TIF districts can utilize incremental sales taxes as well as real property taxes, which adds greatly to the tax increment available to retire TIF bonds in a more expeditious manner.

Tax Abatement Programs

More recently, local governments have also attempted to stimulate local economic development through a variety of tax abatement programs. As is the case with TIF districts, tax abatement programs usually require a prior designation by a local governmental body that the subject property is located in a "blighted" or "conservation" area, the latter being an area "on the way" to becoming blighted. Assuming the district's designation is approved at a duly noticed public hearing, the result of the abatement is usually to lower the level of assessment, both for new construction and for renovation. For example, in Cook County, Illinois, commercial property in a qualified "area in need of commercial development" has its assessment reduced from 38% of fair market value to 16% for a period of eight years, followed by a 30% assessment level for the next four years.[3] In Missouri, a similar process has been in use for some time. Under Chapter 353 of the Missouri Revised Statutes, certain urban redevelopment corporations incorporated and operated by the private sector can petition local governments to approve ordinances creating special redevelopment project areas, and providing the Chapter 353 corporation with the right to condemn property by eminent domain. Property owned by a Chapter 353 corporation enjoys a partial real estate tax exemption which is tantamount to a "land only" assessment for a period of ten years, followed by an ensuing 15-year abatement which essentially equates into one-half the normal assessment level of both the land and improvements.

Special Service Areas

Special service areas (SSAs) are a means to create a new taxing district whose levies will be devoted solely for the purpose of providing a service unique to the geographical area in question. A typical example of an SSA is a district created to extend a new utility line to a previously unserviced portion of a municipality. More creative uses of SSAs in recent years have included, in portions of Chicago, the hiring of additional policemen for security purposes.

As is the case with tax increment financing districts, SSAs typically cannot be created absent a public hearing and an opportunity to be heard by affected property owners. Usually, a unified block of affected property owners and electors can exercise what amounts to a "veto" power over an SSA proposal.[4]

Some shopping center developers have utilized the SSA device to finance infrastructure serving their shopping center in instances where the shopping center itself may be virtually the only tract within the boundaries of the Special Service Area. The use of the SSA device in this manner allows the developer to amortize over the long term the cost of badly needed infrastructure. Some developers will also attempt to use the SSA device to "pass through" these infrastructure costs to tenants under space leases by including SSA levies in the definition of "Taxes" in shopping center space leases. Astute tenants, however, will object to this device, because it is an attempt by the developer to charge tenants for what would customarily be one of the developer's normal capital costs.

Impact or Development Fees

Municipally imposed "impact" or "development fees" are the flip side of the public finance incentives just described. In burgeoning suburban counties, highly complex formulas have been devised for charging developers the incremental costs incurred by local government for providing adequate highway, street, and other public improvements, both for new construction and shopping center expansion. These impact and development fee ordinances are usually the result of complex and lengthy negotiations between governmental entities and the development community.[5] In other instances, development and impact fees are charged by municipalities on a rather ad hoc basis, as developers approach the municipality with rezoning, planned development and subdivision applications. In these ad hoc instances, there is more room for disagreement and possible abuse by the public sector.

Legal standards are emerging for judicially determining whether impact or development fees are constitutional. State courts have devised various criteria.[6] In Illinois, the courts have been imposing a rather rigorous "specifically and uniquely attributable" test, requiring local governments to establish that the alleged impact upon local traffic systems or schools is the result of the proposed development, and that the required contribution is appropriate for the size of the impact. Other states merely require municipalities to show a reasonable relationship between the required dedication or contribution and the impact of the proposed development.[7] In negotiating impact fees with municipalities, the development community will seek assurances that the money contributed is actually used for the alleged "need" within a timeframe which will benefit the project.

Recently, the U.S. Supreme Court has attempted to define federal constitutional standards establishing the boundaries of permissible and impermissible regulatory exactions. In *Dolan* v. *City of Tigard*, the U.S. Supreme Court suggested the following approach for determining whether the government may require a person to give up a constitutional property right in exchange for a discretionary benefit conferred by the government.[8] First, the Supreme Court will determine whether an "essential nexus" exists between a legitimate state interest and a proposed condition. If such a nexus exists, the Supreme Court will then determine whether the degree of the exactions demanded by the permit conditions bears the required relationship to the projected impact of the proposed development.

Environmental Regulation

In the past 10 years, new tiers of environmental regulation have created the need for additional due diligence. A developer's primary concerns are with the existence of subsurface contaminants and the possible need to comply with wetlands regulations.

Under federal law, a potential buyer is required to conduct a reasonable investigation of the site in order to enjoy the "innocent purchaser" defense provided by the Comprehensive Environmental Response, Compensation and Liability Act of 1980.[9] Most developers initiate this investigation by obtaining a Phase I environmental report from a consulting firm dealing primarily with the use and occupancy of the site over a period of time, typically 70 years or more, in order to determine if fee title was held by an entity likely to expose the parcel to contaminants. A Phase I report also will involve a visual inspection of the property, a review of certain databases to see if the property has been the subject of governmental attention (i.e., inclusion within, or proximity to, a superfund site), and contact with state and local officials.

If the history of the property and its immediate vicinity seems particularly innocent, many developers will cease their environmental due diligence with a Phase I environmental report. If the Phase I report indicates the possible existence of subsurface manufacturing waste, petroleum tanks, and so on, or the existence of nearby uses which may be discharging contaminants into a subsurface water aquifer, a Phase II set of on-site subsurface soil samples and analyses may be ordered. Regardless of the results of Phase I reports, many developers now order Phase II sampling for subsurface contaminants. It is often the case that Phase II testing results are ambiguous, and a cost/benefit analysis must be made with respect to whether additional sampling is necessary. In making these decisions, it is of course necessary to be familiar with both federal and state hazardous waste requirements, as well as the regulatory authorities' current interpretation of these requirements. Other important parties which must be satisfied with respect to the environmental condition of the property are the developer's potential lender, as well as other sophisticated parties—such as national retailers—who will be subsequently purchasing and leasing portions of the shopping center.

If serious environmental contamination is detected, the developer may well have to exercise its right under a contingent purchase contract to declare a failure of the contingency, or, in the case of an option agreement, to reveal to the seller that it will not choose to exercise the option on account of the environmental contamination. In the absence of a previously negotiated clause respecting the obligations of buyer and seller in the event such contamination is discovered, the parties may find themselves renegotiating the deal to allocate the costs which will be incurred for remediation. At this juncture, both the buyer and seller also may be interested in consulting with environmental attorneys with respect to potential contribution actions against prior owners and occupants in the chain of title who created the subsurface conditions.

A second major form of environmental regulation which affects the development community is wetlands regulation. While the definition of a "wetland" has been in a state of flux, and specialists in this field need to be contacted in order to ascertain how the regulations will be interpreted, a developer who detects even the *possible* existence of a regulated wetland should quickly attempt to ascertain the impact which compliance will have on his development proposal.[10] Additional land may be required in order to mitigate the removal of a wetland at one location with the creation of a new wetland on another portion of the site. A developer also will be very concerned about how wetlands compliance will impact development costs and may seek adjustment of the purchase price with the seller as a result of wetlands regulation.

A more mundane form of environmental compliance which should never be forgotten is the need to comply with applicable storm water regulations. In many suburban areas, flash flooding is a problem during the spring and summer seasons, and local governments have adopted very strict stormwater compliance codes which require that the site's engineering anticipate catastrophic "100 year" storms. These regulations can have a significant impact upon a developer's site plan, because both wet and dry retention ponds may be required to absorb anticipated rainfall. Some municipalities take the "edge" off this impact by allowing the developer to, in essence, "store" some stormwater on slightly depressed parking fields. It is in the developer's best interest, however, not to retain too much water in the parking field, because catastrophic storms literally can flood customers' vehicles.

Vested Rights

At long last, the point arrives when a developer feels comfortable that all necessary governmental approvals have been obtained. Human nature being what it is, however, some developers are more comfortable than others. A few developers and national retailers insist on the issuance of building permits as a condition precedent to their obligation to close. This presumes that the party insisting on the contingency will go to the trouble to file complete building permit applications within the contract contingency period.

Assuming building permit applications comply with applicable zoning, subdivision, building and health safety requirements (i.e., fire and electrical codes), the issuance of the building permit is characterized legally as a ministerial act which can be specifically required by the courts by means of mandamus actions or injunctions. Some developers are nonetheless very cautious because, on occasion, municipal officials will have second thoughts about a zoning approval and in essence, rezone the site between the time of closing and the date the developer proceeds to apply for a building permit. If a developer is anxious about this possibility, the key question is whether applicable state law vests zoning rights where a developer has spent considerable sums in reasonable reliance that a building permit will issue. In some states, zoning rights vest when a developer changes his position in reasonable reliance even if it has not yet entered the land to begin construction.[11] In other states, actual commencement of physical work is required.[12] In short, determination of one's zoning rights requires an examination of applicable state case law.

TRADITIONAL DUE DILIGENCE

During the contract contingency period, the developer will need to engage in several other forms of more "traditional" due diligence which require less time and effort than the pursuit of governmental approvals.

The most traditional form of due diligence is the review and examination of a title commitment issued by a reputable title insurer. The report should be issued in the amount of the purchase price in the name of the potential buyer. In some states, the title company can issue (for an additional price) various forms of zoning endorsements which will insure the zoning classification of the property, as well as the identity of applicable bulk regulations, such as required setbacks, minimum parking ratios, etc. The developer also may seek specific endorsements insuring the contiguity of each parcel in a land assemblage, the contiguity of these parcels to dedicated streets, and access to public streets. Once an REA or COREA has been recorded, the developer should take care to arrange for the title insurance policy to insure the easements created in the REA for the benefit of the developer's parcel.

The title contingency goes hand in hand with a separate survey contingency. A detailed American Land Title Association survey is required if the developer expects to obtain "extended coverage" over survey-related "general exceptions" to an ALTA title policy—notably, the general exceptions respecting encroachments and rights of parties not shown by the public records. These two general exceptions, together with the general exception for unrecorded easements, are important general exceptions for the developer to fully insure. It is sometimes the case that significant utility facilities lie underground, although no easement is recorded. Without the benefit of title insurance protection, the developer's lender will refuse to fund its mortgage loan to the developer, and the developer may find itself incurring the cost of relocating substantial utility facilities which enjoy easements by a prescription or perhaps adverse possession.

Lastly, a developer should be careful to determine whether the seller's conveyance of the subject property is deemed a "bulk sale" under state revenue regulations, and, if so, whether the seller is current in tax payments to the state.[13] This is because several states have applied bulk sale revenue procedures typically applicable to the sale of personal property to the sale of real estate, with the result that if the seller is delinquent in tax payments at the time of the sale, the buyer is charged with liability for the seller's taxes due and owing (limited to the amount of consideration paid by buyer at closing) *unless* the buyer has filed a report of sale with the state prior to closing and the state has affirmatively reported that the seller was not in arrears on its tax obligations.

A WORLD OF PRIVATE REGULATION: THE RECIPROCAL EASEMENT AGREEMENT

While the developer's zoning attorney is busy negotiating the extent to which the public sector will regulate the appearance and operation of the shopping center, the developer and his real estate attorney will be simultaneously initiating negotiations with the private sector—namely, the anchor retail store locating in the shopping center—who will impose an even greater degree of regulation upon the center's use and occupancy in the form of an REA or COREA.

Before analyzing the terms of an REA, it is important to understand how a shopping center typically is subdivided and marketed among retail users. As described above, the shopping center developer ultimately will satisfy itself that it is prudent to proceed to closing. As part of the governmental approval process, the site will be subdivided into separate parcels which comply with the site plan approved as part of the municipal planned development ordinance. Typically, separate pads or parcels will be designated near the core of the shopping center for ownership and/or lease by the anchor department stores. The developer will retain ownership of the land which connects the anchors' parcels, together with ownership of the majority of the parking field, although some department stores insist on owning a portion of the common area parking field in a manner which assures them perpetual compliance with applicable minimum parking ratios under the local zoning ordinance. In addition to the foregoing, the municipally approved subdivision plat typically will lay out separate "outlot parcels" along the periphery of the shopping center adjacent to arterial streets, for eventual use and occupancy by "free standing" users such as restaurants, movie theater complexes, banks, and so on.

Cross-Easements

A primary function of the REA is suggested by its name—to create "reciprocal easement agreements" among the variously subdivided parcels to assure the various property owners that there will be long-term, and sometimes perpetual, cross-easements for vehicular ingress and egress, parking, utility infrastructure, and pedestrian use of common areas, such as sidewalks and enclosed malls. The REA document, which typically runs from 50 to over 100 pages, may state that these easements have varying durations. Essential vehicular roadway easements and utility easements are usually perpetual in nature. Whether the parking easements are perpetual will be determined, in part, on the basis of whether the anchor department stores and the developer each have retained sufficient land to comply independently with applicable minimum parking requirements under the local zoning ordinance. Whether the parking easements are completely co-extensive throughout the boundaries of the shopping center will also depend, in part, on the anchor retailers' determination of whether the outlots should provide their own self-contained parking which complies at a minimum with parking requirements in the zoning ordinance. Party wall agreements respecting mutually shared foundations and structures may have limited durations stated in terms of years, subject to a provision that they will continue thereafter as long as the party wall remains in use. Various other contractual features of the REA, however, may have a less than perpetual duration and may terminate at the end of the term of the REA—such as 50, 75, or perhaps 99 years.

Site Plan Controls

While the use and enjoyment of reciprocal easements seem relatively uncontroversial, difficult issues arise out of the creation of a site plan. In many respects, the site plan attached to the REA is the most important part of the document. The site plan typically will regulate the following matters, and any subsequent attempt by a party to deviate from the specifications set forth on the site plan may well result in either the rapid issuance of an injunction by a court of equity, or the parties' need to negotiate with other parties to the REA in order to obtain an amendment permitting a deviation from the original layout:

1. *Shopping Center Boundaries.* One should not overlook that one function of a site plan is to lay out the external boundaries of the shopping center. Well drafted REAs prohibit the inclusion of any additional property within the boundaries of the shopping center without each owner's consent, and prohibit the unilateral "detachment" of any segment of the original portion of the shopping center from the effectiveness of the REA. As a result, shopping center expansions and renovations almost invariably entail the renegotiation of the REA and the REA site plan.

2. *Permissible Building Areas.* The site plan also will delineate the external limits of permissible building areas within the shopping center. Any proposed building or alteration must exist within these permitted building envelopes.[14] A significant side issue is whether the site plan will permit outdoor sales in any portion of the parking field. In community shopping centers, heated disputes can exist between grocery stores and hardware "category killers," on the one hand, and traditional discount department stores, on the other, respecting the extensive use of outdoor selling areas. Many retailers

feel that the outdoor sales areas become unsightly and remove valuable parking spaces from customer circulation. REAs for regional shopping centers will contain lengthy provisions and harsh penalties for selling or any other activity in the common areas. Often, detailed compromises must be worked out respecting the area devoted to outdoor sales, and the frequency and duration of outdoor sale use. The existence of narrowly drawn permissible building area envelopes also leads to the need to renegotiate REAs in order to accommodate most shopping center expansions and reconfigurations.

3. *Permissible Heights.* Either the REA site plan or the text of the REA may regulate the proposed height of buildings. This issue becomes particularly sensitive with peripheral outlets. Anchor department stores place great value on the visibility of their stores from nearby main traffic arteries and expressway interchanges. If the development of either these outlets or their business identification signs become too high, anchor stores as well as "in line" retailers within the mall may feel that their visibility is unduly obstructed. Height limitations also prevent stores from evading permissible building area limitations by vertically increasing the square footage of a store and thereby gaining a larger, more competitive presence in the shopping center as compared to other stores.

4. *Vehicular Access and Signalization.* The site plan should show, in detail, the main exterior access roadway system within the shopping center, and the curb cuts which will be utilized to connect these roadways with adjacent dedicated streets. Typically these roadways are shaded or otherwise delineated and deemed to be "perpetual roadway easements" within the meaning of the REA. Oftentimes, retailers feel significantly disadvantaged if such a perpetual roadway easement is relocated without their consent, due to fears that traffic circulation will be routed elsewhere throughout the center. This is particularly the case with the occupants of retail outlets along the periphery of the shopping center, who often enjoy access both from a dedicated street adjacent to the shopping center and by means of perpetual roadway easements located within the center. Shopping center expansions or renovations which involve the relocation of internal access roads frequently require amendments to these features of the REA.

5. *Signage.* Nothing is more sacred to a retailer than sign visibility. Much time and effort will be spent negotiating the location of not only the shopping center sign, but also whether the sign identifies more than the name of the center, which occupants are identified on the

sign, the size of their sign panels, and the location of the sign panels on the structure. Similarly, intense negotiation will occur respecting the location, if any, of free-standing pylon signs devoted solely to particular retailers. Of course, only the "anchor" retail presence can negotiate for such free-standing sign rights, especially since zoning authorities usually limit the number of free-standing signs which can line an arterial frontage. Retailers will be particularly competitive about these rights out of fear that a competitor may successfully negotiate with the developer for greater advantage. The dimensions of building signs, size of letters, and general first class standards for signs also are strenuously negotiated.

6. *Minimum Parking Requirements.* A site plan will delineate not only the common area dedicated to parking, but also the layout of parking stalls and either minimum required parking ratios, or a minimum required number of parking spaces. A few site plans also contain an architectural rendering of minimum required parking stalls for typical passenger vehicles, "compact cars," and handicapped vehicles. Lastly, some REA site plans designate specific areas as mandatory employee parking areas. Shopping center renovations which negatively impact available parking usually entail the need to amend existing REA parking provisions.

Common Area Covenants

The term common area was used in ancient England, where villagers shared joint use of certain facilities as as commons—for example domestic livestock's joint use of the local pasture. The same concept applies today to the extensive common areas shared by individual owners and occupants of parcels within shopping centers. A typical definition of common area in an anchor department store lease is as follows:

> The term common areas means all areas within the boundaries of the Shopping Center now or hereafter available for the non-exclusive use, convenience and benefit of all Occupants and their respective permittees.

> Among other things, common areas include: (i) the parking area, vehicular entrances, circulation roads and access roads; (ii) the Enclosed Mall (except for areas thereof occupied by kiosks which are permitted by this Lease/REA); (iii) sidewalks and walkways located within the boundaries of the Shopping Center; (iv) landscaped and planted areas outside the perimeter sidewalks around all stores;

(v) all curbs and lighting standards, traffic and directional signs and traffic striping and markings located within the Shopping Center; and (vi) any common utility facilities servicing the Shopping Center. Common area does not include any community room, mall offices, security offices, and storage area used exclusively for maintenance equipment and supplies for the common area (but such space shall not exceed in total _____ square feet) and any truck unloading, parking or turnaround facilities, appurtenances or improvements such as trash compactors or refuse areas, transformers or transformer pads, or concrete aprons all of which items are adjacent to and for the benefit of an Occupants' building and are intended for the exclusive use of any Occupant.

As one can easily surmise, the common area plays a critical role in the use and enjoyment of a shopping center.[15] As a result, it is not surprising that the following concepts are embodied in nearly every REA:

1. *Changes in the Common Area.* The anchor department stores who, along with the developer, are the original parties to the REA typically will not agree to any substantial changes in common area without each original signatory's consent. Usually, major shopping center renovations and expansions cannot take place without their consent. Highly sensitive areas which cannot be modified without consent include minimum parking ratios, perpetual access roads, curb cuts, and the addition or deletion of property from the boundaries of the shopping center.

In addition to the foregoing, REAs typically contain general provisions against "obstructing" common areas in a manner which impedes vehicular or pedestrian ingress and egress. A frequent area of contention is the developer's belated decision to install kiosks within the interior mall common areas. Adjacent in-line stores often resent the appearance of these facilities, but their ability to protest will be minimized absent specific protection in their space leases. This is because REAs usually state that while the burdens imposed by the Reciprocal Easement Agreement bind and "run with the land" throughout the entire shopping center, the benefits of the REA—including the ability to enforce the same—lies exclusively with the original *parties* to the agreement (i.e., the anchor department stores and the developer), and their successors *in title*.

2. *Alterations to Common Area Facilities Area.* REAs also typically contain rather generic aesthetic controls requiring that the

architectural appearance of common areas, as the same may be altered over time, be consistent with the balance of the shopping center, and provide anchor retailers with the opportunity to reasonably review and approve architectural face-lifts.

Permitted Uses

The text of the REA undoubtedly will list a variety of prohibited, noxious uses deemed completely inconsistent with a first-class shopping center. Of course, there will be grey areas which will be heavily negotiated. As mentioned above, on "tight" locations retailers may be wary of the existence of free-standing movie theaters, entertainment complexes, health clubs, or amusement parks. Depending on the site and the local marketplace, the customers of these facilities may be viewed as single-purpose attendees who will not frequent the balance of the shopping center, although their cars will be parked in valuable common area parking spaces for a significant period of time. Similarly, office uses are often viewed as potentially incompatible with the goal of retail merchandising. Frequently, agreeable compromises can be reached which allow the anchor department stores the protection they need, on the one hand, while providing the developer with sufficient flexibility to market space during various fads and retail cycles that occur during the life of the REA. Compromises typically include putting certain uses beyond the immediate vicinity of the anchor stores, limiting the size of these operations, and requiring outlot uses to be self-contained insofar as minimum parking requirements are concerned.

Obligation to Construct

As the developer nears success in completing its applications for governmental approvals, it will begin focusing heavily upon obligating the anchor department stores which will serve as initial parties to the REA to begin the construction and completion of their stores within a given time frame. Obligating key retailers to commence shopping center construction simultaneously is much like getting your friends to jump into the swimming pool at the same time. The effort takes a lot of time, effort, and persuasiveness. Basically, anchor retailers will not want to commit to construct the store until they are assured that comparable retailers are committed to do so, that the construction time frame is adequate to go "on line" for the next viable "selling season," and that market demand remains "solid." Some retailers simply refuse to open at certain times of the year, and prefer to wait until their next major "selling season" approaches, further complicating the negotiation.[16]

Operating Covenants

A comparable synergy exists among anchor retailers with respect to operating covenants contained in the REA. No anchor retailer will commit to remain open if comparable department stores are not open and operating within the same time period. A compromise is usually reached which not only limits the anchor's operating covenant to a stated term of years, but also qualifies that obligation in the event a certain number of comparable retailers, or a minimum amount of retail floor area, do not remain open and do not honor the same hours of operation. In the context of smaller "community shopping centers" frequently featuring a major discount department store, a major grocery retailer, and a series of "in-line" strip stores, the discount department store chain will only commit to open its door, "for one day only," as its trade name store. This is primarily because these retailers have learned to treat their real estate as a fungible asset which must be capable of being sold off at any time, and because they enjoy the needed leverage over developers to enter community shopping centers without offering an operating covenant.

Collateral tension will occur over issues such as the obligation of an anchor department store to restore in the event of condemnation or casualty. Typically, the obligation of a retailer to rebuild its building will depend, in part, upon whether the original operating covenant is still in place, and whether any of the qualifications to its obligation to continue will remain unsatisfied. Operating covenants may be subject to occasional "permitted delays," such as periodic remodeling for a limited period of time at given frequencies, or perhaps for remodeling in the wake of a change in ownership.

In the event a party fails to honor its operating covenant, a series of potential ramifications will occur. First and foremost, other retailers may no longer be subject to the terms of their operating covenant. In essence, the synergy of the whole center may begin to unravel due to the interrelationship of the covenants. Will a court of equity intervene against the original defaulting department store? Courts in many jurisdictions are reluctant to order a property owner to perform affirmative acts which require ongoing injunctive supervision by the courts.[17] For this reason, many REAs feature "buy back rights," by means of which the developer can repurchase the defaulting retailer's real estate in order to force the retailer out of the center and replace it with a more viable merchant.

Common Area Maintenance Responsibilities

In order to insure uniform standards of maintenance, care and security, shopping center common area maintenance (CAM) usually is provided by the developer.[18] Anchor department stores typically do not bear their pro-rata share of CAM charges, but are rather subsidized by other occupants of the shopping center. In some instances, the anchor stores will not pay any CAM whatsoever; in others, the anchor's obligation is capped at a relatively low rate.

Anchor stores will be wary of the possibility that the developer will fail to adequately maintain common areas according to the "first class" standards referred to in the text of the REA. Developers frequently will grant anchor tenants' self-help rights, *provided* that the developer and its lender have first been provided notice and an opportunity to cure. In community shopping centers, discount department store retailers frequently negotiate for the unilateral right to ultimately "take over" the developer's role in providing common area maintenance within the boundaries of the anchors' parcel, and thereupon be discharged from whatever monetary liability it has for CAM. REAs also provide that, in the event a CAM set-off is insufficient to recoup the anchor tenants' costs incurred in connection with its self-help efforts, a lien is placed against the developer's parcel, which typically will be subordinate to the lien of the developer's first mortgage lender.

Protection against CAM charge abuse by the developer is usually provided in the form of periodic audit rights, which provide the department store with penalty interest rates and the ability to recoup auditing costs in the event a CAM bill reflects an overcharge of more than a couple percent. "In line" tenants are increasingly hostile to paying CAM charges and scrutinize CAM statements to delete capital costs and other items.

Merchants Associations

Shopping center REAs frequently call for the creation of a Mall Merchants Association. Anchor tenants, however, will refuse to join unless there is a comparable commitment by the majority of similar merchants to participate and contribute, and, if they join the required membership, time is limited generally to a few years. In times past anchor stores demanded adequate representation on the Association's board of directors which corresponds to the anchor tenant's proportionate share of the floor area of the shopping center, and possibly a veto right over the amendments to the Association's initial charter and bylaws. Due to antitrust implications anchor stores now favor a one-store one-vote democracy. In any event, the anchor tenants' monetary contribution will be limited.

REA Enforcement

Courts of equity usually are willing to enforce the literal terms and conditions of REA restrictions. In Illinois, for example, appellate cases uphold the authority of chancery courts to enjoin rather minimal encroachments into the pedestrian common area of a mall, and the ability to acquire the removal of common area obstructions which reduce available parking areas within the mall by just a few spaces.[19] Bear in mind, however, that only the original parties to the REA and their successors in interest may have such clear sailing in enforcing the restrictive provisions of an REA. This is because REAs usually contain provisions which state that while the burdens of REA restrictions apply throughout the shopping center and "run with the land," the benefits of enforcing a shopping center Reciprocal Easement Agreement are limited to the original signatories, and their successors in interest to record title. As a result, a disgruntled "in line" small store tenant seeking to enforce the terms and restrictions contained in an REA may find itself constrained to:

(1) scrutinizing its lease diligently to determine if either REA-style restrictions are offered by landlord to tenant in the text of the lease, or whether the lease somehow provides tenant with the right to require landlord/developer to enforce REA restriction for tenant's benefit; or

(2) trying to make new law in the state in which the shopping center is located, establishing that the tenant is a third-party beneficiary to the REA, with the right to enforce the same, notwithstanding language directly to the contrary within the text of the REA itself.

Mortgagee-Required Provisions

A knowledgeable developer will anticipate the requirements of institutional lenders who will be looking at the REA when considering making a mortgage loan that will be secured by a lien on a parcel that is affected by an REA, whether it is a loan to the developer or to an anchor department store company. If a lender's requirements are not included in the REA, the lender may send its borrower back into battle with the other parties to the REA to modify the REA accordingly.

Institutional lenders and their lawyers will require the inclusion of some or all of the following provisions in an REA which affects their security:

1. The lender will want the right to receive notice and to have an opportunity to cure any of its borrower's defaults under the REA (either during the same cure period provided to the borrower under the REA or after the expiration of an extra cure period exclusively for the benefit of the lender, including the time it may take for the lender to obtain possession of the mortgaged property in order to effect the cure), before any other party to the REA exercises any of its remedies under the REA;

2. In the event of a casualty to the borrower's building and a subsequent default by the borrower under the loan, upon becoming the owner of the security, the lender will want to limit its liability for reconstruction of the borrower's building to the extent that the lender receives insurance proceeds payable for such reconstruction;

3. The lender will require a statement that the breach by the borrower of any of the provisions of the REA shall not operate to defeat or render invalid the lien of the mortgage;

4. To satisfy the lender, the parties to the REA must expressly consent to the mortgaging and assignment by the borrower of its interest under the REA and all supplemental agreements, and agree to recognize the lender as a party thereto in the event of the lender's exercise of its rights and remedies under the loan documents;

5. In the event that the REA contains provisions for arbitration of disputes under the REA, the lender will require the parties to agree to include the lender as a necessary party to the arbitration proceedings;

6. In the event that a lender becomes the owner of the mortgaged property, the lender will expect to be able to freely transfer the property and shall be liable under the REA only for the period of its ownership of the mortgaged property, and to be automatically released from liability upon its sale or other transfer of the property to a third party;

7. A prudent developer will also include in the REA an obligation on the part of all parties thereto to execute and deliver estoppel letters to each other and their lenders, potential purchasers and joint venture partners, setting forth the status of the REA and whether any defaults exist thereunder; and

8. Last, and perhaps most importantly, the lender must be released from any trade-name operating covenant that may be binding upon its department store company borrower. While in some department store mortgage financing transactions, the lender will require its borrower to grant the lender a license to operate the store under the borrower's trade name, the use of that license is not always feasible, and the lender must be able to arrange for a replacement store to open as soon as possible. The lender also must be relieved from the performance of any other obligations of the borrower that may be personal in nature to the borrower, such as delivering confidential financial statements of the borrower. In addition, some lenders will require that the REA grant the lender additional latitude with respect to permitted uses to which its borrower's parcel can be put after foreclosure and subsequent transfer of the mortgaged property. Lenders can and often do begin their negotiation of this point with a demand that the parcel can be used for "any lawful purpose," but those lenders will eventually find themselves in the same arena of battle in which their borrowers fought in the original negotiation of the use limitation aspects of the REA. This is one of the few cases where the one with the gold does not always rule.

Bankruptcy Concerns

Bankruptcy can have a significant impact on the operation and success of a shopping center. Volumes can and have been written on this topic, though practical restraints limit the depth into which this chapter can address shopping center-related bankruptcy issues.

One interesting topic relates to a retail tenant's ability to assign its lease of space in a shopping center. Tenants and owners of all types of shopping centers—whether regional mall, downtown vertical mall, part of a resort or exclusive hotel, power center, strip center, or even the simple corner in a small town—should always keep in mind that retail tenants in these centers, and/or their parent corporations, may at some time file for bankruptcy protection. Many of the anchor tenants in a regional mall, for example, enjoy below-market lease rental rates which they were able to successfully negotiate from developers or managers because their "high fashion" image was thought to be attractive to potential "in-line," specialty store tenants. In bankruptcy, these anchor leases may be a debtor-in-possession's or a trustee's most valuable asset *if* assignable—for a substantial premium—to another retailer desirous of the location and/or the lease terms.

Some of the questions that arise as to shopping center tenant lease assignments are:

1. Can a debtor/tenant assign its lease to another retailer—even to a retailer having substantially different merchandise and customers—over the opposition of the shopping center owner?

2. What control does the owner have to prevent assignment to a potential replacement tenant thought to be incompatible with the mall's "image," existing tenants, and/or plans for future expansion?

3. If the landlord objects, what approaches can the bankruptcy court take to determine whether or not assignment is appropriate.

The Bankruptcy Code contains a provision that specially limits the trustee's (or debtor-in-possession's) power to assume and assign an unexpired lease of real estate located in a shopping center.

Most fundamentally, the trustee must provide adequate assurance of future performance. Although the Code does not define "adequate assurance," it does contain several requirements that must be met in order to assure adequately the performance of shopping center leases. These requirements are based on the recognition that a shopping center is a carefully planned enterprise consisting of a particular tenant mix designed to attract higher patronage of stores. These requirements are also based on the fact that the lease agreement in a shopping center often gives the landlord a percentage of the tenant's gross receipts as the rental. In order to protect the investments of the shopping center owner, the financier, and the other tenants, it is necessary to provide assurance that the tenant mix will not be adversely affected by a tenant's bankruptcy.

Specifically, the trustee or debtor in possession may not assign a shopping center lease under which the debtor is a tenant unless there is adequate assurance:

1. Of the source of future rent and any other consideration due under the lease;

2. That any percentage rent due under the lease will not decline substantially;

3. That assumption or assignment is subject to all the provisions of the lease, including but not limited to provisions on radius, location, use, or exclusivity, and will not breach any such

provision contained in any other lease, financing agreement, or master agreement relating to the shopping center; and

4. That assumption or assignment of the lease will not disrupt any tenant mix or balance in the shopping center.

If any of these assurances cannot be made, the landlord may insist on rejection of the lease so that the premises may be rented to a new tenant who is in a position to make such assurances. A leading published decision, *In re Federated Dept. Stores, Inc.*, 135 B.R. 941 (Bankr. S.D. Ohio 1991), refused to permit assignment of a Jordan Marsh store to Mervyn's. The Court strictly construed the "mix and balance" requirement in the mall owner's favor and stressed that the owner's long range plan to upscale the mall had to be honored.

The concept of tenant mix and balance is not defined in the Bankruptcy Code. The legislative history says only that the concept has to do with generating maximum retail sales volume in the shopping center, which in turn translates to maximum rents paid to the landlord. That little piece of legislative history is significant, however, because it tells us that the mix or balance concept is designed financially to protect the landlord and is designed to protect more than the landlord's ability to receive the rental on the store that is being assigned. That is, it is designed to protect his financial position as to the mall as a whole.

The mix and balance concept has a lot to do with the very idea of a shopping center—another term that is not defined in the Bankruptcy Code. But we do know from the legislative history and recent precedent that the shopping center concept pertains to a situation where there is a combination of leases, all leases held by a single landlord, purposeful development of the property as a single unit, joint advertising, and contiguity of stores—in short, a synergy of the stores so that each adds to a greater whole.

Bankruptcy issues also arise in the context of other shopping center-related issues, but all the multi-faceted aspects of bankruptcy remain beyond the scope of this chapter. .

SUMMARY AND CONCLUSION

The typical shopping center is the subject of intense regulation by both the public sector, which polices health and safety concerns, and the private sector, which attempts to impose its own "vision" upon the use and development of the mall. When the restrictions imposed by both the public and private sector are fully understood, the range of permitted operations within the shopping center proves to be very limited, requiring any person involved in the use, occupancy, or financing of shopping center facilities to be alert to the legal constraints applicable to this unique type of property.

ENDNOTES

1. *See Spaulding School District No. 58* v. *City of Waukegan,* 18 Ill. 2d 526 (1960); *Metropolitan Housing Development Corporation* v. *Village of Arlington Heights,* 616 F.2d 1006 (7th Cir. 1980).

2. *See LaSalle National Bank of Chicago* v. *County of Cook,* 12 Ill. 2d 40, 145 N.E.2d 65 (1957); *Sinclair Pipe Line Co.* v. *Village of Richton Park,* 19 Ill. 2d 370, 387, 167 N.E.2d 406 (1960); *Wilson* v. *County of McHenry,* 92 Ill. App. 3d 997, 1002, 416 N.E.2d 426 (2nd Dist. 1981).

3. Cook County Real Property Tax Assessment Classification Ordinance, last amended December 18, 1989 (effective January 1, 1990), Section 2.

4. *See,* for example, 35 ILCS 235/0.01, 35 ILCS 235/9.

5. *See,* California, Cal. Gov. Code WP. 66000-66009 (Deering Supp.); Florida, Development of Regional Impact and Growth Management Acts, 1988 Fla. Laws 164, 1988 Fla. Laws 393, 1988 Fla. Laws 121; Illinois Complied Statutes Annotated 605 ILCS 5/5-902, et seq.; Georgia, O.C.G.A. Sec. 36-71-1-26-71-13; DuPage County, Illinois Fair Share Road Improvement Impact Fee Ordinance, ODT-021D-89; Nevada, Nev. Rev. Stat. Sec. 278B.010 to 278B.320; New Jersey Transportation Development District, 1989 N.J. Laws 573; Oregon, Or. Rev. Stat. Sec. 223.297 to Sec. 223.314; Tennessee, Tenn. Public Acts 1988, Chap. No. 1022, House Bill 1956, effective 5/12/88; Texas, 1989 Texas Gen. Laws 1.; Virginia, Va. Code Sec. 15.1-498.1 to 15.1-498.10; Washington, Wash. Rev. Code 82.02.020, 36.73.120; 35.72.040, 35.43, 36.88, 39 (Wash. Laws, Ch. 179).

6. *Broward County* v. *Janis Dev. Corp.,* 311 So. 2nd 371 (Fla. App. 1975); *Emerson College* v. *City of Boston,* 462 N.E.2d 1098 (Mass. 1984); *Hillis Homes, Inc.* v. *Snohomish County,* 650 P.2d 193 (Wash. 1982); *Albany Area Builders Ass'n* v. *Town of Guilderland,* 534 N.Y.S.2d 791 (Sup. Ct. App. Div. 1988), *aff'd in part,* 546 N.E.2d 920 (1989); *New Jersey Builders Ass'n* v. *Bernards Township,* 528 A.2d 555 (N.J. 1987); *Oregon State Homebuilders* v. *City of Tigard,* 604 P.2d 886 (Or. App. 1979) *review denied,* 288 Or. 527 (1980); *Weber Basin Home Builders Ass'n* v. *Roy City,* 487 P.2d 866 (Utah 1971); *Strahan* v. *City of Aurora,* 38 Ohio Misc. 37, 311 N.E.2d 876 (1973).

7. *Compare Rosner* v. *Village of Downers Grove,* 19 Ill. 2d 448 (1980); *Pioneer Trust* v. *Village of Mt. Prospect,* 22 Ill. 2d 375 (1960) with *Simpson* v. *North Platte,* 206 Neb. 240, 245, 292 N.W.2d 297, 301 (1980).

8. *Dolan* v. *City of Tigard,* 1994 U.S. LEXIS 4826. *See also, Nollan* v. *California Coastal Commission,* 483 U.S. 825, 837 (1987).

9. 42 U.S.C. §9607(b)(3).

10. Federal regulation of wetlands is implemented by means of Section 404 of the 1972 Federal Water Pollution Control Act, 33 USC §1344, and by Army Corps of Engineers regulations requiring that various environmental guidelines be satisfied. *See* 40 C.F.R. 230. Compliance with state regulation of wetlands should be verified, as well.

11. *See, Cannon* v. *Clayton County,* 255 Ga. 63, 335 S.E.2d 294 (1985); *A.A. Profiles, Inc.* v. *City of Fort Lauderdale,* 850 F.2d 1483 (11th Cir. 1988); *Cos Corp.* v. *City of Evanston* (1963), 27 Ill. 2d 570, 190 N.E.2d 364; *Pioneer Trust and Savings Bank* v. *County of Cook* (1978), 71 Ill. 2d 510, 577 N.E.2d 21.

12. *See,* for example, *Alaimo in Town of Greece,* 418 N.Y.S.2d 492, 68 A.D.2d 743 (1979).

13. 35 ILCS 210/2.

14. While the use of permissible building areas in REAs is widespread, express restrictions on leasing or selling space to named competitors have been curbed by a series of Federal Trade Commission consent decrees. In the 1970s the FTC found certain exclusives and restrictive covenants to be *per se* violations of Section 1 of the Sherman Act, 15 U.S.C. §1 (1982). *Gimbel Bros.,* 83 F.T.C. 1320 (1974); *Tysons Corner Regional Shopping Center, City Stores Co., May Dept. Stores Co., Woodward & Lothrop, Inc.,* 83 F.T.C. 1598 (1974); *City Stores Co.,* 85 F.T.C. 870 (1975); *Rich's, Inc.,* 87 F.T.C. 1372 (1976); *Sears, Roebuck & Co.,* 89 F.T.C. 240 (1976); *Strawbridge & Clothier,* 87 F.T.C. 593 (1976); *Federated Dept. Stores., Inc.,* 93 F.T.C. 449 (1979). In 1989, the FTC did modify the 1977 Sears consent decree but it did not modify the prohibition against tenant approval clauses. Consequently owners and their lawyers do not have firm guidelines within which to operate when agreeing to tenant restrictions. See, *The Antitrust Aspects of Restrictive Covenants in Shopping Center Leases,* 1994 Revision, International Council of Shopping Centers.

15. Public access to shopping center common areas for political activity is frequently litigated. Some state courts have followed the theory that common areas are the "new town centers" serving as a public square and require that access be permitted. *Robins* v. *Pruneyard Shopping Center,* 153 Cal. Rptr. 854, 592 P.2d 341, *aff'd,* 447 U.S. 74 (1980); *Batchelder* v. *Allied Stores Int'l., Inc.,* 388 Mass. 83, 445 N.E.2d 590 (1983); *State* v. *Schmid,* 84 N.J. 535, 423 A.2d 615 (1980) (not shopping center property); and *State* v. *Cargill,* 100 Ore. App. 336, 786 P.2d 208, reviewed, 310 Or. 133, 794 P.2d 794 (1990). See also *New Jersey Coalition Against War* v. *J.M.B. Realty,* et al., 1994 N.J. LEXIS 1283 (Supreme Court of New Jersey, 1994). Other state courts permit certain owners to deny access to the public. *Fiesta Mall Venture* v. *Mecham Recall Comm.,* 159 Ariz. 371, 767 P.2d 719 (1988), corrected, January 26, 1989; *Cologne* v. *Westfarms Assoc.,* 192 Conn. 48, 469 A.2d 1201 (1984); *Citizens for Ethical Government, Inc.* v. *Gwinnett Place Associates, L.P.,* 260 Ga. 245, 392 S.E.2d 8 (1990); *Woodland* v. *Michigan Citizens Lobby,* 128 Mich. App. 649, 341 N.W.2d 174 (1983), *aff'd,* 423 Mich. 188, 378 N.W.2d 377 (1985); *State* v. *Felmet,* 302 N.C. 173, 273 S.E.2d 708 (1981); *Shad Alliance* v. *Smith Haven Mall,* 66 N.Y.2d 496, 488 N.E.2d 1211 (1985); *Western Pa. Socialist Workers 1982 Campaign* v. *Connecticut Gen. Life Ins. Co.,* 512 Pa. 23, 515 A.2d 1331 (1986); *Southcenter Joint Venture* v. *Nat'l. Democratic Policy Comm.,* 113 Wash. 2d 413, 780 P.2d 1282 (1989); and *Jacobs* v. *Major,* 139 Wis. 2d 492, 407 N.W.2d 832 (1987).

Shopping center owners differ about whether permitting such access is good for business. If a center decides to limit or restrict access, it should adopt a consistent policy, and be uniformly administered. Owners who wish to restrict access should know that the following factors are considered by the courts in determining whether access should be permitted:

1. the nature, purpose and primary use of the private property;

2. the nature and extent of the owner's invitation to the public for entering the property;

3. the existence and enforcement of the shopping center's policy in prohibiting use of the shopping center as a public forum; and

4. the purpose of the expressional activities.

16. Anchor stores generally will not agree to open during the period from November 1 of any year and January 31 of the following year, during the 30 days immediately prior to Easter Sunday or between May 1 and August 1 of any year.

17. *Security Builders, Inc. v. Southwest Drug Co.*, 244 Miss. 877, 147 So.2d 635 (1962); *Lorch, Inc. v. Bessemer Mall Shopping Center, Inc.*, 294 Ala. 17, 310 So.2d 872 (1975); *New Park Forest Associations II v. Rogers Enterprises, Inc.*, 195 Ill. App. 3d 757, 552 N.E.2d 1215, *cert. denied*, 133 Ill. 2d 559, 561 N.E.2d 694 (1990); *CBL & Associates, Inc. v. McCrory Corporation*, 761 F. Supp. 807 (M.D. Ga., 1991); *8600 Associates, Ltd. v. Wearguard Corporation*, 737 F. Supp. 44 (E.D. Mich., 1990); *Sizeler Property Investors, Inc. v. Gordon Jewelry Corporation*, 544 So.2d 53, *cert. dismissed*, 552 So.2d 372 (La., 1989); *Madison Plaza, Inc. v. Shapira Corporation*, 180 Ind. App. 141, 387 N.E.2d 483 (1979); *Grossman v. Wegman's Food Markets, Inc.*, 43 A.D.2d 813, 350 N.Y.S.2d 484 (1973); *Price v. Herman*, 81 N.Y.S.2d 361, *aff'd* 275 A.D. 675, 87 N.Y.S.2d 221 (1949).

18. Security issues are important, emerging topics in the shopping center industry. *See* "Security Special Report," *Shopping Centers Today*, April, 1994. Shopping center owners are concerned about liability for crimes committed by third parties. This concern is not theoretical; shopping center owners have been subject to civil lawsuits and found liable in certain circumstances. *Madden v. C&K Barbecue Carryout, Inc.*, 758 S.W.2d 59 (Mo. 1988); *Godwin v. Olshan*, 161 Ga. App. 35, 288 S.E.2d 850 (1982); *Bucks Associates v. R. H. Macy & Co.*, 428 F. Supp. 546 (E.D. Pa. 1977); *Royal Neckwear Co., Inc. v. Century City, Inc.*, 205 Cal. App. 3d 1146, 252 Cal. Rptr. 810 (1988); *Craig v. A.A.R. Realty Corporation*, 576 A.2d 688 (Superior Court of Delaware, 1989).

19. *See The Fair v. Evergreen Park Shopping Plaza*, 4 Ill. App. 2d 454, 124 N.E.2d 649 (1st Dist., 1959), where the court required, at the insistence of an anchor department store tenant, the removal of a bay window installed by another anchor tenant which encroached minimally into pedestrian common area. In addition, *See Walgreen Co. v. American National Bank and Trust Company*, 4 Ill. App. 3d 549, 281 N.E.2d 462 (First District, 1972), where the court enjoined construction of a Fotomat kiosk which would have consumed 3 of 400 parking spaces provided at the center.

Five

Analyzing Market Demand for Shopping Centers

Richard Kateley

T he sales potential and resulting cash flow of a retail entity—
whether a single, free-standing store or a 2 million square foot
super-regional mall—is of critical importance to developers and their
financial partners, to retailers, and to institutional investors. For the
developer, market area demand analysis is used to determine what to
build and where to build it. For the retailer, anticipated sales and
consumer research are used to design and locate stores and to define
merchandising strategy. For institutional investors and owners, sales
levels and forecasts are used to evaluate acquisition pricing to analyze capital improvement pay backs, and trigger dispositions.

Retail market demand is conventionally defined as purchases of retail goods by individuals and households, and to a limited extent by
small businesses. Demand is measured in terms of dollar sales for various categories of merchandise ranging from everyday convenience

goods to consumer durables and automobiles. In this discussion, retail demand refers to the primary consumers of merchandise.

The analysis of retail demand has a long tradition that combines both academic and practical approaches.[1] Academic research relevant to demand analysis is especially varied, ranging from economic theories of central place and models of locational behavior of retailers to motivational and attitudinal research on consumer choice. The pragmatic research tradition, fostered by large retailers and developers, stresses rules of thumb and direct use of local data to refine decision making. This chapter includes both analytic traditions, but also recognizes the importance of the changes taking place across the retail industry that will need to be addressed by sharper and more powerful methods of demand analysis. Many of the old tools appear particularly dull in the face of the demographic, socioeconomic, and lifestyle shifts that characterize American consumer behavior. As new development slows and institutional investors command a larger share in the ownership of retail properties, the financial perspective and analytic methods used in portfolio modeling will have wider application in the retail real estate arena.[2]

For clarity and convenience, the methodological and substantive issues of retail market demand analysis are divided into four basic areas as follows:

- Area demand evaluation, or economic base analysis, which is used to identify and quantify the underlying economic and demographic structure of an area and its long term retail sales potential.
- Direct consumer research on shopper attitudes, preferences, and spending habits which is used to translate aggregate data on the economic base into qualitative sales projections based on local realities.
- Analysis of existing and planned alternative retail distribution channels (both in-store and nonstore) which is used to establish the competitive alignment in a market.
- Trade area definition and evaluation which brings information from the previous three areas into focus on a particular location and forecasts sales performance within that context.

Trade area analysis ties together the macroanalysis of the economic base, microanalysis of consumer preferences, and the market analysis of the competition in the selection of the retail location that optimizes developer, retailer, or investor profit.[3] These factors, and the methods used to identify and quantify them, are discussed in terms of the bottom line for demand analysis: attainable sales volume.

AREA DEMAND: ECONOMIC BASE ANALYSIS

The sales potential for most retail venues is a function of the economic and demographic characteristics of the area in which it is located.[4] There are four key variables that define the economic base: employment, population, income, and retail sales.

Employment

Investors, retailers, and developers rate alternative locations in terms of the size, composition, and growth potential of the employment base. Employment data available from government sources and proprietary vendors are used to measure total job growth and employment by industry sector (i.e., services; government; finance, insurance, and real estate). Analysts are concerned not just with the size of the base but in future projections. Employment forecasts are prepared by federal agencies and most state governments.

Because income (buying power) is generated differentially by industry sector and occupational grouping, the composition of local employment is important. Service jobs, for example, may be increasing in number but, because they generally pay less than manufacturing jobs, the total income available in the area may actually fall. Institutional investors, in particular, are attuned to the diversity of the economy. Some economies are well diversified in terms of the distribution of employment across industry classes while others are more concentrated or specialized. Diversified economies are less vulnerable to downturn than more specialized economics which are, therefore, riskier. Analysts also evaluate large employers in an area and assess their ability to grow.

Finally, more and more attention is paid to the job-creating capacity of the economic base. Many new jobs are created in small and medium-sized enterprises. Some economic sectors have more small firms. Financial service companies, for example, are likely to be small businesses. The incubation potential of an area and its business climate for small firm growth plays a role in evaluating future activity. As small businesses become direct retail customers

(making purchases in home improvement centers, office supply discounters, and warehouse clubs), this aspect of economic base evaluation will be more salient.

Population

The area's demographic structure is as important as employment.
The size of the population, past growth experience, and projected future increases are documented by the census. While overall population trends reveal the outline of the demographic profile, there are
five features of populations that are of special relevance for retail
demand analysis:

1. *Households and Household Formations.* The base unit of consumption for retail goods is the household, therefore, the number of households, the distribution of households by age, and
   their average size and rates of growth (or decline) are evaluated (see Figure 5.1).

FIGURE 5.1

U.S. Household Growth

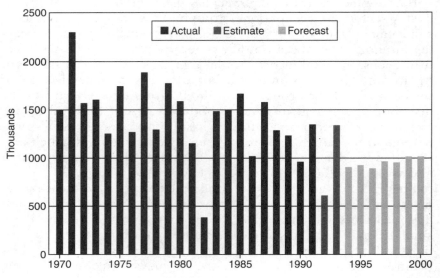

Source: Trammel Crow Residential, April 1994.

2. *Household Composition.* The kinds of households present in the area and more likely to grow are broken down by type: singles, single parents with children, couples with children, empty nesters, and nontraditional households all have different income and purchasing profiles.

3. *Age.* The age structure of populations varies greatly from city to city. The proportion of older and younger people and the numbers at various critical life cycle stages (i.e., teenagers, first-time home buyers) are isolated to understand their impact on merchandise lines (see Figure 5.2).

4. *Race and Ethnic Background.* Although not always well understood by retailers, Asian, Hispanic, and African-American populations, which are majority groups in many areas, have distinct retail preferences and shopping patterns.

5. *Immigrants.* A significant percentage of population growth in major metro areas comes from immigration. The role of these newcomers is too often left out of retail calculations.

FIGURE 5.2

U.S. Population Changes by Age Groups
1990–2000

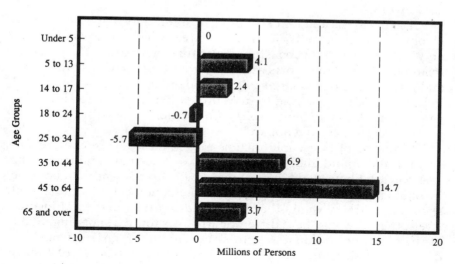

Source: U.S. Bureau of the Census.

Although "quick-and-dirty" demographic analyses use national averages for some of these subpopulation evaluations, that is a mistake. The composition of households varies tremendously from local area to local area and changes in composition are critical to the sales performance of retail outlets. The distribution of the population over age, household status, and income categories is probably the single most important feature of a comprehensive market assessment.

Income

Income is highly correlated with employment and socioeconomic status. (Education is the best predictor of income and is used as a proxy in some demand calculations of high-end retail outlets.) Income is the single best predictor of retail sales.

Unfortunately, reliable and timely income data are difficult to obtain for small areas and for years between the census. The *Survey of Buying Power*, other government publications, and proprietary vendors (e.g., *Sales and Marketing Management*) provide income estimates and forecasts. Many states and some local areas provide household income estimates based on tax returns or special surveys. Care needs to be taken to understand, however, what is being reported in these documents: total money income, personal income, disposable income for example, are all slightly different. Incomes are sometimes denoted per capita and at other times as median household income.

For many areas and for certain types of retail formats, unreported income is a significant issue. In urban areas, the "underground economy" may generate purchasing power that far exceeds that derived from public income reports and estimates. Similarly, in some small and mid-sized cities, a large college student population (unreported in local statistics) can lead to sales projections that are too low. Students spend large amounts locally on big ticket items, such as computers, electronics, and apparel.

The source of household income also plays a role in comprehensive retail demand analysis. With two wage-earner families on the rise, the total household income may be less important than how the income is gained. Dual income households not only have different spending patterns than other households with similar total income levels, they also may have different attitudes toward shopping. Some of the aversion to shopping that is reflected in lower frequency and duration of shopping trips is attributed to the sources of family income.

Some retail market demand professionals focus on area home values and home sale prices as indicators of the wealth of a trade area. While people can't spend their home equity value at the store, this source of potential wealth is used as an indicator of the propensity to spend, particularly on more expensive discretionary items. Home sales data are also used to support projections for furniture and home furnishings.

Retail Sales

Past and present levels of actual retail expenditures are the final variable in economic base analysis. Data on sales by types of merchandise and types of stores are readily available. States with sales taxes augment the federal government data sources. Sales by category (Table 5.1) allow the area to be compared with national averages to determine the composition and strength of local buying power. Sales data over time are used to measure the volatility of consumption patterns.

Retail sales numbers are also compared to income averages to determine if higher or lower (compared to national norms) proportions of income are devoted to different types of goods. A key ratio in this regard is the proportion of total personal income that is devoted to retail sales. Generally, the more affluent the area, the smaller the

TABLE 5.1

Typical Retail Sales Categories

Store Type	Percent of Sales
General merchandise	12
Apparel and accessories	5
Furniture and furnishings	6
Other general merchandise	4
Grocery and food	21
Drugs	4
Home improvement	5
Automobile	20
Gas station	12
Eating and drinking places	11
Total Retail Sales	100

Source: U.S. Department of Commerce.

percentage of income that is spent on retail items. Also, expenditure patterns change with income levels: The proportion of income spent on convenience items (such as food for home consumption) declines as family income increases, while the proportion spent on luxury items increases. Much judgment is required, and used, in most demand studies that rely on sales and income levels.

In sum, the economic base analysis provides the investor or developer with an empirical assessment of the total area size, key elements of the composition of demand, and likely growth trends. Employment and demographic data coupled with available income and retail sales information are combined to estimate the strength of the market in terms of sales volumes.

CONSUMER DEMAND: ATTITUDES AND BEHAVIORS

While area demand analysis provides the context for the overall value of retail sales, this information needs to be translated into forecasts of attainable sales volumes. In effect, the economic base analysis *quantifies* demand, consumer research *qualifies* demand. With the demographic and economic segmentation just described, bottom-up analysis that starts with individuals will be much more important than the aggregate analysis that starts with broad employment or population categories and uses that information to make inferences about smaller areas.

Changes in consumer attitudes toward shopping and on what goods shoppers decide to spend their money are occurring not only as demographic and socioeconomic diversification intensifies but also within traditional purchasing profiles. Thus, high-income single individuals who in the 1980s might have purchased expensive designer apparel may in the future eschew conspicuous consumption in favor of value-oriented, private label merchandise.

Therefore, expectations about expenditure patterns and merchandise lines will have to be recalibrated to meet changing behaviors. Table 5.2 shows results of a survey of patronage at different types of stores and illustrates the volatility in shopper behavior. The "new" consumer will move back and forth across retail formats and price points as lifestyle dictates.

Telephone surveys of consumers, intercept interviews with actual shoppers, and focus groups are the tools that are used to measure the propensity to spend, loyalty to stores, and attitudes toward

TABLE 5.2

Changes in Shopping Habits

Frequency of Shopping (1993 vs. 1991)	Retail Format				
	Catalog	Off-Price	Warehouse	Discount Dept. Store	Traditional Enclosed Mall
More often	23%	26%	31%	50%	18%
Same	29%	35%	34%	35%	47%
Less often	47%	33%	31%	15%	34%

Source: ICSC Research Bulletin, June 1994.

shopping. Microanalytic techniques have long been the province of retailers and regional mall investors, and they will find a larger role in market demand analysis. Income and age, which were the major analytic dimensions in the past, are no longer very good predictors of sales and will be augmented by individual level, bottom-up data gathering.[5]

Although there is no way to predict what directions different consumer groups will take in the future, there are at least two areas of agreement among retailers and shopping center owners. First, people have less time to shop. Some retailers and shopping center developers have reacted to this by focusing on shopping formats that get consumers in and out of stores quickly and provide a high degree of reliability that shoppers will find exactly what they need. Power centers and category killer stores are examples. Others are taking pains to convince shoppers to stay longer and take their time to enjoy the shopping experience. Bookstores with coffee areas and home improvement warehouses with McDonald's franchises inside are examples. Outlet malls and some in-city specialty centers have long combined recreation and entertainment with shopping.

The second reality is that consumers appear able to fulfill different personal and shopping requirements in different retail venues (see Table 5.3). Although some individuals will focus only on price or convenience, most consumers are able to segment their retail purchases along a variety of dimensions including service, selection, and entertainment values as well as price and convenience. This reinforces the notion that retail demand is much more specific, much more targeted than in the past. The end of the mass market and the

TABLE 5.3

Consumer Attraction to Retail Formats

Customer Attraction	Regional Mall	Power Center	Outlet Center
Price		▲	▲
Quality	▲	▲	
Selection	▲	▲	
Convenience		▲	
Service	▲		
Entertainment/ Recreation	▲		▲

Source: Heitman Investment Research.

rise of multiple, segmented retail markets means that demand analysis will have to refocus on smaller and smaller subsets of consumers in order to accurately predict their shopping needs and their potential expenditures.

Finally, in addition to consumer surveys, many market analysts use existing store performance and productivity as a clue to the magnitude and direction of primary demand. If stores catering to specific market segments do not do well—as measured by high turnover, low rents, meager sales averages—that may indicate that the market is saturated in that category and cannot support existing merchants, no less new ones. If data on sales volume per square foot and occupancy are available in a market for specific merchandise or store types, they can be compared to national averages. The Urban Land Institute and ICSC both publish norms and benchmarks for sales performance of different types of shopping centers.[6]

Care must be taken in making inferences, however, because historic store and shopping center productivity is not solely a function of consumer acceptance or underlying demand. Many chain stores opened too many units, overcapacity has reduced operating margins, some stores are poorly managed and merchandised, others have financial leverage burdens. As a result, performance is impacted by factors outside the local market. Market demand inferences drawn from rental rates, vacancy, and store profitability should be looked at critically.

The rapidity of these changes and the difficulty of predicting them is clear evidence that retail investment and development is moving further out on the risk spectrum. Increasing volatility among retailers portends lower occupancy, more turnover, and higher operating costs. These dynamics also place a higher premium on management skill, especially in monitoring sales trends and preemptively moving to attain the most profitable tenant mix.

Competition: Market Share Analysis

The third component of retail market demand is the analysis of the competitive alignment. Traditionally, retailers and shopping center developers assessed markets to see if they were saturated with similar stores selling similar merchandise. If not, they measured the share of the existing market and projected market sales volume that they could capture. These calculations draw heavily on the analysis of the economic base and on locally prevalent shopping habits and predispositions.

The first part of this calculation is becoming more complicated. As recently as the mid-1980s, the traditional array of stores was relatively narrow and well-defined and the range of retail venues, or formats, was similarly constrained. Looking forward, the channels of retail distribution (Figure 5.3) are diverse and merchandise manufacturers have many options to distribute their merchandise to consumers, ranging from outlet stores, to specialty and department stores, to catalogs and interactive television. Therefore, assessing the in-store competition in a local area no longer exhausts the alternatives that shoppers have before them.

At the same time, and responding to the same underlying forces, store types have also multiplied. Discounters now challenge department stores, warehouse clubs vie with supermarkets, outlet stores and off pricers proliferate. As a result there is a general blurring of trade lines, pricing, and store images. This raises the question for demand analysts of what constitutes the "competition"?

One reaction to the segmentation of retail demand markets has been to create more and more retail product. As seen in Table 5.4, the square footage of retail space per capita has increased from about 14 feet in 1970 to over 18 feet in 1990, to an estimated 20 feet by the mid-1990s. This growth came during a period of slow population and household growth and almost no growth in real incomes. Much of this development was driven by the growth of chain stores in terms of the number of stores and their size, and as a result there is overcapacity in many markets along with declining margins and profitability.

FIGURE 5.3

Retail Distribution Channels

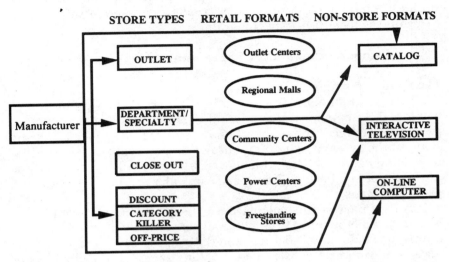

Source: Heitman Investment Research.

TABLE 5.4

Growth in Shopping Center Floorspace

Center Size	GLA per Capita			Percent Change (%)	
(Square Feet)	1990	1980	1970	1980–90	1970–80
100<	4.52	2.75	1.46	64	89
100 to 200	4.81	3.47	2.85	39	22
200 to 400	2.95	2.15	1.80	37	20
400 to 800	2.49	2.11	1.81	18	17
800 to 1,000	1.04	0.99	0.98	5	1
1,000+	1.84	1.67	1.55	10	8
Total	17.65	13.14	10.45	34%	26%

Source: NRB Shopping Center Census, 1991; U.S. Bureau of the Census; F.W. Dodge; and Merrill Lynch.

In this context, investors and developers use a variety of approaches to measure market share. Methods for quantifying sales potential for a retail project include:

1. Comparing the project to competitive shopping centers, using estimates of their sales based on their location and size. The analyst then models project performance in relation to existing and planned competition.

2. Comparing the project to the overall market sales volume, estimated by computing sales estimates based on area income and expenditure patterns, and using an acceptable capture rate to estimate sales for the project.

3. A residual method of calculation where sales of competitive facilities are estimated, then subtracted from the total area sales potential, and the remainder is estimated to be the share for the project.

Each of these methods has merit, but each relies on estimates, on relationships based on past history and on assumptions which may not be valid going forward. Academic analysts, unfortunately, have little to offer in place of the pragmatic approaches to competitive market share analysis.

The competitive alignment for retail properties is emerging as a troublesome area in market demand assessment. New types of shopping formats and the blurring of trade lines and merchandise mix across store types make defining the competition more difficult. Nonstore competition from catalogs, on-line computer services, and even interactive television will also have to be factored into market share equations. As with the influence of individual consumer behavior, quantifying sales potential in a market needs to focus on the microlevel. Inferences based solely on ratios derived from national aggregates or historic performance trends will not provide firm support for investment decisions. Small area dynamics, especially competition, can be understood only in the context of local consumer preferences, historic development patterns, and store loyalty.

TRADE AREA ANALYSIS AND LOCATIONAL MODELS

The final component of market demand analysis is, in many ways, the most important. Defining the trade area in which a store or center will compete draws on the analysis of area demand, local consumer preferences, and the existing and planned competition. For the developer of a retail facility or a retailer entering or expanding in a market, trade area analysis not only includes quantifying and qualifying attainable sales volumes, but also selecting the locations within the area that optimize market share and, therefore, profitability. For institutional investors acquiring existing retail centers, the locations are known and it remains for the investor to appraise the long-term viability of the trade area and the role of the property within it.

Trade Area Definition

The trade area for a retail property (single store or mega complex) is conventionally defined as the surrounding geography from which the property draws 70% to 75% of its total sales.[7] Analysts frequently subdivide trade areas into three components: a primary area which is geographically limited and from which 60% of the sales will be generated; a secondary trade area from which an additional 20% to 25% of the shoppers will come; and a tertiary or residual area from which the remainder of sales will be drawn.

Specifying the trade area involve a number of factors, including:

- Physical and manmade features that delimit areas such as rivers, mountains, freeways, or large scale uses such as military bases.
- Ease of access and driving times that are influenced by roads, congestion, and the like.

There is as much "art" in defining the trade area. With the advent of new distribution channels, the size and shape of trade areas are changing. The penetration of superstores, the draw of outlet centers, the productivity of entertainment-oriented facilities, all challenge traditional trade area definitions. Shopping formats that attract tourists, conventioneers, students, day trippers, and nearby workers require special attention.

Inexpensive availability of computerized geographic information systems (GIS) now allows for the aerial plotting of trade areas as concentric rings of three-, five-, or ten-mile diameters. Rings are *not* reality. There are major differences between a trade area that is carefully defined and is responding to real world issues and one produced mechanically. As in the other aspects of demand analysis, it is important to emphasize the need for microanalysis of the trade area, not simply drawing a ring around it. Techniques such as license plate surveys, drive time analysis, and traffic counts are much more useful than aggregate data displays in uniform patterns.

From the institutional investment perspective, trade area change is a critical issue. Public infrastructure programs and new intervening competition can quickly add to or diminish the sales potential of a trade area. Demographic and socioeconomic shifts occur more slowly, but are ultimately more important. While some merchants and some retail centers can readily accommodate changing trade area fundamentals, some cannot. Anecdotal evidence suggests that hybrid trade areas—where there are two or more distinct economic, social, age, or ethnic/cultural subsegments—are difficult to manage successfully.

Locational Models

The trade area represents the "best" sales potential geography from a demand perspective based on economic, demographic, and competitive conditions. Within a trade area, there is considerable research on retail store location decision making, that is, the places within the market that will optimize sales performance.

There are several distinct themes or traditions in the locational modeling field that are useful in assessing retail demand. One relates to how retailers select the best possible location; another answers the question of how individual consumers choose a particular store or shopping center over another; and a third provides methods to be used by feasibility analysts to assess general market support for sales projections for a given location in a trade area.

Central place theory focuses on the issue of where a retailer should site a facility or where a developer should build a shopping center. In brief, central place theory comprises two variables: the distance of shoppers from the retail location, and the threshold sales required to economically support the facility. The key postulate is that consumers will shop at the nearest place, therefore the threshold location is found by calculating the distance (range) that shoppers will travel. These analyses are based on the simplifying assumptions that shoppers make single trips and seek to minimize the price paid for merchandise in both travel cost and the cost of the goods purchased.

A second academic focus on retail location decisions involves retail agglomerations or clustering. This school of research hypothesizes that shoppers are motivated not only by a price utility but act to

Millstream Factory Shops, Lancaster, Pennsylvania

reduce risk or uncertainty in their buying decisions. Therefore, they will prefer to shop at locations where they can make comparisons among merchants selling the same goods. In central place theory, the lowest price provider wins. In agglomeration research, variables such as selection, convenience, service, and comparability attract consumers and therefore suggest that retailers are best off in central locations.

Both central place and clustering models have been elaborated to extend their initial assumptions. Berry, for example, shows that consumers will travel further than the nearest store for certain types of purchases.[8] The physical attributes of stores and centers are also investigated to differentiate performance. Parking, visibility, and cleanliness are factors that affect consumer choice and retailer location decisions. The role of anchor versus non-anchor tenants in creating demand at a location has also received research attention as a way of better understanding the consumer attraction of retail agglomerations.

While these two academic approaches continue to generate ideas for retail demand analysis, they are still bound by their simplifying assumptions. In the real world, single-purpose shopping trips are not the only generator of retail sales. Indeed, many trips are multipurpose, some are spontaneous, and others are associated with activities such as tourism. In addition, these models are based on consumer preferences for existing types of retail facilities, which means they are less useful for charting the prospects for innovative distribution channels or nontraditional merchandisers.

The third retail location tradition involves the application of probabilistic models of consumer choice derived from the marketing literature. The gravity model is most frequently used to determine the market potential of one or more alternative locations in a trade area. Gravity models[9] in their simplest form relate the attractiveness of a center or store directly to its size and inversely to its distance from the shopper. A center is likened to a magnet, with people represented by iron filings, such that the attraction of the center can be expressed mathematically as a bivariate function of mass and distance.

The basic gravity method of sales potential analysis has been extended to include shopping center features other than size. Pricing, quality of stores, variety, curb appeal, visibility, and many other factors are used to differentiate retail facilities. From the consumer perspective, demographic status, income, and other economic variables are used to add predictive power to travel distance. These factors are used to explain the number of trips individuals are likely to make to a center. Estimates of expenditures per trip are then used to calibrate the model to derive attainable sales estimates.

Gravity models have the same shortcoming as the central place and agglomeration approaches in that the base assumptions are not necessarily valid in today's retail environment. However, these academic studies bring together research findings that practitioners can use to perfect their studies.

CONCLUSION

Trade area definition and assessment of the best location within the market require seasoned judgment and many assumptions about consumers, retailers, and economic optimization. With the changes that are occurring in retail distribution channels—especially the blurring of distinctions between trade lines, pricing, and store types—retail demand analysis will be more and more challenging. The diversity of demand represented by changing demographics, new employment patterns, and shifting attitudes towards shopping further complicate the puzzle.

Accordingly, both the old rules derived and used by practitioners and the simple demand models explored by academics will need to be merged and refocused. In general, attention to segmented consumer profiles and local market peculiarities as opposed to the analysis of past trends and socioeconomic aggregates will pay off in the accuracy of sales projections. For institutional investors, retail volatility adds to the risk of retail real estate investment. But, as retailers, developers, and their financial partners, and academic researchers grapple with these new demand realities, the methods of forecasting attainable sales will improve and so will actual performance at the store, shopping center and portfolio levels.

ENDNOTES

1. An excellent recent survey of the academic literature is by M.J. Eppli and J.B. Benjamin, "The Evolution of Shopping Center Research," *Journal of Real Estate Research*, 9, Winter, 1994. The best review of the application of basic economic models to retail location is by R.A. Roca, *Market Research for Shopping Centers*, ICSC, New York, 1980. The *ICSC Research Quarterly*, and the research papers sponsored by the ICSC Research Advisory Task Force feature the most rigorous theoretical and applied analyses of market demand.

2. Although only a small share of the nation's shopping center inventory is in institutional ownership that share is increasing. REIT ownership of retail property is also rapidly expanding and public market pricing models will influence the evaluation of retail real estate. See, for example, M. Young and R. Kateley, "Retail Revisited and Dissected," *Russell-NCREIF Report*, 8, 1993, and L. Graham, "Community Shopping Centers: A REITs Eye View," Salomon Brothers Real Estate Research, March 1994.

3. Two survey articles summarize the economic optimization models of location theory: A. Ghosh, et al., "Models of Retail Location Process," *Journal of Retailing*, *60*, 1984, and K.D. Vandell and C.C. Carter, "Retail Store Location and Market Analysis: A Review of the Research," *Journal of Real Estate Literature*, *1*, 1993.

4. Exceptions to this basic tenet of retail demand analysis include outlet centers that are located at a significant remove from major metropolitan areas and draw from long distances and certain downtown retail settings (specialty malls, mixed use complexes, entertainment oriented centers) that depend on tourists, visitors and downtown workers rather than on residents for patronage.

5. The diminished role of age and income as predictors are discussed by R.F. Hokenson, "Incorporating Consumer Demographics into Retail Industry Analysis," AIMR, *The Retail Industry*, 1992, and D. Kutyla, "The Shopping Preferences of Teen Agers," *ICSC Research Barometer*, 4, 1993.

6. ICSC *The Score*, ICSC, New York, 1994; ULI, *Dollars and Cents of Shopping Centers*, New York, ULI, 1992.

7. J. Chapman, "Some Pitfalls and Pratfalls of Market Demographics," *ICSC Research Quarterly*, *1*, May 1994 describes definitional issues.

8. B.J. Berry, *The Geography of Market Centers and Retail Distributing*, Englewood Cliffs, NJ, Prentice Hall, 1967.

9. D.L. Huff, *Determination of Intra-Urban Retail Trade*, Los Angeles, UCLA Press, 1962 is the leading exponent of this approach.

Six

Analyzing the Specifics of Retail Markets

Micromarket Demand and Supply Factors

Cynthia T. Ray

B asic supply and demand factors frame the opportunity for retailers and service businesses in a market, but the ultimate selection of a site or location focuses on a number of more explicit factors. Detailing these criteria can be misleading because it makes the retailer's site selection process appear more scientific, or perhaps more simplistic, than it really is. There are nearly as many exceptions as there are rules. Certain site deficiencies can be compensated for by various accommodations. Signage, for example, can enhance suboptimal visibility, or public funding mechanisms can be used to offset high land or site development costs. Access to public transit can reduce parking requirements, while proximity to major tourist attractions can compensate for low residential densities.

123

Market and location factors that dictate the opportunity for retailers similarly influence shopping center development. This chapter takes a brief look at how shopping centers have evolved over time in response to changing micromarket factors and retail concepts.

RETAILER OBJECTIVES

A retailer seeks locations convenient to prospective customers in order to maximize sales penetration. To achieve economies of scale, the retailer also strives to provide comprehensive market coverage through a network of stores.

UNDERSTANDING THE CUSTOMER AND SHOPPING PATTERNS

To identify productive locations, a retailer first must have a thorough understanding of the customer and shopping patterns for the relevant merchandise categories. Even grocery stores, which sell basic commodities, need to appreciate the shoppers' time and distance tolerances for convenient shopping trips. A more complex task is faced by retailers selling unique products and catering to niche markets because of the difficulties in measuring the depth and adequacy of the market for their product. Extensive research is undertaken by many retailers to understand both the demographics and lifestyle characteristics of shoppers, as well as the drawing power of different formats and locations. Sales estimates, along with the project's specific economics, will be the key determinant of whether or not a site meets corporate financial objectives.

ESTIMATING SALES

Sales estimates for a new store or shopping center are derived using various techniques, ranging from entrepreneurial hunches to sophisticated mathematical models. The models, by their very nature, are driven by common denominators that generally reflect the depth of the market, the competition, and a retailer's proven ability to generate sales or capture a share of the potential market. Models are not particularly efficient at reflecting more elusive considerations.

Sales Estimating Procedures[1]

The most common site location and sales forecasting tools utilized by researchers today include gravity models, regression models, and analogs. Rather than replacing analyst's judgments, however, each of these approaches requires creative application because the models cannot reflect the nuances of competitive and site location factors.

Gravity Models are commonly used for convenience good retailers such as supermarkets and drugstores. The sales projections for these retailers are highly dependent on their proximity to a significant population base. The gravity model attempts to simulate a market place as it currently exists, measuring the density of individual trade area sectors, the sector's distance to competing stores, and the strength of the competition. Once the market place is deemed to be in "balance," the analyst introduces the proposed store into the model and assigns a weighting that indicates its strength relative to each competitor. Based on the significance of these weights, the gravity model then calculates the market share that each competitor should achieve in each sector and aggregates over the trade area to produce a sales estimate for the proposed store.

Regression models are a commonly used sales forecasting application, especially for destination-oriented retailers. A regression model utilizes multivariate statistical analysis to isolate those variables that appear to be the strongest predictors of sales. These variables are then assigned a value in an equation,

$$Y = 73.5 + .7A + 1.2B - .6C$$

where Y is sales per household, A is the median age, B is median household income, and C represents competition.

For each future location, the predictive variables are input and a sales estimate is produced based on the arithmetic calculations. *Enhanced Analogs and Normal Curves* are two common approaches used in retail sales forecasting that have proven successful when bundled together. The conceptual approach to enhanced analogs is that a snapshot is taken of each store's sales performance, and those performance levels are analyzed to determine significant predictors of sales. Similar to regression analysis, a simple correlation analysis is conducted to identify the variables most closely associated with strong and weak sales. Sales are typically analyzed by small geographic areas, typically ZIP codes.

Once predictive variables are identified, a series of analog tables are produced summarizing the variables and associated sales performance by corresponding geography. Whenever a new site is introduced, the analogs are queried to identify the set of existing stores that best match the new situation. The analyst then selects a subset of existing stores that closely replicate the characteristics of the new site.

After analogs are determined for each geographic unit in the trade area, normal curves are used to validate the analog approach. Normal curves are graphic depictions of distance decay of sales penetration under varying conditions. For example, one curve is produced to reflect the distance decay for the retail chain as a whole. Then, typical curves are produced for situations where certain predictive variables differ, such as areas with low (or high) incomes, or intense (or weak) competition, as shown below.

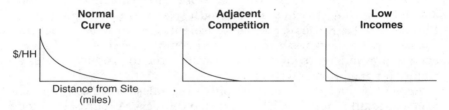

The distance decay curve implied by the analogs can be compared to these norms to ensure that the projections do not deviate substantially from experience without appropriate justification.

MICROMARKET FACTORS

The specific criteria and location standards for different retailers focus on the characteristics of the site and setting, the demographics of the market, and, in the case of existing buildings, features of the structure. Competition is another important consideration that factors into decision making at several stages, including selection of which markets to enter, identification of established retail nodes (and, correspondingly, underserved areas), as well as calibration of sales estimates.

Site and Location Criteria

Many factors influence the character and desirability of a given site for retail use. Several important considerations are discussed, but this is not a comprehensive list. The order is not indicative of relative importance, but the first three items are fundamental.

Visibility

Visual access is the most basic form of marketing and communication and stimulates unplanned shopping trips and purchases. Visibility can be achieved through a large, imposing, or distinctive structure, as well as by signage. Signage is an integral part of a retailer's identity and encompasses logos or other features on the building. While signage is a necessity for retailers, over-sized, over-illuminated, or cluttered signs can detract significantly from a location or development.

Access

Retailers universally seek to expedite shoppers' movements to and from a property. Ingress and egress are facilitated by multiple points of entry, curb cuts directly onto the site, turn lanes, acceleration lanes, median cuts, and traffic lights with turn signals. Driveways should be situated so that they are not blocked by backups at traffic lights or stop signs. Accordingly, major retailers often seek "far corner" locations, rather than "near corners." Other considerations include the width of driveways and the depth (length) of driveways and turn lanes, which influence the "stacking" capacity for cars entering or exiting a property.

Traffic

Retailers typically seek locations on major arterys and often impose various traffic count standards. Minimum average daily traffic (ADT) counts are often required and may be specified for either the "A.M." or "P.M." side of the street. Some retailers also specify desired peak hour volumes. High speeds are not particularly desirable because they reduce the visibility of businesses. Conversely, extreme traffic congestion is a deterrent to shoppers.

Site Size and Character

The site must be adequate to accommodate the store prototype, the minimum frontage, and parking and loading requirements. Store prototypes have been evolving rapidly, which has accelerated the obsolescence of relatively new facilities unable to accommodate expansion.

For most freestanding retailers and strip centers, a relatively flat site is desirable, only about one foot above the crown of the adjacent roadway. A slope not to exceed 5% is another rule of thumb. However, greater slopes sometimes facilitate construction of multilevel regional shopping malls.

Parking

While standards vary and can be influenced by the availability of abundant shared parking, major retailers typically require dedicated spaces adjacent to their entrance. A parking standard widely used in the shopping center industry is 5 spaces per 1,000 square feet of gross retail area. In many cases, this factor has been lowered without adverse effect. In other cases, a higher ratio is required. For example, a major freestanding toy store strives for a parking ratio of 7 spaces/1,000 square feet of store area to accommodate heavy seasonal demands. When shared parking is available, this requirement is lowered to 5.5 spaces/1,000 sf.

Co-Tenants

Combinations of retail businesses can create productive synergies, resulting from cross-shopping among various stores, or simply from the exposure and recognition gained from the other retailer's advertising and draw. Some co-tenancies, however, may have a neutral effect or, in the worst case, be predatory. Relationships also can change as retail concepts evolve. Historically, supermarkets and drugstores were highly complementary uses, but with the evolution of the superstore (concepts that include both groceries and pharmacies), the relationship becomes redundant and unproductive.

Off-price apparel retailers (e.g., T.J. Maxx) favor locations with leading supermarket chains. However, apparel retailers are not always considered advantageous co-tenants by supermarkets because shopping for food and clothing seldom is done on the same trip. Apparel shopping also occurs less frequently and the apparel stores promote less often.

Activity Generators

Employment centers (e.g., business parks and hospitals), college campuses, convention centers, major tourist attractions, casinos, and large hotels are all activity generators that can have synergistic benefits for retailers, much like those of co-tenants. Activity generators often can compensate for deficiencies in the quality or size of the underlying residential market.

Demographics Characteristics

The most basic source of demand for a retailer's product is the surrounding resident population and, in some cases, businesses. Understanding the depth and character of this market is essential to ensure adequate support and profitability for an enterprise. Key factors are not only the absolute number of customers, but the attributes of this customer base.

The magnitude of a prospective market has two distinct dimensions—one geographic, and the other, a measure of demand. The geographic extent of a market is a critical assumption in the site evaluation process. The range of a retailer's draw will depend on the specific business and store prototype, the density of surrounding development, and the location of competing businesses.

Sources of Demand

For most retailers, demand is generated by individuals or by households, so these are the most common measures of a market's depth and adequacy, while anticipated household or population growth is indicative of future opportunity. Many retailers set threshold population requirements for a trade area. Some retailers cater to businesses, particularly small businesses with fewer than 100 employees. Wholesale clubs and office supply companies are particularly sensitive to the number of these businesses within a given area.

Income

Income is a frequent consideration in evaluating a market because household incomes are positively correlated with total retail expenditures, as shown in Figure 6.1. Income is measured in a variety of ways. Many retailers simply consider the median or average household income in the trade area and compare it to established thresholds or targets. Other retailers seek a minimum number of households within an income range or over a certain level, while others consider the distribution of household incomes.

Using income or the presence of high-income households as the sole measure of a market's taste level can be misleading. High

FIGURE 6.1

Consumer Expenditure Patterns, 1993

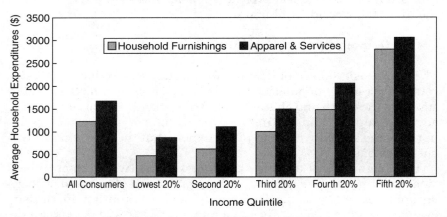

Source: U.S. Department of Labor, Bureau of Labor Statistics.

average household incomes are common in areas with many young, dual-income families, who also may be saddled with new homes, large mortgages, and young children. High incomes also are prevalent in markets dominated by high-wage union workers.

Lifestyles

Market research companies have addressed the shortfall of simple income measures by developing lifestyle segmentation systems, based on a broad range of demographic variables, as well as lifestyle characteristics and consumption patterns. The resulting classification schemes, with categories such as "Lap of Luxury" or "University USA"[2] can provide useful qualitative measures of a market.

Age

Certain retailers cater to distinct age segments, so this becomes another consideration in site evaluations. Toy stores and fast-food outlets, for example, tend to do well in areas with high concentrations of children under age 18. Drugstores thrive with an older population, and many apparel retailers cater to women between the ages of 25 and 50. In general, average annual retail spending (in absolute terms)

FIGURE 6.2

Consumer Expenditure Patterns, 1993

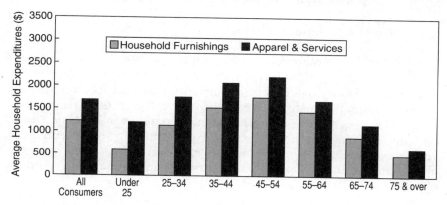

Source: U.S. Department of Labor, Bureau of Labor Statistics.

declines notably for households headed by persons over age 55, as shown in Figure 6.2.

Education

Educational attainment is closely correlated with income, so many retailers rely on income as a surrogate for education. One notable exception, however, is bookstores, which look for above-average education and concentrations of people with college educations or experience.

Occupation

The concentration of white or blue collar workers is another indicator of a market's taste level. Office supply stores and large music and video stores are particularly sensitive to the occupational profile, while many other retailers use it as a qualitative measure.

Ethnicity

Ethnicity is seldom designated as a site selection criteria, but it is critical in the subsequent merchandising and operation of a retail business or shopping center. It can influence staffing considerations, size assortments, fashion orientation, advertising media, signage, and product selection (e.g., music assortments, or the availability of Spanish language books, foreign language cards).

Housing Characteristics

The level of home ownership and the pace of housing development and turnover in a market influences the opportunity for several types of retailers. Home ownership has a strong correlation to expenditures for home furnishings and equipment. Based on a recent government survey,[3] home owners annually spend over 2.2 times more on home furnishings than renters. Correspondingly, beneficiaries of active housing markets are home improvement stores, retailers of consumer durables such as furniture and appliances, and retailers of other home products.

Competition

Competition is an important consideration in the formulation of a retailer's expansion program. First, it influences which markets are targeted for growth. Once a market has been targeted for entry, the location strategy and performance of competitors provides a valuable guide to identifying the number of stores required for comprehensive market coverage. Teaming up with a competitor also can help establish new retail nodes at the suburban fringe. In such cases, concentrating retail activity at one location is more advantageous than having a low-density market diluted over several different retail nodes.

Competition is a key consideration in sales projections. The proximity, size, and quality of competition are all factors which in some manner are reflected in the sales estimates.

SPECIFIC CRITERIA OF SELECTED RETAIL BUSINESSES

Various types of retailers have their specific needs, at the micro-market level, both in terms of site and building requirements, location preferences, and market characteristics. Key market criteria for dominant types of retailers are summarized in Table 6.1 on pp. 134–137. The organizing principle behind the categorization is the type of product and the store format. On the most fundamental level, there are convenience goods, such as food and health and beauty aids which are purchased with high frequency, and then other types of merchandise purchased less frequently, including consumer durables (or, "hard" goods) and apparel ("soft" goods).

Convenience Good Retailers

Retailing of basic essentials has undergone substantial change in the past ten to 15 years, spurred by technological innovation and competitive intensification, as discounters and wholesale clubs vie for an increasing share of these sales. Many supermarkets have added pharmacies, delicatessens, bakeries, liquor departments, and even banks and restaurants. Likewise, drugstores are offering more food and general merchandise products. With this diversification, the long-standing synergy between supermarkets and drugstores is being eroded, causing both retailers to reassess location strategies.

Supermarkets

Prototypes for supermarket/pharmacy "combo" stores range from 50,000 to 75,000 square feet. The stores require a site of about five to six acres, but creative accommodations have been made to smaller sites, particularly in dense urban settings. Chicago, for example, has supermarkets with rooftop parking, and in Washington, DC, a leading supermarket occupies subgrade space in a high-rise building. A price-driven superstore concept also has been developed to respond to competition from wholesale clubs and discounters. The stores are larger (typically 90,000+ square feet), and require more land and parking (about 6 to 7 spaces per 1,000 square feet of store area).

Supermarkets prefer to be freestanding, or in close proximity to a leading discounter, but not in or near regional malls. Easy ingress and egress are essential because the store formats can generate from 20,000 to 40,000 trips per week. Efforts are made to avoid directly competitive co-tenants, such as pharmacies, liquor stores, delicatessens, and bakeries. In an urban setting, the draw can be limited to one or two miles, but in the suburbs, the trade area can extend three to five miles. The superstores have a slightly broader draw, regularly attracting customers from five miles away. For a traditional combo store (supermarket/pharmacy), a population of about 50,000 to 70,000 would be considered minimal, assuming standard competition.

TABLE 6.1

Market Characteristics and Criteria (1)

	Convenience Goods		General Merchandise		
	Supermarkets	Drugstores	Wholesale Clubs `	Discount Stores	Department Stores
Examples (2)	Jewel, Safeway, Von's	Walgreens, Rite Aid	Sam's, Price/Costco	Wal-Mart, Kmart, Target, Venture	J.C. Penney, Sears, Macy's, Marshall Field's
Prototypes	"Combo" stores: 50,000–75,000 sf Superstores: 90,000+ sf	9,500–15,000 sf, but vary widely	80,000–135,000 sf	89,000–135,000 sf Supercenters: 136,000–199,000 sf	Metro stores: 125,000–260,000 sf
Site Size	Combos: 5–6 A. Supers: 7 A.		10–15 A.	10–12 A.	10–15 A.
Parking Requirements	Combos: 5 spaces/ 1,000 sf Supers: 6–7 spaces/ 1,000 sf		5.5–6 spaces/1,000 sf	4–6 spaces/1,000 sf	5 spaces/1,000 sf
Trade Area Extent	Urban: 1–2 mi. Suburbs: 3–5 mi. Supers 5 mi.+	Urban: 1 mi. Suburbs: 2–3 mi. Rural: county	8–10 mi.	Suburban (f'stdg): 8–12 min. drive time or about 5 mi. Near regional mall: 15–20 min. drive time	Metro areas: 5–8 mi. Fringe area: 8–25 mi. Isolated Mkt: 20–60+ mi.
Threshold Size	Min. for combo: 50–70,000 pop.	Min. for 12,000 sf: 20–25,000 pop.	Min.: 75,000 pop.	Suburban minimum: 100,000 pop.; prefer 150,000–200,000 Rural: 10,000 in city, 40,000 in county and 75–100,000 in market	Metro area: min. of 250,000+ pop.
Preferences Location	Freestanding Neighborhood or Community ctrs (Avoid regional malls or areas)	Freestanding Downtowns Strip centers (Often avoid power centers)	Freestanding Community ctr	Freestanding Corner location near dominant retail node. Community centers	Regional malls
Traffic/Access	Easy Ingress/ egress essential Trips/Week: Combos: 20–30,000 Supers: 30–40,000		Major arterial	Major arterial (e.g., 40,000+ ADT)	Regional accessibility
Co-Tenants	Leading discount Some hard goods stores (Avoid delis, liquor stores; combos avoid pharmacies)	Non-combo groceries		Dominant supermarkets, promot'nl apparel stores, electronics stores. (Avoid deep disc'nt drug stores).	Department stores Fashion specialty stores. Entertainment uses. Some hard goods specialty stores.
Demographics		Older pop. Higher incomes		Varied. Some seek hi % with HH inc. $25–60,000 (Avoid income extremes, hi or low)	Concentration of better income households (e.g., $35,000+ or higher, above avg. educ., home ownership, income, white collar. Hi concentration in 35–54 age group

[a] This summary is representational; criteria are not standard for all retailers within the classification. The information, likewise, does not correspond to a single retailer, or necessarily to the retailers given as examples.

[b] The stores listed as examples are simply used to help define the category, and are not necessarily the source for the information elsewhere in the table.

134

Specialty Soft Goods				Entertainment	
Large, Apparel Specialty	Small, Apparel Specialty	Large, Off-Price Apparel	Linens	Theaters	Children's Entertainment
Neiman Marcus, Kohl's, Mervyn's	The Gap, Tolbot's, Footlocker	Filene's Basement	Linen & Things, Bed, Bath & Beyond	AMC, General Cinema	Discovery Zone
75,000–200,000+ sf	Varies widely. 1,500–12,000+ sf	30,000–50,000 sf	35,000 sf	Varies. 12–24 screens with 3,000–5,000 seats. (Screens have 100–600 seats.) / Varies. 50,000–75,000+ sf	13,500–17,000 sf
5 spaces/1,000 sf	Same as mall	5 spaces/1,000 sf	5 spaces/1,000 sf	Varies. Freestd'g: 1 space/2.6–3 seats. If shared pkg: same as mall.	Min. 75 spaces (about 5.5 spaces/1,000 sf)
Fashion Stores: 8–15+ mi. Value-oriented: 5–8 mi.	Same as mall, often 5–10 mi. in suburbs	Suburbs: 5 mi. Urban: 2–3 mi. Rural: 30–40 mi.	5–7 mi.	Varies. Approx. 4–5 mi. or 20 minutes drive	5–7 mi.
Fashion Stores: 450,000+ pop. Value-oriented: 100–150,000+ population	Varied. Some have min. pop. of 100,000. Some want 10,000 HHs $50,000+	100,000–150,000 pop.	125,000–150,000 pop. 10–20,000 HHs $50,000+	Min. 150,000–200,000 pop.	Min. of 30–50,000 children age 2–12
Regional malls Specialty centers Active downtown Large community centers. Near regional malls.	Regional malls Specialty centers Downtowns Urban nghbrhd.	Varied. Strip centers, with nat'l tenants Neighborhood ctrs with lead grocer Close to regional mall. (Some avoid power centers.) Active downtowns Some regionals	Power centers Freestanding Near reg'l mall	Freestanding at periphery of regional mall.	Near regional malls Power centers or Community centers
Hi-traffic. Regional access					Hi traffic with min. of 30,000 ADT
Department store	Comparable specialty stores, Dominant dept. stores.	Department store Some discounters Quality grocer Home Improvement Soft home goods			Toys "R" Us, wholesale clubs, discounters, grocery superstores, large specialty apparel
Fashion; Hi % HHs $75,000+, Well educated White collar Value: Young families	Varied. Often look for above age inc., select age groups, ethnic compos'tn	Mid- to upper inc. Hi % white collar Hi % females 25–50 Hi % HHs $35,000–$50,000	Growth Hi housing turnover		Hi median inc. NOT required. Presence of families w/young children

(Continued)

TABLE 6.1 (Continued)

	Specialty Hard Goods				
	Home Improvement	Electronics/ Appliances	Toys	Sporting Goods	Books
Examples (2)	Builder's Square, Home Depot	Circuit City, Best Buy	Toys "R" Us	Sports Authority	Barnes & Noble, Border Books
Prototypes	110,000– 135,000 sf	45,000+ sf	45,000 sf	40,000–45,000 sf	25,000–45,000 sf
Site Size	11+ A.		3–4 A.	Approx. 4 A.	
Parking Requirements	5.5 spaces/ 1,000 sf	5 spaces/1,000 sf	Freestd'g: 7 spaces/1,000 sf In ctr: 5.5 spaces/1,000 sf	5 spaces/1,000 sf	5 spaces/1,000 sf
Trade Area Extent	Suburbs: 4–8 mi.	Suburbs: 5–10 mi.	Suburbs: 20–30 min. drive (about 5–8 mi.) Small Towns: 50–60 min. drive	Suburbs: 7–8 mi.	Suburbs: approx. 5 mi.
Threshold Size	Approx. mini- mums: 150,000 pop. & 70,000 single family HHs	Approx. 250,000 pop.		Approx. 400,000 pop.	High density
Preferences Location	Freestanding Strip centers	Freestanding Community centers Near regional malls	Freestanding Near regional mall or power center 100% corner	Freestanding Strip centers	Strip centers, endcap position Freestanding, near regional mall
Traffic/Access	Major arterial	Major arterial	Major arterial Corner w/2-way access	Major arterial	High traffic
Co-Tenants		Other promo- tional retailers	Home Improvement Major discounters Wholesale clubs (Avoid groceries)		
Demographics	Growth areas. Above avg. inc. Home ownership SF vs. MF housing		Hi kid count (e.g., 18–20% under age 14) Median inc. > $30,000 Hi family presence	Mid- and upper inc.	Above avg. educ. and incomes Slightly older

[a] This summary is representational; criteria are not standard for all retailers within the classification. The information, likewise, does not correspond to a single retailer, or necessarily to the retailers given as examples.

[b] The stores listed as examples are simply used to help define the category, and are not necessarily the source for the information elsewhere in the table.

Specialty Hard Goods (continued)		Food	
Office Supply	Music	Fast Food	Restaurants
Office Depot, OfficeMax	Blockbuster	McDonald's, Boston Chicken, Carl's Jr.	Olive Garden, Chili's
23,500–30,000 sf	Metros: 5,000–15,000 sf	Very diverse. Typical Freestd'g: 2,500–3,000+ sf, with seating for 50+ and drive thru	Varies. 5,700–9,200 sf
Approx. 2.5 A.		Varies. Frstd'g: Min. 20,000+ sf with pad of 7,000+ sf	Varies. 60,320–120,000 sf
5 spaces/1,000 sf	5–6.5 spaces/1,000 sf	Varies. Can range from 1 space/1 seat to 1 space/every 2.5 seats.	Varies. Approx. 1 space/1.5 seats
Suburbs: Approx. 5 mi.	Video stores: Approx. 7 min. drive (2–4 mi.) Music stores:	Varies, but residential support comes primarily from 1–2 miles in metros.	Varies. Approx. 2–5 mi.
150,000+ pop. & 5,000 small businesses	Video stores: Min. pop. 20–25,000 Min. HHs 7–10,000	20,000–30,000 in immediate trade area 15,000 daytime pop.	Varies. 2 mi.: 25–30,000+ pop. 3 mi.: 40–75,000+ pop. 5 mi.: 100,000+ pop.
Well-anchored strip Freestanding near regional mall or business area	Videos: Freestanding Strip centers, endcap position Music: Freestanding near regional mall Community center Urban nghbrhds	Freestanding Near freeways, regional malls, power strips Food courts Satellite locations Near activity generators	Freestanding Corner sites Near regional mall Near offices
Major arterial Hi traffic counts	High traffic Videos: 20,000 ADT minimum Music: 30–50,000 ADT	Main arterial with 20–35,000 ADT min. "Far corner," often on home-bound (p.m.) side.	Hi traffic (e.g., 30,000+ ADT)
Grocery stores Frequent advertisers Wholesale clubs Discounters	Videos: Grocery stores, fast food, drugstores Music: Theater, bookstores, restaurants		Near other restaurants
Growth area 50% of HHs with inc. > $25,000	Median age < 35 Mid- to upper inc. White collar Above avg. educ. Young singles Young families Growth areas Homeowners	Above avg. median income Kids favorable 25+% of pop. age 8–34 Growth (Avoid older age, very hi incomes)	Varies. Median income about $30–35,000

The sales opportunity for a supermarket is determined by its anticipated share of per capita weekly food expenditures within the trade area. Store chains use mathematical models which take into account population, competitors' size, proximity and quality, the character of the road network, accessibility of the site, and natural barriers. The sales potential is aggregated from small geographic areas to derive a total market potential.

Drugstores

After recent expansions, many of the established drugstore chains have settled on store sizes ranging from 9,000 to 15,000 square feet. Deep discount formats can be considerably larger. Preferred locations for the traditional concepts vary, including freestanding sites on corners, downtowns, small strip centers, or larger strip centers anchored by supermarkets (without pharmacies).

Trade areas for traditional drugstores are slightly smaller than those of supermarkets. In urban areas, the draw extends about one mile, but reaches two or three miles in the suburbs. A population of about 20,000 to 25,000 is required to support a drugstore of about 12,000 square feet, assuming average competition. Favorable demographic characteristics include an older population and higher incomes.

General Merchandise Retailers

The general merchandise category covers a wide variety of stores from wholesale clubs to traditional department stores. As a mature retail concept, general merchandise store prototypes have tended to be more stable, although there continues to be fine tuning. Many retail companies have multiple prototypes, gauged to particular market opportunities or settings. Most conventional discount stores and wholesale clubs range from 80,000 square feet to 135,000 square feet, but several discounters also have developed supercenter concepts which sell food and general merchandise in stores of up to 200,000 square feet. Traditional and chain department store prototypes begin at about 90,000 square feet and range up to 200,000 square feet, or larger in dense urban markets.

Wholesale Clubs

Wholesale clubs require parking ratios of about 5.5 to 6.0 spaces per 1,000 square feet, and sites of 10 to 15 acres. The clubs typically draw from an 8- to 10-mile radius, catering to both individuals and small businesses.

Discount Stores

A typical discount store of 125,000 square feet requires a site of about 10 to 12 acres for both the store and parking. Parking requirements vary by retailer, but ratios ranging from 4 to 6 spaces per 1,000 square feet of store area.

Discounters often describe the extent of trade areas in terms of drive times, rather than distance, which takes into account traffic conditions near the site. The primary trade area for a freestanding discount store in a suburban setting can range from 8 to 12 minutes, which translates into about five miles. If the discounter is located near a regional shopping center, the trade area extends to about a 15- to 20-minute drive time.

The population threshold within a trade area varies based on the store prototype and location. Minimum population requirements begin at 100,000, but concentrations of 150,000 to 200,000 people are preferred.

Department Stores

Department stores and many of the fashion specialty stores favor regional mall settings. The trade area for regional malls can be extensive, depending on competition, natural barriers, the road network, size of center and the uniqueness of the tenant mix. On the suburban fringe or in smaller markets, the draw may extend 20 miles or more, while in major metropolitan areas, the trade area is focused generally within a 5- to 8-mile radius.

Except in small markets, department store trade areas typically have a population of at least 250,000, with a minimum of 150,000 living within the primary trade area where the mall has little direct competition. While the most productive regional mall and department store shoppers have high incomes (above $75,000), market potential is measured on a broader base, often focusing on households over $35,000 for traditional department stores, and above $75,000 for fashion stores.

Specialty Hard Goods

The retailing of hard goods has undergone a dramatic transformation. Large specialty stores focused on specific merchandise themes (e.g., books, toys, electronics) have sustained exceptional growth. The stores offer broad assortments of merchandise at competitive, if not promotional, pricing. These formats have experienced phenomenal growth and rapid evolution since the mid-1980s. Home Depot, for example, opened its first store in Atlanta in 1979 at 60,000 square feet. During the 1980s, the prototype continued to expand from 70,000 square feet, to 80,000 square feet, to 100,000 square feet, and by 1994, to 135,000 square feet. Store prototypes continue to evolve, so references to specific market requirements may become quickly dated.

Home Improvement Stores

Home improvement stores, such as Home Depot and Builder's Square, are a distinct category of specialty hard good retailers that use a warehouse format. Store sizes and characteristics closely parallel wholesale clubs. Store prototypes are beginning to stabilize at about 110,000 to 135,000 square feet. Preferred locations include freestanding pads and strip centers on heavily trafficked arterials. Sites of at least 11 acres are required to accommodate the building and associated parking at a ratio of about 5.5 spaces per 1,000 square feet.

The trade areas for home improvement stores were initially thought to extend about 10 to 12 miles, but more recent experience suggests that the core market (in a suburban area) may be concentrated within about 4 to 5 miles, while the total trade area extends 8 miles.

Demographic criteria focus on the population and single-family housing within about 8 miles of a prospective site, with a threshold population of about 150,000 and 70,000 single-family households.

Other Hard Goods Formats

The other hard goods specialty retailers operate smaller prototype stores, ranging from 15,000-square-foot music stores to 45,000-square-foot electronics and appliance stores. The various types of stores share many of the same site and location preferences. Prominence is a key criteria for all of the retailers and meticulous attention is paid to signage. The stores prefer freestanding sites or strip centers in regionally accessible locations. Proximity to regional shopping centers is a plus. Within strip centers, the stores prefer endcap positions and will rarely take inline space, unless signage and architectural treatments ensure high visibility.

High traffic locations are important. This measure is relative to each market, but some retailers set definite standards ranging from 30,000 to 50,000 cars per day.

The draw of these power formats is regional in scope, but to evaluate the quality of a site, most retailers focus on the demographics within a 5- to 8-mile radius. The population requirements within this area can be quite different. One electronics retailer looks for an average population of 250,000 per store, while a large sporting goods store seeks a population of 400,000 in the primary trade area. These population thresholds are associated not only with retail expenditure potential for the designated type of merchandise, but also typical market shares.

Most of the specialty hard good retailers focus on population density and household characteristics, yet office supply retailers also consider the number of small businesses in the area. One office store for example, looks for at least 5,000 small to medium size businesses within close proximity, in addition to a population of 150,000. A variety of other demographic factors are considered for different concepts. One toy retailer, for example, requires a large "kid" count, with 18% to 20% of the population under age 14. A large music store also looks for youth, but defines it more broadly. The company seeks a median age less than 35, middle to upper incomes, a large white collar professional group, above average education, young singles and young families.

Specialty Soft Goods

The category killer formats such as Linens & Things and Kids 'R Us, as well as the major off-price apparel stores, operate large prototypes and seek dominant retail locations. Smaller off-price apparel retailers have greater flexibility because they also locate in large neighborhood centers and serve a more localized population. Apparel specialty stores have adapted diverse strategies, some favoring strip centers, while others mainly locate in regional malls, on the street in dense urban areas, or in exclusive specialty centers.

Prototypes for the category-killer, soft goods retailers range up to about 5,000 square feet, with most falling in the 30,000 to 40,000 square foot range. Similarly, the latest prototypes for one linen store is 35,000 square feet, while children apparel formats are smaller at 15,000 square feet.

Most prefer shopping center locations, including strip centers with a strong national tenant mix or anchored by a leading supermarket and drugstore chain. Within a 5-mile radius, the major soft good re-tailers look for a population ranging from 100,000 to 150,000. Be-yond that, demographic criteria vary. One linen retailer looks for a minimum of 10,000 households with incomes over $50,000, accom-panied by high housing turnover or growth. Off-price apparel stores favor middle to upper incomes, above average white collar employ-ment, and a concentration of women between the ages of 25 and 50.

Food Services

Prepared food is offered in fast-food outlets, restaurants, food courts, and increasingly, within other retail formats such as discount stores, grocery stores, and warehouse stores like Home Depot. Fast-food retailers, in particular, are developing a number of "satellite" concepts that occupy a few hundred square feet, offer a limited menu and can be incorporated into other retail stores, food courts, or other business locations (e.g., airports). These satellite operations often are adjuncts to larger free-standing units nearby, which provide management, storage space, and back-up kitchen facilities.

Most free-standing food operations seek highly visible locations on major arterials, or near regional activity generators, including malls, business parks, large hotels, or tourist attractions. While many food operations rely on business generated by passing traffic, the resident market also is important. The trade areas for restaurants and fast-food outlets vary substantially, but close attention is paid to the population within 2 to 3 miles of a site.

Entertainment

Entertainment encompasses familiar concepts such as theaters, video arcades, and amusement rides, as well as new high-technology formats involving virtual reality, motion simulation, and other games. These newer concepts have yet to be implemented in suffi-cient numbers to establish an understanding of the retail dynamics, consumer profile, or market requirements, so the following discus-sion is confined to theaters and children's entertainment formats.

Economies of scale have impacted entertainment operations as much as other retail formats. Theater chains are now focusing on locations where they can operate a minimum of 12 to 24 screens. The complexes range in size from about 50,000 to 70,000 square feet, with an assortment of theaters offering anywhere from 100 to 600 seats. Larger facilities and more screens allow theaters to provide a changing assortment of films, while running leading films longer.

Woodfield Village Green, Schaumburg, Illinois

Due to the nature of the movie distribution business, the potential of longer runs gives a theater an advantage in securing first run movies within a given area.

Many chains seek locations either in or near regional shopping centers. Some operators prefer free-standing pads on the periphery of major malls to avoid competing with food courts for concession sales, which are a key source of profits. Others are amendable to locations within regional centers, as long as adequate parking is accessible to the theater entrance. Parking requirements for theaters vary, but to accommodate peak demand, a ratio of one space for every 2.5 to 3.0 seats is targeted in free-standing, suburban settings. During most times of the year, theaters can effectively share parking with shopping centers because peak theater demand seldom conflicts with the busiest shopping hours. The holiday seasons, however, can be a critical exception to this pattern.

The trade area for a typical multiscreen theater extends about 4 to 5 miles, or farther if associated with a regional shopping center. Assuming standard competition, a target population of at least 150,000 to 200,000 would be sought.

While theaters serve a broad section of the population, more specialized entertainment concepts, such as Discovery Zone, have a specific target audience of children, ages 2 to 12. These play centers occupy 13,500 to 17,000 square feet and incorporate a number of activity areas and party rooms. Within the trade area, the retailer looks for a minimum of 30,000 to 50,000 children in the targeted age range. High median incomes are not required.

SHOPPING CENTERS: REFINEMENT OVER TIME

Micro-market factors not only influence retailers' location decisions, but also the merchandising of shopping centers, both at inception and over the life of the property. Merchandising is not a static concept, because a shopping center has a continual rollover of space with the expiration of leases and inevitable failure of certain businesses. The mix of tenants in a shopping center establishes a distinct personality for the property. Over time, the center's character can be altered in response to demographic shifts, as well as changing retail formats. This adaptability distinguishes retail properties from other classes of real estate assets, but also magnifies the need for active management and leasing.

A vivid example of regional shopping center evolution is found in the mature, first ring suburbs of major metropolitan areas. Properties in these locations were the first generation of regional shopping centers to emerge in the 1950s and 1960s as post-war suburbanization accelerated. Two generations later, these retail properties seldom resemble the homogenized, small centers that first opened, often anchored by one traditional department store, a national chain store like Sears, and sometimes a grocery store. Propelled by favorable demographics and a quality location, a few of these centers have become the dominant retail hubs of the 1990s; less fortunate properties have been undermined by an erosion of the quality of the customer base or severely hampered by sites that are no longer regionally accessible.

While shopping center owners and managers cannot control demographic change, there are constructive ways to monitor, anticipate and opportunistically respond to these trends. Several factors might suggest an opportunity to introduce better price, fashion apparel, along with a complement of stores that help to distinguish a regional mall from value-oriented retail concepts. Higher discretionary incomes are typically found in stable neighborhoods characterized by relatively low housing turnover, a slightly older population, smaller households, few young children, and above-average educations. In contrast, residents in an area marked by swing sets, new middle- and upper-income housing and a high percentage of dual-income households may have sophisticated taste levels, but rarely the discretionary income to support them. A center located in a more mature, stable suburb may be a candidate for better tenants, while a newer suburb, though more upscale in character, may respond more favorably to promotional retailers.

Malls which in their early years cannot support fashion department stores still have the opportunity to respond to a sophisticated element in the trade area by incorporating a collection of upscale tenants. For many developers and shopping center owners, the merchandising of the small tenant space remains more art than science. However, the process is guided by many of the same micro market characteristics considered by retailers during the site selection process. In the end, the retailers must be convinced of the inherent suitability of the location and market for their product, or else economic inducements will be required to influence the site location decision.

CONCLUSION

In developing a retail project, the various micromarket factors influencing the potential for a given site must be well understood. These factors determine not only the size and nature of a potential retail project, but also influence the marketability of the site to tenants. Since the ultimate success of a retail development hinges on the individual successes of the tenants and the synergy created by the merchandise mix, evaluating a site from the retailer's perspective can be expedient. An understanding of retailer requirements and sensitivities will help formulate both a targeted leasing program and marketing strategy. An accurate assessment of micromarket factors can help optimally position retail developments from inception, avoiding false starts with unsuitable tenants. And ongoing monitoring of these factors helps to adapt the center to changing demographics and retail formats over time.

ENDNOTES

1. Source: Mark Zygmontowicz, Thompson Associates.
2. These are MicroVision segment names. MicroVision is a registered trademark of Equifax® Marketing Decision Systems, Inc., a division of Equifax National Decision Systems.
3. U.S. Department of Labor, Bureau of Labor Statistics, *1993 Consumer Expenditure Survey.*

Seven

The Role of Feasibility and Investment Analysis in the Investment Decision

Glenn J. Rufrano and A. Joseph Traum

The go vs. no-go investment decision with respect to a retail real estate project calls for two basic forms of analysis. First (and foremost) is feasibility (or objective) analysis: the development team deals with factors such as the availability of a developable parcel of property, access and visibility of the site, the probable land and building cost, the supply of competing real estate and the demand for the project (from retail users and from consumers). The financial analyst, on the other hand, has traditionally focused on investment (or subjective) analysis, which concentrates on rates of return, appreciation potential, income tax considerations, and the investor's ownership structure and investment philosophy. The analyst must be able to interrelate the two types of analysis by weaving aspects of feasibility analysis into the customary investment analysis.

FUNDAMENTAL FACTORS

Any experienced financial analyst will undoubtedly have developed a personalized approach in studying a potential investment. Such methodology would have merged the various types of critical factors—those that focus on a project's feasibility and those that concentrate on a project's investment returns from the owner's special viewpoint. Before such critical factors come into play, the analyst's work must initially take a serious look at three questions, the *fundamental factors*, all of which must be positive before proceeding:

- *Viability Factor.* When a future acquiring entity asks "if it wasn't already built, would it be built again today," will the answer be "yes." A positive answer to the question "should the project be built?" conveys, more than any other answer, a chance of success. This answer is not based on a hunch, or only on experience, but on a hard cost/revenue analysis.

- *Capability Factor.* A project should not be undertaken unless all the requisite skills are part of the developer's team. It is not necessary that all team members be employees—third-party advisors (lawyers, architects, appraisers, engineers, marketing consultants, etc.) can serve equally well or better. In today's environment, with an ever-growing list of rules and regulations that have to be dealt with, only the most skilled practitioners will succeed.

- *Financeability Factor.* Before any serious work on the project begins, it is important to determine if the funds that will be needed are already available (for example, ownership equity funds), or if it is a certainty that they will be available from third-party sources, to enable the project to be seen through to completion. In the early stages of a project, perhaps the analyst can do no more than make an educated guess based on conversations with the company's traditional financing sources and leading real estate investment bankers.

CRITICAL FACTORS

Once the analyst is satisfied that the fundamental factors are fulfilled, the analyst next identifies the critical factors that will ultimately result in making a recommendation to the development team that, in the analyst's view, the project should proceed.

In performing this step, the analyst must deal with both *economic/financial* and *entity-specific* considerations. These are the critical factors in a decision that should be considered by all developers prior to proceeding with a real estate investment. They examine whether the investment meets: (1) requirements for current returns on investments; (2) capital appreciation expectations; (3) income tax planning goals; and (4) compatibility requirements with the developer's strengths, current portfolio holdings, and potential for diversification. Entity-specific considerations are those that are unique to the decision-making body. They include: (1) commencing, maintaining or improving relationships with co-investment entities or key retailers; (2) internal growth requirements, either in gross assets owned or managed or of investor/shareholder returns; (3) competition with other entities; (4) availability of personnel; (5) product mix, including entry into a new part of the business; (6) insider knowledge; and (7) social responsibilities.

Making the Decision

After the economic/financial and entity-specific considerations are defined and established, the process concludes with the selection of those critical factors that are to be emphasized in the decision-making process. Key matters that must be understood in the selection process are:

- Each investment should, ideally, stress at least one and perhaps more than one of the critical factors (whether economic/financial or entity-specific).
- The selected critical factors may be different for each investment.
- Knowing which critical factors to focus upon results from experience and understanding how to balance economic/financial and entity-specific criteria.

With all the information assembled, the analyst is ready to complete the work that will enable a recommendation to be made to the development team. The presentation could take the form of a Critical Factors Worksheet (Figure 7.1).

FUNDAMENTAL FACTOR CONSIDERATIONS

Viability Factor

Demographic data are very necessary when approaching the study of the *viability factor,* but not sufficient. In the mid-1980s, when over-building became rampant, the "Rule of 100" was used—if, say, 100 residential apartments are needed in a marketplace, then 100 developers will each build 100 residential apartments. This "rule" conveys the notion that each developer has studied the appropriate demographic data and reached the same obvious conclusion. Therefore, the analyst must obtain an understanding of two key additional determinants of the potential for overbuilding:

- Competition—not only from currently existing projects, but equally important, from ones in the pipeline or likely to be built in the foreseeable future.

- Political considerations—not only the growth and real estate development perspectives of current office-holders, but equally important, the perspectives of persons likely to hold office in the foreseeable future.

At this phase of the analysis, the demographic data that the development team has gathered should be reviewed carefully. Matters such as population growth and stability, changes in household size and income levels, planned transportation improvements and employment trends must be assessed to establish that the reasons for going forward with a project continue to exist.

One key factor that should be calculated at this point in the analysis is the *ratio of retail square feet to delineated trade area population,* which is helpful in creating a numerical standard to illustrate supply and demand. Assume the project is a 1.5 million-square-foot regional mall and there are two existing malls in the trade area. Furthermore, assume that the two malls have one million square feet each and all will serve a delineated trade area of 500,000 persons. The current factor is four (1,000,000 plus 1,000,000 divided by 500,000), meaning that there are 4 square feet of regional mall retail space for every person in the trade area. The analyst must determine if the addition of the proposed project, the third regional mall, which will increase

FIGURE 7.1

Critical Factors Worksheet—Retail Project

Project Name: _____
Type of Center: _____
Land Area: _____ Acres
GLA: _____ Square Feet
Location: _____

Development Team:
   Project Manager: _____
   Leasing Director: _____
   Construction Supervisor: _____
   Financing: _____

Cost:	*Estimate*	*Contingency*	*Total*
Land			
Hard Costs			
Soft Costs	_____	_____	_____
Total	══════	══════	══════

Net Operating Income:		*Stabilized*
Income		
Vacancy	____ %	_____
Net		
Operating Expenses		_____
Net		
Capital Expenses		_____
Net Operating Income		
Annual Debt Service		_____
Net Cash Flow		══════

	Target	*Upside*	*Projection*	*Downside*
Stabilized Return on Investment	____ %	____ %	____ %	____ %
Internal Rate of Return	____ %	____ %	____ %	____ %

IRR Assumptions:
   Lease-Up Period   ____ Months
   Appreciation Rate   ____ %
   Renewal Percentage   ____ %
   Holding Period   ____ Years
   Terminal Cap Rate   ____ %
Other: _____
                          _____

FIGURE 7.1 *(Continued)*

Other Comments:
Income Taxes: _____

_____

Potential Tenancy:
Committed Majors: _____
Potential Majors: _____
Committed Tenants: _____
Interested Tenants: _____
Other Financial Comments _____

_____

Competition:	Center 1	Center 2	Center 3
Name of Center	____	____	____
Owner	____	____	____
GLA	____	____	____
Distance	____	____	____
Major #1	____	____	____
Major #2	____	____	____
Major #3	____	____	____
Major #4	____	____	____

Trade Area Data:
Population: _____ persons
Households: _____ households
Average Household Income:
Total Competitive Retail _____ square feet
Sq. Ft. of Retail per Person:

Entity Specific:
Relationships: _____

Potential Competition: _____

Other Factors: _____

_____

_____

_____

Prepared by: _____
Date: _____

the factor to seven, will result in a factor that is acceptable for the trade area. This factor, although useful, does not operate in a static environment. In assessing it, the analyst must take into consideration the population growth levels and employment trends data.

Another statistic that will help in assessing the viability factor is the GAFO (General Merchandise, Apparel, Furniture and Other) sales in the trade area and, importantly, in the adjacent trade areas. If GAFO sales are below the benchmark for the trade area under study, this is a clear indication that demand is out of balance with supply. On the other hand, if GAFO sales for the adjacent trade areas are in excess of the same benchmark, a reasonable conclusion is that persons in the trade area being studied are shopping elsewhere and could be captured by the project.

There are other considerations, as well. For example, management should determine the identity of the targeted major retailers; the analyst should judge (just as the retailers will certainly do) if the trade area profile is compatible with that which is traditionally served by such retailers. Consideration should also be given to the reliance of the trade area on a particular industry or business (and the likelihood that the industry will be stable, grow or decline).

We relate the story of a corporate meeting where the institutional sales division of a company discussed a new assignment—the sale of a mixed use project in the Midwest. It had been built at a cost of over $100 million, subsequently foreclosed upon, and the division was estimating that the institution could recover only $20 million from the sale. When management challenged how such an enormous decline in value came about, the answer was that "the project was a little ahead of its time." The chairman thought about this for a moment and then responded, "yes, perhaps by a century." Here was a clear case of the viability factor being ignored and the repercussions that resulted. The analyst should have taken whatever steps were available at the time to prevent the project from proceeding. Those three little words that developers are famous for having adopted as their personal guide—"Location, Location, Location"—may be enough to start the development process. However, the analyst must do much more before declaring that the viability factor has been met.

Capability Factor

In today's environment, the developer likely faces a difficult entitlement process with a sophisticated and wily zoning authority, which expects the developer to assist it in achieving political goals. Once approved, pre-development activities will certainly have to clear significant added hurdles. Then, construction will probably be filled with daily challenges and leasing will likely prove to be extremely difficult. Finally, when the project is built and leased, day-to-day management will undoubtedly be fraught with problems. The skills to resolve these matters professionally must be at hand, otherwise it makes no sense for the development team to pursue the project and it should be, at best, deferred.

The analyst must focus upon the difficulty of the project and those aspects of the real estate business that will be most severely challenged by the project. First, assess the experience of the development team. For example, if the most critical hurdle to overcome is entitlement and the in-house staff is not up to the task (and the right third parties have not been employed), a lot of time and money will be wasted with nothing to show for the process except, perhaps, an overpriced piece of land. Another example of inexperience: a well-capitalized company decided to diversify into the real estate business. Their neophyte real estate operation was able to purchase an extraordinarily well-located land assemblage at a bargain price because it was, historically, swampland. The availability of persons with the capability to build real estate in such a tough physical environment existed; however, the company hadn't hired such skills nor bought them. After the development was completed, there were severe settlement problems (due principally to the pilings not having been driven deep enough) and the company was sued for construction deficiencies. Although the suit was settled out of court, the company lost both money and prestige. The analyst's role was to either make company officials understand the need to form a team that could complete the job right the first time or otherwise, to take a pass on the deal.

Another personnel factor that the analyst must face head on is the reasonable availability of the appropriate project team members. A leading realtor used to say how proud he was of the fact that if need be, he was prepared to work 24 hours a day—and if that still wasn't enough, he would work nights. The development team members cannot be overloaded with work, because if too many balls are in the air, all may fall to the ground. The capability factor must be dealt with on a basis which is both honest and tough.

Financeability Factor

The permanent financing of a real estate project is generally not completed until several stages of the development effort have occurred. Completed means a written commitment—with respect to financing, it is important to remember what a union leader once said about a labor agreement with management, "the best hand-shake agreements are the ones that are in writing." It is unlikely when the project is first presented to the analyst, the developer will have even a handshake. Only when the land has been purchased (or otherwise tied up), the entitlement phase has been completed, and pre-development activities have begun, along with, often, some pre-leasing, is the real estate investment banker usually able to approach the capital markets seeking a written commitment for the necessary funds. When the initial analysis takes place, this point will often be far off. Therefore, if obtaining third-party financing is a critical factor in the development process (and it usually is), the analyst must be satisfied with identifying the expected source, probably only generically, and be comfortable that its risk of availability is tolerable. An experienced analyst may be able to get key input from conversations with real estate investment bankers with whom the analyst has cultivated relationships.

To advance satisfactorily over the hurdle of the financeability factor, it is only necessary that the analyst be satisfied that funds will likely be available to the developer for such a project in such a location with such a targeted tenancy for delivery in such a time frame. The amount of funds and their cost is not yet factored into the analysis.

Are the capital markets active, and if so, are they seeking this kind of project? To respond to this point, research is required. The second aspect, similar to the study of the capability factor, requires that an honesty pill be swallowed. The track record of the developer in raising financing for similar products must be assessed. The desirability, credit-worthiness, and historic performance levels of targeted tenants have to be reviewed carefully. The analyst must determine if the location is "investor-friendly" or if the logical financial participant(s), equity or debt, have had previous negative experiences in the specific marketplace. It is not the analyst's job to raise capital, but if there is any question as to whether it will be made available, the question must be asked and answered, and the answer must be positive before proceeding.

ECONOMIC/FINANCIAL CONSIDERATIONS

Satisfied that the development makes sense, the required skills are on board, and the required funds will be available, the analyst now gets down to business. It is time to study the economic/financial considerations and, thereby, determine the financial returns that can be expected from the prospective project. Throughout the process, the analyst must focus on keeping an objective and detached point of view.

As an initial step, the *stabilized return on investment* should be determined and carefully reviewed to assess whether it is in line with the return requirements of the developer for the risk and commitment of resources involved: If not, the analyst must determine what, if anything, can be done to adjust the return. The stabilized return on investment is determined, simplistically, by estimating post-lease-up net operating income and calculating its ratio to development cost. The percentage calculated should be assessed against the developer's minimum requirement, or target.

In the late 1960s at a real estate seminar, a famous developer told those assembled that the stabilized return on investment will always pro forma out at 12%. "Always?" he was asked. "Always," he said. "If it is less than 12%, don't do the deal because it won't work. And if it is more than 12%, you're kidding yourself." The essence of the developer's wry comment is that land owners, third-party contractors and tenants all have the capability to study the marketplace, having access to the same available information, and it should not be supposed that any of them could be duped into making the kinds of concessions that would enable the developer to squeeze out a higher return than 12%; alternatively, if any of them got an edge on the developer that presented too great an attack on the developer's incentive, the deal would be scratched. In the 1990s, the 12% standard has been as low as 9% and as high as 15%, but the concept has basically remained the same—returns are measured against perceived relative risk.

In assessing the stabilized return on investment, there are two numbers to be calculated, as noted above. First is projected development cost. Second is estimated net operating income. A few comments about how to obtain the appropriate data and pitfalls to avoid warrant a brief discussion.

Projected Development Cost

The entire cost of the project's completion must be included in the analyst's estimate, including all three major categories—land, hard costs, and soft costs—each with an appropriate contingency factor added in. In today's sophisticated environment, it is easy to leave something out, so the analyst must be very careful, especially in estimating soft costs. The contingency factor should be just that—a component to compensate for a low estimate or to protect against a circumstance impossible to foresee. It should not cover for a sloppy analysis.

Land cost is fairly straightforward as it normally includes only the direct cost of purchase, and the amount should be known. Hard costs, if the analyst is fortunate, will be based on the architect's preliminary design drawings, but in any event are obtained from the in-house development team who, in turn, provide input based upon their best estimate or, better yet, bids submitted by the candidates to be the general contractor or construction manager (and in the latter situation, should include the construction manager's fee).

Estimating soft costs, on the other hand, will probably test the analyst's mettle. Such costs include those development costs that are not direct costs of land purchase and hard costs (so-called bricks and mortar). Typically, they contain the cost of pre-development activities (zoning and entitlement), architecture and engineering, and all legal fees (even those connected with land procurement and construction contracting). In recent years, tenant allowances have become common and they are part of soft costs, as are leasing commissions and other tenant procurement costs, and the cost of pre-opening marketing activities. Carrying costs during construction must be estimated (typically real estate taxes, ground rent (if any) and interest on the construction loan, offset by any income earned from temporary uses of the project, say for parking during the pre-construction period). The analyst must take care not to leave out any of the costs that will be incurred in obtaining financing, whether they be the fee to the real estate investment banker arranging the financing, the lender's fee, loan administration fees, and in today's volatile interest rate environment, the cost of interest rate hedges or other protective devices. Finally, a reasonable factor to provide for the developer's overhead should be included—direct with respect to personnel assigned full-time and indirect (usually, by including a developer fee) for part-time members of the team.

It is essential to understand that several skills within the developer's organization will be involved in the estimate of soft costs—for example, the development department must estimate architecture and engineering costs and the leasing department should provide their best projection of tenant allowances and outside leasing commissions. Before the advent of volatile soft costs, caused principally by unpredictable interest rates and highly negotiable tenant allowances, a real estate rule of thumb was often used to calculate soft costs, as a percentage of hard costs. This technique is no longer credible.

With regard to the contingency factors for land, hard costs and soft costs, they are usually highest (8%–10%) at the initial stages of estimating. As deals are made (land cost) or bids come in (hard costs), the contingency factor is usually reduced, perhaps to 5%. The best means of estimating the correct amount of contingency is the analyst's experience, based on the developer's track record. The analyst should understand that the term developer is applied to a person or an entity that develops, not one that sits on the sideline. It is generally easy to pick out the developer's car—it is the one without the rear view mirror. Therefore, caution is the watchword.

Estimated Net Operating Income

The estimate of net operating income requires the analyst to focus on line items of income and expense. The foremost income item, and the most important one for the analyst to estimate accurately is, of course, projected rents from tenants. There are various approaches to obtaining this estimate. Sensibly, the analyst will interface with the in-house leasing team (or the third-party broker expected to head up the leasing effort), who will have ideas to advance regarding the expected merchandising of the project and the rents that can be achieved from the various types of targeted tenants. The analyst should obtain the leasing team's thoughts and review their back-up, and then arrive at his own judgment about rent levels.

In performing this step, the analyst should keep in mind that for most retail tenants, there is a sensitivity with respect to the ratio of total occupancy costs—base rent, percentage rent, real estate tax and expense recoveries, contributions to marketing funds, utilities—to store sales. For regional malls, it is generally 12% to 18%, with the lower end of the range applying to low-volume stores like home furnishings and the higher end of the range applying to both high volume stores, such as food court tenants, and high level of sales stores, such as jewelry merchants. For community and neighborhood centers, the ratio of occupancy costs to sales is lower, perhaps 8% to 10%. The analyst should obtain from the leasing members of the development team their estimates of what they expect their targeted line-up of merchants to achieve in sales and test the estimated rent levels by verifying that the ratios are in order. When working on this phase, the analyst must be aware of two things. First, when it comes time for the actual leasing effort to take place, each potential tenant will ultimately agree to pay the rent level that they believe they can afford, which is not necessarily what the leasing team estimates. Therefore, the numbers should be examined with an appropriate degree of skepticism. Second, the project will not be leased to only high volume tenants such as food court tenants and jewelry stores.

Rent Estimates

An alternative, riskier way of estimating rent levels is to approach leading local market makers for their estimates of what the deals are that are occurring in the market. Performing this work, provides the analyst with a good test of the information provided by the leasing members of the development team.

One of the more controversial elements of any analysis of a retail real estate investment is the projection, or lack thereof, of income from percentage rents. In most cases, it makes no sense to include them, despite the sales estimates obtained from the leasing members of the development team. This is because percentage rent is dependant upon the tenant sales level and the negotiated percentage factor which normally sets the sales breakpoint, and it is a leap of faith to reasonably estimate both of them at such an early phase of development. An exception is normally made, however, in the case of a percentage-rent-only lease, such as a department store and probably pursuant to a letter of intent either under negotiation or executed at this stage of the analysis. Here, the percentage factor should either be known or reasonably known, so the analyst needs only to come up with a reasonable sales estimate. The best means of establishing such an estimate is to talk to a representative of the store and ask for their sales projections, as well as comparable sales from the department store company's similar operations.

It is customary that a vacancy factor (often called a collection loss factor or down-time) be deducted from revenues. Here the analyst must balance three elements—the developer's track record, the current vacancy levels in the marketplace, and the analyst's own experience—in coming up with a number. In the calculation, the analyst should apply the vacancy factor only to those elements of revenue that are uncertain estimates. For example, if a tenant is required to pay a share of expense recoveries based upon its percentage of occupancy to actually leased space (as opposed to leasable space), the factor would not be applied to its recoveries.

Estimating Operating Expenses

To estimate operating expenses (the basis on which the revenue from expense recovery for common area maintenance would be calculated), the analyst has several resources to turn to, for example, the developer's track record for similar projects or BOMA or ULI reports for the market. For real estate tax expense (the basis on which the revenue from tax recovery would be estimated), information about tax rates is usually obtainable from the taxing entity and the estimated rate is applied against the data generated for the calculation of development cost. For marketing and advertising, the analyst should not fall into the trap of assuming that the expense will be equal to the collections from tenants joining the marketing fund. The project's marketing and advertising cost should be set at the appropriate level to generate business for the project, and this amount could easily be above the amounts that the leasing department generates in its negotiations with tenants. Other expenses that must be estimated include management fees (easy to do if a third-party manager will be used; otherwise a factor for in-house overhead should be provided) and administration (accounting, tax return preparation, tenant sales' audits, etc.).

An important consideration is whether the stabilized return on investment is calculated with the inclusion or the exclusion of capital expenditures. It is often calculated with such costs excluded, and therefore, is often overstated. Ongoing capital improvements are a fact of life and should be a part of any analysis. It is essential to include an annual reserve requirement, based upon either a percentage of revenues or a factor of so many cents per square foot.

Comparison to the Target

The project's stabilized return on investment has now been reduced to a single number. It's a simple task to compare it to the developer's targeted return to see if there is a fit. What is not so simple is setting the target in the first place—our developer friend's 12% notwithstanding.

Targeted returns are addressed in various manners by different industries. For instance, the securities markets are assisted by various rating services to help in the pricing of offerings—a bond, is rated with letters and numbers and the price that has to be paid to purchase the bond reflects such rating. In the real estate industry, letters are often used as well, such as in setting the different investment returns expected from Class A, B or C office buildings. For retail real estate, however, characterization is somewhat more exotic as investment ratings are based principally on the physical description of the product, and often on its quality. The project may be an enclosed or an unenclosed regional or even super-regional mall, a power center, a community, neighborhood or highway center, a free-standing store, and so on. Furthermore, it may be a boutique property or a "trophy." Its trade area may be considered superb, or it may be marginal. Each type of project carries with it a panache—it joins a class of product that investors will consider acquiring based upon the property being within a certain price range that provides a specified stabilized return on investment.

In setting the target, therefore, the analyst must carefully assess how the project will be characterized by the marketplace. Determining whether a project will be perceived as a regional or super-regional, as a community center or a power center, is often in the eye of the beholder and anyway highly subjective. Nevertheless, the analyst must, as the marketplace would, blend the project's features (type, size, quality of construction and tenant roster) with market conditions (location, level of competition) in coming up with the target. A feature that complicates the analyst's assignment is that the cost of financing that may be utilized or is otherwise available has to be factored in, as must be the pricing of recent comparable acquisitions or sales by the developer or in the marketplace. The reasons for this are that (i) the targeted stabilized return on investment clearly should be at a level that will enable the developer to compensate the capital that will be employed in making the project a reality and (ii) an "exit strategy," which would normally be a sale of the completed project, should be available to the developer in case things change.

There are several sources to assist the analyst in setting the developer's target. The most important is the market, particularly recent closings involving transfers of real estate. Another is that several companies, including investment banks, real estate advisors and real estate investment bankers, publish periodic reports on the market. The relationships that the analyst has formed with leading market makers are critical. Finally, the developer must address this issue, irrespective of what is happening in the market, based on its internal needs and capitalization.

Producing a Market or Higher Return

If the stabilized return on investment doesn't measure up to the target, the analyst must determine if there are steps that can be taken to cure the deficiency. The analyst should have a reason to believe that either development cost will be lower than projected or that net operating income will be higher. Even if the target is equalled or exceeded, this analysis should be undertaken. There are various means of lowering development cost, ranging from renegotiating land acquisitions to value engineering of construction methods and materials to laying off parts of the cost (such as off-site road improvements) to the appropriate political entity that is seeking to attract the development. Each possibility should be given consideration. Various members of the development team should assist the analyst in performing this portion of the assignment.

With regard to net operating income, the temptation should be resisted to adjust the numbers (particularly the rental income) to more aggressive ones. Rather, real alternatives should be pursued, such as determining if the project could be expanded as a means of creating more lucrative mall shop space, or determining if it makes sense to develop out-parcels with restaurants, theaters, or the like rather than sell them to others.

Capital Appreciation Requirements

An investment in retail real estate is generally made with a view toward holding it for some defined period of time. The goal is, of course, to take advantage of increases in value caused by higher income from rental increases, percentage rents, or the like, and/or quality construction and operations. Real estate has been considered by many, traditionally, as a means of hedging against inflation. The business plans of most retail developers is to build for cost and sell for value. Evaluating and contemplating improving upon the potential future value of a planned development, along with holding period returns, is, therefore, the next step in the analysis.

Internal Rate of Return

The stabilized return on investment provides only one measurement. A second is the internal rate of return on investment. Unlike the stabilized return on investment which focuses on one particular year when so-called stability has been reached (i.e., the project has been leased up), this analysis focuses on the total return that will be derived by the entity over the period the investment is projected to be held by the developer. The analyst should make certain that the information used in obtaining the stabilized return on investment is used consistently when such similar information is required in determining the internal rate of return. Initial rents, for example, shouldn't be different in the two analyses.

There are several features to the internal rate of return analysis that differ from the calculation of the stabilized return on investment, and each merits a brief discussion:

- *Lease-Up Period.* The length of the lease-up period (i.e., the time frame it will take until the project has reached the same level of occupancy utilized in the stabilized return on investment analysis) must be estimated. The internal rate of return analysis covers a period of years, and the events projected to happen in the earlier years will affect the result with more volatility than those projected to happen later in the analysis. The analyst must determine, therefore, what percentage of the project is expected to be leased by the Grand Opening, and over what time frame the balance of the project will be filled. The track record of the developer and the experience of other developers in the marketplace, as well as estimates from the leasing members of the development team, will be helpful in making this estimate.

  In connection with this step, the analyst should keep in mind that the timing of the Grand Opening will be meaningful. If the project is expected to open in September, it is unlikely that the second series of store openings will occur until March, six months later, for obvious reasons. On the other hand, following a Spring opening, other tenants could be projected to open on a monthly basis thereafter. The analyst should be careful not to be over-aggressive.

  An asset manager, who had several retail projects under his supervision, discussed them with a real estate investment banker. The asset manager told the investment banker that he envied him because when the real estate investment banker presents a project to an investor, in the accompanying pro forma the project is always projected to reach its stabilized occupancy—maybe quickly, or maybe slowly, but eventually it is reached. In the asset management business, which the asset manager called "real life," there were spaces in some of his properties that he did not expect to lease until every other space was leased in the entire marketplace. Such real life considerations should find their way into the analyst's work.

- *Appreciation Rates.* A critical element of the analysis is the selection of the appreciation, or growth factor(s), which will be applied to the elements of cash inflows and outflows. Again, caution is in order. If different factors are applied to different elements (e.g., rents will grow by 5% per year while expenses will increase by 4%), the analyst should have a firm and valid basis for these assumptions. General inflation expectations provide a benchmark for assumptions.

- *Tenant Renewal Assumptions.* The estimate of the percentage of tenants that are expected to renew will have an important effect on the result of the analysis. Given that the project hasn't been even initially leased at the time the analysis is being performed, an aggressive renewal assumption can be risky. Many factors enter into a retailer's decision to renew (profitability of store, competing locations, quality of mall, compatibility with other mall tenants), yet none of these can be relied upon at the point of the analysis. The only reasonably reliable indicator at this point is the developer's track record in retaining tenants in its other projects, and this information should correlate to the percentage chosen.

- *Holding Period and Pro Forma Sale.* When discounted cash flow analyses first came to be used in the real estate business, most analyses were performed assuming a 10-year holding period. Today, holding periods vary. Many entities use short-term holds—three years to five years—while others use terms even longer than 10 years. The length of the holding period should affect the analyst's estimate of the pro forma sale. The longer the holding period, the higher the terminal capitalization rate should be, given that the project is older and that the operating agreements with major tenants could be nearing (or past) their term of expiration.

Comparison to the Target

Just as the stabilized return on investment must be compared to its target, so must the internal rate of return. With respect to the developer's own funds, the same factors are taken into consideration in setting both targets, and normally they relate to each other in some way (e.g., the internal rate of return target is, say, 200 to 300 basis points above the targeted stabilized return on investment). Details on IRR capitalization techniques may be found in Chapter 20.

Additionally, the overall cost of third-party capital with an equity kicker, if such funds are expected to be deployed in the investment, must be taken into account. In fact, the internal rate of return analysis is the key means of determining if the appreciation expectation, if any, of the entity providing third-party capital can be reasonably met, without resulting in the development being uneconomic for the developer. This analysis can lead to a decision whether such third-party capital can be justifiably utilized for the project. The analyst must understand that typically, real estate projects do not provide sufficient returns on equity investments during their first few years of operation. Lease-up, the burn-off of concessions such as free rent, the phase-in of negotiated rent step-ups and the generation of percentage rents are usually needed to bring the return to levels that are consistent with those that attract equity investors. If the analyst projects that the returns from the project will not be available within the time frame required by the third-party capital, it is important that the analyst explain to the development team that they run the risk of losing the project, perhaps even early on.

Risk Analysis

If the internal rate of return analysis fails to meet the target, the analyst should determine what, if anything, can be done about the deficiency. The typical means of approaching this issue is to utilize a range of analytical assumptions to enable two or three internal rate of return analyses to be completed, which would range from the most conservative, or downside analysis, to the most aggressive, or upside analysis. Even though the downside analysis will probably produce results which are below the expectations of the development team, a careful study of it may reveal that it is marginally acceptable. This may, in turn, give the developer considerable confidence in the project. On the other hand, the upside analysis may show overly high returns. The development team may be willing to take the risk of proceeding in order to try to achieve this case.

Example Illustrating the Comparisons

In order to illustrate (a) the comparison of the stabilized return on investment and the internal rate of return to the target and (b) the risk analysis, an example has been created. A regional mall is planned with two major department stores (300,000 and 250,000 square feet), a specialty department store (100,000 square feet) and mall shops (200,000 square feet with a 4,000 square foot food court). The larger department store has agreed to pay for a portion of the land cost and build its own store, while the smaller major will lease its store from the developer.

Construction financing is assumed at 60% of the cost of the project, which the lender will fund after the entire 40% equity has been infused. For simplicity sake, it is assumed that upon completion of construction the loan will convert to a permanent loan, there will be a 9% coupon for both the construction and ten-year permanent loan periods, and a 30-year amortization schedule will be in place following the project's opening. The equity is assumed to be provided by a sophisticated capital source who has negotiated a dual-based cumulative preferred return (11% during the construction period and 9% after the regional mall opens). Any excess over the preferred return would be shared by the equity source and developer, with the equity source receiving 85% of remaining cash flow and the developer retaining 15%. Upon sale, the 85/15 sharing would remain in effect until the equity source has achieved a 12% return, at which point the balance of any remaining funds would be allocated 75% to the equity source and 25% to the developer.

The targets set by the analyst include:

1. First year cash flow sufficient to pay debt service, so no additional funds to carry the property will be required from the equity source;
2. Stabilized return on investment at or greater than 10%; and
3. Internal rate of return at or greater than 12.5% overall, and 12.0% to the equity source.

The cost to construct the mall, including land, carrying costs, rate protection on construction financing and contingency, has been projected in this example or $100 million.

With regard to operations, the analyst has prepared three estimates based upon varying assumptions as to potential future events (controlled and uncontrolled), which have been given titles which make their content self-explanatory. (For simplicity in presentation, the only items changed among the three analyses are rent and sales projections. Typically, many more estimates would be varied.) Highlights of the estimated cash flow forecasts for the mall's operations are shown in Table 7.1.

The analyst's comparison to the targets and risk analysis can be summarized as follows:

1. The first goal, a positive first-year cash flow, appears to be comfortably met even under the downside analysis (despite the analyst's conservative assumption that first year occupancy is only 85%);

TABLE 7.1

Estimated Cash Flow Forecasts

	Downside	Realistic	Upside
First year cash flow:*			
Before debt service	$ 7,551	$ 7,978	$ 8,291
After debt service	1,758	2,185	2,498
Return on equity	4.4%	5.5%	6.2%
Stabilized return on investment (Year 4):			
Before debt service	$ 9,335	$ 9,800	$ 10,138
After debt service	3,541	4,007	4,345
Return on equity	8.9%	10.0%	10.9%
Pro forma to determine sale price:			
Gross cash flow	$ 11,846	$ 12,510	$ 13,076
Sale cap rate	9.25%	9.00%	8.50%
Net sale price	$128,068	$139,005	$153,830
Internal rate of return:			
Overall	10.76%	12.53%	14.37%
To equity source	10.43%	11.86%	13.38%

* Cash flow is defined as net operating income after capital expenditures (including structural reserves, tenant renewal/replacement allowances, and leasing commissions for renewing/replacing tenants) but before depreciation and amortization and mortgage interest, unless otherwise indicated. All numbers are in 000s.

2. The targeted stabilized return on investment is 10.0% in the realistic analysis, and therefore meets the target. There is some comfort with regard to risk in that in the downside case, the target is missed by only 110 basis points;

3. The internal rate of return is 12.53% in the realistic analysis, and also meets the target. However, the analyst must be cautious here, because the downside case is below the target by 177 basis points. Furthermore, the analyst must carefully study the ability to induce the equity source to proceed, because the internal rate of return to the equity source is below the 12% target; although the return is a mere 14 basis points away, in the downside case, the return is well below the target (by 157 basis points) the realistic case. In this regard, the analyst will be helped by the upside analysis, because the returns

are shown to be potentially well above the target (by 138 basis points) the realistic case.

If this example were a real transaction, the focus on the realistic case would show that the cash flow over an 11-year period ranges from close to $8.0 million in the first full year to close to $12.5 million in the eleventh year and tends to support a value in the $140 million range at the end of the tenth year. If the analyst has confidence that future market conditions will be favorable in this location, and that the upside case estimate has a reasonable chance of being achieved (with the ultimate sales price reaching $150 million or more and the internal rate of return being 14.37%), there is a very good chance that the analyst would be pleased with the outcome of this analysis.

Income Tax Planning

It is important that the analyst understand the effect of the investment upon the developer's income tax status, as well as the developer's income tax status upon the investment. The goal of the analyst here is to assure that the tax effect of the investment results in enhancing the opportunity. At the very least (as could be the case where the developer is a tax-exempt entity such as a pension fund or, perhaps, offshore), the tax effect should be neutral. Specifically, an equity owner can generally shelter, for income tax purposes, some or all of the income from a project because depreciation (deductible for tax purposes) usually exceeds mortgage principal amortization (not deductible). Certain techniques in tax return preparation, as well as tax elections (for example, component depreciation), can further enhance the post-tax reward of proceeding with the investment.

The analyst should not rely too heavily on income tax considerations that positively affect an investment opportunity and tilt the scales in its favor. A development undertaken because its positive tax effects offset its failure to achieve targeted levels for the other financial/economic factors should be avoided. A colleague once asked us to show him a real estate opportunity that we would describe as an excellent "tax deal" and he promised he would show us, in less than five years, a project that is owned by the mortgagee.

Compatibility Requirements

A series of economic/financial considerations emphasizes understanding the developer's strengths, improving the developer's portfolio holdings including enhancing diversification potential, and avoiding over-competitive situations. In this stage of the work, the analyst could be said to be "analyzing the analysis."

Retail real estate is different in several respects from its brethren, investment in other types of real estate such as office, industrial and residential. The most obvious difference relates to tenancy. If an office, industrial or residential developer attracts a tenant to its project, the developer has probably succeeded in preventing other developers from obtaining the tenancy. With respect to retail, the situation isn't quite the same. Absent radius clauses and a reasonable understanding by a tenant of its trade area, any tenant is fair game for any retail development. Furthermore, there are times that a developer can induce a tenant to sign even where the project may be marginal by the tenant's standards. The ability of a developer to attract such a tenant, despite evidence that the tenant's situation may be unfavorable, is often referred to as the developer's clout.

In order to reflect this characteristic of the retail real estate business, it is critical to understand the developer's strengths—type of project (mall, strip, etc.), geographic location, urban vs. suburban, clout. If the situation is one in which the developer is strongest, whether in terms of the type of development, the location, or the targeted tenancy, it may overcome a failure of the stabilized return on investment or the internal rate of return to hit the target by a few basis points. Another kind of risk analysis is portfolio review. If the developer has not diversified in terms of type of product, geographic area, or dependence upon one industry, there is the possibility that a single event can trigger a portfolio catastrophe. Geographic diversification is one way of overcoming this problem. Another is by building a portfolio of real estate investments tailored to retail centers with differing price points (or emphasis on types of products sold).

ENTITY-SPECIFIC CONSIDERATIONS

Financial/economic considerations apply to all investment opportunities, regardless of the type of retail investment, its location, and the identity of the developer. On the other hand, entity-specific considerations require the analyst to look at each development opportunity as unique. Aspects to be considered are highly subjective and difficult to measure. It is the analyst's job to confront and deal with these issues.

Relationships

The first entity-specific consideration that might cause a developer to consider proceeding with a project, absent financial/economic criteria that support its development, is relationships. Key retailers may want to be represented in a marketplace for competitive reasons, and their relationships with the developer may be such that they want to enter the market in a project together. Another factor could be capital—entities that have had success in investing in the developer's projects may want to diversify in terms of product or geographic market and may want to do it with the developer rather than establishing a new relationship. If there are non-economic factors involved, in other words, if feasibility is not the issue, as it will affect the reading of the financial/economic considerations.

Company Growth Requirements

Another entity-specific situation that must be addressed is one in which company growth requirements (whether in terms of gross assets owned or managed, or investor/shareholder returns) encourage proceeding despite marginal financial/economic numbers. For example, it was previously related how a 12% pro forma return was required. If a developer's public offering was underwritten, however, at an 8% investment return, it would clearly be tempting for that developer to modify its requirements (let's say the targeted stabilized return on investment is 10%) and to proceed with a deal that would yield, say, 9.5%.

Items the analyst should look for include:

- *The Entity's Business Plan.* The developer's internal requirements, based on the goals set by its key investors (or in the case of a public company, by Wall Street), may set a level of investment criteria or thresholds that are different from those of an otherwise unaffected entity.

- *Growth Commitments.* The entity may have made commitments to its investors regarding such matters as entering new markets (for diversification reasons) or concentrating on different investment direction (such as the entity's first regional mall development).

- *New Directions.* The developer's senior management may chart a course for the entity into new waters. A private company may want to go public, a small company may want to become big, or a local entity may want to become regional or national.

- *Income Tax Considerations.* Although the analyst must exercise extreme caution and not overemphasize the importance of income tax considerations to the feasibility of the basic investment itself, the entity's tax position may be so critical that the effect the development under consideration could have may require review. For example, the entity may have the opportunity to sell other assets but such sale may produce such large taxable income that the deal would be uneconomic. A new real estate development that produces taxable losses which would shelter the expected surge of taxable income could be welcomed despite the real estate development's questionable economic merits on a stand-alone basis.

To best deal with the issues raised here, the analyst must obtain an understanding of the developer entity equal to the understanding obtained of the real estate project.

Business Competition

A successful analyst is one who goes beyond the numbers in understanding a proposed project. The analyst must determine if an investment will accomplish certain important entity-related, market share goals.

Any marketplace is, at any given point in time, relatively finite. For instance, the trade area is measurable, as are the number of existing projects and the need for growth in the number of retail opportunities that serve it. If the developer is currently a force in the market, but the particular development being analyzed is on the cusp (meaning that it is arguable whether or not it is feasible), one factor that may cause the developer to want to proceed is to keep a particular competitor, who is looking at the same opportunity, out of the market.

Each developer should understand its competition—those entities that compete with it currently and in the future. With this understanding, any analysis should include as a "given" that key competitors will also be looking at the market, maybe even the same potential development, and that the such entities may lower their investment targets in order to justify proceeding into a competitive situation. A developer defending its turf may therefore be prepared to go forward with an otherwise marginal opportunity. This type of thinking could manifest itself in tying up the land across the street from the developer's major regional mall and then building, say, a community center or even a cinema. The new project may not "pencil out," but it may bring additional traffic into the market to patronize the mall and increase percentage rents.

Personnel Policy

Developers are in the business of development; in connection with this situation, a developer may not be willing to risk the loss of key personnel who are temporarily inactive because there are no projects on the board that meet the criteria established for financial/economic considerations. As a result, the developer may be willing to proceed with a project that marginally misses the targets.

Another consideration may involve the desire of the entity to diversify. By proceeding with the development of a new type of project or one in a new geographic location, the developer may be improving the skills or contacts of its staff, which could prove invaluable with respect to future opportunities.

Product Mix

If the entity understands its portfolio and determines that it is too dependant upon a certain product (e.g., malls) or a certain geographic area or tenant, the result may be a need to enter another part of the real estate business. Financial/economic considerations, in such cases, may be less relevant or even insignificant. (This is a situation with respect to which the analyst should act, not react. A skilled analyst is often the trigger in pointing out to the development team the need to diversify.)

Still another situation could be that the developer (with, perhaps, the analyst's prodding) may believe it has discovered what will be the next growth concept in the retail real estate business. For example, some developer had to be the first to develop a so-called "power center," and another had to be the first to put together an "outlet mall." In such an instance, an economic/financial analysis becomes rather difficult (if not impossible).

Special Knowledge

Sometimes, the developer has a special knowledge about a market or a situation that compensates for apparent failures to meet financial/

economic considerations. The developer, using its resources including its initiative and creativity, may determine that a market exists that others have failed to perceive. Even the leasing members of the development team may underestimate the income levels the project will attract. Similarly, a retailer may choose to enter a new market and may advise the developer (hopefully not other developers) accordingly. Relationships with real estate investment bankers may prove fruitful, as such professionals may point out a marketplace where financial sources have determined investment makes sense. Also, information may be obtained by the developer from politicians or lobbyists. For example, the city in question may implement a program that offers a series of development initiatives, which may interest the developer in an otherwise unattractive marketplace.

Social Responsibility

A final entity-specific consideration, which cannot be ignored, is that the developer is part of a community and as such, has responsibilities that may go beyond earning a profit. There may be reasons that a developer may seek to proceed with a marginal project that could bring honor and prestige to the entity and to the community. The analyst must understand if this is the case.

CONCLUSION

The analyst's role on the development team is to connect the work performed with respect to feasibility with the real world that is the real estate business. By providing a focus upon the "numbers" and their linkage to the many and varied non-monetary concerns that a developer must consider, the analyst will provide the team with sensible, useful input which will play a critical role in the development decision.

Eight

The Formats Employed in New Retail Strategies

Howard C. Gelbtuch

I n the late 1980s, and even more so in the early 1990s, consumer preferences shifted away from conspicuous consumption (designer jeans, expensive cars, etc.) to more value-oriented shopping. While it became more fashionable to buy goods at "bargain" prices than to flaunt one's wealth, "value" has also been defined to include ". . . good quality, fair prices, selection, and service."[1] This gave rise to the value-oriented formats described next.

- *Factory Outlet Stores*, owned and operated by manufacturers, sell directly to the consumer, eliminating interim markups in pricing. Among the manufacturers choosing this route are Levi Strauss & Co., Nike, and London Fog.
- *Department Store Outlet Stores*, operated by well-known national and regional retailers, typically sell both excess inventory and out-of-season merchandise. In some cases, department stores purchase excess inventory from manufacturers for resale in their outlet stores. Among the best known are Nordstrom Rack and Neiman-Marcus Last Call stores.

- *Specialty Outlet Stores*, operated by the specialty chains, are increasingly found in outlet shopping centers—neighborhood or community-sized centers tenanted exclusively with value-oriented stores. Tanger Outlet Centers, McArthur/Glen, and Factory Stores of America, Inc.—these centers are frequently tenanted by Nine West, Ann Taylor, VF Corp., Levi Strauss & Co., and Nike, among others. Since 1988, the number of factory outlet centers in the United States more than doubled from 131 to 294 in 1993. They are generally situated away from large metropolitan areas so as not to compete with the manufacturer's larger customers, such as department stores and mass merchandisers. Average sales of outlet retailers increased by 10% in 1993 to $264 per square foot (see Table 8.1).

- *Off-Price Retailers and Super Savings Stores* are often larger in GLA than the specialty outlet stores and are well-known for discount prices. Retailers in this category include Burlington Coat Factory, Syms, and Marshalls.

TABLE 8.1

Average Sales per Square Foot for Outlet Retailers (1984–1994)

Year	Sales	Percentage Change
1984	N/A	
1985	N/A	
1986	N/A	
1987	$196	10.7
1988	211	7.6
1989	233	10.4
1990	235	0.1
1991	243	3.4
1992	240	(1.2)
1993	257*	N/A
1994		274*

* Weighted for chain size.

Source: 1994 Outlet Retail Directory, Value Retail News, March 1994.

- *Catalog Outlets* are retail stores operated by the major catalog merchandisers such as Lands' End and L.L. Bean, and offer discounts from their standard pricing. Mail order retailers are well positioned to target the increasing number of people working at home, particularly the retailers offering casual styles. Lands' End, reportedly dubious about going on the home shopping channel, has been experimenting with other means of selling its wares electronically.

Although the era of marketing to Yuppies came to a close at the end of the 1980s, both high-end and low-end stores will survive future decades, often catering to the same customer who is both price and quality conscious. The remainder of this chapter examines several different approaches to capturing the consumer's attention and dollars.

CATEGORY KILLERS

Category killers offer a dominant selection of products in a single, specialized category, such as office products (Staples), sporting equipment (The Sports Authority), or white goods (Bed, Bath & Beyond), all at attractive pricing, and at the expense of independent retailers who cannot compete in price or inventory, nor offer the occasional bargains. The store environment is usually spartan and self-serve with merchandise boldly displayed. Additional examples of retailers in this category include Marshall's, Linens 'N Things, Home Depot, Toys 'R Us, Oshman's SuperSports, Circuit City, and Best Buy; the latter is the subject of the case study below.

Case Study

Best Buy is a $3.6 billion sales retailer of electronic goods including stereo equipment, televisions, and computers. It is known for its aggressive pricing. To a base of 151 stores at year-end 1993, the retailer is planning to add an additional 45 stores in 1994, 30 in new markets, with the majority being 45,000 square feet in size. Six to seven of these stores will be in Los Angeles, (growing to as many as 25 ultimately) a market where competitor Circuit City gets over 10% of its sales, and Good Guys generates 40% of its volume (including Orange County) highlighting the competitive nature of the industry. Plans also call for the expansion of 25 existing 28,000-square-foot stores into 45,000-square-foot formats. Each store averages about $23 million in sales. Interestingly, Best Buy's traditional sales base of consumer electronics goods and appliances has diminished to less than 40% of goods sold. Home office equipment represented 35% of sales in 1993, and is expected to increase to 40% in 1994, and software, which accounted for 12% of sales in 1993, is expected to account for 15% of sales in 1994. As a result, Best Buy, traditionally viewed as an electronics retailer, now has as its foremost competitors computer retailers CompUSA and Computer City. Its next generation of stores, known as Concept III, will contain a higher degree of interactive displays and video games in an effort to attract younger customers.

Wall Street analysts expect Circuit City, which competes in 50% of its markets with Best Buy, to respond by focusing on more expensive products, and Good Guys to continue its strategy of opening stores next to Tower Records.

WAREHOUSE CLUBS

Warehouse clubs are a major form of mass retailing rivaling department stores, discount stores, and supermarkets. These clubs, which include such leading names as Price/Costco and Sam's, sell quality brand name goods at sharply discounted prices. Categories stocked include groceries, office supplies, appliances, electronic equipment, and hardware among others. They are typically situated in nontraditional locations offering good access; visibility is not important as they are true destination retailers. Physically, the clubs are spartan 100,000+ SF industrial buildings capable of generating sales volumes three times that of normal discounters.

Customers are charged an annual membership fee to shop and must bag or box their own goods and carry them to their vehicles. The majority of purchases are made by small business owners such as vending machine operators, restauranteurs, and service station owners who are frequently allowed into the store before others. Another important category is families, some of whom travel long distances to take advantage of the price savings, often by making joint purchases of bulk goods with other families.

Operating cost savings are achieved by operating these no-frills facilities on a self-serve basis. Many items are stocked only in large sizes, making comparison shopping difficult. Important to their success, items are turned over frequently, approximately every three weeks, compared to every three months for typical discounters. This

contributes to the "excitement in shopping" feeling in that a particular book, appliance, or food item may not be available on the customer's next shopping trip. Most clubs carry only about 5,000 items
(known as Stock Keeping Units or SKUs) compared to approximately
50,000 SKUs in a typical discount store.

From an operating perspective, the clubs provide a limited selection of high quality merchandise, often as a result of direct relationships with brand name manufacturers. Restricted membership
reduces the risk of bad checks and shoplifting. Costs are contained
through minimum staffing, low rent, absence of deliveries, incidental use of credit cards, and minimal advertising.

AUTOMOTIVE AND CAR CARE MALLS

Not all retail strategies are successful or long lasting. A headline in
the April 1987 issue of *Venture* magazine reported "Developers Are
Racing to Build Malls Catering to the Auto Service Market." First developed in 1984, car care malls contain a variety of services such as
an oil-change station, a tune-up shop, or a car wash. Tenants can be
franchisees, multilocation nationals, or local independents. Heavy
duty businesses such as body shops are generally excluded, whereas
cleaner uses like automotive detailers are welcome.

Dual attractions to the development of these facilities are (1) the
synergy created by offering the customer the convenience of a variety of uses at a single location; and (2) an attractive environment in
a pleasant neighborhood instead of the stereotypical unappealing
surroundings. Newer facilities are designed to be more appealing to
women (more than half of all car owners) who can sometimes be intimidated in an automotive repair environment. Also driving the development of car care facilities is the lack of old style service stations
(the number of service stations declined by nearly 50% between 1970
and 1988) since replaced with convenience stores and the like. Particularly during the 1980s, the ever-escalating price of suitable land,
(major arterials with daily traffic counts of 20,000 or more) made it
more economical to spread the cost over a variety of tenants.

Unfortunately, this concept seems to have fizzled, either as a result
of the real estate recession of the early 1990s, or more likely, the realization that merely because one's car is in need of a tune-up does
not mean it needs to be re-upholstered as well.

Auto malls are agglomerations of car dealers in a single location—
shopping centers for car buyers. Frequently part of redevelopment

projects, they have particularly proliferated throughout California. One of the nation's largest is Stockton Auto Center, a 108-acre, $80 million project that houses 15 dealerships as well as related uses.

This concept was spurred by two factors (1) the price of property in urban areas (San Francisco's Van Ness Avenue is one example) is escalating, particularly important to an auto dealership where large amounts of land are required to store and service vehicles, and because auto malls truly do generate customer traffic since most potential purchasers visit more than one dealership when shopping for a car; and (2) municipalities generally favor development of auto malls because of the jobs and sales tax revenue that they create, as well as the opportunity they give planners to convert former "automobile rows" into more desirable uses.

THE MILLS

Among the first real estate developers to anticipate the shift to value retailing was Herbert S. Miller. After a stint at the Taubman Company, Mr. Miller founded Western Development Corporation in 1967, which, following some financial engineering in the early 1990s, became a publicly traded Real Estate Investment Trust (REIT) known as The Mills Corporation. Named after its most notable developments, the four "Mills" super-regional malls combine the major categories of value retailers into a regional mall format. Table 8.2 provides an overview of each of the existing Mills centers.

Typical major or anchor tenants at the Mills include category killers like Burlington Coat Factory, Waccamaw Pottery, Office Max, Sports Authority, and Bed, Bath & Beyond. Among the specialty stores are chains owned by Melville Group including Chess King, Kay Bee Toys, and Marshalls; Footlocker including Footlocker Outlet and Lady Footlocker; and several versions of Dress Barn including Dress Barn Outlet and Dress Barn Woman.

Overall, the four Mills centers were 97% leased at year-end 1993 with average sales of more than $290 PSF. Occupancies ranged from a low of 93% at Gurnee Mills to 99% at Potomac Mills, and sales ranged from approximately $240 PSF at Gurnee Mills to $375 PSF at Sawgrass Mills.

The combination of a large concentration of value-oriented stores in a festive Main Street environment coupled with aggressive marketing, including bus tours, and in at least one case—Gurnee Mills, an in-house television studio that produces programming for video

TABLE 8.2

The Mills Shopping Centers

Name/Location	Metropolitan Area	Year Opened	GLA	No. of Stores	Specialty
Potomac Mills Woodbridge, VA	Baltimore/ Washington	1985	1,541,000	16	202
Franklin Mills Philadelphia, PA	Philadelphia/ Wilmington	1989	1,553,000	19	194
Sawgrass Mills Sunrise, FL	Miami/ Ft. Lauderdale	1990	1,513,000	16	201
Gurnee Mills Gurnee, IL	Chicago/ Milwaukee	1991	1,269,000	14	176

Source: The Mills Corporation Prospectus, Merrill Lynch & Co., April 14, 1994, p. 6.

monitors with ads for tenants, updates on mall events, and fashion shows—has contributed to the success of these centers.

Although Western economized during construction by building Gurnee Mills out of corrugated steel with square windows and sky-lights, meant to suggest a modern industrial building, they spent heavily on the details. The floors, for example, are designed with more "give" than typical corridors, and a voice reminds shoppers where they parked their cars as they enter and leave the mall's nine entrances. Inside, stores are arranged according to price point: high-end designers, moderate to better, and moderate to low, to enable shoppers to cover the more than one mile of corridors efficiently.

The primary trade area of a Mills center ranges from 25 to 40 miles, with a secondary trade area of as much as 100 miles. Potomac Mills, for example, is the top-rated tourist attraction in Virginia, and Sawgrass Mills is second only to Walt Disney World in the state of Florida. Franklin Mills is reported to be the number one shopping center destination in the Delaware Valley, and Gurnee Mills draws more visitors than the next three Illinois tourist attractions combined.

Because of the 3,500 jobs as well as real estate and sales tax revenue generated by a Mills project, municipalities often assist the company with direct grants, infrastructure financing, and tax abatements.

More Mills centers are planned; on the drawing boards are the re-development of an existing 630,000 SF single-anchor regional mall in Orange County, CA into a 1-million-square-foot plus regional mall with 12 majors and 169 specialty stores, and a similar conversion in San Mateo, CA. New Mills malls have been proposed for the New York Metropolitan area, as well as Boston, MA, and Riverside/San Bernadino, CA.

WAL-MART

Wal-Mart is the largest retailer in the United States with total 1993 revenues of more than $67 billion. Its success is legendary. From a single store in 1950, Sam Walton grew the chain to 15 locations in 1962. By 1980, the chain had $2.4 billion in sales. Ten years later, Wal-Mart passed Sears as the nation's largest retailer, reporting $32.6 billion in sales volume. Current Wall Street estimates call for the retailer to pass the $100 billion revenue mark in 1995 (Table 8.3).

As Table 8.3 above indicates, in absolute terms Wal-Mart is expanding even faster today than it has in the past, particularly as it enters the supermarket industry with its supercenter stores.

Wal-Mart also announced its first store in a regional mall, a 125,000-square-foot facility in a mid-market mall in Phoenix, AZ, after "ringing" the city with additional stores, a strategy it has

TABLE 8.3
Number of Wal-Mart Operated Stores

Year	Discount Stores	Super-centers*	Sam's Wholesale Clubs	Total Stores	Net Increase
1989	1402	—	123	1525	161
1990	1573	—	148	1721	196
1991	1714	6	208	1928	207
1992	1850	30	256	2136	208
1993	1953	68	332	2353	217
1994	2063	133	439	2635	282
1995	2203	213	529	2945	310

* Supercenters are 150,000 SF hybrid stores combining a traditional Wal-Mart store with a supermarket.

Source: Research Growth Retailers, Alex. Brown & Sons Incorporated, February 23, 1994, p. 8.

successfully employed in Chicago, St. Louis, and Dallas. Wal-Mart has announced plans to build a 75,000-square-foot store in Vermont in an attempt to appease anti-development and small merchant groups, the smallest it has built in years; Vermont is the only state where the retailer does not have a store. As Wal-Mart continues to expand in the Northeast, its opponents have become more vocal.

If the Mills represents entertainment in shopping, then Wal-Mart stands for efficiency. It generally builds stores on rural sites offering sizable acreage, high visibility, and access via a major thoroughfare, located outside of incorporated municipalities where property taxes are lower. Wal-Mart typically options or buys the site, has the building constructed, and then sells it and becomes a tenant, giving it control during the construction phase, and flexibility afterward. Tax incentives from municipalities frequently accompany Wal-Mart's entry into a community. Reinforcing this strategy is the fear that if one town doesn't secure Wal-Mart, a neighboring town might, which could result in a loss of sales in the first community.

Cash registers are connected via satellite to a computer system at the company's Arkansas headquarters, which combined with a network of regional warehouses, enables the company to boast the lowest inventory and distribution costs in the retailing industry. Wal-Mart also utilizes a monthly tabloid of sales and specials, preprinted in Arkansas and sent to local newspapers or distributors via direct mail thirteen times per year, less costly than the weekly format most retailers use. As a result, Wal-Mart has the highest ratio of sales to advertising costs of any of the nation's top 100 advertisers.

The demographic characteristics of traditional Wal-Mart locations necessitate drawing from a large trade area. The average 1990 population of an Illinois Wal-Mart community was under 19,000 people.[2]

"Wal-Mart thrived by locating its stores in rural areas, where people were traditionally underserved by retailers. Thus they were willing to drive 30 miles not just to shop but to indulge, as well, in the postwar cornucopian experience of walking into a store the size of a hanger, stacked to the rafters with consumer goods."[3] Wal-Mart also appeals to buyers seeking good value, particularly lower to middle income households. In 1990, fully 40% of its customers had household incomes of $20,000 or less.[4]

What should a retailer do when Wal-Mart comes to town? Is it cause for excitement or alarm? Several studies have been undertaken to evaluate Wal-Mart's impact, with near uniform results: positive for some retailers, negative for others, and generally beneficial to the municipality. When this powerful retailer enters a small community, it quickly captures a disproportionate share of business, and expands the trade area. Firms selling complementary products usually benefit because of the additional traffic generated by Wal-Mart; examples include restaurants and service stations. Businesses that sell products competitive to Wal-Mart generally suffer, such as lower price point apparel retailers, merchants selling small appliance items, electronics goods, and household items like disposable diapers and formula; and drug, jewelry, auto parts, hardware, and grocery stores. The net impact on a community is positive, however, particularly when sales tax revenues are included. Wal-Marts have also been found to have a stabilizing effect on communities, reinforcing the community's position as a regional trade center.

One thing is clear: when Wal-Mart comes to town, a retailer must do *something*. In March 1988, Wal-Mart opened a Supercenter, a 126,000-square-foot store combining groceries and discount goods, in Washington, MO, population 12,000. Within weeks, sales reached an annualized $50 million, and a nearby IGA supermarket was forced to close. An ineffective strategy is to try to compete on price; Wal-Mart's high volume and low costs preclude such a move. A competitor would be better suited to try to find a market niche, for example, carrying harder to find or more expensive items aimed at higher income customers. Another way to compete is to improve service, by offering delivery, installation, and alterations where appropriate since Wal-Marts are large stores and, to a certain extent, impersonal. Competing retailers should also consider extending their hours, changing their product mix to one that complements rather than competes (by carrying maternity clothes, for example); and perhaps most importantly for many retailers, prepare for a period of declining sales until the adjustment process can be mastered.

MALL OF AMERICA

Arguably the most famous regional mall in the United States, and the second largest in North America, Mall of America is a 4.2 million square foot mega-mall/entertainment center—the equivalent of four regional shopping centers—located in Bloomington, MN, a Minneapolis suburb. Developed jointly by Indianapolis-based Melvin Simon & Associates, and the Ghermezian family's Triple Five Corp. of Edmonton, Canada, it was financed with a $625 million permanent loan replacing a construction loan from a consortium of

Japanese banks. It opened, after seven years of planning and negotiations, on August 11, 1992. The lender also has a 55% equity stake in the project.

Entertainment plays a big part in attracting visitors to the mall; in fact, a significant amount of Mall of America is devoted to entertainment in the form of the mall's centerpiece, a 7-acre landscaped indoor Knott's Camp Snoopy, with 400 trees, a 70-foot waterfall and 16 rides including a roller coaster and log flume, a proposed aquarium, and a LEGO Imagination Center. The mall is a combination retail facility and tourist attraction, offering dozens of restaurants, 14 theatres, eight clubs, and other miscellaneous uses.

Conceptualizing, developing, and financing a megamall such as Mall of America was a bold undertaking that will not work in every environment. Among the criteria for success are the following:

- *Family entertainment* is necessary to attract visitors from long distances. Industry research has shown that entertainment in conjunction with traditional retail uses can increase mall attendance by as much as five times, as well as increase the length of a shopper's stay.[5] Furthermore, rides and games attract customers without making a huge dent in their shopping budgets. At West Edmonton Mall in Canada, visitors routinely stay for several days at a time, drawn to attractions such as the world's largest indoor lake and more submarines (4) than the Royal Canadian Navy. West Edmonton Mall attracts about 23 million visitors each year, reportedly twice as many as visit Disneyland. Houston's 4-million-square-foot Galleria complex boasts both an ice skating rink and movie theatres; many of the shoppers first come to Houston because of the Texas Medical Center, one of the largest medical facilities in the world.

  Forest Fair Mall in Cincinnati is another good example. Shortly after its March 1989 opening, developer L.J. Hooker filed for bankruptcy protection, taking with it three major tenants, Bonwit Teller, Sakowitz, and B. Altman. By the fall of 1990, occupancy had declined from an initial 75% to 47%. Now, despite being situated only five miles from two other regional malls, occupancy is at an all-time high of 78%, largely due to a $5 million expansion in 1993 that added six rides (including a full-size carousel), a miniature golf course, and an enclosed play area for children. Entertainment uses, including a two-story strip of seven bars and restaurants, occupy as much space as three floors of an anchor department store.

- *Convenient access* is a must, especially to attract visitors from abroad. Northwest Airlines offers a four-day air and land package from London to Mall of America, including coupons for mall purchases. In contrast, Edmonton, home of West Edmonton Mall, has a population of only 600,000 and is located 350 miles north of the Montana border. Mall of America is located on a key interstate freeway only 1.5 miles from Minneapolis/ St. Paul International Airport, and 10 miles from Minneapolis. The city of Bloomington financed $101 million in infrastructure improvements, including acquisition of the site formerly improved with Metropolitan Stadium and an adjacent 33-acre parcel to be used for expansion, roadways, utilities, and the two parking structures, the largest parking facility in the United States. Similarly, Houston's Galleria attracts shoppers from nearby Mexico. To be successful, a mega-mall must have a domestic trade area of at least 100 miles. At Mall of America, 70 percent of shoppers come from within a 150 mile radius.[6]

- *Aggressive leasing* is necessary as the megamall concept is still relatively untried. At Mall of America, the financing commitment did not contain a minimum occupancy requirement, enabling the Simon group to be selective about recruiting retailers. Nevertheless, the developers believed that at least 1 million square feet leased by opening day was critical to the project's ability to attract and sustain shoppers. Many retailers signed multiple leases for different chains because of their confidence in the Simon organization, including Minneapolis-based Musicland Group, Inc. and a 100,000-square-foot commitment from The Limited for various divisions. Many retailers opened larger stores than usual, or used the mall as a testing ground for new prototype formats.

- *Local shopper habits* must be conducive to a megamall. Prior to the opening of Mall of America, despite 17 shopping centers with more than 350,000 square feet each, Minneapolis was deemed under-retailed. Several retailing professionals doubt the viability of such a large project for example in New England, where provincial shoppers are thought to be reluctant to travel the long distances necessary to the success of the mall, although Toronto and Buffalo, NY, are sometimes mentioned as candidates for a mega-mall.

An article in *Chain Store Age Executive*, citing a study by Stillerman Jones & Co. points out[7] ". . . 2.8 people are in each car that visits the Mall of America, far exceeding the industry average of 1.9 Customers stay an average of three hours, three times the industry average, and spend $84 per visit (compared with $35 at a typical mall). Ninety percent of visitors make a purchase, and 66% of visitors make a food purchase." The same article reports that the first year's annual sales were estimated to be between $1.2 to $2.0 billion, far above both the city's original estimate of $900 million, and the developers' estimate of $650 million.

THE DYNAMICS DOMINATE RETAILING

Some retailers such as Wal-Mart have withstood the test of time, prospering in good times as well as bad. Others appear to be off to a sound start, such as new formats in Mall of America, but most, like Best Buy, are continually evolving. Retailing is a changing business, and what is currently popular now may not be in vogue several years from now. Schroder Real Estate Associates, in their Summer 1994 Commentary, provides the following summary (Table 8.4) of current retail trends.

Some retailers seem to have been able to incorporate the best of all worlds into their operations. Following three years of test marketing, Toys 'R Us plans to open Books 'R Us departments in more than half its 620 stores. Category killer Bed, Bath & Beyond began experimenting with large 20,000-square-foot stores in 1985 after fourteen years of operation. Their timing was perfect as, at the same time, department stores were cutting back on housewares in favor of apparel. Watching the bottom line, the retailer kept advertising to a minimum, and located in power centers rather than malls where occupancy costs were less. Now riding the housewares boom, sales in the company's 49 stores are expected to increase by 35% in 1994 compared to a year earlier. Bed, Bath & Beyond is planning on adding approximately 15 stores annually for the next five years, including a mamouth 82,000-square-foot store in Manhattan that will incorporate yet another recent trend, a coffee bar.

Restauranteurs, too, continue to experiment with new concepts. As the retail bakery business has become more competitive, T.J. Cinnamons, Inc., one of the first operators and franchisors of retail bakeries specializing in gourmet cinnamon rolls and related products, has begun experimenting with mini-food courts at service stations and convenience stores. Next on their agenda are modular units in less traditional and perhaps less competitive locations such as airports, train stations, stadiums, and military facilities. In a similar

TABLE 8.4

The Goods

What's Hot	What's Not
Bookstores with coffee bars	Tobacco shops
Highly targeted specialty stores	Unfocused ma and pa operators
"Career casual" apparel	Men's suits
Home fashions and furnishings	Conspicuous consumption
Flannels	Furs
Everyday low prices	Sales hype
Knowing your market	Offering everything to everybody
Ethnic-sensitive retailers	Undifferentiated mass merchants
Customer service	Buyer beware
Regular soda (with sugar)	Hard liquor
Self-service access	Locked-up display cases
Weekend delivery	8 to 5 mentality
Family fun at the mall	Shop 'til you drop
Computerized product information	Untrained sales staff
Roasted chicken	Fried chicken
"Vintage" clothing	Designer chic

Source: Commentary, Retail Trends: Consumers, Goods, and Real Estate, by M. Leanne Lachman and Deborah L. Brett, Schroder Real Estate Associates, Summer 1994, p. 19.

vein, McDonald's operates nearly 200 "satellites," offshoots that are smaller with limited menus, in hospitals, schools, and general merchandise stores like Wal-Mart. McDonald's plans to open 500 more satellites annually for the next several years.

Some Wall Street analysts are bullish on casual dining restaurants such as Buffets, an "all you can eat" chain that charges patrons according to the age of their children, forty cents per year up to age twelve. The attraction is value and an aging population for whom dining out is both routine and affordable.

Themed restaurants are one of the fastest growing segments of the $14 billon casual dining industry, and some of the most visible players in the industry are the twelve Planet Hollywood restaurants, cafes filled with movie memorabilia, including one at Mall of America. The original, in New York City, has 250 seats, and was deliberately constructed on a small site so that the line of patrons qued up behind velvet ropes would create an aura of exclusivity. With the average Planet Hollywood restaurant generating $15 million in annual sales (including about one-third from apparel) it is not surprising that up to 24 more are planned by the end of 1995, in locations as diverse as Tel Aviv and Paris.

As this is being written, the prognosis for retailers, like the real estate industry in general, is favorable. Employment is increasing as is consumer confidence, and personal saving as a percentage of disposable income is declining. California's economy appears to be bottoming. Even the weather has improved over a year ago, leading to higher sales and greater profits from less markdowns. The environment appears set for a retailing recovery, and astute retailers will benefit the most.

CONCLUSION

Expect to find more and more retailers in less traditional locations. Examples range from Tommy Hilfiger shops in department stores to a McDonald's kiosk at the base of New York's World Trade Center. Urban retailing will continue to become more pronounced.

Also expect to see more examples of entertainment in retailing. Musicland Stores Inc. is opening 50,000-square-foot Media Play stores, featuring story hours for children as well as community programs on family fitness and safety, all in an effort to keep shoppers in the store longer.

Stores are getting larger, and multilevel formats, once shunned because of the perceived reluctance of shoppers to travel between floors to buy full-priced merchandise, are becoming more common. In downtown Chicago, much of the recent absorption of space is a result of leasing-up space in the numerous vertical malls that line North Michigan Avenue. Driving the trend has been (1) a lack of street level space; (2) improved merchandising skills by retailers, especially in making the upper and lower floors more visible to shoppers from street level; and (3) landlords' desire to maximize revenue; owners can often obtain a higher rental for basement and/or second story space by linking it with a retail lease for the ground floor. The trend toward larger stores is not limited to urban areas. For example, Kmart recently announced it would close 110 of its 2,350 stores, nearly 5% of the chain. But because these are mostly smaller outlets, averaging 40,000 square feet compared to many of its newer models that approximate 110,000 square feet, the reduction in square footage is only 2%.

Convenience will remain important to consumers. Most of Dress Barn's 700 stores are in strip centers rather than malls "where a woman pressed for time can pull off the highway, park directly in front of the store, and be back on the road in twenty minutes."[8]

Consolidation will continue in the department store industry, particularly with the merger of Federated Department Stores Inc. and R.H. Macy & Co. Furthermore, many department stores which had largely given up the apparel business to specialty stores in the 1980s, have now introduced more moderate pricing in the 1990s as they attempt to regain market share. Sears will be adding about 4 million square feet per year to apparel for the next three years, almost equal to The Limited store division's total 4.5 million square feet of retail space.

What will happen to the traditional retail formats, the neighborhood and community centers, regional malls, and Main Street locations that have survived and prospered for so many years? A shopping center is a collection of businesses. Like any enterprise, some will survive and others will fail. The advent of power centers, (community centers greater than 250,000 square feet with three or more anchor tenants accounting for 60% to 90% of the space)[9] with their category killer anchors has taken away market share from regional malls and strip centers alike.

Following spectacular growth of warehouse clubs in the 1980s, from only 21 stores in 1983 to more than 400 in 1990, we are now witnessing the inevitable consolidation in the industry as retailers fight for market share. The value these clubs offer to consumers, particularly in the price-conscious decade of the 1990s ensures that this format, if not each club, will continue to prosper.

Operators of regional malls have added entertainment, community facilities, and convenience to the unparalleled diversity of specialty shops they offer, often in a climate-controlled setting, in an effort to retain market share. However, they will remain dependent to a large degree on the ability of their anchors and specialty shops to attract shoppers. In many instances, the large specialty chains such as The Limited, Inc. with its Limited, Limited Express, Victoria's Secret, Lane Bryant, and Lerner stores, among others, occupy almost as much leasable area as a small department store, with significantly more drawing power.

To the extent retailers can merchandise their wares effectively, there is no reason to believe that traditional retail formats cannot survive. To prosper will require a combination of astute merchandising skills and the right format. Perhaps the most explosive growth of all will come from overseas. More than one-third of the 14,000 McDonald's restaurants are on foreign soil, and within a few years, more than half of the company's revenues are expected to be generated overseas. Wal-Mart recently acquired 120 former Woolco stores in Canada for $300 million, and formed a joint venture with CIFRA to operate Wal-Mart stores in Mexico.

Lastly, we have entered the age of electronic shopping. Although the ultimate effect this will have on traditional retailers remains to be seen, it is clearly a force to be reckoned with, especially in light of the social changes described earlier in this chapter, such as the trend towards working at home. QVC already has 48 million subscribers, and Home Shopping Network 1 and 2 collectively have 43 million subscribers.[10] As the quality of merchandise continues to improve, and interactive technology becomes more widespread, electronic shopping will continue to increase exponentially.

The combination of improved merchandising skills by retailers and new shopping formats has made the competition for shopper's dollars more intense. Structural changes in United States demographics are well documented, while changes in consumer preferences such as the shift to casual wear may or may not become permanent. New concepts are continually evolving, and unless retailers and property owners alike monitor changes in the industry, they will surely lose market share.

ENDNOTES

1. Commentary, Retail Trends: Consumers, Goods, and Real Estate, Schroder Real Estate Associates, Summer 1994, p. 6.
2. What Happens When a Large Discount Store Comes to Town, *Small Town*, March–April 1992, p. 21.
3. When Wal-Mart Comes to Town, *Inc. Magazine*, July 1993, p. 77.
4. Wal-Mart Versus Main Street, *American Demographics*, June 1990, pp. 58–59.
5. Mall of America: Confounding the Skeptics, *Urban Land*, April 1993, p. 82.
6. Mega-Mall Shows Promise, Exceeding Its Projections, *Shopping Centers Today*, Volume 14, Issue 8, p. 3.
7. Time for a Megamall Update, *Chain Store Age Executive*, March 1993, p. 43.
8. Recovery in Store, *Barron's*, August 1, 1994, p. 19.
9. The Dictionary of Real Estate Appraisal, 3rd ed., *Appraisal Institute*, 1993, p. 272.
10. Slicing It Thin, *The Wall Street Journal*, September 9, 1994, p. R8.

Nine

Planning, Designing, and Renovating Retail Properties

Lance K. Josal and Joseph J. Scalabrin

M any in the industry—developers, lenders, property managers, and retailers among them—think of architecture and design as a scanty aesthetic overlay instead of as a crucial component to the efficient and successful functioning of a retail project, just like tenant mix, retailing strategy, and other factors.

To the contrary, we believe that good architecture is integral to the efficient functioning of projects. Retail projects, more than any other, require consensus. Developers, lenders, anchor tenants, in-line tenants, government officials, neighborhood and environmental interest groups, architects, engineers, and a multitude of others must come together around a retail project, even though all of them have goals that may conflict in some way. All of those goals must be brought into alignment before any project can come to fruition. This consensus requirement explains why retail development has been relatively strong and steady through decades of ups and downs in the American economy, despite the field's extreme competitiveness: Most of the projects that get built are pretested; they are not speculative whims. Architecture is the physical expression of the decisions and agreements that go into creating each project. When that architecture results in a shopping experience that meets the needs of shoppers, it succeeds.

SITE SELECTION: WHAT MAKES A GOOD SITE

Retail-development projects start with site selection, and the three most important factors determining what makes a good site for retail development are traffic flow on adjacent roadways, visibility, and size.

Traffic flow—in our predominantly suburban culture, this most often means vehicular traffic—is the basis of retail-site selection. Without flow patterns that match the requirements of a given project type, from neighborhood center to regional mall, no project can succeed. But careful consideration must be given not only to the raw number of cars going by, but to three additional factors: ease of access from adjacent thoroughfares, ease of access from the local community served, and capacity within the project to handle the project's anticipated traffic levels and parking.

Many sites have excellent nearby traffic flows but lack easy access from adjacent roadways. Those developers and retailers who proceed with a project despite this fact are running a great risk. Shoppers, who are unlikely to visit a retail site frequently and who want a clearly visible path to their destination, are typically scared off by an approach sequence or circulation pattern that they perceive as illogical or daunting. A driver who can see a project, but can't figure out how to get there simply won't go. A recently built specialty center in Massachusetts, was driven into bankruptcy by access problems, despite strong traffic flows and an affluent surrounding neighborhood well suited to its high-fashion retail tenants. Not only were there no convenient drive-offs from the adjacent freeway, but the site was surrounded by a chainlink fence that seemed to make the site unapproachable. This situation, unfortunately, is not unique. There are numerous potential sites around the country with excellent nearby traffic flows, but restraints on access that can lead to problems, even failure. One of the first tasks of an architectural team, in studying a potential site, is to spot such restraints.

If shoppers who live one-half mile away from a mall find that they can only reach it by getting on a freeway, they may be less likely to visit. While the aversion to such a situation seems to be less strong than that confronting centers with poor freeway access, it is nevertheless beneficial to have easy access from secondary points as well. In general, the more access the better.

Capacity to handle the anticipated traffic levels is just as important as access. A project can have excellent access to both primary and secondary feeders, but can be, in effect, strangled, if its entry, parking, and circulation capacity are not up to the demands of the traffic the project will generate. Experience shows that, if potential shoppers see a stack of cars backed up in a project's entrance magazine, they won't visit the project. They may even avoid that area of town altogether. Circulation and parking patterns and capacity within a project are also important. Experience shows that shoppers will probably look for a more convenient place to shop, if they reach a center but find its circulation pattern convoluted due to the configuration of the site (requiring that they turn at right angles away from their destination stores in order to reach a parking space, for example) or gridlocked due to insufficient capacity. In testing the site plan for a project, the architect should make sure that such problems are avoided.

Visibility, for retailers deciding whether they can justify development of a site, is the first criterion to evaluate after traffic flows. In general, retailers want to maximize sight lines to their buildings and, in general, they would prefer 100% corner conditions for their sight lines. Such a condition is seldom available, however: The architect's job in site design is to work with a project's developer and retailers to plan the optimum visibility that the site affords. With this in mind, today's retailers aren't bashful about using graphics and signage to catch the eye of nearby motorists; they have become proficient at developing prototypical building types that themselves act as signs for their projects: IKEA, Circuit City, and Home Depot are all nationally known stores with signature building forms, materials, and signage adapted for freeway-side sites. Retail projects are sited best at the eye level of potential shoppers, which means, typically, at the grade level of the adjacent roadway. Building on top of a flattened hill seems to work for office-building projects, but if motorists find themselves looking out their windshields at a hillside instead of at the buildings and signage of a retail development, the image projected may not be enough to draw them in.

Visibility can also be affected by the landscaping of the site, and this is an example of the innate conflicts that affect most sizable retail projects, since retailers don't want their buildings and signs obscured by plantings and walls—a forest of mature oak trees, for example—while neighborhood groups and municipal officials usually want as much greenery around a project as possible, specifically so that trees, walls, and other landscaping features will block views of the project's signs and light standards from the surrounding residences. Cities without landscaping requirements in their ordinances are rare and growing rarer. Compromises have to be worked out among the parties to a development, and skillful treatment of the landscaping, to maintain optimal visibility for retailers while providing a buffer that neighbors and municipal officials can accept, is an important task for the retail architect's team. Randomized massing increases the visual impact of the landscaping and supports the illusion, as the plantings mature, that the trees and other greenery were part of the existing site conditions that were saved in project development.

The size of a potential site is the third factor that will determine its suitability for retail development. A rule of thumb applicable to most projects is that retail sites require approximately one acre per 10,000 square feet of gross leasable area, based on yet another rule of thumb: one car space is required for every 5,000 square feet of retail lease space. This rule requires somewhat more land than the standard underlying relationship of parking to leasable area, because it takes into account a number of additional factors. Customers prefer to be able to drive into spaces that are slightly angled, versus the 90-degree turn required for the tightest parking arrangements. Meeting such a customer preference requires a bit more room. Compared to office situations, where users will be familiar with the circulation and layout of a parking surface or structure, parking bays for retail projects need to be both wider and deeper, to allow for easy turning radiuses, preferred parking angles, and the other factors of ease of use that are so crucial to customer perception of a retail project. A one-acre/10,000-square-feet rule derives from these factors. There is a constraining element related to size that also affects parking, however: Spreading a center's parking out to accommodate angled parking and wide turning lanes quickly reaches a point of diminishing returns. In general, people don't want to park more than 300 feet from the entrance of their destination store. To test a site plan, architects project radiuses out 300 feet from each of the entrances, generating a diagram of the optimal parking arrangement. Because of size and configuration, not every potential site can achieve the optimal parking diagram, and this factor has to be carefully considered by the design and development team in evaluating sites.

Regulatory and Other Issues

While traffic flow, visibility, and size are the major determinants of a good site, regulatory issues can also make or break a site's suitability for development. These are changes to prior zoning or current uses, as well as utilities and regulations covering signage, site coverage, building heights, curb cuts and site access, proximity to other uses, buffers and restrictions that derive from adjacent property-line zoning classifications, and environmental matters, including wetlands restrictions.

Whether a developer is considering a virgin site, a redevelopment that involves clearing away existing buildings and even replatting an area's streets and utilities, or an adaptive reuse of an existing facility, the first regulatory issue to be investigated by the architectural and development team is prior zoning restrictions on the site and what they will permit in terms of new development. Retail development of virgin sites, with their typically relatively unrestrictive zoning, is rare. As a rule, retail follows rooftops: that is, retail development comes in after new residential neighborhoods are settled, or following changes in roadways and other patterns that have the potential to affect the density of population and traffic in a given area. But residential neighborhoods often show a love/hate relationship with retail development. Residents of a community may want a convenient place to shop, but they are often leery of the associated traffic congestion, noise, light pollution, and other problems they see lying behind that convenience.

A potential site's existing utilities must also be checked for adequacy. Rezoning and replatting an existing site—for example, to clear the houses from residential streets, with extensive future plumbing capacity, and convert them to use for a retail center—may or may not be approved for one-to-one utility-capacity exchanges by local officials, or may be permitted only after additional utility upgrades, to be paid for by the developer, are made. Such potential hidden costs of redevelopment need to be searched out by the architects in the earliest stages, and they rank with size, visibility, and traffic flows in the importance of the role they play in determining suitability for development.

Another factor is the local sign code, which may limit the total square footage and height of any or all signs on a given site, and may go so far as to specify the materials, configuration, and colors that can be used for signage. Municipal sign codes typically are not in themselves deal-breakers, since, if a city has a restrictive sign ordinance, all retailers are affected by it and no one development bears the ordinance's whole brunt. But when a developer has a choice between sites of comparable size, traffic flows, and visibility, where one permits 300-square-foot signs up to 40 feet high and another permits only 100-square-foot signs up to 10 feet high, unfortunately, the developer will usually opt for the opportunity for greater signage. In all cases, architects need to be involved in working with local officials from the earliest stages on approval of signage that meet higher levels of artistic taste, by becoming familiar with local restrictions on size, height, materials, and other matters, and gaining approval from both government officials and retail-project tenants.

Unlike local sign ordinances, local ordinances governing site coverage—the percentage of a property that can be occupied by building or parking—*can* be deal-breakers. Site coverage ordinances are really zoning under another name, and they vary from jurisdiction to jurisdiction. Sometimes they are very specific, allowing building on a site to equal no more than 16% of the total area or permitting only 40% to be covered by parking, for example. In other cities, a less sophisticated measure may be used, in which authorities draw limits in terms of total floor-to-area ratios or total coverages allowed, without restricting the mix or relationships of building and parking within that total. Developers and architects need to have a firm grasp on such regulations when they are evaluating properties for suitability.

Similarly, developers and architects must know from the start about any ordinances or city rules restricting the number or location of curb cuts. Typically, because of concerns about traffic safety, local authorities require that access points from a normal feeder street (with 35-mile-per-hour traffic) be at least 250 feet apart. If the access is from a high-speed roadway with traffic moving up to 55-miles-per-hour, curb cuts will typically be limited to 1,000 feet on center as a minimum. Proximity to the closest intersection can also be a factor, as can be the service levels of such intersections. Or the location of a given curb cut can be determined by its equivalent at an existing property across the street, since local authorities, again for traffic-safety reasons, will want facing properties to have facing entry and exit points.

If a property is limited to a single access point from a major thoroughfare, there can be potential problems for the perceived ease of access of a project, but such problems are not necessarily insurmountable. Indeed, limited access is simply a fact of life for almost every site, something that architects and developers must deal with routinely: Access points for most available retail sites are predetermined before a single development or architectural decision is made about them. In dealing with sites limited to a single access point, architects have to do innovative things to increase ease of access to the whole site. One technique is to connect the entry to a ring-road loop that maximizes circulation around the project, so that traffic is not stacked into a shopper-scaring traffic jam adjacent to the roadway. If a ring road is used, care must be taken to eliminate any parking directly off the main access to the site. Otherwise, a single driver, by misjudging a turn and causing a traffic accident, could cut off the project's life-blood, its access to the adjacent traffic flows. With any technique used to deal with limited access, architects and developers need to keep in mind the rules derived from customer behavior related to entry and parking: People expect to be able to progress logically to their destination store, and they want to park as near it as possible. Any violation of these expectations runs the risk of turning customers off. Asking customers to make a leap of faith—"Just follow the signs and we'll get you there!"—makes them nervous, and they may react by not coming back.

Building heights are often restricted by local ordinances, but it is rare that such restrictions have any impact on retail locations, particularly in the spread-out, horizontal world of suburban retail. This is because shoppers typically don't like to climb stairs. It is unusual to find mixed-tenant retail projects in North America, outside established urban centers, that go up to three stories. In many cities, two-level centers are hard to lease, and those strip and neighborhood centers with second levels have upper floors rented predominantly to insurance agents, karate schools, and nail-care salons—tenants who don't generate much traffic and who don't pay much rent compared with the retailers on the first floor. Regional and super-regional shopping malls, however, are often built on two levels. In such centers, it is best to bank the parking so that a majority of the shoppers come in through, for example, the second level of the anchor stores and walk down to the remaining stores; shoppers, while showing an unwillingness to walk up stairs, seem to have much less objection to traveling down an escalator or stairs to look around. Until consumer behavior changes and 10-story retail centers become the norm, it is unlikely that building-height restrictions will play an important role in determining the way most retail sites can be developed.

Proximity to other uses can also have a significant impact on the suitability of a site for development. When sites are adjacent to affluent neighborhoods, residents can almost always be expected to resist the creation of a new development, creating potentially costly delays and regulatory barriers. One of the most difficult of these, which must be identified as part of the site-evaluation process, has to do with buffer requirements and other restrictions on site development due to adjacent property-line zoning classifications. Many local authorities require setbacks of 50 feet or more from the property lines of adjacent residential neighbors, a fact that can greatly increase the difficulty of making a site plan work. When a developer has already been told that a site's coverage and heights are restricted, the discovery that he can't be closer than a certain number of feet to the property lines of adjacent residences further erodes the developable area of the site, hence its profitability. In addition, when there are abutting noncomplimentary zoning classifications—usually retail centers and neighborhoods, although in some areas it also applies to churches where they adjoin neighborhoods—local zoning boards typically require the creation of a masonry wall or a landscape buffer to segregate uses, putting the burden of the separation on the commercial developer.

But not all uses in proximity to a proposed center create adverse consequences. If a retail project can serve the several thousand workers accommodated in a large suburban office complex, for example, it will gain the benefit of their foot traffic. A third type of use, in proximity to a retail center, can also provide the center with a major benefit: the "swing" use, of which the best example is a movie theater. Retail customers tend to frequent centers in late morning and late afternoon hours, while theater-goers tend to come in the evening. Having an existing theater nearby your center provides an additional draw to your location, for several extra hours of the day; this is why so many movie theaters are built as part of retail center developments, either within the center or at its periphery. As a collateral benefit, the parking spaces for retail can be used to serve the movie patrons, and vice versa, since they tend to be used at different hours.

The last of the critical regulatory issues affecting site selection is environmental considerations. These may take the form of green space requirements for a given site, including prescriptions for preservation of original trees and other vegetation, or rules for the number and placement of trees in a parking lot; here the greenery is being treated not as buffering landscape but as an end in itself. Other regulations may address the amount of impervious cover and storm drainage the project will be allowed to have, or its impact on local ground water recharge zones.

Authorities and interest groups have become both "greener" than before and more specific about a range of issues from tree types, spacings, and sizes to storm runoff impoundment designs. Those outside the development have an increasing desire to participate in determining its environmental impact, prescribing how green the site is to be, partially in reaction to the mistakes or bad-faith gestures some developers have made in the past.

Wetlands restrictions have become among the most important environmental criteria affecting potential development sites. Other environmental issues can often be resolved by amelioration or substitution, moving or replacing trees and green space to other parts of the site so that its most usable parts can be developed. But if a developer has a 20-acre site with a 3-acre wetland in the middle, federal officials have been directing that such wetland cannot be disturbed or substituted for. As a result, a number of prime locations in Northeastern and Southeastern states, where flat, damp plains abound, are undevelopable.

In other states, the presence of birds, wildlife, and insects protected under the federal Endangered Species Act can make sites undevelopable. Environmental issues are almost always contentious, pitting the goals of developers and retailers against those of local officials, neighborhood groups, and environmentalists. Only knowledgeable evaluation and careful planning and presentation on the part of the architectural and development teams, along with a willingness to engage in the consensus building that results in successful projects, will solve these and other issues where goals seem so often to be mutually exclusive.

SUCCESSFUL RETAIL ARCHITECTURE: DESIGNING TO SUPPORT THE SHOPPING EXPERIENCE

There are five major considerations with respect to basic architectural design and construction of retail properties: cost, appearance, durability, flexibility, and security. Judging how to combine these considerations in a given retail project is far from simple, and such judgment can play a major role in separating successful from unsuccessful retail operations. Development dollars are perennially scarce, so holding down first-dollar costs is always the primary factor in making decisions about design and construction. But low-cost materials may not have the appearance that a developer desires for a project. Or they may not be durable enough to handle anticipated traffic volumes. They may be so costly to maintain that tenants will be unwilling to take on the expense of common-area maintenance fees. They may be insecure. Secure architectural planning and materials may have an unpleasing appearance. Durable materials may not be flexible enough, and so on. There are endless possible combinations of benefits and problems in dealing with these five considerations. How is a developer or retailer to proceed in choosing architectural solutions for retailing properties?

Similarly, retailers must respond to the needs of their customers, and customers are nothing if not diverse. Indeed, there is a fascinating industry devoted to studying and analyzing the consumption patterns and trends shown by market segments of shoppers who differ by age, gender, ethnicity, income and educational level, marital status, attitude toward technology, and a host of other factors. How can retailers and property owners best create shopping experiences to respond to the needs of this fragmented market? And how, in doing so, can they make decisions about juggling the cost, appearance, durability, flexibility, and security of their facilities. It is preferable to start with a simple classification system, focusing on three types of customer purchasing behavior: demand shopping, comparative shopping, and impulse shopping. Each of these shopping-behavior types requires a different retailing strategy, and as part of that strategy, each type requires a different architectural response in terms of materials and construction techniques, plan form, exterior expression, interior finishes, and lighting. At the same time, since each of these shopping patterns generates a different amount of traffic, the requirements they place on potential sites for retail development will vary.

In demanding shopping, the customer has thoroughly thought through the purchase to be made at the appropriate time and the appropriate price. A consumer in demand mode goes to a destination to get what he or she wants, whether it be a quart of milk, a Montblanc fountain pen, timbers for building an outdoor deck, or a twelve-speaker home-theater system. Grocery stores, name-brand specialty stores, and "big box" or "category killer" retailers are among the stores most clearly designed to serve demand shopping.

The outward appearance and interior arrangement of Circuit City stores, just like the chain's merchandising strategy and its print and electronic advertising, are designed to support the customer's perceptions of the store's place in the market. In general, big box or category killer stores have facades that are simple and cleanly detailed, providing neutral backdrops for the stores' prominent nameplates: The buildings are billboards. Typically, tilt-wall concrete or concrete-masonry-unit walls covered with an exterior insulating stucco finish are used for the building shell. Such inexpensive construction materials allow for bold visual strokes appropriate to the freeway-side locations and wide expanses of parking lot on which these types of projects thrive (demand shopping locations typically generate a large volume of customer traffic). Circuit City is among the category killer retailers that have most successfully refined these parameters into a formula; Circuit City stores are easily identifiable, with their iconic entry tower (rotated 45 degrees to the plane of facade) and standard palette of colors. Inside the store, materials and display techniques support customer perceptions. The merchandise displays emphasize the wide variety of items for sale, as well as the functionality and price advantage that each item offers. The interior finishes of the store are inexpensive and low-maintenance (qualities the store managers have no qualms about displaying to customers, since they are attributes that support the shopping experience of the store). Instead of a dropped ceiling, for example, the store's roof structure is open and painted a dark color to decrease its visual impact. The floor is inexpensive carpeting or painted concrete. But at the same time that low-cost, easily maintained materials are used, colors, lighting, and merchandising displays establish that the store is different from a warehouse discounter.

The demand-shopping mode of Circuit City customers also affects the plan form of the centers in which the stores are located. As with other big box retailers, Circuit City stores generate very little cross-shopping between tenants in a center, so typically these retailers are stacked in centers with separate and distinct shopping fields for each retailer, and very few accommodations are made for customers to traverse the site from one store to another on foot.

The plan form needed for the comparison-shopping mode of consumer behavior are unique, as are the retailing strategy and merchandising techniques, along with the architectural response that they require. Here, center developers, retailers, and architects must support customers who are searching for the best value and price in the category of merchandise they have in mind.

Comparison shopping is, in fact, the raison d'être for the creation of the shopping mall as a building type and a social institution that has come to play a central role in American life. Shoppers before World War II typically went to a single, vertically arranged downtown department store for nonfood purchases; there they could browse in separate departments for clothing, furniture, appliances, and other items. Contemporary shopping centers, from the neighborhood center to the regional mall, are like exploded department stores, spread out, so that what had been departments in one store are themselves separate in-line stores with smaller areas and more focused merchandise lines—specifically to make comparison shopping easier. Shoppers go there for information on which to base purchasing decisions, as well as to act on those decisions. In the case of a regional mall, shoppers will probably be attracted to a given center first by the presence of an anchor store with aggressively advertised or widely identifiable lines of merchandise. Having visited that first store, the shoppers then head into the mall to engage in "cross-shopping"—to see what other comparable merchandise is available and at what prices. They may be thinking of making substitute or complementary purchases.

Cross-shopping of a kind also occurs in neighborhood centers that have a grocery store at one end and a video store anchoring the other, with a dry-cleaner, a music store, and a shoe-repair place in between; the difference is that, in such situations, the cross-shopping tends to have less to do with comparison than with convenience. On the other hand, cross-shopping seldom seems to happen with big box retailers; they are seldom included in the mix of a center that emphasizes cross-shopping in its retail experience. Developers and property need to be careful: There are certain stores that, when paired as anchors, don't seem to generate much cross traffic.

In designing retail centers for comparison shopping, architects need to pay attention to those features that make shoppers feel welcome to take as much time as they like, while making it possible for shoppers to see as much merchandise as possible, displayed in ways that enhance the merchandise's perceived value. The plan form of a center designed for comparison shopping flows from this consideration: Ease of circulation and a comfortable, safe, climate-controlled environment are the first elements. Double-loaded corridors take shoppers through in-line stores, with their large, well-lit store windows and openings that invite shoppers to inspect different types and combinations of items. Fountains, pools, and other court elements break up the plan of the pedestrian walkways, producing a scale friendlier to relaxed browsing (and pushing the customers out of the middle of the corridors toward the store fronts, closer to the merchandise). Food courts invite customers to make an evening of it, structuring shopping around a convenient place to have an informal meal, and to bring the whole family.

The product displays used for comparison shopping are a far cry from the wire and wood racks of the discounters and neutral backgrounds of the category killers: Retailers know that if you display a cotton T-shirt on a marble statue under a theatrical spotlight, you enhance the shirt's perceived value, and thus raise the price point at which consumers are likely to consider it a worthwhile purchase. Like the display techniques, the materials of a center for comparison shopping need to be upgraded from those of demand-shopping venues. While they must be tough enough to withstand large traffic volumes, and not difficult or expensive to maintain, they must also be value-enhancing. Brick and decorative stone are more commonly used for exterior elevations. Floors are typically of tile, decorative concrete, or stone, set in colored patterns that break up the scale of corridors while unifying the overall project. Ceilings are softer and more refined in treatment, allowing for the best presentation of the retailers' merchandise, commonly using drywall enclosures and grid systems. Skylights are also often used, since filtered daylight brings with it a park-like, holiday atmosphere, and it makes the merchandise look good. In some centers, clerestory windows make the light less directional and cut down on heat gain from the sunlight.

The third type of shopping behavior, impulse shopping, can happen both in centers aimed at demand shopping and in those designed to support comparison shopping, and it is integral as much to the success of grocery stores as it is to that of the largest super-regional shopping centers. Indeed, the techniques used in a typical grocery store to stimulate impulse shopping, familiar to just about everyone, are those used at all retail levels. The grocery store's circulation pattern is deliberately organized around product types, and aisles are laid out so that customers who visit the store in demand mode for a single typical purchase—milk, eggs, or beer, for example—are forced into a circuitous route that takes them past displays for a variety of products, prompting them to buy additional items beyond the demand purchase that brought them into the store. Product manufacturers who supply groceries with goods to sell pay a premium to have their products displayed in the most advantageous locations and at the most eye-catching shelf heights. It's a determined shopper who leaves the grocery store with no more than the items on his or her original list. Because so much effort is expended by retailers in stimulating impulse shopping, such behavior is often, and more accurately, referred to as "influenced shopping." In shopping malls, where purchases tend to have higher sticker prices than those at grocery stores, the influence exerted by retailers to stimulate impulse buying behavior is even more extensive.

In terms of architecture, the techniques used to influence impulse shopping are similar to those used for comparison shopping; the focus is on enhancing the value of products through display, making them look more appealing, and showing how they can work in combination with other items. As with comparison shopping, the basic planning goal is to make circulation as simple as possible while moving customers in front of as many merchandise displays of the center's tenants as possible; the standard method—unsurprisingly, since its flexibility and efficiency as a planning device are so well tested—is to place anchor stores, the major strengths of the center, at opposite ends, with in-line tenants in between and common-area attractions, such as food or entertainment courts, in central locations.

Other architectural and planning techniques for stimulating impulse shopping may be as simple as optimizing adjacencies within a given store's sales area, so that customers who come in a demand mode for a sports jacket have only to take another step to see well-lit displays of shirts, ties, belts, and pants, all on the way back to the sales counter. Or they may be as extensive as designing a complete mall signage, graphics, and lighting system that plays off unique features of the mall building's structure and plan. To stimulate impulse buying, the aesthetic emphasis goes beyond supporting an atmosphere of nonthreatening relaxation to shaping one full of sparkle and freshness that turn a trip to the mall into a family holiday.

As seen in high-fashion regional malls and festival retailers, which are likely to have the highest impulse-shopping quotient of any retail venue, the emphasis is usually on glittering light, high-quality finishes, bright and harmonious colors, and stirring changes in vertical and horizontal scale. Ceilings need to be high, with a character that goes beyond minimal construction, evoking an image of quality and value. Floors and wall treatments, as always, should be easy to maintain and durable enough to handle high-volume traffic, but should show both a pedestrian scale and a pleasingly "designed" quality, and they should look costlier than those used to support other types of shopping behavior. There should be an atmosphere that will attract and hold people with disposable income and some time to spend. Impulse shopping is shopping as entertainment, and it has become a growing part of the recreational time of families in recent years. The elements of the architecture must take on a more active and important role in the overall drama of the retail experience. Architects, developers, and retailers have begun routinely thinking of their projects in dramatic terms, creating themes and story lines that are played out in the merchandising strategies and architecture.

Fashions change over time, and these mall-level visual stimuli to impulse buying will eventually need be updated and replaced with others emphasizing different qualities that customers will respond to. In addition, in a market area saturated with brightly lit, festive malls, it may be advantageous for a developer to adopt an "anti-mall" strategy, in which some or all of the visual code of the standard mall is inverted. The beginnings of such a change can currently be seen in the merchandising strategies of retailers who focus on sales to teenagers and "Generation X" young adults, and who have brought the rough textures, muted colors, and industrial/primitive materials of the "grunge" look of recent fashion into the fixturing and display materials of their stores. Such dynamic changes, to which architects, developers, and retailers must pay careful attention, are what give retail venues their currency and excitement, qualities crucial to influencing impulse shopping. It has been said that nothing obsolesces faster than a mall interior and its store fronts and displays so architects must be alert to real changes and avoid fads.

RENOVATION AND REPOSITIONING: NEW LIFE FOR OLD RETAIL

A retail property endures wear and tear and must be maintained; every retail property is part of a competitive market place, subject to the economic and cultural changes that affect the whole retail industry. Customer expectations and preferences shift, sometimes seemingly overnight and sometimes slowly. Who would have predicted, halfway through the 1980s, that the styles of the 1970s would be considered cutting-edge among young, fashion-conscious female consumers in the mid-1990s? Or that upper-income consumers would show a willingness to shop at discount and big box stores? Retailers have had to update their merchandise to keep up with these different customer perceptions, and property owners and architects must, in a more generalized way, follow suit by updating their properties. Shopping has become an important mode of entertainment for many American families. This is good for retailers in many ways, since an entertaining atmosphere attracts people, but it also poses some new challenges, since entertainment, more than any of the other categories of things on which consumers spend money, demands constant updating. Consumers don't want to see the same movie over and over again; likewise, they want their retail environments to change, showing a new retail mix and perhaps even a new dramatic premise or story line. It is hard to predict exactly how long or short a cycle is required for updating a given store or retail center's image. Some centers can go as long as 10 years, while others need updating after as little as 5. In the architectural experience, 7 years seems to be a working average. Whatever the period, updating of retail properties is absolutely essential to hold a center's customer base.

Updating of a property's image is also required for tenant retention. To a degree, tenant success is a function of the overall property's success, and, in a retail situation involving a cluster of independent stores, the property owner owes it to the tenants not only to maintain the physical plant of the center, but to try to keep a competitive edge in attracting customers, altering the envelope in terms of architectural design. A generation or two ago, tenants often tried to cut corners on design and finishes in their stores, and property owners routinely had to write restrictive leases, insisting that tenants maintain standards comparable to those of benchmark stores in the same space or in other locations. Today, tenants are much more likely than ever before to understand that good design is good business, and they are likely to be updating their own spaces, along with their merchandise, on an even shorter schedule. Good retailers try to make each new store better than the last one. The changes may not be readily apparent—they might involve better security, better cabinetry or other fixtures, or better adjacencies within a store's layout. Knowledgeable tenants will push property owners just as hard or harder, not only to fix the roof leaks, the bent door frames, and the potholes in the parking lot, but to redo the major design elements that shape the image of the overall property, to keep up the freshness that attracts customers. A knowledgeable architect is absolutely essential to updating or repositioning a property's image, since that image is crucial to the bottom line of the retailers and property owners involved. Image updating is where design in all its subtleties comes into play.

Typically, on a budget of less than 10% of the overall value of a given property, only minor cosmetic changes can be made; such a budget usually will not cover any structural changes, any new roof penetrations, or any new mechanical equipment. Architects have observed that when the cost of renovating a project exceeds roughly 10% of a property's value, owners stop thinking of the project as a cosmetic renovation, and start planning to add skylights, new entries, and new court elements, or to reorient circulation. At that 10%-of-overall-value demarcation line, when the undertaking turns into a major renovation, most owners begin looking for ways to expand revenues from the property, either by recapturing unused or inefficiently used space within the existing footprint of the center or by adding new leasable space.

The best circumstance that calls for expansion occurs when a property is at 95% occupancy. A property owner in that happy situation is already doing much better than the national average for leasing, and should naturally think of expanding his or her capacity, as a way of capitalizing on the center's already demonstrated popularity, and of increasing revenues.

Repositioning of retail space is a major renovation, usually accompanied by expansion, aimed at bringing in a different or enlarged set of customers. It can be applied to high-fashion malls that have not succeeded, as a way of attracting tenants and customers who may be less fashion-driven and may have lower relative incomes, and thereby increasing the malls' profitability. More often, however, repositioning is undertaken for centers that are a little rundown and no longer "fashion-forward." It usually involves raising the level of the finishes, lighting, and landscaping (exterior and interior), so that new, higher income customers can be attracted and lease rates can be increased. Neighborhood and even strip centers are sometimes repositioned by resurfacing them with stone wainscoting or other upgraded materials. In larger properties, repositioning often additionally involves ending the leases of some long-term tenants: Nothing wears down the image of a center so much as writing leases for in-line tenants that run too long and that turn over too little. As much as property owners want the security of long-term leases, they are much better served, within reason, by keeping their options for change and growth open, when the opportunity arises. Otherwise they may see their customer base erode.

Depending on local market conditions and the relative strengths and weaknesses of competing retail centers, an expansion, renovation, or repositioning can be aggressive (to capture market share from a competitor) or defensive (to maintain market share). For whatever reason, the work involved in renovation, expansion, or repositioning must be planned carefully, since no retailer can afford to be shut down for the months or even the year that a major construction project can take. This makes the task of the architect and construction contractors very challenging, since they must work around the ongoing normal operations of the project in such a way as to disrupt them as little as possible. Phasing of the construction under such circumstances is both delicate and crucial. Phasing is also critically important in another way: If development of retail properties is a consensus operation, in which all the parties must reach agreement, construction on an existing property is doubly so. The tenants and all other interested parties are partners to the problems that will be encountered as well as to the rewards that will be realized; they must be made aware of what is going to happen and when, and they must be able to make necessary adjustments with plenty of warning.

Perhaps the most amazing thing, given the difficulty of construction under such circumstances, is that we have found it to produce a completely unexpected phenomenon. Not only is shopping entertainment, but, in our experience, shopping-center construction is regarded as entertainment by a significant number of mall visitors. Surveys showed that customers would actually return to see how center construction was progressing—and to do some shopping. The surveys showed that sales fell for the first month or so of construction, but that, soon thereafter, sales picked up and actually increased over the levels achieved before the start of the construction. If the architects, contractors, and property owners have done their homework and avoided creating any real inconveniences that will keep people away, our experience indicates that, far from hurting sales, the construction activity may become an attraction that brings people to the center.

CREATING RETAIL SPACES FOR CHANGING CUSTOMERS AND TENANTS

Change is constant in retailing, and it drives the strategies by which stores attract and keep customers, along with the architecture of retail spaces. But certain types of architectural change are of particular note, and promise to make up a large part of the demands for renovation work to be done in the near future. These include changes to vertical circulation, changes to facilities in increase security, changes to decrease the cost of maintenance, and the provision of features that cater to the structure of today's families.

Of these, changes in the patterns of vertical circulation are the most interesting because they trace a demographic arc of some importance to retailers. During the 1970s (to use the broad strokes that cover phenomena affecting mass-market retailing locations), American families didn't have enough surplus income to do much shopping, and so they spent less time at centers of every type than they had during the 1960s. During the 1980s, a rising number of households added a second income when the wife went to work. With more income, these families offset the problems that had kept them from spending much time in retail centers in the 1970s, but they created a new set of problems for themselves and retailers: They had too little time for shopping, so they shopped through necessity, making fewer trips to centers, visiting fewer retailers within the centers, and, again, spending less time in the centers each trip. In the 1990s, however, people have more income and somewhat more time than they had in 1980s. The new problem is that, because of the relentless pace of life today and its demands on men and women alike (but particularly on women, who have full family responsibilities in addition to their jobs, and who typically are in charge of shopping as well), shoppers now find themselves out of energy when they reach the mall. There they are faced with stairs installed during the days when stairs were a cost-effective means for getting people to cross-shop in malls, and, even when they see a store they might like to visit upstairs, they get discouraged at the prospect of having to walk up. Too often, they get in their cars and go home.

To solve this problem and induce shoppers to spend more time in their properties, center owners are installing more automated means of vertical transport—escalators or elevators. To have both is the ideal. We have found that, to function effectively for customers, these must be positioned conveniently, which means considerably closer together than was the past norm for stairs. Not only don't people want to walk up, they are getting to where they don't want to walk across.

Security a Major Concern for the Architect

Designing to support increased security has also become an important issue for property owners, retailers, and architects. Malls have become fully integrated fixtures in the social life of America; unfortunately, this means that malls also have their share of violent crime, from shootings to muggings and carjackings. Customers feel safer in brightly lit spaces. As a result, property owners are asking architects to design new lighting systems that change the look that used to be thought appropriate to almost all shopping situations. Common areas, particularly corridors, were previously given low light levels to make them contrast with the brilliantly lit storefronts, now lighting levels are being raised throughout centers. Even parking garages are being brightly and evenly lit, to eliminate the shadowy spots that make shoppers nervous. Parking-lot landscaping presents particular problems: a 50-foot light candle standard over a 20-foot-tall tree casts a deep shadow that has to be eliminated. In some extreme cases, architects are being called on to design rooftop workspaces for security personnel engaged in surveillance of surface parking areas and store entryways.

Concern over the cost of maintenance has led tenants increasingly to request a different set of changes in retail centers, particularly regional malls, where the fees for common-area maintenance that tenants pay, in some cases, become almost as high as the monthly rent. Tenants want architects to specify low-maintenance materials that can take the stress of high-volume public use. This means stone, tile, terrazzo, or even stained concrete for floors instead of vinyl flooring, and it means almost any practical substitute for drywall on vertical surfaces, which typically can't stand up to the demands placed on it. High construction costs, however, contribute to higher rents, so architects must help owners and tenants achieve an optimal balance.

Finally, changes in the makeup of families visiting retail centers are leading to the creation of new ways to provide service to customers and make them feel welcome. Information kiosks, often joined to gift-wrapping areas, are now common in medium-sized centers and up, and fold-up diaper-changing tables are now routinely found in both women's and men's restrooms. A recent innovation following from this is the creation of what is called the "family restroom." This is a single-fixture restroom that makes it possible to serve the needs of family members with small children—a father who might not feel comfortable either letting a young daughter go into a women's restroom unattended or taking her into a men's restroom, or a mother with a young son—without having to create a gender-specific restroom area. Usually these types of restrooms require a key available from a security or manager's office. Architecturally, this is a small gesture with a large impact. As such facilities become more common, other innovations will emerge that will help make retail centers more accessible to a changing public.

CONCLUSION

From the initial study of the accessibility, visibility, and size of a site being considered for retail development; to the shaping of the environments that support demand, comparative, and impulse shopping; to the incremental improvements that make construction work better and centers more accommodating to tenants and an ever-changing public; architecture and design play a central role in bringing success. In retailing, good design is good business.

Ten

Developing and Investing in Local and Community Centers and Highway Retail

Ron Sher and Merritt Sher

T here are rapid changes taking place today that impact local and community center and highway retail development in many ways. The changes range from environmental and land use regulations, to the flexibility of credit markets and the availability of financing. Consumer demands and attitudes are driving retailers to change their formats, as are changes in technology and distribution. Customers demand more every day as they seek better values, improved systems, more convenience, and more sophisticated presentation. This means that today's retail developer must understand marketing, merchandising, critical mass, circulation, synergy, and aesthetics in addition to the more traditional aspects of the development process.

210

These rapid and ongoing changes can have a profound effect on the viability of retail property. The retail property that just a few short years ago was considered a valuable asset that would only increase in value may now be a vacant property with little hope for the future. On the other hand, some properties have appreciated dramatically in the midst of all this change, thriving as they adapt to the forces that mold the evolution of retail.

Today's developer is challenged at every turn throughout the entire investment and development process. One way to better understand the complexities and hazards of the developer's journey from land acquisition to the establishment of a thriving shopping center is to relate the retail development process to the categories in a pro forma statement of development expense and operating income. These familiar tools will serve as especially useful metaphors, since they quantify all aspects of the development process and are applicable to an assortment of retail types. Simplified pro formas for a hypothetical neighborhood shopping center are included as exhibits in this chapter. As much as 95% accuracy can be achieved with such pro formas if the information they convey is supplied by a knowledgeable decision maker, with adequate due diligence.

HISTORICAL PERSPECTIVE

Starting after World War II, the downtown core was comprised of department stores, small retailers, restaurants, service businesses, and public buildings. People shopping and gathering at that time were to a large extent centered downtown. When automobile usage became so widespread after World War II, the nature of retail started to change dramatically. First to evolve were the highway commercial stores, which opened at random locations for the convenience of motorists. Later, the shopping center developed. This was an agglomeration of stores that usually included a place to purchase food.

Actually, retail merchandising and retail real estate development evolved in tandem—when one changed, so did the other. For example, as retailers moved out of the downtown core, suitable real estate became more plentiful and less expensive. People had more mobility. Stores grew. A small grocer had a 10,000-square-foot supermarket. The 10,000-square-foot supermarket then grew into a 25,000-square-foot supermarket. This 25,000-square-foot model was basically the retail standard for the 20-year period from about 1955 to 1975. It became the anchor for retail commercial development and marked the birth of the neighborhood center, which was closer to the suburban population. As these communities grew, the neighborhood center was joined by the community center; it was distinguished not only by size, but also by the range of services supplied. Principally, the arrival of this type of center meant that merchants now sold soft goods as well as services and food. The first neighborhood centers were approximately 6 to 8 acres, while community centers were approximately 20 to 30 acres. The large regional center discussed in Chapter 11 was the next to evolve.

At first, as the neighborhood and community centers grew, other elements of downtown retail moved to them, especially the small retailers, or "mom-and-pop" stores. There would be one, two, perhaps three large anchors (in those days totaling 20,000 or 25,000 square feet) in a center, while stores of 1,000 to 3,000 square feet would be plentiful. Generally, the small spaces paid considerably higher rent than did the anchors. There would be some intermediate-size tenants (5,000 to 10,000 square feet) and they would pay rents between the small stores and anchors. The profit in a project generally came from the small stores.

Changes continued in retail, and the small stores began to disappear. Over time, specialty stores grew from 2,000 to 5,000 square feet, then climbed to 10,000 or 20,000 square feet. Today, for example, the new sporting goods prototypes are 43,000 square feet. This change and growth played havoc with many small mom-and-pop stores. Even within the sporting goods category, specialty retailers have split up into stores of 5,000 feet or more that specialize in categories such as golf or bicycles. Some small, individual stores, such as fly fishing shops or climbing shops, continue to exist, but even these very specialized stores are finding it harder and harder to compete.

As the nature of the tenants continued to change, so did the shopping centers. Some of the stores that began to specialize in categories derived from the department stores started moving from downtown out to the highway commercial areas. Then in the mid-1960s came the concept of taking those category tenants, which we called promotional tenants, and aggregating them in a promotional center, a term that Terranomics (the authors' company) trademarked. The promotional tenants were the forerunner of the "category killer." They specialized in categories of 5,000 to 10,000 square feet; occasionally they were smaller, as in the case of Wallpapers to Go. The promotional center usually took these tenants, all destination retailers, and grouped them in a dynamic retail center that ranged from 20,000 to

100,000 square feet. This was one of the first centers that was not anchored by a market or drugstore of 30,000 square feet or more, and it set the tone for some of the more recent developments. As the size of those specialty retailers grew, they acquired the name category killer. The name reflected both function and form: They specialized in a category, had a complete selection at a good price, provided knowledgeable service, and were destination retailers. They also were "killer" competition for other tenants.

BIRTH OF THE POWER CENTER

With the growth in size of category killers, the power center was born. In 1984, 280 Metro in Colma, California, was developed by Terranomics, the first "power center." This was the next logical step: Assembling a collection of larger tenants on a big piece of property. The power center also came to include a limited number of smaller interest tenants, such as restaurants and yogurt shops, as a convenience for customers. The result was a center with the power and strength to draw people from a long way for destination shopping. Power centers were generally located near freeways on a high-visibility site, which encouraged people to travel long distances to shop there.

After power centers came the "big boxes," which include Price/Costco, Home Depot, and Sam's. (Big boxes are sometimes called power parks when they exist in clusters designed to make them more attractive to city dwellers.) Offshoots of the various categories also were developed. Some promotional centers focused on one product type, such as home, apparel, or recreational products. Then came the outlet center, most often located far from regionals since the tenants were usually manufacturers, and department stores did not want to compete with their manufacturers.

Originally, shopping centers were defined as neighborhood, community, and regional shopping centers, but these definitions no longer work today. Community centers and power centers are now the two dominant terms for shopping centers in the industry. There are far more community shopping centers than power centers, which have received the bulk of public attention because they are so innovative. Yet, the community center, anchored by a supermarket, drug chain, and (in some instances) a junior department store, remains a strong and viable competitor. The old regional center of less than one million square feet often has been reconfigured to become a form of community center. A power center, on the other hand, is more than 300,000 square feet, and serves a trade area of 100,000 people or more. Its principal tenants are the large promotion retailers and the big boxes.

Lifestyle centers—a concept that we believe to be one of the biggest shopping center development opportunities through the year 2005— is basically a type of center or store where consumers can purchase items that define who they are, how they live, and what they believe in. The Grove at Shrewsbury, developed by Terranomics in Shrewsbury, New Jersey, is a 145,000-square-foot lifestyle center that offers activities and merchandise that are personally relevant to shoppers. The stores there include Williams Sonoma, Victoria's Secret, the Limited, Gap Kids, Ann Taylor, and Eddie Bauer—all typical of lifestyle retailers. This constellation of retailers appeals to a strong market segment comprised of shoppers with discretionary income who are attracted to these products.

For the purpose of this chapter, everything other than community centers, power centers, outlet centers, and regional centers will be considered convenience retail, highway retail, or special situation retail. Centers need not be true to type. A good developer can mix, and often should, components of each.

WHAT MAKES A GOOD LOCATION

Because the initial investment decision is so important, consider some factors that influence it. The first might be location, but to mention location alone is simplistic: what is a great location for one type of project might not work at all for another. Location is so complex it could be the subject of an entire book.

Some of the simple fundamentals of location include visibility, access, proximity to neighborhoods, and traffic patterns: Is it on the going-home or going-to-work side of the street? What is happening in and to the neighborhood? It is important to know if a location is right for a particular project. It must be convenient to the neighborhood and accessible to the population it serves. The size, demographics, and the amount and quality of the competition are also important.

With location, there is a trade-off between convenience and regionality. It generally is better to be convenient. However, when a larger trade area is being served, the location must be reasonably convenient to the expanded trade area. Major shopping trips are encouraged when both the project and the stores are larger. Big stores do well in destination locations serving larger trade areas; whereas small stores do not unless they are well located in an integrated regional shopping experience. Stores that are frequented more often can exist in smaller trade areas, but that same location may be too small a trade area for a larger store. A good location for either type of retailer is generally in a commercial pocket. In some cases, the project itself may be large enough to create the pocket. This, for example, explains why the power center needs to locate in a larger trade area at an interstate highway site.

The process of choosing a location can begin several ways. The developer may begin with a project in mind, then look for a location; or begin with a location in mind and look for a project. To effectively maximize economic gain and create a development that will endure, the site should be matched with its best use. A small project in the heart of a community would generally be a neighborhood site. A large piece by a freeway interchange would more often be a power center, entertainment center, location for big boxes, or a combination thereof.

Retail property with the best location is generally the most valuable. This rule usually applies unless the more powerful tenants locate elsewhere. Then the property that has the strongest critical mass is the most valuable. If better retailers locate on a lesser property, the owner of the best real estate could be in trouble. You have a better chance to recover when you have the best property. There are many times when weaker retailers survive on the best property, but they prevent the best location from functioning as the best property.

Other than the requirement (in some instances) for different types of sites, the guidelines for the location of community centers, power centers, and other retail projects are similar. However, there are very few absolute rules—only guidelines.

When identifying sites for successful shopping centers, the proposed use must be considered. In addition, the following criteria are important:

1. *Appropriate Critical Mass.* Is the project big enough to draw the traffic necessary to make it successful? Size is very much a function of use. Is it big enough for its intended use (i.e., can it accommodate enough tenants to provide the consumer with a selection)? This determination is based on the subsequent site selection

criteria. Sometimes a project that is too small for the site will fail, but would have succeeded had it been larger.

2. *Traffic Circulation.* How accessible is the site? How fast is the traffic? Is it too fast? Or too slow? Is it on continuous right turn or is it a difficult left turn? Also, how easy or difficult is it to exit?

3. *Visibility.* Can the property easily be seen to allow enough time to turn in? Even if the use is a known destination, the shopper likes to be able to see where he or she is going. Does the location of the building itself have a presence and an ease about it that makes it a comfortable destination?

4. *Site Planning.* This involves circulation on the site. It must be relatively easy to park near the stores. There must be enough parking, so that customers will expect to find a space. It must be very easy to get in and out and must not be dangerous. This does not mean that all of the people must be able to park all of the time. The ratio of parking to retailers will vary.

5. *Signage.* The signage must have appropriate impact. Signs should be easily visible, and they must be of the size and graphic presentation to reflect the appropriate store image. This includes balancing the needs of tenants with the scale of the center. The signs must relate in a way that makes the store entrances and the stores appear inviting and hospitable. They must relate to the building so that the store looks large enough and the relationship with its neighbor appears appropriate. Signage that is too uniform tends to make the center look dull and boring. Pylon signs should be located to draw attention to the center and major tenants. They are not necessary unless visibility is weak.

6. *Exterior Elevations.* The major stores should have a strong individual identity, but that identity should relate in an interesting way to adjacent stores. The customer should be able to get a slightly different feeling in different parts of the center. Smaller stores that have similar markets can be grouped together with similar types of building design and signage elements. The colors and the elevations should add interest to the center. Even the smaller stores, if possible, should have interesting, individualized characteristics. The big stores should be designed to have a presence that reflects their size, and the smaller stores to look inviting but smaller. Visibility is very important to tenants, as is presence, and it is difficult to lease a large store that does not look large. Only so much presence can be provided, and it should be allocated to the greatest square footage.

7. *Tenant Mix.* Does the project have a unique authority that gives it drawing power beyond what would normally be expected on this site? A number of factors influence the draw. The strongest concentration of the best retailers that appeal to the same customers will expand it. A center with a specialty focus tends to boost the draw. The more interesting the tenant mix, the more unique the identity and the larger the draw. Mix also can serve to fill the deficiencies in nearby shopping centers. This will make all of the centers stronger and tends to create a shopping district comprised of several shopping centers. As a corollary, shoppers like to get used to driving in the same traffic patterns. If there is a good mix, they will drive it more often.

8. *Security.* Do people feel secure going to this property day and night? Lost night-time business can cause a project to fail.

9. *Environment/Site Feasibility.* You must determine whether the site can be developed. Will you be able to get the zoning approvals and building permits that you require? Is it a site that will be controversial? Was it a toxic waste dump? Will there be flood plain issues? Traffic issues also should be considered. Ask yourself if the use you have in mind is one that the community will accept. Do you intuitively think that? Here your gut feeling is very important. Time is money, and working on a project—especially if you have put hard money down—can be a mistake. Trust your intuitions and don't pursue a project that you doubt will work.

10. *Zoning and Enactments.* Zoning and enactments can take a long time and may involve a great risk, but when successful can be very profitable. The best approach is to buy the property only if successful in obtaining the desired zoning and enactments, but this strategy requires controlling the property with an option or contingencies for a long time. The process can tie up capital and organization. It is almost a separate business operation in many cases; and projects requiring re-zoning, changes in a comprehensive plan, variances and enactments should be carefully considered.

11. *Pre-Leasing.* If a project meets the criteria described in (9) and there is a very strong confidence level, a pool of equity or a lot of cash, and a very tight market, then a developer might consider going ahead without pre-leasing. But when financing is necessary, or any doubts remain, then pre-leasing is a necessity. Sixty percent pre-leasing on a project is usually sufficient, but on rare occasions an exceptional site may be purchased without a tenant.

MODERATING RISK

When considering development, you must consider risk. The more risk, the more return will be required. Also, the more risk, the more difficult it is to obtain financing. Many believe that there is a direct relationship between risk and reward in development. This relationship, in fact, often is not the case. Usually the use for a parcel and the rents a retailer can pay in a project have a maximum level, and the development risks can be mitigated with little impact on return. Control risks: zoning, environmental, leasing, construction, financing. Controlling these risks does not necessarily mean less return.

The best way to control most of these risks is to have a sufficient feasibility period, under a purchase option with extension provisions, when buying the property. Hopefully, the developer will be able to build the project as planned, while discovering environmental problems, zoning and traffic problems, and often building-permit problems, before assuming ownership. A purchase option also allows pre-leasing during the option period; this is the time to arrange financing.

Usually it is not possible to have everything perfectly arranged prior to closing. At some point, you must assess the risks and close the purchase, pay significant nonrefundable dollars, or possibly lose the property. Often a quick purchase results in a better price. This usually increases your return, but it also increases risk. If concessions are wanted from the seller, you normally have to make a reciprocal concession, and frequently that concession is to pay more for the property—often the full asking price. One tactic when negotiating the purchase of land for a new development is to offer the full asking price and negotiate on the terms and conditions. The developers who have done well are the ones who controlled their risks and built sound projects, rather than those who speculated on land.

TYPES OF DEVELOPERS

For the sake of explanation, we will distinguish between the proactive and reactive developer. (Most developers are a mix.) Usually the proactive developer operates from one of the following perspectives when looking for land:

1. *Project-Driven.* These developers want to do a project in a certain area, and thus look for a parcel of land there. In this case,

developers usually have in mind the type and size of investment and property they are looking for, and this will guide the search. For example, you may feel that there is a need for a small automotive center in a certain neighborhood, so you would look for a site of 1½ to 3½ acres. You may just be motivated by a general shortage of retail, higher than normal rents, low cost, strong demand, or a shortage of services. There would be a specific reason for identifying a certain area as the right site for a profitable project. A key player in this arena is Homart, which builds more power centers nationally than any other developer. Its ties to Sears provide this company with a built-in system for developing many projects and also keep it well capitalized.

2. *Tenant-Driven.* Here, the developer is working with a tenant. This can either be seeking a location for a tenant or even sites specified by the tenant. It may be a build-to-suit, a remodel, or a purchase. This potential site could incorporate additional tenants. In fact, the tenant may wish to anchor a center, or at least be the catalyst for one. In this case, the demographics and selection criteria would be based on the needs of the tenant. Often, the developer can create business by working with a tenant to help them penetrate areas. At times the tenant may even be a partner with the developer in these projects. We have worked on joint ventures with The Gap, Starbucks, and Millers Outpost. Kornwasser Friedman is a tenant-driven developer that works in tandem with Price Club, developing new outlets nationally for this warehouse store. The alliance enables Kornwasser Friedman to raise money for development by soliciting Price Club shareholders, thus leveraging off of a publicly traded company to fund major projects nationally.

3. *Land-Driven.* This is the perspective of the developer who may own, control, or be fascinated by a piece of land that is sitting fallow and who wants to determine how to make it productive. How often have we seen the sign, "Will Build to Suit"? Possibly the developer knows something advantageous about the land or has a relationship with the owner, a neighbor, or government officials. Or the site can have a special characteristic like a view or water setting. Alexander Haagen, for example, is a land-driven developer in Southern California skilled at identifying and transforming intriguing pieces of land into interesting power and community centers. This developer has a keen sense of what interests retailers and can put together projects with unique characteristics determined by a specific marketplace. An example of this is the old Sears building on Geary Street in San

Francisco, which was transformed into a promotional center offering major retailers that included Mervyns, The Good Guys, and Toys 'R Us.

Instead of being proactive and looking for land, the developer also can be reactive—as when an interesting and available piece of land or project is presented to you. Then the developer may ask such questions as, "Is this the type of ground I would want to use for the kind of project I would like to build?" or "Is it right for a tenant I know?"

A piece of property doesn't always come in a nice, neat package. In fact, if it did it probably wouldn't be there anymore—at least not if it is in the path of development or obvious fill-in. Usually there are problems, such as zoning, access, easement, environmental, and ownership. It may be too small, not have enough frontage, or the configuration may be wrong. It may have environmental or title issues. However, overcoming these problems also creates opportunities, especially if you see a solution that is obvious to no one else. Controlling a piece of property gives you a comparative advantage. It may be necessary to assemble two- or three-piece parcels. Is one parcel key to the assemblage? Can you tie up that property long enough to acquire the other two or three? Possibly a building can be torn down. A tenant's lease may be expiring. Can you relocate a tenant to help recapture a building and create an assemblage? Could you arrange joint-use parking with an adjacent parcel? Sometimes there are special costs attached to land acquisition, including buying out existing tenants, demolishing existing buildings, or being in a situation where the buyer rather than the seller pays the commission. Despite such costs and the many questions that always should be asked, when you spot the opportunity you must do what is necessary to capitalize on it. Remember that parcels rarely come in nice neat packages, and problems can create opportunities.

In-Fill Development

Certainly one example of this is in-fill development, that is, filling in after the obvious sites are done and development has been substantially completed. In-fill development presents interesting possibilities and often results in some of the best projects. However, it usually requires more creativity. Generally such a property has unusual circumstances and often is in its second or third incarnation. This often leads to special problems, including environmental issues, demolition, lease encumbrances, municipal covenants, and multiple ownerships. But in-fill properties, if chosen wisely, are less likely to be subject to variations in the economy or future over-supply of retail, which in the long term can be harmful to retail's strength and value. We, particularly in our lending company, prefer in-fill or urban locations—projects in dense areas without more competitive sites available for retail. Projects in the path of development often are more of a commodity. There is plenty of land available and only so much rent a retail site can command. Thus margins will be tighter, and you are faced with competition from others possibly doing a similar project.

Are Pads a Sound Idea?

Another item to consider with local, community, and highway retail development is whether or not to sell pads. Pads are small outparcels, not part of the major tract, which are usually located at curbside and which may be sold or leased. Selling off pads is often short-sighted and can be detrimental for many reasons, including a loss of control. Future purchasers will want to control the entire property, and this will affect the price. If you lose control of what happens on the pad, this can devalue the entire center. The amount of square footage on the pad is usually only a small fraction of that of the center, but it can block visibility and make the land less efficient for parking. While the sale of pads may provide more equity, in terms of the overall project, it is usually very expensive equity in the long term. A poorly developed pad in front of a center can negatively affect the image of the entire property behind it.

Free-Standing Retail

Developing a free-standing retail building for a single user on a highway may appear simple, and there is no doubt that it is less complicated than developing a shopping center. However, many of the same issues arise, including a decision on the location, determining the feasibility, controlling the property, and determining who the tenant is before construction begins and preferably before the property is purchased. Permitting has become a major problem for developers. Certainly one of the most important considerations is to pre-lease such a building. To speculatively build a free-standing building rarely makes sense. Financing would be impossible, and the building might not be exactly right for the tenant that does come along. There may be no cash flow for a significant time, and the use of borrowed money means a negative cash flow.

When constructing a free-standing retail building it is extremely important to consider the tenants' credit. Credit becomes less important as the tenants proportion of the project decreases. The terms of the lease also are important, and the tenant should not have kick-outs. In the greatest extreme, leases should be true triple net, with all operating costs and taxes the responsibility of the tenant. Even if the tenant is strong, but particularly if they are not, it is important that the building generally be useable for another tenant. It is hard to lease a White Castle, a Shari's, or an IHOP to just anybody. When determining if a building with rent substantially above market rent is a profitable investment, always discount the over-market rent due to the cost of any specialized tenant improvements paid by the landlord.

The dollars-per-square-foot cost of a free-standing retail building can sustain the market value of the building. There is a limit to what price per square foot a certain project or market can sustain. So, when determining the value of a property rent should be discounted significantly, which is achieved by landlord concessions such as high tenant improvement allowances or free rent. However, because there is an income stream, rent should not be discounted completely. Tenant inducements increase the cost per square foot of a project, and lenders and investors are more comfortable with a lower cost per square foot.

SITE COSTS

We usually break site costs down into on-site and off-site. Off-site costs are those expenditures required of the developer by the city. The developer may have to widen an overpass because traffic counts are too high, or perhaps contribute to the cost of traffic signals. Significant storm drainage fees may be required, or the widening of a street. There are a myriad of things that could happen here. The city may have extensive improvement plans that include requiring the developer to pick up a share of a local improvement district. (This expense occasionally can be passed on to the tenant—but not always.)

On-site construction costs also must be factored into the retail real estate development equation, for example, bringing in or exporting dirt, retaining walls, environmental cleanup, demolition of existing buildings, and provision for or relocation of utilities. The developer must ascertain all of the many on-site variables that can drive up the cost of getting the land into buildable shape. Some cities have large landscaping provisions and parking requirements. All of these factors will effectively cut down land productivity and force up your land price on a per square foot basis.

On-site costs also involve parking lot construction. How fancy do you want to make the parking lot? We believe in cutting some costs, but not too many, for example, double striping is more expensive than single striping but it helps to keep people in the middle of parking spaces, making the parking lot function better. Scrimping on lighting is false economy. Sufficient lighting enhances the appearance, increases the desire to shop, and will discourage crime. If you want to build projects that will sell at low capitalization rates to institutional buyers (discussed later), you must also have excellent landscaping. Other kinds of projects require lower on-site costs; much depends on the neighborhood, tenants, and your personal goals.

BUILDING COST FACTORS IN
DEVELOPMENT PLANNING

After determining general site costs, which cannot entirely be done without a plan, you next need to conceptualize your shopping center. (These steps don't necessarily come in this order, but tend to evolve simultaneously.) When planning a shopping center, it is important to know what you want—rather than relying solely on consultants. Many projects where developers assumed that consultants, including architects, were knowledgeable and relied on them resulted in serious mistakes. The developer should check the work of consultants and consider their input but remain the ultimate decision maker. Site planning is an extremely important part of the development process. Not only is it necessary to lay out the center to maximize the gross leaseable area, but the space must be leaseable. This means that the stores must have visibility, access, sufficient parking, and reasonable dimensions. Also, circulation in the center must be viable, with easy ingress and egress. We do countless sketches, changes, and fine-tuning before we end up with our ultimate site plan.

Once the plan is in place, you need to determine what to build. However, it is important to gauge the cost and quality of the building to your needs and the project needs. Building very inexpensive buildings is, we believe, nearly always false economy. Essentially, most shopping center buildings are boxes with different kinds of facades.

The incremental cost of making a project look attractive is very little compared to the advantages gained by positioning it well in the market—to say nothing of one's responsibility to the neighborhood. The pay off is two-fold: signed leases and a positive reputation in the community. Often developers will overbuild. This is when money is spent that will affect neither the income nor the long-term success.

It is possible to divide building costs into three categories: Base Shell, Vanilla Shell Improvements (VSI), and Tenant Improvements (TI). The shell is basically the box with a facade. For one redevelopment project in Bellevue, Washington, the first part of our redevelopment involved constructing a new building on the prime corner. We felt this was so important to the image and momentum of the project that we built a shell and facade far beyond the demands of the tenants.

Vanilla Shell Improvements (VSI) involve taking the store from a base shell to a vanilla box—an industry term that means a store with walls ready to be painted, a concrete floor, a drop ceiling with lights, electrical outlets, HVAC, and restrooms. The amount allocated for this varies somewhat according to the store size, but runs approximately $10 per square foot.

A Tenant Improvement (TI) allowance is given to a tenant for work they intend to do on the store. This can be from $2 per square foot for flooring or a partition wall and painting, to more than $75 per square foot for an important image tenant with strong credit that will be a strong draw for the center. The amount of the TI will vary greatly with the type and size of the project, the store, and the landlord negotiating leverage. The line where the VSI ends and the TI begins is often blurred during budgeting. If the developer does the construction and goes beyond the vanilla shell, then TI has shifted to VSI. On the other hand, if the tenant takes the building in base shell condition the VSI has become TI. Actually, the sum of the two is the most important number.

Landlord improvements and rent are clearly a trade-off. Tenants usually want the landlord to finance their store improvements and are willing to pay interest and amortization in the form of higher rent. If lenders treat the rent as over-market then most of the additional tenant subsidy will be in the form of additional developer equity. We always budget some TI money. This is "mad money," enabling us to entice the right tenants into the project. Unless you make some money available, you cannot be a major player and bid for the key tenants that will create the nucleus for a dynamic shopping center.

SOFT COSTS

Another category listed on our pro forma is that of soft costs. This is actually a catch-all for items not included elsewhere. It includes leasing commissions—which could be the subject of another book. As developers also involved in the brokerage business, we value brokers and pay commissions gladly. Good brokers work hard and deserve to be well-compensated. Maintaining a good relationship with the broker and promptly paying fair, but not excessively high, commissions is recommended. In the long run, this will help position the developer favorably in the market. Soft costs also include loan fees and legal fees, which tend to be underbudgeted in pro formas. Other soft costs include architectural and engineering fees and the development fee, which constitute development overhead. We tend to budget development fees as more than our time, assuming development fees must cover office overhead. Permit fees vary greatly from jurisdiction to jurisdiction. We also include marketing as a soft cost. Sometimes it is included with commissions if it is the responsibility of your agent. Ideally, all soft costs should be identified and included, no matter how small. Ordinarily, construction interest and lease-up, which we describe below, also are included in soft costs.

Construction/Development Interest

A very important part of the retail real estate pro forma, and probably the most difficult to pinpoint, is the construction interest. This can be divided into (1) the land carry and cost of money during the construction period and (2) the time during which the center is not earning sufficient income to cover debt service. In terms of the first, purchase of a property that doesn't generate income means that interest on the acquisition price must be carried. Mainly this is during the planning and entitlement stage, but could be longer. Certainly it is preferable to plan and obtain permits prior to closing, but that is the exception rather than the rule. There also is the period when the center is under construction, where construction expenditures generate a substantial amount of interest. Construction interest is a significant charge, which illustrates the importance of minimizing the time from purchase of the ground to completion of the store.

The second part of construction interest occurs during the time that the center is not earning full income. Most projects take 3 to 12 months to fully lease after construction is completed. Even if this leasing is completed right away, time usually must be allowed for the tenant to perform tenant improvement work, stock the store, and train employees. Sometimes there is a period where the tenant must be given free rent. It is important to identify an interest number that reflects the income shortfall during the lease-up period.

This entire area is one of the most difficult to estimate, and often in real cost it is the greatest problem to the developer. Interest cost is real. Working quickly to control interest is very important to success, because time costs money. We recommend breaking contingency down by category. As you hone in on your pro forma you also can hone in on and reduce your contingency. Hopefully, it will be realistic in terms of total project costs.

INCOME AND EXPENSES

Another important part of the pro forma is the income and expenses breakdown. The income statement for determining the value of property has changed greatly. Now when determining income value, buyers are including re-leasing commissions and tenant improvement allowances as expenses. Deferred maintenance is a bigger issue when inflation and the ability to refinance capital improvement cost do not exist. Design has become more important, resulting in the need to remodel centers more often. How predictable is the upside? With rents in many places only equal to and often less than those of ten years ago, it is very hard to predict appreciation. Hence yields have increased. Greater equity is required than before—often 40% or more. Capitalization rates on market drug centers and freestanding buildings have ranged on first-year rents from 7% to 12% return. The yields on less stable properties have increased in the last five years more than with other types of properties, principally due to the lack of institutional buyers and lenders. More properties than ever before have become obsolete. Essentially, it is the stability and predictability of the income stream that has had the principal effect on value.

Income primarily consists of minimum rent. Percentage rent is not much of a factor for the pro forma, because with few exceptions it is difficult to project. It can affect the cap-rate, however, and is important with a property that has a history of percentage rent. Historic percentage rent will be counted, but may be discounted when a property is sold. Other miscellaneous income comes from sources such as fireworks stands, telephones, rides, and billboards.

When discussing income, it is important to understand the development of retail as it also affects pricing and rental structure: The sector of retail industry that is growing most rapidly and appears to be the most profitable can pay the most for land or rent. But the developer also must look at competition. A shortage of large retail space occurred in the mid-1990s. The obsolete 25,000-square-foot supermarkets, which were supplanted by the 35,000- and 50,000-square-foot supermarkets, have been absorbed. There is more than sufficient small retail space, because there is not much demand. But there is great demand for large space. Thus it appears that when developing a center today, the rents you can get for large spaces are often as high as they would be for small ones. Another source of income is reimbursement by tenants for expenses such as property taxes, insurance, the cost of maintaining the shopping center common area and buildings, and security. Leases should be structured so that nearly all of the costs of operating the shopping center are reimbursed. Management fees are not usually reimbursed by the tenants of strip centers.

The expense portion of the income statement includes the costs of maintaining the common area and buildings, insurance, property tax, and management fees. These fees can be paid to an outside management company or be used to cover the developer's cost of managing the center. Partnership expenses are another consideration and are not reimbursed by tenants. Other expenses attached to a property are levies from local improvement districts, off-site parking, and leases. For pro forma purposes, expenses are deleted. The assumption is made that the tenant leases require the tenant to reimburse the landlord expenses, so that they don't affect the income statement. However, in most long-term cash projections, it is customary to report all expenses on a line-item basis as well as the line items for reimbursement of expenses.

Vacancy must be considered and shown as an expense. It is unrealistic to assume 100% occupancy. There will be tenant turnover. Even if the spaces don't stay vacant long, there is lost rent during lease-up time, and the construction period to be calculated, along with a possible rent-free period.

Re-leasing costs must also be included. They are particularly important when considering an existing rather than a new project. Re-leasing usually requires remodeling the space, providing tenant improvements, the cost of commissions, and possibly marketing—all costs that frequently are ignored or underestimated on the expense side of the pro forma. Another cost that has been ignored over the years, but is especially important to include when buying a project, is the amount of money required to keep that property in the vanguard and positioned well ahead of the competition. Too many people think that once you build a shopping center you don't need to go beyond merely maintaining it. It is essential to keep a shopping center contemporary and competitive, and the cost of doing so must be included.

IMPORTANT PRO FORMA FORMULAS: RETURN ON INVESTMENT TO RETURN ON EQUITY

These formulas are shown in Figure 10.3, and are applied to our hypothetical example. The presentation here is simplistic, but works very well. A sophisticated analysis might involve a 10-year projection of net operating income (NOI), discounted according to the cost of capital and any risk factors. While this type of analysis is good, it is not imperative. After calculating income and expenses, the NOI can be determined by subtracting nonreimbursed expenses from income.

Dividing NOI by total project costs will yield return on investment (ROI)—an extremely important number for the retail real estate developer. We want it to be higher than our interest constant so as to avoid negative leverage (despite amortization). We know it must be higher when interest rates are higher, higher for risky projects, and for projects that will not be of institutional quality.

In analysis of the project's potential profit, you divide NOI by a capitalization rate to determine market value. Once the market value is determined, selling costs must be subtracted to yield a number representing net market value. Net market value minus the costs of the project result in projected pre-tax profits. The capitalization rate is perhaps best described as the rate of return the project would yield if sold on the open market. A project is considered investment grade if it meets the following criteria: low vacancy, strong credit, excellent location, good neighborhood, well-maintained and nice looking, high sales per square foot, and little competition. It usually is the type of property that a conservative institution will purchase. The value of the property will be higher if it is attractive to that type of purchaser. This means that they would buy it to yield less, thus at a lower capitalization rate. To develop such a property requires a smaller ROI, as it sells at a higher price. Conversely, if a property is in a lower income area, is leased to noncredit tenants, and is in an area of oversupply with high vacancy rates, it will need to sell to yield a higher return on investment (at a higher capitalization rate).

To analyze the profitability of a project, a developer must consider the end result. A lower sale price means the development's profit expectations at the outset must be much higher. This is important to remember, for in the development "equation" one eventually compares the net market value to the initial cost in order to determine profit. When determining how to develop, you need not consider whether you are going to sell the project, but you should ask yourself these important questions: "Would it be saleable if we need to sell, and to whom and for how much? We build and lease to the same standard, whether it is our intent to sell or keep the property.

When we undertake a project we always ask ourselves if this will be something that an institutional investor would want to own. If we don't feel that a properly developed and leased property will have the quality to be valued at a lower than market cap rate (i.e., higher price), we pass on that project—unless the profit potential seems outstanding or there is another special reason. With development, something unexpected always surfaces—and usually it is negative.

When beginning a project, the developer has a tendency to think that everything is going to go well and be positive, but always consider risk, downside, and what will happen if things don't go as expected. The rate of return on investment also must be considered. What rate of return will be necessary? The return depends on a lot of factors, including the capitalization rate at which the project should be or may be valued. It involves the cost of capital, which is generally a reflection of current capital markets. Clearly, the rate of return has to be above the cost of capital so that positive leverage exists. How much positive leverage is necessary? Again, it all depends on where interest rate levels are historically: If they are higher, less positive leverage is necessary since expectations of an increase in rates would be less than for a decrease. Another consideration is the relationship of equity to debt. More equity means less positive leverage is necessary—even negative leverage is possible at some point, because the equity portion has a greater effect and returns required on equity are not as interest-rate sensitive. Much depends on your opportunity cost of capital (the higher it is, the higher the return you need). It may also be affected by how long you intend to hold the property, or how soon you need your capital. Sometimes, too, there are noneconomic considerations.

Projects rarely are built for all equity; even if this does occur, there is usually an intent to finance later. There are two measures to determine how much of the project costs can be financed. One is based on debt service coverage, and the other is based on loan to value. One must compare the calculated amount of financing based on debt service coverage with that based on loan-to-value ratio, and then take the lesser amount of the two. Lenders usually will require a certain debt service coverage ratio, which depends on a number of factors including the project, lender, developer, and whether the loan is recourse or nonrecourse. The ratio required generally is in the range of 1.25 to 1. To determine the amount available for debt service, divide NOI by the debt service coverage ratio, a rate that takes into consideration the amortization period and interest rate. To compute the loan amount available, divide the amount available for debt service by the debt service constant. For example, if there is a 10% interest rate and 20-year amortization, the amortization constant would be the amount of money necessary to amortize the loan at 9% over 20 years. In this case, it is 10.80% per annum, paid monthly. The other way to arrive at the value of the loan is to take the project value and multiply this by the maximum percentage loan to value permitted, generally from 60% to 75%.

The final steps in the pro forma analysis are to determine the equity needed in the project by subtracting the amount of the loan available from the cost of the project and to identify return on equity by dividing the cash flow after debt service by the equity required; the latter also is called the cash on cash return.

Today, it is more important than ever to assess the long-term value of retail real estate. It is not merely a question of cap-rates, but a question of identifying the underlying characteristics that determine long-term stability and future increases in value. Traditionally, institutional investors have been most interested in purchasing regional centers. However, many of these centers once thought to be invulnerable have become financial disasters. As a result, there is more demand for supermarket drugstore centers and freestanding, net leased property. The stronger the tenant, the lower the yield. Markets have changed and residual values have disappeared. Even some of the seemingly strongest retailers have gone through reorganization, allowing them to terminate leases.

THE PRO FORMA IN DEVELOPMENT PLANNING

The pro forma is designed to determine the feasibility of a development. Each development is very different, and the pro forma in a sense is a synopsis of the development. It details how development is expected to go—with a contingency, of course. Throughout the process, developers need to do their best to achieve or exceed the pro forma. This goal is never without problems; developers are in the business of problem solving.

A typical pro forma for a simple neighborhood shopping center is shown in Figures 10.1 and 10.2.

The line items in both exhibits are the important factor, rather than the costs, for these line items and their subcategories are the main aspects of the project for discussion. Assume that the land is already zoned retail commercial. One street is a main arterial, and the other feeds directly into the neighborhood. Figure 10.4 is a site plan of the shopping center. The 36,800-square-foot building is pre-leased to a strong grocery chain. A 4,000-square-foot restaurant is committed for the corner building. A building is also planned to have a 6,400-square-foot video store and 7,100 square feet of small stores perpendicular to the market. There is also a lease to a 12,000-square-foot drugstore, and 6,700 feet of additional small stores between the market and the drugstore. Prospective tenants for the stores include a dry cleaners, mail box store, hair salon, and a beauty supply store. The project has a good mix; not too many shops in relation to the major, but enough for it to work. We have provided the parking field required by the market and ample parking for all the stores. The restaurant is placed so that the view of the in-line store is not blocked too much. The land price of $2,704,000 reflects a good useable site without unusual problems or the requirement of excessive on- or off-site work.

The site costs reflect a slightly uneven site that requires some leveling work, so there is money in the on-site category for exporting dirt and building a retaining wall. The other on-site costs at $2.50 per square foot on the land not occupied by buildings covers the cost of the paving, landscaping, all the standard utilities, lighting, and so on. Off-site costs include one-quarter of the cost of a traffic signal and a storm water contribution to the city. Normally storm water shows up as a cost for retention on-site or as a contribution off-site.

The deal with the supermarket in this example is for them to build their building, with an allowance from the developer. The same applies to the restaurant. This is usually disbursed as monthly draws through our loan, but sometimes it is a reimbursement to the tenant upon opening for business. In this case, for simplicity the market and restaurant will front their costs. The video building, which also has space for other uses, is estimated at $42 per square foot to complete.

FIGURE 10.1

Development Pro Forma

	Sq. Ft.	$PSF	Total
LAND:	6.21 acres	10.00	$2,704,000
SITE COSTS			
On Site			
Grading & Site Preparations			80,000
Retaining Wall			20,000
Parking Lot Lighting &			
Landscaping			
2.50/sf			494,000
Off Site			
Stop Light Contribution			35,000
Storm Water			100,000
CONSTRUCTION			
Allowance for Market	36,000	$40	1,472,000
Allowance for Restaurant	4,000	45	180,000
Video/Stores	13,500		
Shell		42	67,000
Tenant Improvements		10	135,000
Drug/Stores	18,700		
Shell		38	710,600
Tenant Improvements		10	187,000
Pylon Sign			20,000
TENANT IMPROVEMENT			
ALLOWANCE	32,200	5	161,000
CONSTRUCTION CONTINGENCY			
5% Not Inc. Market & Rest.			
Construc. Allowance			125,000
SOFT COSTS			
Leasing Commissions	73,000	3.5	256,000
Loan Fees		1.25%	78,000
Legal & Consultants			80,000
A&E			120,000
Permits			35,000
Marketing			5,000
Development Fees			180,000
TOTAL EXPENSES			$7,745,000
INTEREST			
Construction Interest (Land Amounts @ 10%)			125,000
Negative Cash Flow to Break-Even Leaseup			125,000
TOTAL PROJECT COSTS			$7,995,000

FIGURE 10.2
Pro Forma Income Statement

Tenant	Sq. Ft.	$PSF	Total Rent
Market	36,800	11.00	$ 404,800
Restaurant	4,000	24.00	96,000
Video	6,400	19.00	121,600
Stores/Video Bldg	7,100	16.50	117,150
Drugstore	12,000	14.00	168,000
Stores/Drug Bldg	6,700	16.50	110,550
TOTALS	73,000		$1,018,100

Other Income—	
Telephone, Xmas Trees, Fireworks	$1,500
Less:	
Management Fee 4%	(40,700)
Vacancy (5% excluding Market)	(30,700)
Reserve for structural, releasing and	
Tenant Improvements	
(5% excluding Market)	(30,700)
	($ 102,100)
Net Operating Income	$ 917,500

We presume that all common area costs are reimbursed, as well as taxes and insurance, and that there are no owner payments not reimbursed to the landlord as local improvement districts. Although most leases will have percentage rental provisions, on a project of this type they probably should not be included when determining the feasibility of a project.

It's more expensive than the other building because it is smaller and shallower, with more demising walls. The other 18,700 square feet is estimated at $38 per square foot for base shell. To these estimates is added $10 per square foot for completing the building through a plain, or vanilla, shell.

Tenant Improvement (TI) allowances should be in the budget. Budgeting for them allows much more flexibility when dealing with tenants. When you budget this expense you also can expect, on the income side, to get more rent. The $5 per square foot TI will probably allow you to average 75 cents per square foot more in rent for those tenants receiving them, but the main thing is to be able to use it to make deals.

FIGURE 10.3

Pro Forma Formulas

$$\frac{\text{N.O.I. (Net Operating Income)}}{\text{Total Project Costs}} = \text{Return on Investment} \quad \frac{917{,}500}{7{,}995{,}000} = 11.48\%$$

$$\frac{\text{Net Operating Income}}{\text{Capitalization Rate}} = \text{Sales Price} \quad \frac{917{,}500}{0.095} = \$9{,}657{,}895$$

$$\text{Sales Price less Sales Cost @ 4\%} = \text{Net Sales Price} \quad 9{,}657{,}895 - 386{,}000 = \$9{,}271{,}895$$

$$\text{Net Sales Price less Project Cost} = \text{Before Tax Profit} \quad 9{,}271{,}895 - 7{,}995{,}000 = \$1{,}276{,}895$$

$$\frac{\text{Net Operating Income}}{\text{Required Debt Service Coverage}} = \begin{array}{c}\text{\$ Available for}\\ \text{Debt Service Coverage}\end{array} \quad \frac{917{,}500}{1.25} = \$734{,}000$$

$$\frac{\text{Available for Debt Service}}{\text{Debt Service Constant*}} = \text{Amount of Loan (1)} \quad \frac{734{,}000}{0.109044} = \$6{,}731{,}228$$

$$\text{Sales Price} \times \text{Loan to Value**} = \text{Amount of Loan (2)} \quad 9{,}657{,}895 \times 65\% = \$6{,}277{,}632$$

Lower of (1) or (2)

$$\text{Project Cost Less Amount of Loan} = \text{Equity Required} \quad 7{,}995{,}000 - 6{,}277{,}632 = \$1{,}717{,}368$$

$$\text{N.O.I. less Debt Service} = \text{Cash Flow} \quad 917{,}500 - 734{,}000 = \$\ 183{,}500$$

$$\frac{\text{Cash Flow}}{\text{Equity Required}} = \begin{array}{c}\text{Return on Equity or}\\ \text{Cash on Cash}\end{array} \quad \frac{183{,}500}{1{,}717{,}368} = 10.68\%$$

*Assume 10% interest and 25-year amortization

**Assume loan to value 65%

A 5% construction contingency for items (not including the market and restaurant) has been included. This is a "safety net," and is strongly recommended. Leasing commissions have been estimated at $3.50 a foot. They will be higher on the small stores and lower for the supermarket; this is an average number. The 1.25% loan fee is an estimate based on the loan amount of $6.25 million. The other soft costs are reasonable estimates for a project of this size. Interest costs in this case are based on the following: a land-hold of eight months from the time of purchase through completion of construction with a construction loan interest rate of 10%; a six-month construction period with a 2½ month outstanding average on the other construction costs, and payment of the market and restaurant TI allowances upon their opening for business. We have also provided $125,000 to cover debt service shortfall during the lease-up period. It is presumed that $1.75 million in equity is contributed day-one, and does not accrue interest. On the income side, we assume pre-leasing of the market, the video store, drugstore, and the restaurant. After taking out management, vacancy and reserve, you are left with $917,500 in net operating income. This, divided by the cost of $7,995,000 provides a 11.48% return.

After reviewing the implications of this investment (Figure 10.3), it is evident that nearly $2 million in equity is required to accomplish this project: For those of us who are used to working with other peoples' money, the required equity is considered to be a substantial sum for a project of this size. The debt service constant at 10.9% is not much less than the return on investment of 11.48%. This means that there is almost no positive leverage, including amortization. Unless the developer has a lot of cash, this project would generally not be a good idea if the intention is to hold. Thus, it might make sense to build this project with construction financing and sell it upon completion, thereby making a profit.

The preliminary pro forma can also be used for sensitivity analysis. What would happen if more rent could be obtained? Can we get more rent? What is the risk? How much pre-leasing is necessary? Can we do a pre-sale of the project by identifying a buyer before we build? On the cost side, is a contingency necessary? How much certainty can be attached to costs? Can firm contractor bids be obtained for some work, that is, can money be taken out of the site-work estimate or any of the other cost projections? With this pro forma, a developer might pursue this project and still not know whether to go forward. This type of project has many advantages: it is attractive to lenders, and very marketable (if well located). On the down side, it requires

FIGURE 10.4

Neighborhood Shopping Center Site Plan

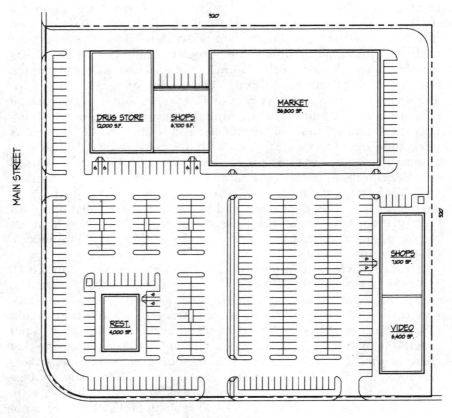

much equity and has a marginal profit. It is very typical of initial pro formas.

DEVELOPING FOR THE FUTURE

Today, it is more important than ever to assess the long-term value of retail real estate. It is not merely a question of capitalization rates, but also a question of identifying the underlying characteristics that determine long-term stability and future increase in value. Traditionally,

Carmel Mountain Plaza, San Diego, California

institutional investors have been most interested in purchasing regional centers. However, many of these centers once thought to be invulnerable have become financial disasters. As a result, there is more demand for supermarket drugstore-anchored centers and free-standing, net leased property. The stronger the tenant, the lower the yield. Markets have changed and residual values have disappeared. Even some of the seemingly strongest retailers have gone through reorganization, allowing them to terminate leases.

Retail changes so quickly. The changes have to be anticipated. The developer must interpret retailers' advertising and other signs to understand the latest merchandising concepts and how they are affecting retail real estate development. Prior development formulas aren't necessarily helpful. Retail changes quickly, and if the developer or retailer is not changing or going forward, they will be going backward, resulting in loss of value and market share. View the big picture and build projects that will not only be successful, but will, with constant attention, maintain and increase their value in the future.

Eleven

Developing and Investing in Regional and Super-Regional Malls

Martin Bucksbaum and Matthew Bucksbaum

Developing and investing in regional and super-regional malls is much like being a conductor of a major world symphonic orchestra. The parts are diverse, the players are individualistic and often temperamental, and there can never be an end to the interpretations. Yet, all the pieces have to come together to make beautiful music.

Success and profitability are the harmony that comes from the well-developed mall. There must be a submission of egos; it takes a lot of hard work, creativity, and ingenuity. Timing and coordination create the beautiful music that is reflected in a profitable regional mall. But even with the best plans and efforts, there are factors beyond the owners' or developers' control.

Over the past two decades, malls have been very profitable businesses—requiring much effort, thorough analysis, and never-ending new thinking. The 1970s and 1980s were periods of rapid development and almost assured profits. The growth of America's suburbs along with massive inflation virtually guaranteed success in most every project.

SHOPPING CENTER MATURATION PROVOKED PROBLEMS

After the tax law changes of 1986, the mall business began to hit a wall of maturity. The lending industry was forced to retreat from its freewheeling practices of 100% financing. This drastically reduced the number of developers who had the financial backing to develop regional malls. An era of over-building had occurred and it began to appear this was to be a one-generation business. New activity and new development came to a grinding halt and, by the mid-1990s had begun to progress at a very slow pace.

The surge of unlimited new capital to the mall development business was over; knowledgeable developers recognized that this period would probably never recur in their lifetimes. When liquidity returned to the marketplace, it would be from new sources and the terms and standards for both equity and debt financing would probably be changed for an indeterminate time.

Within a short period, consumers developed changing views about shopping and retailers moved quickly to adjust to meet the updated needs and desires of these new consumers. Competition became significant as the financial returns began to shrink. The mall business became a completely changed business; once dominated by the owner and developer, the customer and the retail tenant began to dictate.

The development segment of the mall industry was forced to respond to *demand* rather than to financing availability. It was no longer a "cost plus" business. New buildings had to be designed and built to accommodate prevailing rents, not arbitrarily established rents based on development costs plus guaranteed profits. The development of new retail malls came to a virtual standstill, but the *redevelopment* of regional malls continued. Renovation, modernization, and, where essential, a change in the tenant mix, became the standard for the 1990s. The acquisition of existing regional malls that had expansion of remerchandising potential thus became the new focus.

REDEVELOPMENT CAN REPRESENT A COMPLICATED INVESTMENT

Redevelopment, however, can be as complicated and time-consuming as developing a new center from scratch. The environmental concerns are just as great, and asbestos abatement or the cleanup and removal of underground storage tanks can prove to be quite costly. Acquisition of additional land can be time consuming, complicated, and very expensive. The approval process, both from governmental and environmental agencies, may be as complicated and time-consuming as a new project. Major tenant approvals may also cause delays and increase costs. If, however, the expansion of an existing regional mall will eliminate the potential of a new competing center and increase the dominance of the redeveloped project, the investment may well be worthwhile.

The redevelopment of some centers is becoming increasingly major in scope. Usually, the existing projects have enjoyed the best locations, so when possible, a redevelopment can become a highly profitable venture. When renovations or improvements are made, they usually go beyond mere cosmetic changes. Major renovations can entail making additions, double-decking a project, or even tearing down existing structures and replacing them with more modern and efficient retail space.

Inevitably, these major changes reflect substantial changes in the mix of tenants. The more aggressive retailers, who continue to look for new, larger, and more modern facilities, are often the new tenants for a redeveloped project. They easily replace the merchant who hasn't been able to keep pace with the new merchandising techniques and adjust to changing consumer demands.

Are there too many malls? There is no simple answer to this question. Certainly there is a good future for the well-designed, quality mall that is dominant in its markets. There will always be a need for a marketplace for goods and services, but as never before, there is now an added need for good management. No longer does this business consist of just receiving rental checks and making the mortgage payments.

EFFECT OF COMPETITIVE FORMATS

There has been much published about regional malls losing their market share of retail sales because of the proliferation of other types of retailing, such as television retailing, power centers, and factory outlet malls. To offset these changes, many of the country's retailers, including many department store chains, are restructuring and gearing up to meet this new competition. The retailers that were for many years handicapped by bloated cost structures, over financing, and a lack of retail focus have been restructured through a disciplined, long-term plan with new management, a streamlined structure, plus new efficient, low-cost distribution systems. Many retailers today are re-emphasizing their dependence on regional malls and are anxious for new locations. The leading merchants already have the mall locations; they've learned that they must find the merchandising to fit. Today's cost-conscious retailers are proving they can compete effectively with the power center, the factory outlets, or any new type of value retailing.

For the developer, however, the competition from the changing retail format means a tightened rental budget. There is continuing pressure for lower rentals from all users of retail space. The so-called value merchants, with their obsession for a lower cost of distribution, are insisting on substantially lower rentals than had been the norm for the industry. In many cases, developers are converting vacant department stores to multiplex theaters, large food courts, or other types of retail space. Real ingenuity is required to retain the same economic returns and, in many cases, the profit margins are reduced for the owners. The cost of converting the department store space, which is usually a big unknown, but always expensive, continues to be the huge impediment to the developer.

THE SHOPPING MALL OF THE FUTURE

Marginal shopping mall projects, those with too little land for expansion, those that have built-in obstacles for growth, or those where changing demographics or traffic patterns negate their long-term value, have and will continue to suffer. Lack of financing will seriously erode future values as new projects demand continual new and added cash investments. Lenders are willing to lend only on the strongest and best projects. Weaker projects are extremely difficult to finance at any price. Depreciation is real and no place is it more pronounced than in the operation of regional and super-regional malls. Any major project needs a continual infusion of cash for normal maintenance, major improvements, as well as tenant allowances.

Future malls will be substantially different. Research for new projects will be of prime importance in identifying the successful mix of tenants that will differ substantially from the make-up of centers of the 1970s and 1980s. It will no longer suffice for a developer to "eye ball" an area to determine if it is the right location. Future projects will not only need to be analyzed for existing conditions and demographics but will also have to project the future. New projects will have to be analyzed and planned for what is expected to happen in the next ten to twenty years.

New issues continually add to the complexity of new development. Environmental issues are certainly at the head of the list. This is an area of concern that was almost unheard of only a few years ago. Substantial concerns are usually raised concerning how the new project will affect the area, both environmentally and economically. Wetlands and storm water retention are continuing issues; the larger the market, the more development has taken place, the more environment becomes a concern. Traffic, too, is included in this area as many markets are finding their highway systems are inadequate for today's traffic flows.

The permitting process for a new regional mall can easily take from a minimum of two years to as long as ten years, and there is no guarantee that the developer's efforts will be successful. Special interest groups (which include owners of existing malls) representing diverse "no growth" interests can be expected to attack each step of a developer's permitting process. These well-organized efforts can further extend the time period and add greatly to the costs of developing a new regional mall. This can also have the same impact on expanding or attempting to up-grade or change existing centers.

NEW ANALYSIS TECHNIQUES ESSENTIAL

The economics of new development continue to change. Costs for new projects continue to escalate, not only because of continuing inflation, but because today's competitive markets require a much higher quality of construction. Older shopping centers were often built in the cheapest way possible—a box with a few cosmetics added to the entrances. Today's markets require much more attention to detail and amenities. Consumer safety requirements, the disability act requirement, and added structural standards mean higher completion costs and more equity investment dollars.

To satisfy today's new consumer, service has become the byword. The more services that can be offered to make shopping easier, more convenient, and more exciting, the more satisfied the customer. It's a competitive game; your project has to be better than the facility down the road.

INTERIOR AND EXTERIOR
DESIGN CONSIDERATIONS

Today's shopper is more sophisticated, choosing to shop in malls that offer convenience in addition to tenants who are compatible with each other. In the past, it did not matter how tenants were aligned. Today, the design and layout are very important. Merchants themselves are encouraging developers to create more excitement and interests in the malls. Bookstores and record shops should be close to each other. Fashion ready-to-wear stores should be in the same vicinity where there is activity and where stores offer complimentary merchandise that is attractive to their type of shopper. This kind of consideration and planning add to the complexities and, ultimately, to the costs of today's projects.

The mall tenants' store interiors and their storefronts were usually a cookie cutter type installation. Today, successful merchants have learned that well lit and spacious interiors make more sales and better profits. The use of pop-out storefronts has added more interest to the typical tenant store unit and creative signing has become more attractive to the customer. All of this is extremely costly. It's a continuing battle between the developer and/or owner and the tenant as to who will pay for the cost of these improvements and who will perform the work. In most cases, the owner and/or developer provides a cash allowance and the tenant does the work. This can vary significantly.

Food and entertainment continue to increase in importance. Both areas require new expertise in planning and space utilization. Food and entertainment play a big part in attracting customers to a mall and also in keeping a customer in the mall for a longer period of time. However, if not properly designed and managed, food and entertainment can weaken the quality image of a mall by attracting patrons who are not serious shoppers or who may create a poor image.

Shopping center signage takes on a greater significance in today's regional mall. In the past, department stores were insistent that there be strict limitations on pylon signs and exterior signage. With the incorporation of category killer retailers and off-price merchants, there is a need to provide adequate identification for them.

Landscaping, which was once almost totally ignored in regional centers, has now become more significant. Now, more than ever, a well-landscaped property makes it more inviting for shoppers and sends a signal that ownership is concerned about the environment and the beautification of the community.

In the early development of regional malls, department stores often dictated the overall design. As in the past, department stores drive the development of any new regional mall and still have a major say on the overall design of the development. Visibility is a key concern of any department store, and the earlier the department store commits to the project, the more choices it has to a preferred location. Today's regional mall caters to a more diverse group of retailers than in the past, which has somewhat moderated the department store's control over the design and layout of the center. The total center must function as an integrated unit and no single department store can dominate. The department store, like all of the smaller tenants, is interested in increasing the foot traffic and attracting more shoppers to the centers.

The department store is also required to shoulder a more equitable role in the owner's development costs. Developers believe that without participation by the department stores in the owner's acquisition and infrastructure costs, many regional malls simply will not be developed. The department store firms are well aware that a developer can no longer fully leverage the costs of developing a center. Unreasonable department store demands for subsidization by the developer may create too large an equity investment for the developer to assume. With fewer national and regional credit retailers available to fill up the necessary mall shops' square footage at market rates and with the need to attract larger space uses in the value merchant categories, it is very difficult for a developer to project a profitable financial pro forma for a new regional mall.

EFFECT OF RECIPROCAL EASEMENT AGREEMENTS AND OPERATING COVENANTS

Of utmost importance to the successful development of a regional mall is the commitment, called an *Operating Covenant*, by each department store to conduct its business operations for a given period of time. This is true whether the department store is a tenant or owns its own facilities. The covenant is contained in the department store's lease or reciprocal easement agreement. Without such operating covenants, the developer cannot insure the mall shop tenants that the main customer drawing powers will remain open. The owner should also be given the right to recapture the department store facilities should the department store elect either to cease operations or assign or sublet its interest to a third party after the period of its required operations. This enables the owner to protect the tenant mix to the benefit of all of the merchants in the center. Without such recapture rights, the department store could seek to lease its vast square footage to a multitude of small retailers in direct competition to top owner's mall shop tenants.

THE DYNAMICS DOMINATE REGIONAL MALL OPERATIONS

It is also very important to keep in mind that a regional mall is a constantly changing real estate investment. The concept of future changes must be anticipated and incorporated in any department store lease or reciprocal easement agreement both of which are long-term agreements that can easily extend 40 years or longer. The department store will typically attempt to restrict future changes to the initial site plan of the center, since changes which affect access, parking ratios, or site lines are legitimate concerns. However, too often department stores attempt to use site plan approval rights for the sole purpose of keeping out competition. There must be a reasonable balance between the legitimate concerns of the department stores and the owner's need to have the flexibility to make future changes that will continue to make the center the desired place to shop in the marketplace. Tensions often exist between the developer and the department stores.

The major questions and concerns that apply to the department stores' involvement in new projects are equally applicable to attempts to change, expand, or upgrade existing centers. The owner has to cope with the egos and jealousies that often exist between the major chains.

There has always been a question about the need for department stores as anchors. From a competitive standpoint, experience has proven that department stores are still needed to establish the center as the major shopping facility for the area. Keeping a maximum number of department stores in one complex adds to the attractiveness of the center as a one-stop shopping facility. Initial planning to accommodate additional department stores helps prevent competition and provide built-in growth as the customer and market demands increase.

The benefits of regional mall ownership begin with the locating of the anchor department stores. In most cases, the department store will build their own store and enter into an operating covenant for a limited period of time. Attracting the right anchors means exactly what the term describes. "Anchors" enable the developer to attract other merchants as well as offering assurance of ample financing.

There has never been a uniform consensus on the number of department stores that are desirable for any specific center. Without question, however, at least two department stores are a minimum, with three or more being desirable creating better attraction for smaller tenants, better profitability for developers, and less chance for future competition. It is usually the developer who has the final say on the number of department stores for each center.

The mix of department stores—value-oriented, fashion-oriented, conventional, major chains, or newly started—is another matter. There has been a continuing debate about the best mix. There is no one best arrangement since each market varies in size, income, and consumer preference. One thing is clear: the value-oriented stores are now being included in virtually all projects. The idea today is to give the customer a full range of choices. This concept seems to be receiving good acceptance from developers, department stores, and shoppers. Most tenants recognize that keeping the shopping in one location is preferable to fragmenting a market with fashion stores in one project and value stores in another center down the road or across the street.

THE QUESTION OF SECURITY

A new concern for regional malls is security. Whether there are problems or not, there is often a feeling of insecurity at some of the larger regional malls. The need for added and upgraded security is a result of today's social problems. Malls attract people, all kind of peoples, sometimes undesirable elements. Most malls have given security their highest priority.

At new shopping centers, more emphasis is going into the design to maximize the security for the shoppers as well as for the tenants. At one time, the use of video cameras was frowned on because shoppers felt someone was spying on them. Today, shoppers seem pleased to know that television cameras are there to assist in making their shopping visits safer and more secure. The increased staff of security personnel, while costly to the owners and the tenants, is essential.

Lighting has become a much more important factor in regional malls. Improved lighting can add to the aesthetics as well as provide better security. This is particularly true in parking areas.

Security has become such a major concern that most owners and managers have full-time staffs for the protection of their properties. In larger malls, the security department works with the local authorities. In small centers, the common practice is to hire off-duty police officers for the security of the mall.

Most centers utilize cars or roving patrol carts for parking lot security. In some extreme cases, management has had to install "crow's nests" look-out stations to properly police the external lots.

VERTICAL INTEGRATION OF MULTIPLE
SHOPPING CENTER OPERATIONS

In centers that are being developed or improved, larger and more successful developers have found that it is necessary to integrate all the various functions within their own organizations. This includes design, construction, financing, leasing, and management. Proper management of regional malls is itself a very highly concentrated operation that requires much expertise.

Many developers have and are continuing to work out alternate anchors for their developments. Food courts, movie theaters, and amusement centers all fit into this category. They add to the appeal of the project. Also, many developers are attempting to add more value merchants that normally would be located on the perimeter of the centers or on freestanding pads close to existing centers. All of this makes today's shopping center a much more complete, more competitive, and more interesting and attractive shopping facility for the consumer.

DEPARTMENT STORES AND MALL SHOPS MAY
MARCH TO DIFFERENT DRUMMERS

In the past, new development was dictated by the demand and needs of the anchor department stores. This was during the period when there was no shortage of mall shop tenants. Today, the number of viable department store chains has dramatically decreased. Many department stores have reorganized, adding the newest high-tech facilities, and restructured their balance sheets. They need added volume. This has created pressure on the developer/owner to develop new centers and expand existing centers. As a result, department store managements are aggressively pushing for new locations.

For the mall shop tenant, this is not necessarily the case. Bankruptcies, changed customer demands and shopping habits, and more competitive conditions make leasing smaller shop space much more difficult. Many mall shop tenants, particularly in the ready-to-wear category, are no longer in business, and many that are still operating are struggling to regroup under reorganization plans. The national and regional small shop chains (The Gap, The Limited, Banana Republic, etc.) have replaced to a great extent the local fashion and specialty mall tenants.

Developers are now faced with finding new categories of tenants to replace the specialty shops that have fallen behind in their competitive battle with the revived department stores. As a result, the supply of new projects is growing at a very modest pace. It is now necessary to be assured of demand not only from anchors, but also from a significant number of smaller merchants, many of which are first timers to regional malls.

Regional malls are facing new forms of competition from manufacturers' outlet centers, off-price retailers, category killers, and electronic retailing, a field in which even the department stores are entering. While department stores are finding that they can compete price-wise with discount merchants, many typical mall shop tenants cannot. Finding new replacements for the typical mall shop tenant of the past is one of the major challenges facing today's developer. Any new regional mall should have adequate acreage to assure pad space for off-price retailer and category killers.

DECLINE IN RATES OF RETURN

Another factor that has a significant impact on the number of new projects is the investment return. At the height of the developer mania, the developer rarely had to invest any significant amount of equity. Today, this is not the case. The return on investment has shrunk considerably. Whereas many developers used to be assured of 12% to 15% returns on new projects, this has now slipped to sometimes as low as 5% to 6%. It will take some time before the industry again sees a high rate of return on its investment. The developer in the 1990s has to rely on continued growth in his market, develop a high-quality marketing program, and have confidence that interest levels will not increase too dramatically.

In the past, most regional malls have been financed by conventional first mortgage debt. This leverage has minimized the equity requirements and has created satisfactory returns for the owners and developers. With reduced loan values, it becomes much riskier to project a future return.

Construction debt for new or renovated centers has become more difficult to obtain. Most lenders limit the percentage of cost they will

Grand Traverse Mall, Traverse City, Michigan

lend. They are reluctant to assume excessive risk for this or any type of real estate projects. This has forced many developers to look for financial partners to provide the equity investment. Other developers have turned to the public financial market for sources of equity.

The evolution of financing for the industry has already begun to make publicly owned shopping centers and real estate available to a wider range of investors. In the past, the price of publicly traded real estate shares has not necessarily reflected the true value of the underlying real estate. Calculating true value has been very difficult. Part of the problem was that the accounting treatment of development and high leverage investments made it extremely difficult for the average investor to understand.

Much of this new growth from public companies will probably come in the form of publicly traded real estate investment trusts (REITs). REITs are very similar to mutual funds except they own real estate instead of securities. We are already seeing a substantial number of REITs being formed and sold to the public with listings on the major stock exchanges. Some are being done privately. REITs are very tax efficient and the mandatory dividends that are paid to the shareholders are taxed only once. The recipient pays tax on the dividend but the dividends are not taxed to the REIT so long as they conform to certain requirements.

Permanent financing has varied considerably over the past few years. It became virtually nonexistent in the early 1990s, but beginning in 1993 commercial banks, insurance companies, pension funds, and other types of lenders have re-entered the market and are now willing to arrange a long-term loan of approximately 75% of value.

If there is one word that would sum up the desires of a regional mall investment, it would be "franchise." To own a dominant regional center that has a franchise in its market offers the owner an outstanding investment. This is true even if it requires a continual reinvestment for upgrading and maintaining its dominance. With the right anchors and the right tenant mix, a major regional center can truly establish itself as the dominant marketplace for a major geographic region.

CONCLUSION

The regional mall business continues to be a well entrenched part of today's business world. It continues to thrive even though it has its share of competitive pressures as well as suffering from some of the social repercussions of our current society.

It is obvious that there is no wholesale demise of this industry in sight nor will this merchandising medium be replaced in the foreseeable future. There is a good future provided ownership remains *innovative, creative,* and *adaptable* plus has ample financial backing to stay current with the rapidly changing trends of the retail scene.

The profitability will perhaps be a bit less than was experienced in the industry's earlier days, but the future continues to look bright.

Twelve

The Competitive Position of Central Business Districts and Main Street Retail Property

Kevin D. Gray and Diane C. Melish

D owntowns—both Main Streets for small towns and Central Business Districts (CBDs) for large cities—are the setting for a wide variety of individual store and multistore retail developments. The real estate occupied by retailers in CBDs and on its Main Streets does not lend itself to easy categorizations or measurement of supply and demand; no industry measures exist as they do for shopping center owners.

For this analysis, the nation's top 50 metropolitan areas are considered to have CBDs as their core. Main Street is defined here as the CBDs of smaller MSAs (less than 1 million persons) and shopping streets of satellite communities within larger MSAs. Suburban communities are generally characterized as secondary to the CBD. Even the smallest of these MSAs, which is Greensboro—High Point—Urban Street in North Carolina has several fully developed suburbs with Main Street retail areas. Large metro area CBDs can further be categorized as "24-hour cities" or "9-to-5 cities," based on the extent of residential and retail week-end and nighttime activity.

THE HISTORY AND EVOLUTION OF DOWNTOWN RETAIL

America's downtowns remained the focus of economic and social life through the early twentieth century. Accessible, concentrated, and diverse, downtowns provided synergy and excitement. With the development of streetcars, suburban residential neighborhoods were created. By the 1930s, department stores and other major retailers followed their customers outside of the center with suburban branch units. However, the focus of retailing and the flagship units of department stores remained downtown until after World War II when rapid changes in demographics, transportation, and economics began to significantly alter downtown's competitiveness. The demand for new homes, resulting from the lack of new housing constructed during the Depression and the postponement of new family formation during World War II, together with a new definition of the "American Dream," accelerated the movement of population centers from the cities to the suburbs.

The exodus to the suburbs was largely a middle and upper class phenomenon. Remaining in downtown residential neighborhoods were the poor, minorities, and recent immigrants. Retail and office building development followed the residential movement to the suburbs. For retail, it was simply the pursuit of the customers and a recognition that, at the time, most shoppers were women who shopped near where they lived. The development of the shopping center industry, with its responsiveness to the suburban American consumer, represents one of the great eras in value creation in American real estate. Most of this book is devoted to such retail real estate. However, concurrent with this development, by the early 1960s, department stores and specialty shops (with the exception of a few fashion-oriented stores) began to close downtown flagship units and expand into more profitable suburban regional shopping centers. The economics were clear, by the early 1970s, shopping center sales accounted for 60% to 80% of total sales volume for the largest department stores.

Main Street's response to the exodus of customers to the suburbs varied by city and town, but most were slow to recognize the threat to their commercial activity, slow to get organized, and lacked centralized ownership or management. Cities generally ignored the importance of parking and access to downtown shopping districts and were driven instead into experimental forms of development, such as the ubiquitous conversion of downtown shopping streets into pedestrian "malls," often with disastrous consequences.

Government policy for cities throughout the post-World War II period has been contradictory. Programs to facilitate purchase of suburban housing, the construction of interstate highways, and public housing projects in inner cities all have had the effect of encouraging the decentralization of cities (in contrast to the redevelopment of most European cities after the war). Government intervention has gradually evolved from an emphasis on housing (Housing Act of 1949) and transportation (Federal-Aid Highway Act of 1956) which encouraged the exodus to the suburbs, to large, single-purpose "urban renewal" projects in the 1960s with little or no retail component. Funding shifted from federal to state and local levels in the mid-1960s. New Community Block Grants in 1974 merged federal programs into a single funding source that decentralized federal control. The Housing and Community Development Act of 1977 provided for Urban Development Action Grants (UDAG) as an incentive for private investment. UDAG funds combined with private financing did not necessarily provide dollars for retail, but provided funds for projects that created retail markets.

By the 1980s, public funding for such large scale projects had virtually disappeared. Loans rather than outright grants became more commonplace. During the mid-1980s, both new and abolished federal programs dictated a new direction in funding for the public portion of downtown projects. The Tax Reform Act of 1986, for example, restricted the tax exemption for state and local bond issues assisting private businesses. In the 1990s, new public financing sources were therefore developed using local sources and future project income as a financing technique. These sources include revenue and tax increment bonds, special use taxes, loans from city agencies, and cash advances from developers.

Public funding has been critical in developing downtown retail projects and should remain so in the future. Since the 1970s, cities themselves have become developers, and often to attract and benefit nonresidents such as tourists and downtown office workers. In the future, the same techniques for financing and attracting new investment capital are also available to suburban edge cities, who will aggressively compete for such retail projects. For many older cities, a strong emerging "edge city" may preclude a return to past dominance of the Central Business District, no matter what their government policy.

DEFINING DEMAND FOR CBD AND MAIN STREET RETAIL

Population

Population is the most basic measure of market health and size. The top 50 major metro area differ greatly in their distribution of population. Mature markets, such as older East Coast cities, generally have established CBD retailing. Younger markets, which often are the fastest growing markets, often have no historic CBD—these are cities in the West or so-called "edge cities" of major metro areas where suburban growth is occurring. Such areas typically lack any shopping, transportation, or employment focus of any importance. Most of them have some core historical downtown, a vacant department store or two, and retailing that is increasingly oriented to office, government or daytime worker populations.

A recent survey of executives indicated that New York, Chicago, Atlanta, Miami, and San Francisco offer the best business environments among U.S. cities. Other major metropolitan areas may be grouped into satellite cities of these major metro areas; regional centers, such as Atlanta, Denver, and Seattle, and smaller markets, ancillary to these major markets. While arbitrary and subject to disputes, a classification of these cities is essential to an understanding of the competitive positioning of CBD markets for retail development and investment. Resident population and its distribution provides the first, most basic tool for analysis. Beyond these statistics, there is a "hidden" population in cities comprised of immigrants and others, often resulting in an underestimate of the city population.

Office Workers

The size of the CBD office market as a percentage of the total metropolitan area office market is another useful measure of demand as a proxy for the daytime worker population within America's CBDs. There is a relationship between the daytime CBD worker population and the health of CBD retailing. The density of daytime workers is also a factor in predicting the level of retail development. Can office workers reasonably walk between buildings either at street level or via an artificial system, such as a people-mover or light-rail system? Office worker data is a strong predictor of healthy CBD retailing in established office cores of cities such as Boston, Chicago, New York, and San Francisco.

Tourists

Tourism can also be a significant factor in supporting retail development. Chicago, New York, and Los Angeles are major tourist destinations. Some major markets, such as San Francisco, Seattle, Boston, Baltimore, and Washington, DC, benefit from a steady influx of tourists that supplements the expenditure potential of daytime office workers. Tourism also includes conventioneers and spectators at sporting events, and the presence of a large convention or sports complex in the CBD can also increase the strength, duration, and mix of shopper demand. In many cities, unfortunately, convention and sports complexes are poorly located to assist in creating a healthy downtown. Even in Chicago and New York, as well as in San Francisco and Washington, the size of convention facilities has dictated their placement on the periphery of the CBD, in isolated, quasi-industrial locations. In this regard, New Orleans and San Antonio are better examples of new and old retail centers within an easy walk of convention facilities and tourist attractions. In the future, new retail development will also be related to the proliferation of gambling operations. The success of the Forum Shops at Caesar's Palace in Las Vegas has generated plans for similar shopping/entertainment complexes related to casino development in Atlantic City and other downtowns.

Inner City and Ethnic Populations

No demographic trend has greater implications for the competitive positioning of CBD retail development than the growth in ethnic populations that has occurred in the cities. By some estimates, 75% of projected population growth will occur among minority groups. In less than a generation, whole areas of the nation's cities have been transformed by the growth of ethnic populations. While the trend is most pronounced in coastal cities, such as San Diego, Los Angeles, Houston, Miami, and New York, significant ethnic populations are present even in small and mid-sized cities. Ethnic populations are reinvigorating CBDs and Main Streets with a new demand for retail shop space and a new class of building owner. At least in the initial phase, the shops being opened in these enclaves bear little resemblance to conventional shopping center retail. They may be the source of new formats in the future.

Suburban inflow into ethnic enclaves is also occurring. For example, Japanese from throughout metropolitan New York drive to Fort Lee to shop, and Asian Indians drive to Jackson Heights in Queens from throughout the East Coast. On the West Coast, growth in Asian populations has created submarkets with an active investor class, eager to purchase and develop retail property. Institutional investors seem largely unaware of this market and unable to capitalize on it. Whether it is a temporary one-generation phenomenon prior to assimilation or a more sustained, dominant trend (as appears to be the case in Miami), demand from ethnic groups can revive and sustain a retail environment. Understanding this change will be a major challenge and opportunity for the investor and developer of CBD retailing in the future. Expect a surge of interest driven by demographic trends, as numerous ethnic enclaves expand. Those cities with large, vibrant ethnic populations should benefit in the form of more varied and stable downtown retailing, as these groups may be the closest resident population to the CBD, and the most dependent upon it, probably more inclined to value-oriented retailing and more inclined to view shopping as a social activity. In some metropolitan areas, the original downtown may simply be bypassed in favor of a suburban location, such as the growth of Hacienda Heights and Westminster, California, with Asian population growth that has no effect on downtown Los Angeles retail development.

Measures of Main Street Demand

How does Main Street demand differ from the demand for retail space in large cities? Smaller cities are both more numerous and more dispersed. With some exceptions, the population is ethnically more homogeneous, and development land is generally available and less expensive. Does the smaller city population favor true Main Street retailing on the traditional model? The worker, inner city and suburban population together comprise the source of demand for retail goods in small cities. Most small cities (even county seats, university towns and medical centers) don't have a sufficient worker base downtown to support retail without the patronage of residents, and if the nearest major metropolitan area is a sufficient distance away, the draw can encompass an enormous distance (even extending to shoppers who spend the weekend, in places such as Amarillo or Spokane). College towns such as Appleton (Wisconsin) and Burlington (Vermont) can have a healthy, vibrant downtown, even with competition from a suburban shopping center. The presence of a college or university is not an automatic guarantee of a well-retailed shopping district, as evidenced by Knoxville (Tennessee) or Lubbock (Texas). Demand within the smaller cities is a relative constant, with supply of new retail development in the suburbs being the wild card. The "Wal-Mart Effect" has been the subject of controversy and grass-roots protests throughout the United States; this dominant retailer has the power to shift demand outward to the outskirts of even the smallest town.

DEFINING THE SUPPLY OF CBD AND MAIN STREET RETAIL

While measures of demand are available, based on statistics from various agencies and chambers of commerce that track such data, measures of supply are far more subjective. The supply of CBD retail space is contained in a few free-standing stores, in shopfronts, in enclosed shopping centers, such as vertical or festival centers, and in fully developed shopping malls with department store anchors that are located on downtown sites. The department store is the original source of supply, together with street-level retail that is related to it. Together, the department stores and shopfronts make up the formula and the historic basis of both CBD and Main Street retailing.

The Role of the Department Store

For most residents and visitors to a city, the department store is still the defining symbol of CBD retailing. To lose a department store is to symbolically lose the core of downtown shopping, while to have a healthy department store is considered evidence of a successful, strong downtown. The presence of the traditional department store is related to the historical development of the downtown. Almost every city at some point had a local department store in its CBD. The emergence of the catalogue stores (Sears, J.C. Penney, and Montgomery Ward) provided a department store presence in even very small towns. As the industry consolidated through buying cooperatives (such as

Allied Stores, Mercantile, and Belk's) and mergers and acquisitions (a process that is still going on with the merger of Macy's into Federated) department stores have become more efficient, national chains. Just as department stores followed their customer base to the suburbs as anchors of regional shopping centers, they also exited the downtowns when the customer base no longer existed. Few cities now have viable department stores in the traditional downtown, as consolidation in the industry and a decline in market share has necessitated more efficient operations. A notable exception is the presence of Saks Fifth Avenue and other fashion specialty department stores in some CBD locations, such as the Saks locations in downtown Pittsburgh and Cincinnati, where centralized locations serve a fashion conscious clientele from throughout each metropolitan area. But in most metro areas, the fashion-conscious shopper is served from a suburban location. Each bankruptcy of a chain has resulted in a reduction in downtown units. (The 1992 bankruptcy of Macy's resulted in the closing of Macy's in downtown New Haven, New Rochelle, and Newark, for example.)

In the East, where public transportation infrastructure is more prevalent and land for new development is scarce, there are still a number of smaller cities that have a department store in the traditional downtown. But, for most cities, the decline of the department store mirrors the department store's own declining share of market (department store sales for Carson, Pirie, Scott; Dayton Hudson; Federated/Macy's; May Company and Mercantile combined are far short of Wal-Mart's) (Figure 12.1). As department stores left all but the largest cities, there was a mostly futile attempt by local government to retain them. Some new department stores have been built as freestanding stores, such as Hecht Co. in Washington and Barney's in New York and Beverly Hills, but for most vacant department stores, an alternative use has to be found (see Figure 12.2).

Retail Space in Office Buildings

In many cities, the presence of office workers, rather than residents, is the driving force behind CBD retailing. The retailing can be either at, above, or below street level and is often linked with an underground pedestrian system or mass transit. In the late 1980s, as office markets weakened, retail development became a factor in the amenities needed by office buildings to attract tenants. Examples are not limited to large cities, even smaller cities have retail service centers catering to the needs of the office population. The most

FIGURE 12.1

Downtowns that Lost Department Stores (A Partial Listing)

City	Department Store
Los Angeles, CA	Bullock's Wilshire
New York, NY	Alexander's, B. Altman, Gimbels, Ohrbach's
Chicago, IL	Wiebolt's
Philadelphia, PA	Gimbels, Lit Brothers
Washington, DC	Lansburgh's, Kahn's, Garfinkels
Detroit, MI	Hudson's
Houston, TX	Joske
Atlanta, GA	Rich's
Dallas, TX	Joske, Sanger-Harris
San Diego, CA	Walker-Scott
Orange County, CA	Buffum's
Baltimore, MD	Hoschild-Kohn, Stewart's
Phoenix, AZ	Goldwater's
Seattle, WA	Frederick & Nelson
Cleveland, OH	Halles
Newark, NJ	Bamberger's/Macy's
Denver, CO	The Denver
New Haven, CT	Macy's, Edward Malley
San Francisco, CA	City of Paris, Liberty House
Cincinnati, OH-KY-IN	Pogue's, Mabley & Carew
Norfolk, VA	Miller & Rhoads
Fort Worth, TX	Frost Brothers, Diamond's
Indianapolis, IN	Lazarus, L.S. Ayres
Charlotte, NC	Belk's, Ivey's
Buffalo, NY	Sibley's, Ames
Hartford, CT	G. Fox

Source: Dougal Casey, Jones Lang Wootton

complete and successful example is the mall underneath the plaza of the World Trade Center in New York. Thousands of workers pass through this transportation hub each day to work on Wall Street. Successful retailers operate without a department store anchor in one of the most heavily trafficked sites in the United States. At night and on weekends, the area is practically deserted, as there are only a few, relatively new, residential areas in lower Manhattan. In other developments, such as Century City in Los Angeles and Water Tower Place in Chicago, the siting of these projects makes them accessible

FIGURE 12.2

Alternative Uses for Closed CBD and Main Street Department Stores

Alexander's, White Plains, NY, *Westchester Pavilion, Urban Power Center*
B. Altman, St. David's, PA, *St. David's Square, High-End Community Center*
B. Altman, New York City, *New York Public Library Offices*
Belk's, Charlotte, NC, *Residential Condominiums*
Bloomingdale's, Stamford, CT, *University Extension Building*
Garfinkels, Washington, DC, *Proposed Office Building*
Gerber's, Memphis, TN, *Apartment Building Parking Garage*
G. Fox, Hartford, CT, *Proposed Community Social Services Center*
Hudson's, Detroit, MI, *Proposed GSA Records Center*
Ohrbach's, New York, NY, *Office Building*
Sears, Bridgeport, CT, *Vocational Community College*
Sears/Younkers, Council Bluffs, IA, *Proposed Community College*
Macy's, New Rochelle, NY, *Proposed Urban Power Center*
Edward Malley Co., New Haven, CT, *Flea Market*
Rich's, Atlanta, GA, *Proposed Federal Office Building*
Walker-Scott, San Diego, CA, *Mixed Use Office/Retail*
J. Wanamaker, Philadelphia, PA, *Mixed Use Office/Retail*

Source: Landauer Associates and Company Reports.

to both office workers during the week and nearby residential areas on weekends.

Above-grade or below-grade shopping areas are usually associated with a transportation system or are related to local climate. Rockefeller Center in New York (which inspired Penn Center in Philadelphia, Embarcadero Center in San Francisco, Place Ville-Marie in Montreal, and the World Trade Center concourse) is still the model of this form of development. Other transportation-related projects (some of which have an office component) include Union Station in Washington and Tower City Center in Cleveland. A major renovation and retail development is also planned for Grand Central Station in New York. Few cities can support such a large underground complex, which requires pedestrian traffic both at street level and below grade. It would appear that connection to a rail line is essential, with the exception being Houston, where a hostile climate has encouraged an extensive network of underground passages and related retail. Above-grade retail can also be a function of climate: Minneapolis, St. Paul, and Spokane have extensive pedestrian walkway systems above street level, which interconnect department stores, retail projects, and office lobbies. Indianapolis, while not in an extreme climatic zone, is in the process of linking its pedestrian system to the new Circle Centre, an enclosed shopping mall that will provide an extensive system of walkways above grade. Charlotte, although bereft of department stores (both Belk's and Ivey's closed their downtown units) has an excellent pedestrian system above street level that caters almost exclusively to daytime office workers.

What is the optimum relationship between retail square footage and office worker population or CBD office space? In Charlotte, the office population of 60,000 persons is served by Founders Hall, the City Place market and other venues, but substantial vacancy even with a healthy office market suggests that there is too much retail for the current population of workers. In Houston, the daytime population of 200,000 is served by The Parks at Houston Center and scattered tunnel-level retail. It would appear that each worker can support as little as one to perhaps three square feet of daytime retail space.

These above-grade and below-grade systems appear to be related to the determination of the municipalities where they exist to support them. Extensive zoning and regulatory barriers have often been removed in these cities to encourage participation in the pedestrian network by building owners.

Festival Retail Centers

Festival Retail is a product type that was inspired by the marketplaces of Europe, envisioned by Jim Rouse, and developed by The Rouse Company. It introduced into America's CBDs an alternative to the traditional department store/shop street of the past. Festival retail projects almost always incorporate historic buildings, a water feature, and a tourism district into the design, and the more successful ones have been able to appeal to both office workers and tourists, giving them a more year-round appeal than a tourist attraction, with more weekend traffic than a typical office-related project. South Street Seaport (New York), HarborPlace (Baltimore) Faneuil Hall (Boston), and Riverwalk (New Orleans) are examples, all developed by The Rouse Company. Although hugely successful with customers, high land acquisition and operating costs have made further new projects difficult. Moreover, few cities have the convention business, feature (such as a harbor, aquarium, or historic site) and above all, civic support, which are the necessary elements.

Anchored Malls in Urban Locations

In some markets, particularly on the periphery of major metropolitan areas, the scarcity of land and the attractiveness of a satellite office center have encouraged the development of shopping malls in CBDs and "edge cities." Some of these projects, such as the developments of The Taubman Realty Group of Beverly Center in Los Angeles and Stamford Town Center in Stamford, Connecticut, are very similar in size and concept to the traditional shopping mall, but they have a more fashion-oriented merchandise mix. These projects are vertical, with multilevel parking garages. Typically, these centers have higher sales productivity than more traditional regional malls because they are located in densely developed submarkets and benefit from both office workers as well as from affluent residents. Successful examples of these "urban" regional centers include Prudential Center in Boston, Century City in Los Angeles, and Columbus City Center (Figure 12.3). While security is often cited as an issue whenever multistory parking garages are necessary, the reported high sales productivity of these centers suggests that shoppers are not intimidated by the complicated access and multistoried garages that usually accompany such projects. Moreover, the relative newness of many of these projects indicates that developers are returning to centralized locations for development when anchor alignment is unique or fashion-oriented, when little or no retail sales growth is occurring in outlying areas, or where suburban sites are not readily developable. Many of these new developments would probably not exist without public assistance or financing from the cities.

Urban shopping centers (whether in old CBDs or in new "edge city" CBDs) aren't usually designed to accommodate an existing streetscape, and so they are often criticized by urban planners as fortresses within the CBDs they inhabit. However, they are also among the largest taxpayers in these cities, and the developments were generally encouraged at the time of the zoning and permitting process. For most of the cities that have subsidized CBD mall development, the alternative—that department stores and development would go elsewhere—is far more troublesome than any attempt to accommodate existing streetscape retail. In newer developments, notably The Westchester in White Plains, Circle Centre in Indianapolis, Tower City in Cleveland, and Downtown Plaza in Sacramento, more of an effort has been made to be both a self-contained shopping experience and a bridge to existing urban context beyond the "four walls" of the development. Recent renovations of Santa Monica Place, Horton Plaza in San Diego, The Fashion Show in Las Vegas, and Biltmore Fashion Center in Phoenix have attempted to relate restaurants and entertainment to the surrounding streets and to animate them.

There is another type of "central city" development best exemplified by Walden Galleria in Buffalo, Carousel Mall in Syracuse, and The Mall at Steamtown in Scranton: these centers are located on industrial sites with excellent, centralized arterial freeway access from all points of a metropolitan area. As such, they are not really part of a CBD or Main Street, but take advantage of the strategic location of the interstate system (at or near the historic downtown) with convenience to the largest possible customer base. As a strategy for increasing the tax base of a city, these centers can effectively take market share from many—perhaps all—of the suburban regional malls in the metropolitan area by virtue of their superior regional access, large size, and merchandise presentation, without a positive impact on the historic center.

Single-Anchored and Unanchored Vertical Urban Centers

The single-anchored or anchorless urban center, exemplified by Lafayette Place in Boston, Herald Center in New York, as well as others lacks the possibility of cross-shopping advanced by the traditional "dumbell" shaped, anchored shopping center. Exceptions are found in Minneapolis, Portland, Spokane, and a few other cities, where the skywalk systems function like a mall concourse, linking projects and anchor stores under different ownership, for the benefit of all.

Most unanchored vertical urban retail is another matter. Even connection to the skywalk system was not sufficient to ensure the success of The Conservatory in Minneapolis, since the pedestrian system does not lead to a destination beyond it. In Scottsdale, Arizona, the unanchored, multistoried Galleria is basically vacant and slated for redevelopment after a substantial capital investment was lost. In New York, Herald Center, which used a food court destination on the upper level, was unable to attract a multitenant mix and is now largely leased to a single user: Toys 'R Us. In smaller cities, the loss of the anchor in a single-anchor center can often spell the end of the center in its current configuration. Manhattan's Trump Tower, while connected to the former Bonwit Teller store (subsequently converted

FIGURE 12.3
Anchored CBD Shopping Centers

Name	Size[a]/Year Built	No. of Stores	Parking	Anchors	Tenants[b]
Prudential Center Boston, MA	462,000 1965/1993	40	3,000	Lord & Taylor Saks Fifth Avenue	Brooks Bros., FAO Schwartz, Giorgio Armani, Louis of Boston
Cambridgeside Galleria Cambridge, MA	800,000 1991	150		Filene's Lechmere Sears	Ann Taylor, The Limited, J. Crew, New England Sports Museum, Guess, Bombay Co.
Water Tower Place Chicago, IL	613,703 1975	131	667	Lord & Taylor Marshall Fields	Charles Jourdan, Dunhill, Guy Laroche, Rodier
Tower City Center Cleveland, OH	1,000,000 1990	95	1,390	Neiman Marcus	Gucci, Liz Claiborne, Polo/Ralph Lauren, Fendi
Columbus City Center Columbus, OH	1,300,000 1989	160	4,700	Lazarus Marshall Fields	B. Dalton, The Gap, Godiva, Natural Wonders, Nordic Track, Warner Bros.
Fort Lauderdale Galleria Fort Lauderdale, FL	1,300,000 1980	150	6,000	Burdine's Lord & Taylor Neiman Marcus Saks Fifth Avenue	Ann Taylor, Brooks Bros., Disney, Nature Co., Wet Seal, Williams-Sonoma
Circle Centre Indianapolis, IN	787,000 1995	100	3,000	Nordstrom Parisian	The Limited, The Gap

Center / Location	GLA	Year	Stores	Mall GLA	Anchors	Specialty Tenants
Beverly Center, Los Angeles, CA	900,000	1982	200	3,000	Broadway, Bullocks	Ann Taylor, Brookstore, Eddie Bauer, Mondi, Pacific Sunwear, Warner Bros.
Century City, Los Angeles, CA	762,000	1964/1987	142	2,800	Broadway, Bullocks	AMC, Gelson's, Bueno Bueno, Nature Co., Disney, Imaginarium, Dive!
Manhattan Mall, New York, NY	506,000	1989	56	n/a	Stern's (formerly A&S)	9 West, Athlete's Foot, Wilson's, Au Bon Pain
Downtown Plaza, Sacramento, CA	927,000	1971/1993	120	3,800	Macy's, Weinstocks	Ann Taylor, Gap, Gymboree, Morton's, Suncoast, Structure, Warner Bros.
St. Louis Center, St. Louis, MO	1,180,000	1985	150	4,800	Dillard, Famous-Barr	August Max, Gap, GNC, Radio Shack, Payless Shoes
RiverCenter, San Antonio, TX	551,000	1988	150	1,600	Dillard, Foley's	AMC, Limited, Cignal, Naturalizer, Zookeeper
Horton Plaza, San Diego, CA	694,000	1985	150	2,400	Broadway, Mervyn's, Nordstrom, Robinsons-May	Banana Republic, Eddie Bauer, Gap Kids, Disney, Sam Goody, Williams-Sonoma
San Francisco Center, San Francisco, CA	1,100,000	1988	100	2,600	Nordstrom, Emporium	9 West, Boxerbay, J. Crew, Sacha of London, Wet Seal, Williams-Sonoma, Z-Gallerie
The Westchester, White Plains, NY	1,000,000		160	4,000	Neiman Marcus, Nordstrom	Tiffany & Co., Williams-Sonoma, The Limited

[a] Includes anchor GLA.
[b] Small sample only.

Source: Laudauer Associates, Inc., Company Reports.

FIGURE 12.4

Suburban Specialty Shopping Centers (Associated with Main Street Shopping)

Name	Size[a]/Year Built	No. of Stores	Parking	Anchors	Tenants[b]
Suburban Square Ardmore, PA	275,800 1928	60	1,150	Strawbridge & Clothier	Ann Taylor, Banana Republic, TCBY
Roland Park Shopping Center Baltimore, MD	60,000 1907	11	50	n/a	Victor's
Highland Park Village Dallas, TX	237,507 1931/ 1987/ 1993	65	982	n/a	Chanel, Hermes, Pierre Deux, Polo/Ralph Lauren, Calvin Klein, Guy Laroche
River Oaks Shopping Center Houston, TX	233,000 1937	116	2,300	Jos. Bank Kroger	Crown Books, La Griglia
Country Club Plaza Kansas City, KS	c. 1929 1992	140	5,000	Dillard Saks Fifth Avenue	Eddie Bauer, The Limited, Gucci, Brooks Brothers
Market Square Lake Forest, IL	71,205 1929/1982	33	n/a	Marshall Fields	Talbots, Laura Ashley, Starbucks, Williams-Sonoma, Rodier
Hampton Village St. Louis, MO	198,000 1941/1987	22	2,000	J.C. Penney National Super	B. Dalton, Walgreen's, Kidsmart

a Includes anchor GLA.
b Small sample only.
Source: Laudauer Associates, Inc.

to Galleries Lafayette and now scheduled to become NikeTown), functions effectively as a multilevel unanchored center, because of its exceptional location (on Fifth Avenue in New York) and its notoriety, which make the center an attraction in its own right rather than a prototype for other cities.

Main Street Retail

The supply of retail on Main Streets in America's small cities is a moving target. Not only is there a tremendous supply of street level retail in existing buildings, but there is also a gradual change in use constantly taking place which makes any estimate very subjective. In larger markets, brokers have monitored the retail space on Michigan Avenue, in Chicago's Loop, in downtown Santa Monica, along Rodeo Drive, Madison Avenue and Fifth Avenue in New York, and around Union Square in San Francisco. Top shopping streets in the United States indicate a strong correlation between a large office and tourist population in the CBD and the health of the streetscape.

In the suburban areas, there are also successful Main Street shopping areas. The affluent suburbs of most major cities have quaint shopping streets which cater to the local residential population, whether it is New Canaan or Westport, Connecticut; Ridgewood, New Jersey; Winnetka or Lake Forest, Illinois; the towns on the main line in Philadelphia; Grosse Pointe, Michigan; the Park Cities in Dallas, or elsewhere. Increasingly, the presence of national retailers is becoming predominate. In many of these communities, small and often very successful shopping centers exist. Indeed, the very oldest prototypes for the ubiquitous modern shopping center are found in suburbs of Roland Park, MD; Ardmore, PA; and Lake Forest, IL (Figure 12.4). Retailers are also moving out of the controlled environment of the shopping center into the traditional streetscape. In Rye, New York, for example, where no national retailers were present ten years ago, there are now Boston Chicken, Coffee Tree, The Gap, Gap-Kids, Sam Goody's, and Starbucks. Greenwich Avenue in Greenwich, a town of 65,000 persons, has even more units of national retailers typically found in enclosed shopping malls. Recent growth on Main Street generally has not resulted in an increase of supply of space on any given Main Street, but reflects the ability of national credit tenants to crowd out locally owned stores when a desirable demographic mix is available. With the top suburban malls in any market at or near full occupancy, these retailers must look elsewhere for growth.

Discounters Revive CBD Retailing

The growth of discount and value-oriented retailers in recent years has been nothing short of phenomenal. New retail formats (see Chapter 8) have increased their market share and numbers of new formats dramatically, with their origins and growth in suburban locations. It is logical that these retailers, in need of sales growth in a highly competitive environment, would seek this growth in new store openings in locations where a dense, value-oriented, and often under-served population is available. Ironically, this phenomenon doesn't apply to smaller towns and cities, where downtowns, if anything, are under more pressure than ever.

Some of these retailers are regional players looking to insulate themselves from stronger competition. Witness the bidding for the vacant Alexander's department stores on Long Island (New York) by Bradlee's and Caldor, in part as a preemptive move to lock in scarce sites with densely populated trade areas before Wal-Mart completes its saturation of the New York suburbs (although both chains entered bankruptcy in 1995). Likewise, successful suburban chains such as Bed Bath and Beyond, Today's Man, Marshall's, and Sports Authority have opened stores in Manhattan and other CBDs. Higher costs in downtowns should be offset by greater volume for these new formats to work. In the case of the Wooster Galleria, a conventional, but unsuccessful one million square feet enclosed shopping center in downtown Wooster, MA, was completely repositioned by New England Development as a factory outlet center in 1994. History is repeating itself, as one of the earliest post-war re-uses of vacant retail and industrial space was for factory outlet stores in such secondary markets.

SUCCESS FACTORS FOR CBD AND MAIN STREET RETAIL PROPERTY

What are the success factors for Main Street and CBD retail property? What distinguishes a successful project in one town from a similar project which was an abysmal failure in another? While government policy and financial support can distort the forces at work in a market, the successful projects seem to have several factors in common:

Trade Area Demographics

Whether affluent or ethnic or both, whether resident or office workers or tourists and convention-goers, there has to be latent demand present in the shopper base. Perhaps this latent demand is unsatisfied with the traffic or congestion at the nearest regional mall, or perhaps there is an influx of immigrants reviving a once moribund neighborhood. Whatever the circumstances, and public desire for a project notwithstanding, demand cannot be created by fiat. It must be present or potential in the shoppers themselves and currently unsatisfied. The emphasis of many downtowns is on fashion-oriented retailers, which traditionally required a trip to the suburbs. Helpful, but not always essential, is the overlapping presence of daytime workers and tourists or convention goers and residents, all of whom have different shopping needs and different schedules, which can provide a more even distribution of business and sales.

Critical Mass and Critical Continuity

One store does not a shopping district make, and whether it is an enclosed regional center in a CBD location, or a free-standing department store in an historic downtown, the shopping area has to be of sufficient size to provide a full range of goods and services. Critical mass also means concentrated mass. Pedestrians will not easily be induced to walk several blocks of "dead" streetscape between stores or shopping destinations. At the pedestrian level, continuity is key. (On Greenwich Avenue, in Greenwich, CT, the Old City Hall and Post Office interrupt the flow of pedestrian traffic, but the size of retail both north and south of this break is sufficient to overcome it.) In many older CBDs, such as Atlanta and Dallas, the lack of critical mass is very negative for the future viability of downtown retail, and what remaining retail there is has little or no continuity.

Access for People and Cars

The fad of closing off streets for shoppers had a disastrous effect on Main Streets both large and small throughout America, leaving in its wake deserted and dangerously empty pedestrian malls. Successful Main Streets must have easy and affordable parking within a short walk—especially at peak shopping periods such as Saturday morning, and must not conflict with office worker weekday parking. If garages are necessary, as is usually the case with vertical urban malls, every attempt at ensuring a feeling of security is critical. In markets where the customer doesn't typically drive (or even own a car in some urban settings), or where car access is prohibitively difficult, then good bus and subway access directly into the project is essential. The correlary to access is security—perhaps the major issue confronting the shopping center industry in the 1990s and reflective of the increasing concern over public safety. Security in downtown settings, like access, is complicated by several modes of transportation, diversity of the customer base, and multiple points of access.

Public Support

Both in the form of direct subsidies, such as tax-increment financing, and indirect benefits, such as zoning which facilitates new skybridges or tunnels to other projects or parking garages, municipal support is essential. Property ownership is often fragmented, and statutory authority is limited, but much can be accomplished through friendly persuasion and peer pressure to coerce owners and tenants to attract customers, and hence, increase sales and rents. A strong Chamber of Commerce, like a strong merchants association in a mall, realizes the importance of a coordinated merchandising and marketing plan.

Credit Retailers

The success of any project will be short-lived if the retailers lack the commitment or financial ability to see it through. This is especially true of urban projects, where development and operating costs are typically higher than in suburban locations. A common characteristic of successful retail projects in downtowns is the presence of committed and well-known regional or national merchants. Certainly, not all or even most merchants need to fit this description, but there needs to be a commitment to the downtown by high-profile merchants. The lack of a commitment is a self-fulfilling downward spiral. Which comes first: the commitment of the retailer to the city, or the commitment of the customer to the city, or the commitment of the city to both of these constituents? No one sequence appears to be predominant, and in the case of Circle Centre in Indianapolis, for example, a combination of business and civic leaders was able to bring a major project to fruition, without the participation of the two hometown department stores (Lazarus and L. S. Ayres) but with two new department stores (Parisian and Nordstrom). Conversely at St. Louis Center, the commitment of May Company (based in St. Louis) and Dillard's (successor of Joseph Horne Co.) were instrumental in the completion of the project. Credit retailers also need credit landlords—landlords willing to work on behalf of their tenants with the financial strength to provide support.

Sales Productivity Consistent with Operating Costs

No retailer can survive in an environment where operating costs are not supported by sales productivity. Sustainable downtown retail projects must have sales potential sufficient to support the usually higher taxes and other costs of doing business in an urban location. If sales are not going to be greater than those at a typical unit, is the retailer willing to accept a lower margin and profit at a downtown unit? Not likely in the long run, so taxes, garage costs, and other expenses have to be kept down—by public subsidy if necessary—if the downtown retailer is to remain competitive. High sales aren't necessarily an indicator of an ability to pay costs, but are also a function of the individual retailer's typical gross margins. Discounters, for example, can experience sales per square foot in excess of $400, even up to $1,000 or more for some categories; the nature of this business is high volume, low margin, and their ability to pay rent as a percentage of sales is actually less than for many specialty stores with lower per square foot sales volumes.

CBD AND MAIN STREET RETAIL AS AN INVESTMENT

Do the success factors for CBD and Main Street retailing translate into investment vehicles for the real estate investor? Historically there has been money, primarily European on the East Coast, Asian on the West Coast, Middle Eastern in Texas, and Latin American in Florida, interested in acquiring storefront buildings on well-occupied shopping streets, but the investment experience has been variable. Trophy retail properties, such as the Tiffany Building on Fifth Avenue in New York, were sold to foreign investors at the peak of the market at cyclically high prices. For well-located buildings on strong shopping streets, especially in major CBDs or in affluent suburbs, there seems to be a consistent level of demand by investors. There is a belief by investors that the residual value on Union Square in San Francisco, along upper Madison Avenue in New York or Newberry Street in Boston is secure well into the future. But Main Street fortunes can change: witness the fall in rents and occupancy on once-trendy Columbus Avenue on New York's Upper West Side and in Georgetown, in Washington, DC.

More easily analyzed because they are part of the family of regional malls, urban shopping centers are more typical institutional investments. During the past few years, South Bay Galleria (Redondo Beach), Fort Lauderdale Galleria, and RiverCenter (San Antonio) have been acquired by institutional investors, and a number of other urban shopping malls are owned by real estate investment trusts (such as Simon, Taubman, and Urban). Each situation is unique, and no discount or premium for an urban center compared with a traditional shopping center can be assumed. In the case of free-standing buildings, the credit of the underlying tenant is probably as critical as any real estate factor. In theory, such properties should trade at a premium to similarly occupied suburban properties, assuming that the residual has more lasting appeal in a location which is permanently valuable, as opposed to an infinitely reproducible suburban site. No conclusive data is available to support this hypothesis. The stability of ownership for most urban sites and the long-term hold of these investors make an analysis of sales transactions very difficult. Like all infrequently traded products, the market for urban retail properties is inefficient, and highly variable. But also, like all types of real estate, investors must consider the timing of their investments within the cycle.

THE FUTURE OF CBD AND MAIN STREET RETAILING

What does the future hold for the nation's Main Streets and the CBDs of our large cities? With the movement of population and jobs to the suburbs, most American downtowns have lost their diversified base and have become specialized business districts (SBD). As commercial activities have become fewer, operating in more concentrated hours, less intensive and narrower levels of retail development have become the norm. Hospitals, universities, courthouses and government offices should remain downtown indefinitely, as will businesses relying on direct personal contact, including financial, professional and medical services. For many cultural and educational facilities, relocation is uneconomical, so expect art museums, schools, and sports facilities to also remain in cities.

Forum Shops at Caesar's, Las Vegas, Nevada

Downtown business leaders and advocacy groups should continue to view the status of America's downtowns with alarm. Just as much of the downtown festival and other retail development was possible because of public grants or loans, most future downtown development, to be competitive, will probably require some form of public/private joint venture, with profit sharing, tax abatements, and other incentives for developers that minimize municipalities' up-front costs, while encouraging private equity.

For Main Street, the impact of Wal-Mart and other so-called category killers will put continued pressure on the nation's small town mom-and-pop businesses and historical downtowns. But just as McDonald's has advanced from its early stages to its Baroque phase, discount department stores and big-box users should become more adept at fitting into Main Streets and developing new formats which can be accommodated in in-fill locations over time. Where ethnic populations predominate, ethnic retailers can breathe life into some Main Streets, even in the absence of significant capital from conventional institutional sources. And as regional malls continue to saturate the suburbs, either with new properties in outlying areas or renovated centers in established markets, expect to see more mall-type retailers looking for other venues, and giving up some of their usual demographic requirements, which can be obtained in a mall, for free-standing and in-fill locations in urban areas with a dense population, high household income, or poor regional access.

For the nation's biggest cities, the picture is also mixed. Investors prefer retail properties in cities with diverse activity from residents, shoppers, tourists, and office workers. Ironically, it is the "edge cities" of the country's largest metro areas that seem to meet this criteria more than many big city CBDs, a trend that doesn't bode well for the influx of institutional capital that is so desperately needed by the nation's troubled downtowns. A few large cities are considered to have 24-hour downtowns, such as San Francisco, Chicago, Boston, New York, and Philadelphia. Other cities, such as Atlanta, Dallas, Detroit, Houston, Los Angeles, and Newark, are regarded by investors as having CBD cores that now function as no more than another satellite of the metropolitan area. With the center of gravity for each of these cities effectively shifted to a suburban location, their continued decline seems inevitable. The future for these "centerless" cities is far more negative than for cities where quality of life and diverse activity and occupations are present. For the healthier downtowns of major metros, expect continued redevelopment, probably from full-price to more value-oriented retailing, which appropriately reflects most downtowns' shopper base, and more regionally oriented, freeway-accessible enclosed mall developments, which will provide strong and aggressive competition to their suburban rivals. As prime suburban areas become intensively developed, congested and expensive, the interest on the part of all retailers and discounters in the nation's stronger CBDs should continue.

For both the CBDs and Main Streets, one thing is clear: No amount of government money or legislative action can completely reverse socioeconomic trends. Rational behavior will always dictate a flight of capital from high cost areas to lower cost ones—and from socially distressed areas to those with fewer people and fewer problems. The nation will continue to struggle with its ambivalence towards the usefulness of cities, even with the usefulness of Main Streets in small towns. Retailers will respond, and there will be a place for retail development in CBDs and on Main Street in the future.

Thirteen

Space Marketing and Lease Terms in Shopping Centers

Department Store, Major Chain, and Independents' Lease Terms

Marc J. Munaretto

M arketing space to retail merchants is a sophisticated endeavor that combines a variety of elements: sales, marketing, legal, construction, and operations. Although the tenant can generally see the physical space he or she is considering, or review space plans prior to construction, both the landlord and the tenant must share a vision of what the space will become when it is fitted with the tenant's improvements, signage, and merchandise. Documenting the transaction with a lease that embraces the business terms of the agreement, together with any specific covenants, conditions, and restrictions is a key element in the process. This chapter will deal with large and small shopping center leases.

THE SHOPPING CENTER LEASE

The most common shopping center leases are percentage leases that make the lease amount equal to the net of the real estate taxes, common area costs, and insurance costs. There may be, on rare occasions, space leases that are not net. For instance, some leases may provide for the excess of real estate taxes to be paid over a base year's amount or may place a cap on these costs. Shopping center leases also include a provision for percentage rent to be paid when the tenant's gross sales exceed a specific sales threshold, in other words, the greater of the minimum base rent or an agreed percent of the tenant's total gross sales from merchandise or services.

Ground Leases

Ground leases can either be subordinated to the first mortgage or nonsubordinated land leases. Subordinated ground leases contain a provision that subordinates the fee simple rights in the land to the mortgagee while nonsubordinated ground leases do not. Subordinated ground leases require the lessor, or fee owner, to pledge his fee simple land as collateral interest to the first mortgage. The note on this mortgage is also secured by the lessee's improvements on the land. In the event of a default, unless the fee owner is willing to cure any nonpayment of debt service, the mortgagee will be in a position to take full title to the collateral in the loan which is paramount because the typical lender in these transactions has traditionally been life companies. Life companies are fiduciaries and they may only be in a secure first priority lien position. The ground lessor, subject to the financial strength of the lessee, may be attracted to this form of transaction because it typically yields a more attractive ground rent. The downside to the lessor is apparent. In the event of a default in the first mortgage, he has risked the fee to the mortgagee.

Reciprocal Easement Agreements/Operating and Easement Agreements

Reciprocal easement agreements or operating and easement agreements are similar to leases insofar as they establish the covenants, conditions, and restrictions between the entities joined by this agreement. They include the terms upon which the department store or anchor store and the developer will:

1. Construct their building;
2. Operate and maintain their facility;
3. Create a standard of operation for the common areas and who will operate them;
4. Agree to operate a store for some period of years, under a particular trade name; and
5. Agree to any restrictions or impositions between the parties such as signage, minimum parking, insurance, preservation of view corridors, controls over the types of merchandise in the center; among others.

The Construction and Reciprocal Easement Agreement (REA) creates precise standards of construction and operation for department stores who are accustomed to building their own facility to very specific design specifications. As owners, department and anchor stores are accustomed to supporting their own operating and HVAC costs. The REA also includes restrictive covenants that are found in leases with both department stores and anchor tenants. These restrictive covenants place some degree of control over the developer's merchandising decisions within the mall be excluding or restricting certain types or categories of merchandise or services. Some of these categories include theatres, restaurants, health clubs, taverns or night clubs, among others. In addition, the REA grants ostensible control over any physical changes to the building or the common area to the developer but notwithstanding, it requires the developer to seek the approval of the parties to the REA before he may proceed.

LEASED VERSUS LEASABLE

A vexatious provision for tenants in the expense recovery section of the lease is the landlord's definition of *proportionate share*. In almost every standard landlord retail lease, the tenant's proportionate share of common area, real estate taxes, and insurance is based on a formula in which the numerator is the gross *leased* and occupied area (GLOA) of the shopping (in contrast to the gross leasable area [GLA] of the center). The leased area method of computing the tenant's share increases the tenants' exposure to these costs and effectively distributes 100% of these costs over the tenants in occupancy. The landlord argues that operating costs should be paid proportionately by tenants who benefit by these costs, exclusive of the vacant spaces in the shopping center. Tenants, of course, have a different perspective, particularly as a result of the significant increases in common area and real estate tax costs over the past 10 years. Tenants are placing increasing demands on the owner to control and reduce these costs wherever possible. One such control may be calculation of proportionate share based on the total gross leasable area [GLA] of the center.

For example:

> GLA: 100,000 sq. ft.   GLOA: 90,000 sq. ft.
>
> CAM Costs: $100,000

GLOA calculation for a 5,000-sq.-ft. tenant:

$$\frac{5,000 \text{ sq. ft.}}{90,000 \text{ sq. ft.}} = .05555 \text{ or } 5.56\%$$

$$5.56\% \times \$100,000 = \$5,560 \text{ annual common area cost}$$
$$(\$1.11 \text{ per sq. ft.})$$

GLA calculation for a 5,000 sq. ft. tenant:

$$\frac{5,000 \text{ sq. ft.}}{100,000 \text{ sq. ft.}} = .05 \text{ or } 5.00\%$$

$$5.00\% \times \$100,000 = \$5,000 \text{ annual common area costs}$$
$$(\$1.00 \text{ per sq. ft.})$$

Radius Restrictions

Percentage rent revenue is a critically important source of future rent that has, in some instances, been eroded by the strategic placement of stores in close proximity. In an effort to stem the potential for this occurrence, developers and owners negotiate for the inclusion of a radius restriction that limits the placement of additional stores in a defined area. The defined area is generally a 1- to 5-mile radius around the shopping center.

SPACE MARKETING

Finding the right tenant, anchor store, or department store depends upon a comprehensive understanding of the needs, wants, and expectations of the retailer. Furthermore, it depends on an ability to match these needs to the physical and demographic characteristics of a specific market area. More sophisticated retailers, such as anchor stores and department stores, and a growing number of national tenants leave as little to chance as possible in selecting a location in which to conduct business. Locations are screened to match certain demographic and psychographic criteria. Complex market research is often performed to estimate the sales potential of the subject site; to determine reasonably what competitor sales and market share may be; and to measure the potential for growth in sales over a defined period of time. Some of these site specific criteria include a minimum population density within a defined area; a specific range of household income levels; and a minimum average age and education. It might also include types of employment and other socioeconomic elements of a homogeneous demographic region.

The mechanisms for influencing the potential tenant's decision to choose your center include:

1. Advertising in trade publications and newspapers;
2. Direct mail distribution either to a proprietary list of targeted prospects;
3. Telephone contact;
4. Canvassing local and regional merchants;
5. Window and building signage;
6. A written proposal format;
7. Consistent follow up over time.

Professionally produced marketing collaterals (printed and audiovisual materials describing the features and benefits of the shopping center) are used to disseminate critical information gleaned from market research. A variety of publications such as *Chain Store Guide,* produce directories of national and regional chain stores and detail what their site criteria are for all types of retail properties. Other directories and publications provide this information for outlet and off-price shopping centers. Finding local tenant prospects, however, requires a higher level of creative effort and considerably more direct canvassing. The source books for most of these tenants is often the local telephone book or newspaper. The end result of marketing retail space is a homogeneous array of merchandise and services that fulfills the shopping needs, wants, and expectations of a target area.

THE EVOLVING ROLE OF THE BROKER

The historic role of the broker in neighborhood, community, and power shopping centers has been that of an agent of the owner. As such, he or she was responsible for procuring tenants for the space either to be constructed, presently vacant, or anticipated to become vacant in a shopping center. Using a combination of marketing, canvassing, and cold calling techniques, the broker sought out and identified prospective new or existing tenants from a broad range of sources, including competing developments and franchisers of new businesses. His efforts where generally devoted to matching a need to merchandise vacant space with an opportunity for a tenant to expand the business. The broker often acts as the exclusive agent of the owner; the broker is governed by the laws of the agency and he owes loyalty to the owner of the property. In this form of relationship, the broker is responsible for representing the interests of the owner and the owner is responsible for paying the broker's fee.

There is no standard commission rate among shopping center brokers. However, it is most common to express commissions on a dollar-per-square-foot basis. Normally, retail commissions have higher commission rates for smaller spaces. A frequent range for retail commissions may be $4 to $5 per square foot for leases up to 5,000 sq. ft.; $3 to $4 per square foot for leases over 5,000 square feet but under 15,000 sq. ft.; $2.00 to $3.00 per square foot for leases over 15,000 sq. ft. but under 40,000 sq. ft.; and $1.00 to $2.50 per square foot for leases over 40,000 sq. ft. These commissions are paid to the exclusive broker who, in turn, is responsible for paying the procuring broker. This is particularly true in instances in which the tenant may be represented by an exclusive broker. Also, it is not uncommon, in instances in which there is a cooperating broker, for the owner to pay a total commission equal to 150% of the stated commission rates. It is a frequent occurrence in some markets to pay the tenant's exclusive broker a full commission. The additional one-half commission is compensation for the owner's agent whose efforts to procure the tenant were no less than they would have been if the tenant were not represented. Some brokers are employed by either the landlord or the tenant in a specific transaction, working in a nonexclusive capacity. In such cases, the independent broker must secure a written commission agreement from the party he is representing in order to assure payment of his commission.

Community shopping centers have considerably more experience working with brokers than regional malls. However, many national retail firms have learned the importance of the broker's knowledge and his understanding of the market and its varying dynamics. Regional mall tenants and leasing representatives have, until more recent times, operated in something of a perfect market. For many years, there was an abundant supply of expanding national and regional retail tenants eager to populate a regional mall, a condition that may have contributed to the claim that most regional malls are similarly merchandised. The economic events of the past five years, including the recession and the consolidation of the retail industry, have begun to alter this condition and although there are still national, regional and local tenants eager to negotiate directly with the developer, conditions in this business are also changing to recognize more fully the important role of the broker or agent.

In increasing numbers, retailers are looking to the professional real estate broker for assistance in locating quality sites, and more traditionally to continue to assist in the disposition of surplus sites. It is possible that this condition has been brought about by: (1) a reduction in the size of corporate real estate departments with no corresponding reduction in their responsibilities; (2) an acknowledgment that brokers know the markets and the available product and can provide a more effective use of the retailer's time; and (3) brokers add value to the process in their understanding of the range of prevailing lease terms in a market. These are especially important factors to expanding tenants who cannot easily generate, in quality or in substance, the same degree of information available to a sophisticated retail brokerage firm. The broker's fundamental product is *information* and its application to the specific market needs of the tenant and the product available in his market.

ECONOMICS OF OBTAINABLE RENT

Each shopping center pro forma reflects the minimum rent expectations of the owner. It is derived from the owner's investment objectives for the asset and is tempered by conditions of the marketplace and the competition. To measure the financial performance of a leasing transaction, a variety of financial analysis tools are employed by owners. This analysis may include an objective evaluation of the discounted present value of the future cash flows generated by the lease; or it may be evaluated more subjectively on the basis of the importance of the tenant to the project and to the potential for attracting other key tenants.

In addition to understanding the finances of each leasing transaction, it is important to employ some form of measurement to determine: (1) how much square footage has been allocated to each category of merchandise in the center; (2) what proportion of fixed rent dollars are generated by each category; (3) what the sales performance of each category is or is projected to be; and (4) what the percentage relationship is to each category's sales.

These data will allow the marketing team to analyze, in existing centers, how much area is invested in each category and how well it is performing from a sales production perspective. In new centers, it is also important to construct a merchandising model that will allow the marketing team to focus its efforts to achieve a specific concentration of merchandise; a desired aggregate fixed rent; and a minimum expectation of gross sales among the various categories of merchandise. Table 13.1, on pp. 284–287, provides a sample measurement tool. The percentages of area invested in each category depend on the type of shopping center and the demand for certain merchandise and price points in the region gathered from market research and an understanding of the competition. An analysis of sales production by tenant and by category can be obtained from published information produced by the Urban Land Institute in the *Dollars and Sense of Shopping Center: 1993.*

DEPARTMENT STORE AND ANCHOR LEASES

The prevailing custom in shopping center developments and in retrofit leasing among anchor stores is the use of the form lease customarily employed by the tenant. Although these agreements vary widely in style and construction, their content is quite similar. Not unlike the document used for satellite store space, the anchor lease establishes the working relationship between the developer/owner and the department store or anchor tenant during the construction or reconstruction of the space and during the term of occupancy. In addition, these documents form the basis of value upon which the center's long-term financial life will be underwritten. Not all anchor or department stores are tenants. In regional malls and in some power centers, most department stores own the land and improvements and are legally joined to the developer's tract and the other department store tracts by way of a Construction and Reciprocal Easement Agreement. Reciprocal Easement Agreements establish the covenants, conditions, and restrictions that govern the relationship of the various entities that form the project. Some of the key REA provisions include: (1) covenant to operate; (2) cross parking and utility easements; (3) the cost and operation and maintenance of the common areas; (4) rights of self-help; and (5) construction. In some instances, department stores may acquire a leased fee with a term of between 50 and 99 years plus options, upon which they construct their own improvements. In this form of leasehold, they are joined with the other department stores and the developer by way of the covenants, conditions, and restrictions imposed in the REA.

The economics of the anchor or department store lease differ radically in concept from small shop lease economics. The developer's risk requires that he or she create a sustainable source of revenue (rent) that reflects the cost to construct a building on suitable land that will produce a desirable profit from capital cost and a competitive return on investment over a period of years. These transactions are more often a model of build-to-suit lease standards in today's terms whereas small shop pricing is more sensitive to supply and demand and market rent conditions. However, the developer can and does provide inducements to entice a department store or anchor tenant into a project. These inducements primarily provide for the developer to construct the space and pay as rent the sum required to amortize the developer's costs over the initial lease term, without interest. In this instance, the smaller tenants are subsidizing the department store. Inducements, however, should not be misconstrued with subsidy. Cash or other monetary consideration is still used on occasion to convince a key merchant to choose one project over another.

While the economic terms of most department store or anchor leases usually follow the convention of normal development economics, some have conjectured that anchor tenants are often subsidized by other tenants in a shopping center. While this conjecture may not apply to fixed rent, does it impact on other financial terms of the lease? Do all tenants pay an equal share of common area, insurance, and real estate taxes? Does each tenant pay based upon the same formula for proportionate share? No, proportionate share methodology can vary. Tenants define common area in different terms. Some elements of insurance are omitted from reimbursement by some tenants. What then defines a subsidy in the context of shopping center leasing? Although it is generally agreed that the common area provisions of anchor leases allow for a lower common area recovery ratio, many national chain stores are equally demanding in this element of the lease negotiation. We need to examine this argument of subsidy from an enclosed mall and strip center perspective.

Department stores and anchor tenants in regional malls typically support 100% of the exterior common area maintenance. Landscaping, snow removal, paving and striping, exterior lighting and

TABLE 13.1

Merchandise and Rent Analysis

GLA: 187,089

	Sq. Ft.	Current Rent $ Psf	$ Rent	Category Rent Psf
Women's Ready to Wear				
Misses RTW	3,540	7.00	24,780	
Junior RTW	3,550	6.00	21,300	
Half size RTW	2,378	7.00	16,646	
Career apparel	3,533	7.00	24,731	
Petite RTW	949	12.00	11,388	
	13,950		98,845	$ 7.09
Men's Ready to Wear				
None	0	0	0	0
Men's & Women's Ready to Wear				
Levis	2,638	8.00	21,104	
Men's and Women	8,960	3.00	26,880	
	11,598		47,984	$ 4.14
Children's Ready to Wear				
None	0	0	0	0
Footwear				
Athletic shoe	2,010	11.00	22,110	
Family shoe	2,940	12.00	35,280	
	4,950		57,390	$11.59
Jewelry				
Credit jewelry	945	23.00	21,176	
Costume jewelry	295	12.00	10,620	
	1,240		32,355	$26.09
Specialty Food				
Candy	435	25.00	10,875	$25.00
Restaurant				
None	0	0	0	0
Fast Food				
Salad/Sandwich	919	4.98	4,577	
Pizza	1,165	10.00	11,650	
Bagel	1,740	10.00	17,400	
	3,824		33,627	$ 8.79

% of Category to Total GLA	Annual Sales 199_		Sales Psf	% to Total Sales	Percentage Rent $	Ratio of Rent to Sales
	$	327,836	$ 93			7.56%
		674,483	190		12,242	3.16
		288,750	121			5.76
		278,897	79			8.87
		158,679	167			7.18
7.46	$	1,728,645	$124	9.85	12,242	5.72%
0		0	0	0	0	0
	$	288,750	$109			7.31%
		621,000	69			4.33
6.20	$	909,750	$ 78	5.19	0	5.27%
0		0	0	0	0	0
	$	198,527	$ 99			11.14%
		195,825	67			18.02
2.65	$	394,352	$ 80	2.25	0	14.55%
	$	323,142	$342			6.55%
		73,367	249			14.48
0.66	$	396,509	$320	2.26	0	8.16%
0.23	$	178,950	$411	1.02	2,988	6.08%
0		0	0	0	0	0
	$	145,650	$158			11.14%
		174,750	150			6.67
		336,533	193		123	5.17
2.04	$	656,933	$172	3.74	7,197	5.12%

(Continued)

TABLE 13.1 (Continued)

	Sq. Ft.	Current Rent $ Psf	$ Rent	Category Rent Psf
Home Furnishings & Housewares				
Art and supplies	6,630	8.25	54,698	$ 8.25
Music, Records, Home Entertainment				
Radio	2,280	10.00	22,800	
Records	2,940	6.50	13,033	
	4,385		35,833	$ 8.36
Specialty Retail				
Alternatives	943	10.00	9,430	
Amusements	2,024	15.50	31,372	
Fabrics	3,600	6.90	24,840	
Picture frames	176	24.00	4,224	
	6,567		65,642	$10.00
Service Retail				
Optical	1,114	14.00	15,596	
Hair salon	1,628	10.00	16,280	
U.S. Post Office	93	23.58	2,100	
ATM Machine	63	60.42	3,806	
Photo	1,104	8.00	8,832	
	4,002		46,614	$11.65
Drug				
None	0	0	0	0
Gifts, Card, Books				
Books	1,950	13.00	25,350	
Cards	1,785	16.00	28,560	
Tobacco	898	10.00	8,980	
Gallery	1,695	11.00	18,645	
Studio	2,280	9.21	20,999	
	8,608		102,534	$11.91
Cinema				
None	0	0	0	0
Department Stores				
Dept. Store #1	121,000	5.58	675,180	$ 5.58
Total Retail:	**187,089**		**$1,261,576**	**$ 6.74**

% of Category to Total GLA	Annual Sales 199_	Sales Psf	% to Total Sales	Percentage Rent $	Ratio of Rent to Sales
3.54	$ 1,170,000	$176	6.67	40,230	4.68%
	$ 272,433	$120			8.37%
	398,400	199		5,138	3.27
2.29	$ 670,833	$157	3.82	5,138	5.34%
	$ 117,300	$124			8.04%
	111,313	55			28.19
	314,313	87			7.90
	44,850	255			9.42
3.51	$ 587,776	$ 94	3.35	0	11.17%
	$ 221,550	$199			7.04%
	363,750	223		5,541	4.48
	0	0			0.00
	0	0			0.00
	116,250	105			7.60
2.14	$ 701,550	$175	4.00	0	6.64%
0	0	0	0	0	0
	$ 517,583	$265		529	4.90%
	398,100	222		681	7.17
	75,000	84			11.97
	329,805	195			5.65
	328,320	144			6.40
4.60	$ 1,648,808	$192	9.40	1,210	6.22%
0	0	0	0	0	0
64.68	$ 8,500,000	$ 70	48.45	0	7.94%
100%	$17,544,106	$ 94	100%	$74,728	7.19%

security, within an acceptable standard of maintenance, are essential services provided to the common benefit of all. However, most department stores provide only a nominal contribution to interior mall common area cost. Their monthly voluntary assessment can range from $500 to more than $5,000. The balance of these costs, after subtracting the department stores' contributions, are distributed among the interior mall tenants who, in effect, provide a subsidy to the anchors by paying an increased proportion of the aggregate common area costs.

In strip centers, however, the anchor stores more typically pay a proportionate share of common area maintenance costs, real estate taxes, and insurance, with certain exclusions. There is a growing trend among power center anchor stores to place limitations on a developer's control of the costs of maintaining the common areas. Limitations are very often placed upon the maximum annual increases in common area costs that the tenant will pay. These increases may be limited to no more than 5% annually. The shortfall from contributions made by anchor stores to recoverable costs become part of the burden of the small shop tenant. In the evaluation of subsidy, the small shop tenant absorbs some part of the cost that might otherwise be supported by the anchor tenant(s).

SMALL STORE LEASES

It is axiomatic that independents lack the bargaining clout and the experience of developer/investor in lease provisions. Leases for small store tenants have evolved with the changing conditions of the real estate industry and the various conditions that have impacted shopping centers. The evolution of the small store lease has been affected by elements such as promotion and marketing, insurance, environmental laws, reimbursements for operating expenses, the use of the premises, access by the handicapped pursuant to the ADA, among others. Developer and tenant influences in this document mirror the important business and legal issues that affect the financial and operating components of their respective businesses. A few examples are discussed next.

Environmental Laws

The inclusion of environmental language in leases is a contemporary example of how leases mirror changing conditions. The emergence of concerns relating to the contamination of soils, HVAC refrigerants, the use, storage, and disposal of certain chemicals by both landlords and tenants have given rise to a whole new level of negotiation in most leases. The essential component in this language between both entities seems to be the dispersion of risk and the avoidance of liability. Since environmental laws such as CERCLA have very broad applications, the parties in a lease are interested in deflecting responsibility for acts in which they have not participated.

Common Area Costs

Common area language among many chain store and regional multiple store tenants is under the closest scrutiny ever and landlords are being forced to be ever more accountable for the tenants' share of operating costs. In some instances, tenants are demanding evidence of these costs in the form of copies of invoices, advance copies of common area budgets, and by controlling the frequency of major repairs in the common areas.

Self-Help Rights

Self-help rights have become unilateral provisions in anchor store and department store leases and REAs. These self-help rights provide that the tenant may perform on the landlord's behalf under some circumstances. Some of these provisions, for example, permit the anchor store to take over the maintenance and repair obligation in the common areas from the landlord. The conditions under which this decision is typically made are a result of the landlord's failure to adequately perform his duties. This is not always the case, however. Some tenants choose to take control of the common areas to reduce operating costs. These self-help provisions are inserted to keep the landlord from becoming complacent in performing his duties although they can lead to tenant abuses. This transfer of power has evolved as a check-and-balance mechanism and the competition for anchor stores and the evolving relationship between developer and tenant have increased the tenant's negotiating leverage in this area. Unless the landlord makes the tenant accountable for a consistent standard of performance, it is possible for the landlord to be at a disadvantage if the tenant chooses to provide substandard performance.

Small store leases are an important part of the fiscal structure of a shopping center. The landlord seeks to control a higher proportion of the revenue-generating provisions of the document. These leases, although they may represent a wide band of credit worthiness, generate the substance of profit in many shopping centers.

ALTERNATIVE LEASE STRUCTURES

Temporary tenants are finding increasing opportunities to merchandise their products and services in regional malls and, to a growing extent, in community shopping centers. These tenants typically rent space for a brief period of time, usually one year or less, at a fixed rent plus a percentage of sales. They can occupy either kiosk locations in the mall or vacant in-line spaces. The landlord chooses not to convey a leasehold estate in the realty by executing a lease with the tenant but, rather, chooses to extend a license to the tenant to use the space for a specific purpose. These are often start-up businesses and some developers and owners have learned to use this program to incubate permanent local tenancies that enrich the center's merchandise selection and character. Temporary tenants are at a distinct disadvantage in negotiating lease terms. The provisions give them few rights beyond a narrowly defined use, required hours of operation, and the need to pay rent.

PERCENTAGE RENT

Percentage rent is rent expressed as a percentage of gross annual sales volume. For the purposes of this chapter, gross annual sales can be defined as the sales prices of all goods, wares, and merchandise sold, and the charges for all services performed by the tenant, any permitted subtenant, licensees, concessionaires, or any other person or entity in, at, or from the premises for cash, credit or otherwise. Items commonly excluded from gross sales include merchandise exchanges made between stores, returns to manufacturers, refunds to customers on transactions included in gross sales, sales of fixtures or machinery, and sales or use taxes imposed by a governmental authority. Early in shopping center development, merchants, feeling unsure of this new shopping center format, leased space on percentage leases with a minimum base rent that reflected the landlord's minimum financial requirement to operate the center and amortize his costs. In an effort to allay the risk in this new shopping format, the developer and tenant became "partners" by sharing in the tenant's future performance over a set threshold of sales performance. Percentages for additional rent were set to reflect what the merchant could afford to pay based on historic occupancy ratios, markups, and the differing types of merchandise. Percentage rents were an enticement to the landlord that his rents would grow over time based upon the tenants' increasing performance and, to the tenant, that his rents would never exceed a fixed percentage of sales. These additional rental dollars would serve to defray the effects of time and inflation on long-term leases at fixed rental rates. Thresholds were established by dividing annual fixed rent by the tenant's percentage rent rate. Table 13.2 provides a range of percentage rent rates, by merchandise category.

While the fundamental elements of this theory are still in place, two things have changed over time: (1) inflation in the 1970s and 1980s had a dramatic impact on growth in tenant sales and percentage rents; and (2) underwriting for financings placed an increasing demand on the developer for more secure income to support the debt. Long-term leases written in the 1960s and 1970s produced attractive

TABLE 13.2

Percentage Rent Rates by Merchandise Category

	Regional Mall Range (%)	Strip Center Range (%)
Women's apparel	3 to 6	4 to 6
Men's apparel	3 to 7	3 to 6
Children's apparel	3 to 7	3 to 6
Shoes	4 to 7	4 to 6
Jewelry	5 to 8	5 to 8
Specialty food	5 to 10	5 to 10
Restaurant	4 to 7	5 to 7
Fast food	8 to 10	5 to 10
Furniture, home furnishings & housewares	4 to 7	3 to 6
Music and records and home entertainment	3 to 6	3 to 6
Specialty retail	5 to 10	5 to 8
Service retail	6 to 9	5 to 7
Drugs	2 to 4	2 to 5
Gifts, cards and books	6 to 10	3 to 7
Cinema	6 to 10	6 to 10
Anchor store, grocery	n/a	1 to 3
Anchor store, nonfood	0.5 to 2.5	1 to 3

Source: The Urban Land Institute—*Dollars and Cents of Shopping Centers: 1993.*

percentage rents that served to hedge the landlord's investment against the effects of inflation and created a windfall for landlords upon renewal. At renewal, it was customary to convert 75% or more of the tenant's effective rent (fixed rent plus percentage rent) into a new base rent producing a long-term secure source of revenue that the landlord could leverage. This convention is dependent upon conditions in the market, not the least of which is supply and demand. In addition, events of the past few years, such as the collapse of the savings and loan industry and the burgeoning supply caused from overbuilding almost all forms of commercial space, have demonstrated that renewal rents can also decline and may not be subject to simple arithmetic.

Lenders and investors have, in varying degrees dependent upon the type of shopping center and the stature of the tenant, heavily discounted the value of percentage rents in computing the finance or investment value of shopping centers. Percentage rents are viewed as an unreliable source of revenue that can be impacted by conditions out of the control of either tenant or landlord and as such the value of this stream of revenue is adjusted for its risk. However, it is possible that capitalization rates are favorably impacted in those centers with a record of producing sustainable percentage rents. Centers with historic levels of percentage rent underscore stability and performance and can often provide a basis for future profit from the conversion of percentage rents to fixed rents upon lease renewal.

The accuracy of tenant sales reporting has always been a question that confronts this issue of percentage rent reliability. Although a well-written lease allows for an audit of tenant sales, this mechanism is costly and can be difficult to apply. While there is some concern about the accuracy of sales data, errors committed in this regard tend to be more a function of the management of different leases with differing definitions of sales than it is outright under-reporting. Chain stores have a considerable challenge managing the exceptions to numerous leases. Under-reporting sales is often a condition driven by the differences among too numerous percentage rent provisions and too numerous definitions of gross sales.

In many small centers, the potential for generating percentage rent is small. High fixed rents in relation to the tenant's sales potential have generally made it impossible for small tenants to reach their sales threshold. This condition is exacerbated by the indexing of fixed rents to a cost of living formula or in the use of graduated steps in fixed rents. Although percentage leases continue to be employed for small and large centers, most of these agreements employ, in addition, an alternative fixed rent structure. There are two frequently used methods of gradually increasing rents in retail leases: (1) periodic stepped rents in which the tenant agrees to pay a graduated rent; or (2) a fixed rent multiplier, such as the Consumer Price Index, that increases fixed rent by the percentage change in the index. The fixed rent multiplier is more difficult to employ among tenants whose experiences with the growth in these indices has been unpleasant.

MECHANICS OF THE RETAIL LEASE

The retail lease form is the contract that binds the tenant and the landlord to perform in a very specific manner over a defined period of time. It is the culmination of the process of creating value and it is a function of the selling event. The lease is also a contract that is written in a careful fashion to blend the needs of the landlord with those of the tenant to provide an effective vehicle for the distribution of the merchant's goods and services in a well-located, well-constructed, and well-operated retail environment.

Use and Continuous Occupancy

Two segments of the lease require special consideration, the use clause and the assignment clause. In combination, they can have a beneficial or a deleterious impact upon the performance of the center and the generation of future sales and traffic. The use clause provides for two important elements in the contract between landlord and tenant: (1) it affirms that the tenant will operate the premises continuously and with the intent to produce maximum sales; and (2) it describes the parameters for the merchandise the tenant may sell while it occupies the premises. This agreement forms a covenant that assures the landlord that the shoe store or apparel store, for example, will always be a specific type of shoe store or apparel store. Furthermore, it creates a covenant that the tenant will always keep the store open during required hours of operation and operate and merchandise it in such a fashion so as to produce the maximum sales from the premises. The developer has studied the needs of the market served by the shopping center and has carefully developed a merchandising plan that combines merchants synergistically to complement each other. It is essential that the developer retain control over merchandising decisions that will influence the future performance of the center.

Developers who negotiate use clauses that are too narrow or focused can create a potential tenant turnover problem by making it difficult for the merchant to produce a satisfactory level of sales production or earn a reasonable profit. This is more often found among independent tenants than among chain stores who have well-developed use clause language. It is essential to maintain a willingness to review the use clause language and to make changes that are warranted.

Assignment Clause

Assignment and sublease provisions generally allow for the legal transfer of the rights in a leasehold estate from one tenant to a successor tenant. The rules allowing this transfer are very precise in most leases and place conditions upon both the assignor (the original tenant) and the assignee. Some of the rules governing assignment include:

1. Written consent of the transfer by the landlord.
2. The use of the premises must not change, unless specifically approved by the landlord.
3. Financial data of the assignee must be provided for landlord review and acceptance.
4. The assignor may not be in default of the lease.
5. The assignor be required to remain liable for the performance under the lease subsequent to the assignment.

In more recent leases, the landlord may reserve the right to terminate the tenant's lease and any future obligations for performance by the assignor, in lieu of permitting its assignment. A new lease can then be negotiated with the assignee as a new tenant. This provision is often employed in tandem with the landlord's agreement not to unreasonably withhold consent in the tenant's request to assign the lease. It provides an acceptable alternative to assignment by permitting the termination of the rights, duties, and obligations of the original tenant (assignor) in its lease in exchange for allowing the landlord to negotiate a new lease with the successor tenant for the premises. The original tenant avoids a contingent liability in the assigned lease and permits the landlord to negotiate a new lease with the successor tenant. It should be noted that anchor stores and department stores possess broad rights to assign their leases to any lawful uses without landlord consent. This same provision can be found in strip center leases among a growing number of chain stores.

Leasing Space to Be Constructed

Leasing space to be constructed presents special challenges. How can the tenant be certain the space will be built? Will the finished shopping center look like the rendering in the developer's brochure? Who will the anchor tenants be and is their commitment certain? How carefully will the developer merchandise the center to maximize the tenant's sales potential and synergize the sales potential of the whole center? These issues are carefully planned in the lease document to reflect the conditions under which the center will be built and what the consequences to the developer are if he is unable to deliver the shopping center in substantially the form contemplated. The ramifications here are clear if the developer fails to perform: tenant cancellation of leases, loss of rents, and the likely loss of or inability to secure permanent financing.

Special Clauses during Start-Up Leasing

Some chain stores prefer and, indeed may require, that only percentage rent be paid until the shopping center achieves an agreed maturity defined in terms of a stated percentage of occupancy, say 80%, or a number of years. Other chains reserve the right to cancel their lease if the shopping center fails to achieve an agreed occupancy within a stated period of time. A developer may negotiate to "kick out" a tenant that fails to produce an agreed annual sales volume within a stated period of time. The permutations, here, are limited only by one's imagination and negotiating skills.

Modernization and Remerchandising

For the leasing representative, modernization of the center is the centerpiece to the leasing and marketing effort and it is an important condition in the decision making of new tenants. It is an opportunity to not only update the merchandise offered by the center but, also, to relocate tenants and reconfigure spaces. Reconfiguration may potentially increase the value of vacant spaces to be leased by (1) increasing the number of spaces the developer has to work with; and (2) by allowing for combinations of spaces that yield the square footages required by new and exciting tenants who are expanding in the marketplace.

As conditions in the retail industry continue to promote consolidation, regional malls are also confronted with the need to retrofit and retenant large spaces. This problem becomes more complex with Reciprocal Easement Agreements that are cross-functional among all parties of the REA. In addition, the department store usually owns and controls the land and building and is joined with the other department stores and the mall shop segment of the shopping center. In these instances, satisfying the varying agenda among the parties in the REA becomes a very complex condition. However, there is a growing trend among secondary regional malls to either transform the enclosed center into an open power center or to replace a vacant department store with a national discount store or category killer. In traditionally merchandised regional malls, these changes can create substantial apprehension among conventional mall tenants and it may be too early to predict how well they will be able to compete with this new class of retailer. For the owner, the choices among replacement department stores can be extremely limited and they may have no alternative other than to lease the vacant anchor to a discount store or category killer.

Lease Cancellation Rights

The influences impacting the use clause in retail leases were discussed earlier in this chapter. There are other topics of the retail lease that are important to address. In a rapidly changing retail industry and among markets equally subject to change, it is becoming increasingly commonplace for chain store tenants in strip centers to demand the right to cancel their lease upon certain conditions. These conditions most often correlate to a specific level of sales production over a specified duration, usually at the end of the 2nd or 3rd lease year. To be certain, this is a problematic condition for the developer who must protect his revenue stream and who must make certain that he is able to cover his operating expenses and debt service. Releasing costs can erode the developer's potential profit and impair the terms of financings and the potential investment value of the asset. At the same time, the dynamic conditions of the retail industry are often reflected in the changing fortunes of the retailer's balance sheet. This condition can be applied in a bilateral fashion in which developers reserve the right to terminate if the tenant fails to perform to a prescribed standard.

How do each of the parties, who possess apparently divergent needs, assure themselves of adequate protections? The developer continues to be tenacious about knowing the relative strength of the tenant's balance sheet. In some instances, this right to cancel can be tied to a specific tenant, minimum net worth threshold. In other instances, the developer can require repayment of some proportion of the unamortized costs of any improvements performed for the tenant if the tenant elects to terminate. Often, the developer accepts the risk that the tenant will choose not to exercise his right to terminate. In these instances, it is most important to negotiate this provision to provide the tenant a one-time right to make this election.

Bankruptcy

The changing fortunes in retail balance sheets have also fueled retail bankruptcies. The trustee in the bankruptcy estate is in control of the assets of the estate and has very broad powers granted by these laws. The trustee may dispose of the lease, a financial asset of the tenant, almost indiscriminately. The only area in which the landlord may have an arguable position in a lease assigned by the bankruptcy trustee relates to the use of the premises. If the use is clearly objectionable or can be proved to impair the center or the performance of its other tenants, it is possible to forestall such an assignment.

Exclusive Use

Exclusive use provisions provide some level of control over a specific category or segment of retail merchandise. The tenant views this provision as a controlling element in excessive (or any) duplication in the landlord's merchandising strategy. It is also a mechanism employed by a tenant to eliminate, at least in a shopping center, any apparent competition. Exclusivity is less often found in regional malls than in strip shopping centers and one must be very specific in the wording of this language. It is not common to include anchor stores or incidental merchandise in other tenants' businesses in this provision. Remember to exclude existing tenants from new leases with exclusivity clauses.

Expansion Space

Chain stores evaluate their space needs with extreme care; some can be very inflexible with respect to size and dimensions. Expansion provisions are infrequently found among these tenants. However, some discount stores such as Wal-Mart, and several grocery chains can require the developer to set aside land for expansion. Leases may include language that establishes the provisions for the construction of the expansion area and the rent to be paid by the tenant. The most common formula places a value on construction costs for the expansion and expresses a minimum rent based on a fixed rate of return. For instance, if expansion costs are to be $42 per square foot (psf) and the return criteria is established as 12.00% then the rent would be $5.04 ($42 × .12% = $5.04 psf). Alternatively, the tenant may choose to lease the land from the developer or owner and invest in constructing its own improvements.

CONCLUSION

Never before has the competition for tenants of all sizes been as intense as it is today. The disparity in retail space supply and demand and the consolidation that continues to affect the retail industry clearly underscore this point. The prominence of marketing and leasing in the global process of shopping center development and ownership should be quite evident. It is in this element of the process that meaningful, substantive, and sustainable long-term investment and finance value is created for the real estate. Moreover, it is a well-conceived and well-executed marketing plan that is essential to restoring the financial value to distressed or underperforming real estate.

The role of the marketing team, especially the leasing representative and the leasing broker, is continuing to evolve to embrace the higher disciplines of marketing. The techniques of this task are growing in sophistication. The skills required to influence the decision-making behavior of retail tenants, who are often deluged with location choices, must continually be adapted to the special needs of the market, the consumer, and the tenant. Marketing success depends upon the ability to carefully match the needs, wants, and expectations of the consumer to those of the tenant. Demonstrating and presenting this match in a succinct and persuasive way is the essence of marketing.

Fourteen

Operating and Managing Retail Centers

Harold J. Carlson

T he increasing competition across all segments of retail has made operation and management of retail centers a critical issue. Controlling costs and increasing sales are the two, often conflicting, goals. Security, in retail properties as in other aspects of modern life, is an overriding issue. Regardless of the form of management utilized for the property, there are three basic needs to be addressed. The first is a strategy. Where is the center in the marketplace today? Where should it be? How will it get there?

The second—specific objectives. Objectives as to leasing and tenant mix, as to operating cost control, as to income forecasts and a bottom-line target, and as to marketing goals.

The third is a management plan—deciding in advance—what to do, how to do it, when to do it, and who is to do it—that bridges the gap from where the center is to where the center should be.

1. Identifying and then meeting the customers' needs.
2. Capitalizing on a center's existing strengths.
3. The creation of competitive advantages.

Experience has shown the success of a shopping center is clearly dependent on a thorough business plan that states the objectives together with short- and long-range recommendations for achieving them. For such a plan to be effective, the manager must:

- Gather all the pertinent information about the center—its location, trade area, competition, market characteristics (size, support, share, and demographic and psychographic details).
- Thoroughly analyze this information and present the results in a useable format.
- Make specific recommendations that will guide the operation of the property in an appropriate direction.

While this management plan represents a professional analysis of the asset, the recommendations must reflect several factors. These include the financial capabilities of ownership (or an outline of methods of financing, if that is a viable alternative), their reasons for owning the property, and their long-range objectives for it. The business plan becomes the guide book and, hence, must be thorough, well-thought-out, and detailed.

A frequently-used outline includes the following ten points:

1. An executive summary.
2. Company history/background.
3. Service description.
4. Industry analysis.
5. Market analysis.
6. Marketing strategy.
7. Organizational issues: ownership and management.
8. Support services.
9. Financial statements.
10. Risk analysis.

A property leased to a single tenant will generally prove to be an easy management assignment. The manager must administer the lease and ensure the tenant is fulfilling all its obligations in both a timely and effective manner. Periodic property inspections are a must, and care must be exercised to be certain the insurance policies are appropriately written and in adequate amounts. The level of housekeeping and maintenance appropriate for the property should consider the tenant's use, the provisions for maintenance, the location of the building and the lease agreement. Under a *gross lease*, the landlord generally remains obligated for the exterior maintenance of the property and for the payment of real estate taxes, operating expenses, and insurance premiums. The rent under a gross lease is often subject to periodic adjustments, usually upward, to reflect the current costs of the foregoing landlord obligations. The lease provisions vary as to the frequency of rent adjustments related to the change in operating expenses. Landlords favor an annual review and adjustment, while tenants prefer less frequent adjustments to permit a more accurate budgeting of occupancy expense.

In many parts of the country, brokers and rental agents will refer to "net," "net-net," and "net-net-net" or "triple net" as they describe the terms of the lease document. Generally under a net lease, the landlord shifts to the tenant the obligation for the timely payment of real estate taxes. When the lease is net-net, the tenant is obligated to pay not only the real estate taxes, but also the insuring costs. There may be some negotiation as to exactly what type of insurance will be included in the tenant's obligations, but most often, it involves the basic property insurance (fire and extended coverages) or some form of "all risk" protection. Under a triple-net lease, the landlord shifts to the tenant the obligation to pay taxes, insurance premiums and the cost and expenses of repair and maintenance of the structure. Two issues that are often the subject of specific discussion and negotiation in a triple-net lease involve the roof and the structural integrity of the building. Many times, upon conclusion of the give-and-take of lease negotiation, the landlord may remain obligated for roof repairs and building structural repairs, particularly if the property is not newly built, and thus the lease is technically not triple-net.

Simple pre-printed property management forms can often be used when the property involved is a free-standing or a single-tenant building. These forms should be scrutinized carefully to be certain all issues are appropriately addressed. Management Agreements involving multi-tenanted shopping centers, however, should not generally be a "stock" form because of the relative complexity of property administration. Any agreement should thoroughly and accurately describe the shopping center including a statement as to the gross leasable area (GLA) of the property and its specific location, including expansion rights; the agency and term; compensation including an understanding of reimbursable and special expenses; and the duties of the agent. The agreement should address personnel assigned, budget responsibilities, leasing obligations and guidelines, tenant contact and frequency, service contracts-negotiation and approvals, participation in Merchants' Association activity, timely payment of utility bills and real estate taxes, enforcement of leases, maintenance responsibility, financial requirements—separate bank accounts, bill payment procedures, monthly statements and operations reports, indemnity and insurance agreements, and default provisions.

GOALS OF MANAGEMENT

Professional management is the effective, efficient, creative, timely, and ethical use of physical, mental, financial and human resources toward the attainment of well-planned, short-term, goals. If the short-term goals of management are well-thought-out and well-planned, they will also lead to the attainment of long-term goals. Management represents an agency relationship between the owner and agent in which the majority, but not necessarily all of the renting, maintenance and promotional functions are delegated to the agent.

NEIGHBORHOOD AND COMMUNITY CENTERS

Generally, neither neighborhood or community centers require on-site management staffs, but they do require management. Experience has shown that owners who believe their centers don't "need" management will have centers that generally underperform, suffer high vacancies, and fail to sustain value in the marketplace.

With competition increasing, the informational needs of the small center owner/manager are becoming more critical. Information about who typically shops at a small center, how they get to the center, where they shop and how much they spend can offer a standard of comparison. Data on shopper characteristics, habits and expenditure patterns among small center shoppers can be extremely valuable to professional center management. Currently available benchmarking information, tabulated by demographic/economic characteristics, when used with data gathered at the center, can provide for the creation of marketing, leasing and management strategies. Astute center managers have found that the more research done, the better direction they can give to what the center offers, what stores the customer would like to have at the center, and how what the center offers is communicated to the customers.

In virtually every center, there are merchants that need help. Whether disappointing store windows, amateurish paper signs, sloppy use of display fixtures and weak merchandise presentations, or anemic sales productivity, it is usually obvious which stores are not adequately serving and selling to their customers. Many small tenants lack professional training, and some "mom-and-pops" may lack shopping center experience. Even some chain store managers are guilty of ignoring retailing basics, requiring a response from proactive center management in the form of market research, marketing and the use of consultants.

MARKETING

Developing a successful marketing theme requires consumer research to determine shopper preferences, perceptions, likes and dislikes. Properly conducted market research provides guidance for fine-tuning the merchandise offerings of the center's merchants.

Through focus groups, managers can be alerted to mismatches between the center's stores and the center's prospective customers. So-called "secret" or "mystery" shoppers are frequently used by the retail industry to test the quality of the products and services being provided by the center's stores. These people then report directly to center management on their impressions of the performance by the stores visited. Good store window displays (visual merchandising) generally will stimulate sales, particularly of newly-arrived, full-price merchandise.

Developer-owners and major retailing organizations have learned that to attain its sales potential quickly, a shopping center must have a well-organized, active merchants' group and an aggressive and continuous cooperative advertising and promotional program based upon sound merchandising and publicity principles. A center marketing program can increase store sales, improve tenant relations, enhance the developer's image, build a long-term "brand" franchise, extend market share, and reinforce brand identity and loyalty.

Effective advertising is focused advertising, the kind that speaks directly to the customer base. Developing a successful marketing theme requires appropriate research to determine shopper preferences, perceptions, likes and dislikes. Consultants can use this data to create messages appealing to the targeted base. Shopping center-sponsored workshops using local management-oriented executives can sharpen the skills of store managers and department heads—again, for everyone's benefit.

OPERATIONS

Operations include customer service, direct-mail advertising, telemarketing, clientele building, managing cash flow, generating publicity, and community involvement. Such programs can be sponsored by center management in the form of workshops with assistance from outside specialists and authorities.

Security workshops and center-sponsored seminars on issues such as shoplifting and self-defense can prove valuable by creating not only an awareness of the issues, but specific steps that can and should be taken in various emergencies. Shoplifting is everyone's problem, for part of the price customers pay for merchandise reflects the added cost to the store in dealing with this issue. Workshops can highlight new anti-theft devices that are more efficient and less expensive. Retail shrinkage and pilferage can be reduced initially with proper security.

It is imperative that center management provide the right programs for the right merchants. Programs should be specifically designed to suit a specific store's information needs—one plan doesn't suit all stores. When possible, work with potential winners, not losers. Tenants respond best to objective outside experts, and a variety of shopping center and retail consultants may be used. Resources include local schools, community and business associations all of whom may have speakers available. Other possibilities include the Chamber of Commerce, trade groups such as the International Council of Shopping Centers, the Urban Land Institute, the National Retail Merchants Association, media sales representatives, advertising agencies, and national seminar presenters.

REGIONAL MALLS

Regional shopping centers are faced with all the issues of administration and management of the neighborhood and the community centers, as well as additional challenges related in part to their much larger size; the importance of their anchors; the larger number and diversity of their tenants; and the role such centers play in the regional marketplace. The basics remain the same, but larger centers require larger management staff and increased supervision.

In an operational sense, a shopping center is a management concept, not a building. As a planned collection of retail outlets, each with its own identity, each separately-owned, but all working together as a single business enterprise, the shopping center has a major impact on our way of life. Current research indicates almost every American adult visits a shopping center at least once a month. Most make about two trips to a center every week. Increasingly, the shopping center is the choice for leisure time activities and entertainment.

Shopping centers have become the new town center in many communities and, as such, are subject to many of the woes of contemporary society. Malls and centers are almost universally considered safe to visit, but that doesn't mean they are above the fray and beyond the multiple and nagging problems that affect community life. When an incident happens at one of these properties, it becomes news and is reported by the media, creating safety concerns for the community.

Competent center management must address the goal of a safe and secure center. Customers and employees both are entitled to the perception, at least, of a safe environment. Some of the shopping center managers' responsibilities toward that end include ensuring physical upkeep of the property, enforcing rules and guidelines, ensuring smooth traffic flow, and maintaining a secure environment.

COSTS

Shopping center operating costs—which the industry refers to as common area maintenance (CAM) costs—have been on the rise. This cost category includes such expenditures as shopping center security, parking lot maintenance, common area maintenance, roofing maintenance, utility costs, snow removal, center insurance premiums, and, in some cases, advertising and promotion.

Each property is an individual challenge as the physical plant, local market conditions, and the competition all play a role as owners/managers endeavor to balance quality and cost control. Excessive costs will often prove detrimental to achievement of a competitive net operating income.

If a tenant has only so many dollars for occupancy, most managers will agree they want the revenue dollars to be in rent, not in common area maintenance (CAM). CAM income is not as bankable as rental income. The owner and management benefits by holding down occupancy charges and maintaining rents. With escalating CAM charges, the ultimate burden goes to the tenant, who has no control over the cost, while the owner, who has some control, is insulated from these charges. Some management companies recognize CAM as another area in which they can gain an edge in the ever-increasing competition in the shopping center industry. Lower CAM charges not only help make center space more attractive to both customers and tenants by increasing occupancy, but they free up tenants' finances, allowing the landlord to charge a higher net rent. Both are important factors in increasing the value of the center.

Whether identified as common area maintenance costs or operating costs, it doesn't really matter. What does matter is components of the costs are passed on to the tenant. Factors to consider are:

- Center configuration as an enclosed, heated and cooled mall or an open-air center;
- The relationship of common areas to gross leasable area;
- Finishes and features requiring maintenance within the center (plants, fountains, inaccessible light fixtures, dark corners, etc.);
- Hours of operation;
- Makeup and size of the center's trade area; and
- Local community standards as to maintenance, cleanliness, decorum, safety.

"Cost cutting" has been the credo and every number on the financial and operating cost statement will come under scrutiny. It is appropriate that the landlord and the tenant be concerned with each others financial well-being. In selecting a manager, owners should review track record, job descriptions, supervision and incentive pay. Some work will be contracted versus performed in-house, and the manager should be aware of trade-offs.

The major goal of maintenance is daily cleaning and minor repair work done consistently and economically. Preventive care is the most fruitful tactic when cultivating a healthy environment—the watch word is to keep an eye out for problems and react immediately. In the competitive climate of today, a poorly-maintained center is likely to lose sales to its competitors. However, just because a center is well-maintained, it does not follow that tenant sales will be above average; customers expect cleanliness and order as a matter of course. Only when the situation slips does the average shopper notice. Consequently, beyond a certain point, timely managerial attention to housekeeping and maintenance work is not likely to pay off in increased store sales.

An important aspect of property management is risk assessment and control. At its most basic level, risk management can be divided into five distinct options, or steps—identify risks, avoid or eliminate them, reduce or prevent the events that cause risk, assume the risks, or transfer the risks to an insurer.

All these techniques can be useful in controlling property and liability insurance premiums. Control is the reduction of hazards, both to people and things, before loss occurs. By employing the proper amount of control, managers can reduce both the frequency and the severity of loss, thus reducing insurance costs.

Management of a shopping center includes financial management, and a first step is the creation of an annual budget. A forecast with a plan is a budget. While the dictionary defines forecast, plan and budget differently, from a center's perspective, they are related.

Most shopping center managers, in short-range financial planning, participate in four tasks—an operating budget, a cash flow budget, a capital budget, and some form of leasing game plan.

A budget is a part of a management system used to accomplish goals or aims. It is a process by which income and expenses are assigned to specific functions or activities that are planned within a designated period—usually twelve months. Effective budgeting can improve decision-making, provide a benchmark for measurement and control, increase the general communication and analysis within the shopping center, and establish an understanding about goals and objectives, with integrity. Budget integrity means the preparation of a realistic and practical estimate of income and expense and then adhering to it.

Forecasting is an essential aspect of both the income and the expense categories. Income forecasting is based on a thorough reading and understanding of the lease and rental terms of the center's existing tenants and an estimate of what rental terms can be achieved on new leases and on lease turnovers. It also requires a forecast of sales productivity of the tenants and, hence, their potential percentage rent productivity. As a forecaster, the manager must take into

account the center's own long-range plans and goals, economic forecasts, industry forecasts, and market share forecasts. In expense
forecasting, management must be alert not only to the aging of the
physical plant, but also to possible changes in such expenses as fuel,
labor, electricity, water, as well as possible changes in the method of
operation dictated by new equipment purchases or new processes.

While there are a number of methods of budgeting, one frequently used is zero-base budgeting, an operating, planning, and
budgeting process which requires each department head to justify
the entire budget request for that department's function in detail
from ground zero.

Most managers can readily identify areas where a concentration
of efforts will have the most meaningful control and, therefore, the
greatest pay-off. In the expense categories, able managers know
where potential errors are likely: what equipment could break down,
what weather or seasonal problems could occur, and what these
might mean. These are examples of "the critical few" which become
barometers of the center's overall performance.

For labor, management must establish the specific tasks and determine how long it should take to do them and the required frequency. To establish this program, the center staff should:

- Inventory the work to be done;
- Define the work routine and time requirements;
- Establish required payroll hours;
- Match, as nearly as possible, scheduled manpower hours to
  scheduled required work;
- Compare in-house costs with outside contractors regularly;
- Establish current earnings per pay period as well as any antic-
  ipated changes during the budget period (include overtime, va-
  cations, and benefits);
- Recognize such allocations as may be necessary to properly
  provide for specific departmental costs;
- Provide an ongoing method for each employee to record his/her
  time.

Management must constantly strive to minimize the maintenance
payroll and yet maintain the center in a clean, attractive, safe and
healthy condition. This can be accomplished primarily in two
ways: first, the mall manager must efficiently schedule maintenance

personnel through exact job descriptions and, secondly, attempt to double-up maintenance and security payrolls by combining these two functions.

It is imperative that good specifications for the work be developed and several bids from qualified companies be obtained. Preventive maintenance programs are extremely worthwhile, for many repairs can be prevented before they happen. Roof-top HVAC units, as an example, can be checked by maintenance personnel on a regular basis. Many areas on the roof, such as scuppers, roof drains, downspouts, flashing, coping, and duct work could possibly rust, and should, obviously, be painted when necessary.

Other steps that can be taken in matters of cost control can involve all of the following:

1. Examine the number of people on each shift and attempt to achieve maximum results with less staff.

2. Bulk ordering and direct ordering of supplies from manufacturers can save dollars.

3. Recycling programs can affect tens of thousands of dollars in savings on hauling costs in larger centers or groups of centers.

4. Each year, competitive bids should be obtained on the insurance program from qualified, sound insurers.

5. Regularly challenge the real estate tax assessment levels.

Many retailers believe owners have no interest in or desire to control CAM expenses. They falsely believe that "common area" is a catch-all which permits the owner to operate his business and improve his property at the expense of the tenants. In actuality, owners have a strong self-interest in controlling common area maintenance expenses, a self-interest with several dimensions. The center which can operate a first-class property on a lean budget by controlling expenses may be able to negotiate a higher minimum rent. By focusing negotiations on "occupancy expense" during the lease, the owner can demonstrate to his prospective tenant that at projected sales levels, expenses will be within acceptable parameters.

CAM charges, at least to many tenants, means eliminate the concept of "fair" and substitute it with "legal." Retailers continue to contend they're not being billed their "fair" share of occupancy costs. That is likely true if they're looking for operating and maintenance costs passed through with no mark-up. Instead, they're being charged the "legal" amount permitted by the language of the lease.

Experienced center management will examine every cost item and ask if this is the best way to spend the money as opposed to the idea of "this is the way we've always spent it." This is the essence of responsibility in management!

There will probably always be disputes between landlords and tenants with respect to what items are appropriately included in common area maintenance (CAM). Landlords have a tendency to interpret the CAM clause broadly, while tenants try to hold to costs that are specifically indicated. In the past, CAM expenses have often been interpreted to include maintenance payroll, lighting, cleaning and repairing the common areas, maintaining the common area drainage systems, snow and trash removal, and maintenance painting. Often such clauses have an open-end phrase that can capture unspecified costs but can lead to serious disputes.

In acknowledging there likely will be unbudgeted costs in keeping a center competitive, landlords often will use a more expansive definition of CAM in their lease form. One effective approach is for the landlord to refer to such expenses as "pass-through costs." This is legally less restrictive than "common area maintenance" (CAM). In fact, the definition may be so worded as to include more of the landlord's gross costs of owning, operating, repairing, replacing and maintaining the center. This definition might also include costs incurred by the landlord for insurance and general improvements, as well as those involved in new or expanded common area facilities. Attorneys representing tenants will often negotiate to exclude capital expenditures such as a new roof or an HVAC system or expenses related to the landlord's management office as well as other "objectionable" items. The final result will be based upon give-and-take negotiation.

A professional property manager will find over time that contact with a variety of agencies will be required. The approach taken with various classifications of tenants will vary. If you are dealing with a mom-and-pop tenant, it will be appropriate to avoid the use of industry "slang" or language or terms that are unfamiliar to someone outside the shopping center industry. It is imperative the prospective tenants clearly understand not only the financial details of the transaction, but the operational requirements, as well. A complete appreciation of the lease-required hours of operation is necessary and, if the lease is on a percentage form, the need to submit accurate and timely monthly reports of gross sales.

Most regional and national tenant lease representatives are well-versed in shopping center real estate and would be expected to have complete familiarity with the general parameters of lease obligations and requirements. Absolute accuracy and candor would be appropriate in all the dealings.

While the representatives of a franchising organization (the franchisor) doubtless know the shopping center and the local marketplace as well as lease details, the individual signing the franchise agreement may not be that well-informed. Since the center's day-to-day contacts will be with the franchisee, it will be most useful to meet with these individuals and explain center operational requirements and policies and to answer questions.

GOVERNMENT REGULATIONS

Over time, it is reasonable for the property manager to anticipate contact with various local governmental agencies, discussing tax assessment levels, filing tax protests, requesting zoning modifications or to process requests for modifications or expansion of the center with the building/zoning departments. The health department will usually be inspecting food-serving facilities and, thus, be in touch with the landlord's agent. The police and fire departments may periodically inspect the premises following which there may be requests for supplemental information or meetings at the site to answer questions. Security concerns may warrant a review by the police department, which may assist the manager in improving the existing programs.

Contact at these several levels should be business-like and professional and supportive of the agency's inquiries and requests. Positive communication will prove helpful as will timely returning of phone calls from community offices.

PREDEVELOPMENT ISSUES

Several things can be done during the developmental stages of the center to optimize property management, if the property manager is given the opportunity to participate in the planning stages.

1. *Design.* It is possible to reduce the grandeur, fanciful amenities, excessive volume, and unneeded widths of malls—if these reductions or eliminations will not impair either the beauty or the functional utility of the center. A careful look at the layout of the parking area, particularly in the snow-belt areas, and

the choice and design of the exterior landscaping will pay dividends in the ongoing operating cost of these items.

2. *Construction.* This obviously is directed to the developer/ building for indiscriminate use of cheap materials and the acceptance of shoddy workmanship results in an unneeded and unwarranted boost in the cost of operation and in early replacement . . . usually totally at the expense of the tenants.

3. *Energy Conservation.* There are available to all center managers a number of methods that can save energy consumption and, thus, save operating dollars.

SECURITY: A MAJOR ISSUE

Today, security ranks second only to tenant mix as the most important consideration about shopping centers, probably to customers as well as to shopping center management. Security issues include parking lot crime, disaster planning and management, gangs in the mall, shoplifting and employee theft, crisis management, and developing and managing security forces.

The fear of crime has had a telling impact on American's buying habits. A national survey by America's Research Group found that 37.1% of those polled said they had changed their buying behavior because they were afraid. Only about half (48.2%) felt their local police department could handle their community's crime concerns.

Some survey ideas for dealing with the problems correspond closely with some of the provisions of the 1995 federal crime bill. Some of the suggestions of those surveyed include:[1]

Very brightly-lit parking lots	71.4%
More police officers walking the streets	59.2%
And in patrol cars	54.0%
Video cameras in plain view in stores	53.1%
Video cameras in parking lots	49.2%
More security personnel in store parking lots	47.3%

Crime and fear of crime are detrimental to profits—of the tenants' stores, of the shopping center's owners, and often of the municipality housing a shopping center. Serious incidents involving harm to individuals do happen at shopping centers; some are grave. These are not every-day events, yet some publicity about the more serious ones suggests they are. Much of this publicity tends to accuse the ownership/management of some failure. Rarely does the owner's consistent ability to prevent crime come to the public's attention. When an incident occurs, the media often seeks either to brand a given location as unsafe or to paint shopping centers in general as unsafe.

Security costs have risen in shopping centers generally and will continue to rise. Recently, proposals have been made to establish laws and regulations compelling center owners/management to assume more police-like responsibilities. Included in these proposals are requirements to staff security personnel at levels that may not be needed and, in fact, would give the false impression in some centers that they are unsafe.

Proactive center management knows that a center's leadership is fundamental to the success of programs that attack the causes of crime. The basic legal principle involved in premises security liability is that property owners are liable for foreseeable criminal acts that occur if they fail to take prudent safeguards to prevent criminal behavior on their premises, thus resulting in someone being victimized by the criminal conduct of another individual. In premises security litigation, the plaintiff must demonstrate that the criminal conduct which occurred on the property owner's premises was foreseeable and that the property owner should have taken measures to prevent the incident which prompted the litigation. If a plaintiff cannot demonstrate this "foreseeability," it is difficult to prove the property owner was negligent in not preventing the incident. The concept of foreseeability requires a property owner to take appropriate action to prevent crime. In many jurisdictions, there is a requirement there be a prior incident on the premises to alert the owner to the possibility such an incident could occur again and measures should have been taken to prevent that from happening. This is referred to as the "prior similar crime" rule.

A job description, security manual, straightforward rules, proper instructions, and training for security personnel are needed. Management must know what is happening in the centers, when and where. Incidents must be reported in detail and senior managers should review each report. Two appropriate and logical steps that can be taken include the following:

1. Mount a site plan and use pins showing location, type, and time of incidents so security patrols can be alert to what is happening and where in the parking lot and in the center.

2. Review the levels of parking lot lighting and if substandard, consider upgrading them. Parking decks can be special problems, even in the daytime. Study the light levels. Consider adding emergency phones. Have adequate signage indicating the location of stairways and/or elevators.

Top-quality regional center management can take advantage of a center's security system as a marketing tool with prospective tenants. A welcome package given to all new tenants should include a section on security and tenant safety education. Include an emergency manual or specific recommendations as to what to do in instances of employee or public accident; tornadoes and earthquakes, however unlikely; fire; bomb threat; unruly demonstrations; and actual witness of crimes.

With the ongoing and desirable frequency of tenant store renovations as well as remodeling of the mall's public and common areas, such plans should be checked for compliance with current life safety codes and for tie-in to existing sensing or monitoring devices. Tenant participation and cooperation is an absolute must. Usually it is also necessary to update any program or procedure on a frequent basis. Often questions asked by new center personnel or new tenants trigger new thinking, which results in modifications or additions to the procedures.

OWNER OR AGENCY MANAGEMENT

There are three principal methods of administering and managing a retail property—management by owner, management by owner in absentia, and agency management.

In the past, the firm that built a center typically managed it. Competition was less keen in those early days, and marketing the center was relatively simple. Over time, institutions began investing in shopping centers in their own right. Experienced property managers often became asset managers who could advertise, in effect, that they managed properties better; they had better-trained people; they had strong key tenant relationships; market knowledge; and, the ability to generate meaningful, high-quality management reports. Agency management at its best offered to property owners a spectrum of desirable qualifications for a fee.

Many owners find comfort in the breadth of services management companies offer and conclude the results are worth the fees. The fees are generally tied to the effective income so there is built-in motivation for the fee manager to do its best to increase that income.

Management by an owner is certainly an option but whether an appropriate one is dependent upon the owner having the time, the knowledge, the skills, the interest, and the contacts necessary to oversee the multiple activities leading toward the achievement of stated objectives. Certainly, the owner can hire staff and/or arrange for contractors of various disciplines to respond to the needs and functions of the property. A large property warranting on-site staff can be employees engaged by the owner, but the ultimate success of the venture will be in very large part directly related to the owner's administrative skills in guiding and leading the people attending to the multiple tasks.

Professional property managers typically are subject either to licensure or certification. Licensure is defined as a process by which an agency of government grants permission to an individual to engage in a given occupation upon finding that the applicant has attained the minimal degree of competency required to ensure that the public health, safety and welfare will be reasonably well-protected (U.S. Department of Health, Education and Welfare, 1977, p. 4).

Certification is the process by which a government or non-governmental agency grants recognition to an individual who has met certain pre-determined qualifications set by the agency. It is a way of identifying individuals who have met some standard. Unlike licensure, a certification law does not prohibit uncertified individuals from practicing their occupations. However, only those who have met the standard set by a governmental agency are permitted to use a designated title.

There is ample evidence that qualified asset managers and property managers have the capabilities to maximize the returns on real estate investment. Real estate is a long-term, relatively non-liquid investment, which combines the virtue of a productive asset with those of a store of value. Rents not only yield income but add to resale value so long as they keep up with inflation.

Management in absentia is arguably no management, and properties "operated" in that fashion can generally anticipate failure to achieve positive results.

Institutional owners—banks, insurance companies, pension funds, and realty trusts—are major purchasers of retail properties and centers. Many of these financial institutions entered into an ownership position inadvertently as they found it necessary to foreclose delinquent loans. Many are in the business of managing funds—not properties (although that is changing as many institutions have created their own management arms as a supplemental profit center).

Some of these institutional owners are still major purchasers of asset and management services. Insurance companies and other institutional investors now own a significant share of shopping centers in the United States. Some institutions elect to manage directly and to build large and sophisticated organizations to do it. Others arrange for management under contract with the seller or with a third party. Whatever the pattern, the new alliance has emerged.

Both the institution and center management have learned new things: how to communicate effectively, how to set up basic rules defining joint and separate responsibility for decision-making. It is generally conceded that retail ownership is considerably more complicated than office building ownership and investors want to make sure that management has the experience and expertise to assure the property operates properly.

Regardless of the managing entity, the long-term success of a shopping center depends, to a great extent, on the relationship that develops between three entities: the property owner, the tenants, and the managing agent. This troika is faced with the responsibility to achieve acceptable management objectives:

- A regular return on the investment;
- A capital gain upon the sale of the property;
- Tax shelter during the term of ownership;
- Use and occupancy of the property (sometimes);
- Entrepreneurial return; and
- Pride of ownership.

To achieve these objectives, a number of issues demanding attention and action must be addressed; namely maintenance concerns, marketing challenges, security matters, employee problems, leasing activities, construction needs, accounting and financial demands, and tenant relations.

ENDNOTE

1. Inside Retailing, Vol. 19, No. 22, September 5, 1994.

Fifteen

The Business and Promotional Aspects of Retail Centers

Weldon "Joe" Larsen

Any study of shopping center marketing should be made with the following factors in mind:

1. The word "marketing" is used differently from industry to industry. In the shopping center business, it generally means creating and implementing a strategic plan to produce the highest possible sales at the mall. There is no marketing counterpart in other types of real estate development or management.

2. Marketing a mall is unusually difficult because the landlord doesn't control the product (the retailers do), and there is essentially no immediate measurement to determine your success.

3. There is a real divergence in mall marketing philosophies without widespread agreement among developers, managers, or retailers.

4. While there are some very successful marketing efforts for shopping centers other than regional malls, for the most part, smaller centers usually have little or no budget and no dedicated marketing personnel. Except for specific areas dealing with small center marketing, the focus of this chapter will be on regional mall marketing.

The Evolution from Merchants Associations to Media Funds

The earliest enclosed regional malls sought to improve on all the weaknesses of central, or main street business districts. In addition to controlling parking, hours, and the physical environment, the center required everyone to belong to and help fund the internal chamber of commerce called the Merchant's Association (MA).

These organizations were quite similar from mall to mall in the late 1960s and 1970s. Most had a group of merchant directors, with the landlord and department store managers being guaranteed directors. Each year a new president was elected. The Promotion Director (PD), as they were called, often reported to the merchant who was president. The MA's board directed its employees to spend the budget submitted by the PD to create sales. There was heavy participation by locally owned stores who found it beneficial to plan their own store activities to be enhanced by mall events.

A group of experienced PDs worked with the International Council of Shopping Centers (ICSC) to create an accreditation program called the Accredited Shopping Center Promotion Director or ASPD. This title was awarded to a candidate who could successfully pass a difficult written exam and an oral review by other ASPDs. Accreditation added professionalism and credibility to the position similar to the already widely respected CSM (Certified Shopping Center Manager) designation for managers.

By the mid 1970s, the evolution of the shopping center industry caused several things to happen. The role of the PD was expanding to include marketing responsibilities, so the position title changed to Marketing Director (MD), which signalled the industry that research should provide the guidelines for budget expenditures. ICSC changed the designation from ASPD to CMD (Certified Marketing Director) to respond to this change.

Also, department stores were beginning to limit their financial participation in the Merchant's Associations. This resulted in their store managers becoming much less involved in mall marketing efforts. For many developers, this change hastened the demise of the traditional Merchant's Associations. The landlord, who generally contributed 25% to 33% of the budget, took control. A new entity called a Marketing Fund eliminated any department store or mall shop managers from the administration of marketing the mall. This allowed the store managers to run their stores while the landlords marketed the malls with marketing professionals.

At the same time, landlords began the widespread use of mandatory advertising clauses in their leases, whereby the landlord required retailers to do a specified amount of advertising. This requirement worked well for nearly a decade, but by the mid 1980s, retailers began to ask to have this requirement eliminated, as costs increased. Marketing directors were producing print sections with heavier, whiter, and glossier paper, soon adding four-color printing. Expanded distribution, usually by direct mail, ultimately made the mandatory advertising clause very expensive for the retailers. Furthermore, with every mall having different themes, deadlines, and print media requirements, national chains with a wide distribution of stores in malls found it impossible to coordinate all the requirements.

The compromise between retailers and landlords was the birth of the "media funds" or "advertising funds" as they are called today. Essentially, the retailers significantly increased their existing contribution from the marketing fund to this new fund in exchange for eliminating the much greater expense of mandatory advertising. Increased contributions gave the landlord a sizable budget to undertake advertising in strategic ways never before possible. The larger budgets, along with greater fiscal discipline, has minimized additional contributions, or subsidies, by the landlord. These were quite common in the 1980s from owners who were strong supporters of shopping center marketing.

How Marketing Creates Value

To appreciate marketing, one must appreciate its contribution to the value creation process. A formula to quantify the value creation potential of marketing illustrates this.

Sales determine rents and rents determine value.

This principal relationship in the value creation equation should be obvious, but was overshadowed when creating wealth was as easy as finding another cornfield in which to build a mall. The more the landlord helps the retailer prosper, the more the landlord prospers. It's strange that marketing is often questioned, even by the most successful developers, but its contribution is rarely quantified. In the simplest terms "What is a 1% sales increase worth?" To answer the question, the relationship between sales and rents must be identified.

The developer has typically needed about a 10% rent-to-sales ratio to make new development feasible. The average mall shop retailer would like that ratio to be 6% or less. For illustration purposes, an 8% ratio is assumed as a compromise.

Problem: What is a 1% increase in sales worth?

Assumptions

Mall Shop Sales	$250 per sq. ft.
Rent to Sales Ratio	8.0%
Mall Shop GLA	300,000 sq. ft.
Cap Rate	7.5%

1. *1% × Mall shop sales = Sales per square-foot gain*

    1% × $250 = $2.50

2. *Sales per square-foot gain × Rent to sales ratio % = Rent increase per square foot*

    $2.50 × 8% = $0.20

3. *Rent increase per square foot × Mall shop GLA = Total rent gain*

    $0.20 × 300,000 sq. ft. = $60,000

4. *Total rent gain ÷ Cap rate = Value creation*

    $60,000 ÷ 7.5% = $800,000

Realizing that a 1% sales gain can be worth $800,000 of value creation in an average mall should cause developers and investors to focus on marketing. In most cases today, sales gains at one property are made by stealing the business from competing properties. Hiring and supporting the right marketing talent for a regional center can pay very large dividends to the landlord.

If a mall is well leased on long-term leases, it will be some years before a sales gain becomes a rent increase and a value increase. It is true that the value gain would be less if the mall were being sold within a year or two. However, the following factors appear to give credence to the validity of the value creation formula, even in the short term:

1. There is always some vacancy; increased market rent can be realized immediately as vacant spaces are leased.

2. Over the past three years, closures have averaged about 5% of gross leasable area. This space can usually be re-leased at the higher rates immediately.

3. Every lease term ends at some time, and all of the annual increases aggregated will set the market rent for the renewal. A present sales gain effectively puts a future rent increase in the bank.

4. The current REIT frenzy is expected to result in longer, even indefinite, holding periods, so those banked rent increases can be realized by the owner who created them.

5. Sales increases will also increase overage rent immediately. Because income is capitalized at disposition, the value creation is immediate.

6. Higher sales create lower capitalization rates, which in turn create enormous gains for the owner.

The value creation of overage rent is quite insignificant compared to the value creation of increased market rent from increased sales. A marketing director would have great bargaining power if, using the earlier assumption, a case could be built showing that the marketing program caused an additional 3% increase for the year or a $2.4 million value enhancement, from the increased market rent rates (Figure 15.1).

FIGURE 15.1

Value Creation for Each 1% Increase in Sales. The Graph Is Based on the Earlier Hypothetical Assumptions.

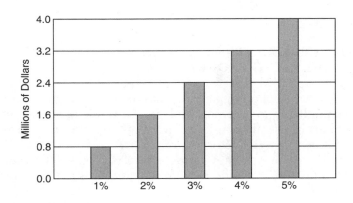

Measuring Results

Some shopping center owners, managers, and tenants believe sales increases are due to inflation, a favorable economy, or many other circumstances, but rarely attribute the results to good marketing. When sales are down, marketing is always suspected as the cause. Marketing's inability to obtain and analyze sales results easily or quickly has led to the development of other types of measurement, including car counts, various types of people counts, random store surveys, and other measures. None have proven extremely accurate forecasters of actual sales. For example, monthly car counts can be up, while certified sales are down. A good marketing director knows what works and what doesn't, but proving it is difficult.

One of the losses that occurred with the disappearance of most of the Merchant's Associations was sales measurement. When MDs met regularly with their merchant board members, the retailers provided the sales analysis for marketing events, a great assistance in determining if and when to repeat an activity. Without the MA, MDs were left to find new measurement techniques. Unfortunately, the monthly sales reports from the merchants arrive 15 to 20 days after the end of the month and lack details to help analyze a week, a weekend, or a day.

Recently, technology has made instant sales results feedback both possible and affordable. At Homart, for example, with the help of the company's information services department, a daily sales reporting system was designed to provide the mall staffs, retailers, and corporate leaders with daily sales results. With this technology, Homart could measure every dollar of marketing expenditure, just like a retailer, in terms of cost of sales. And the retailers received a daily report card to show their results versus their merchandise category and the whole mall (Figure 15.2).

THE ELEMENTS OF A GOOD
MARKETING PROGRAM

To most observers, shopping center marketing is the mall's advertising, merchandising, or promotional events. While these elements are certainly part of the program, they are not the entire program—they are simply the most visible or obvious parts.

The challenge of any marketing effort is to take the mall from where it is to where it should be, and that requires a marketing plan.

FIGURE 15.2

Evaluating Measurements

Evaluating measurements is not simple. Marketing people tend to find one set of measures that seem to justify the expenditure and then ignore or skip the rest. Now that landlords can measure sales like a retailer, Marketing Directors should measure every event using all of the following menu items that apply:

1. GLOA (Gross Leasable Occupied Area).
2. Prior year same day's sales per square foot.
3. Current year same day's sales per square foot.
4. Prior year sale's revenue (1 × 2).
5. Current year sale's revenue (1 × 3).
6. Variance % [(5 − 4) ÷ 4].
7. YTD sales trend line.
8. Additional revenue (5 − 4).
9. Total cost of event.
10. Percentage cost of additional revenue (9 ÷ 8).
11. Percentage cost of total revenue (9 ÷ 5).
12. Participants % increase.
13. Nonparticipants % increase.
14. Percentage of participants.
15. Number of participants.
16. Sales per square foot, same days week prior.
17. Sales per square foot same day during promotion.
18. Sales per square foot, same day, following week.
19. Radio expenditure (if any).
20. Print expenditure (if any).
21. TV expenditure (if any).
22. Print insert number (if any).
23. Direct mail number (if any).
24. Redemption percentage (if applicable).

This information is critical in determining the effectiveness of marketing expenditures. Only by examining all of these items can a clear evaluation be made. If a developer has a large portfolio, corporate-wide analysis is possible. Comparing results from mall to mall will enable great corporate strategies to emerge for repeating similar events in the future.

First, it's important to add perspective to the items that affect sales in the mall.

The Product

Malls range from very strong to quite weak, and, when viewed as products, are diverse. In any form of product marketing, the product makes a big difference, hence, the most important goal of any marketing program is to improve the product. The most important part of any strategy to increase sales is leasing. Replacing an underperforming store or a vacancy with a retailer capable of producing sales in excess of the mall's average sales per square foot will increase sales, and also increase traffic for the other stores.

The pulling power of a mall is the sum of the individual pulling powers of its stores. A vacancy has no pulling power. An underperforming store has little or no pulling power. The MD who assists in the leasing process is pursuing the fastest and most lasting way to increase sales.

Store Management

Next to a good tenant mix, the most important factor in driving sales is good store management. Consider the case of a 1,600-square-foot casual men's apparel store that did $1 million with an effective store manager. The manager left at the end of the year. The following year the volume declined to $560,000, then, to $265,000. The subsequent year the store closed. Over this same period, mall shop sales increased 12%. Obviously, the problem was the particular store management, not mall marketing. But what can be done to ensure good management in individual stores? Here are a few things to consider:

1. Hire MDs who have been successful retail store managers. They can be very helpful in strengthening store management.

2. Require MDs to spend time discussing sales results with store managers, whether daily or monthly. The MD knows what's working well and can be very helpful. The underperforming store hurts the mall.

3. Hire professional consultants to do seminars or provide individual assistance for store managers to make them more effective in driving sales in their stores. The large number of stores in the big chains and the frequency of manager turnover

puts many in management positions who have received inadequate training.

4. Communicate regularly with retailers' district and regional managers and home offices. Provide facts to demonstrate to them why their stores are not getting their share of the business.

5. Make the mall more successful. "A" malls get "A" stores and "A" store managers.

The Marketing Plan

Everyday numerous products are marketed directly. Not all of these products are equally good, but the quality of the product and the success of the product are not synonymous. Good marketing can produce exceptional results for a less than stellar product. This doesn't mean that a $200-per-square foot (in sales) mall can be a $400-per-square foot mall with good marketing. But good marketing can make a big difference.

Like advertising, not all mall marketing programs are successful. The reason for failure may be that the creative process is not based on a strategy. If MDs would ask themselves, "What is the problem I'm trying to solve?" before they start to brainstorm, more relevant messages would result. Uncreative relevant messages are more meaningful than very creative but irrelevant work.

The late Bob Jones started teaching the elements of a marketing plan at ICSC Marketing Institutes over 15 years ago. His message was excellent and is still being taught by others today. His five-step Marketing Plan process included:

1. Situation Analysis.
2. Problems and Opportunities.
3. Objectives.
4. Strategies.
5. Tactics.

The five steps sound technical, but the process is really very simple. It means that the product and competition (Situational Analysis) are researched thoroughly. Weaknesses (Problems) and strengths (Opportunities) are identified. The objectives are what needs to be accomplished to correct the problems and take advantage of the opportunities. It is imperative that the objectives be reasonable, specific, and measurable. A plan (Strategies) is then created to fulfill those objectives. The following step is to detail how and when the plan (Tactics) will be executed. The process is evaluated and revisited again.

Consumer Research

Research is very helpful in determining whether to build a project and in establishing rents, but it is not the same research needed to improve sales at an existing center. Some developers have separate personnel for consumer research, or they utilize an independent research firm.

There are several pitfalls to avoid in consumer research:

1. Information is valuable only if applied. Many mall owners purchase market research data but don't use it to develop a marketing plan.

2. If an MD is not careful, research can create objectives that transfer sales, not create them. For example, if strategies are implemented to increase weekday sales, ensure that it isn't at the expense of weekend sales. Or, if shopping frequency is increased, ensure that it isn't at the expense of visit length or average expenditure. At the end of the measurement period, there is no victory in improving a statistic if overall sales are not improved.

3. Research may indicate that the mall exceeds quoted national demographic statistics. A large number of the malls that purchase research aren't performing well and seek research to help them. So quoted numbers may be heavily weighted by underperforming properties. Also, teenagers who frequent malls and do more and more of the total shopping each year, unaccompanied by adults, are not normally included in the research numbers, which can seriously distort and understate results in every significant strategic planning category. The distortion is not a reflection on the research companies, but rather on those who use it without understanding what the information really means and what other facts need to be considered.

Research companies that provide the majority of mall research have developed national benchmarks, but these benchmarks are not necessarily representative of the entire shopping center industry. When the media uses benchmarks as representative of the entire regional mall industry, it can promulgate erroneous assumptions. Over the past several years, for example, numerous media articles have alluded to the end of the regional mall era, sighting average purchase, shopping frequency, and number of stores visited all being significantly down. But, at the same time, sales figures have indicated that sales at the register were up or flat even during the 1990–1992 recession. Research improperly used, can result in a wrong or incomplete evaluation. Research is only as good as one's analysis and interpretation.

The Budget

Often, the size of a center's marketing budget is evaluated in terms of competing malls' budgets or the cost of local media versus other markets' media. Such standards are relevant, but the most important criteria for budget size is the marketing plan and how much it costs to execute it. Shopping center marketing needs to be approached annually from a "zero-base" philosophy. Otherwise, similar programs may be repeated year after year without consideration of their worth or strategic significance. Malls with relatively small budgets can sometimes produce better results than malls with large budgets when such zero base controls are in place.

Today, marketing fund budgets range from $200,000 to over $1 million, with the average probably around $500,000. It is the MD's responsibility to see that each dollar is spent to produce the highest possible positive impact on sales.

The Retailer Perspective

Most national chains do some national advertising. Those that do so want lower marketing fees. Some retailers ask that marketing funds be eliminated, because they want to use the money to further their own advertising budgets, which they believe will benefit their stores to a much greater extent than mall marketing. Other national retailers argue that since national chains are represented in most malls in a given market, they are indifferent as to which mall the customer shops, whereas developers want to use their funds to compete with other developers' malls.

The Developer Perspective

Typical mall retailers spend 3% of their sales on advertising and, of that, about 1% of sales go to the marketing fund, which still provides considerable opportunity for them to do other advertising.

Unfortunately few of them spend 3%. It is ironic to landlords that retailers locate in malls for their synergistic strengths but want to advertise and promote themselves as though they were free-standing stores. The pulling power of anchor department store advertising is evident from parking lot and pedestrian traffic whenever they do major advertising. The MD sees this same evidence when the mall merchants are combined as a "critical mass" to lure customers to the center. So why isn't the developer's perspective more evident to the retailer that this synergistic effect can and does occur?

Generally, the mall shop retailer's home office is located far from the mall. District, regional, and home office personnel visit infrequently. Opinions of marketing programs by local store management are often invalid due to inexperience, and may be rendered to provide self-glory if the store results are good, or to provide an excuse if sales results are bad. Measurement systems to prove whether a store is under- or overperforming were lacking in the past. Accurate measurement now exists; however, many retailers don't want it or don't know how to use it.

Historically, most of a developer's senior officers also didn't concern themselves with shopping center marketing or its potential. Profits and wealth were presumed to come from development, while marketing was an expected requirement, but couldn't be measured or proven. When marketing personnel ask landlords to dig deeper into their pockets, and go beyond lease-required financial participation to support marketing, the request is not always granted. Similar scrutiny comes not just from the institutional owners, but also the developer owners. Still there are many owners who continue to give strong support for marketing, who understand and stay involved in the marketing process and who require their marketing personnel to provide measurement that has demonstrated acceptable results.

Considering all the costs, including markdowns, would the marketing expenditure have enhanced the retailer's bottom line if the retailer had borne the cost? As long as the answer is affirmative, the MD should spend the budget and look for ways to make the budget and bottom-line profit even bigger. Spending should stop where it no longer makes sense.

New Budget Trends

The budgeting process is normally completed late in the third quarter for the following operating year. Marketing activities are calendared for specific dates with specific funds allocated. The budget summary breaks down the various categories of expenses such as administrative, media, decor, and events. Each activity likewise has a portion of the activity allocated to these expense categories, allowing the MD as well as a supervisor to determine the appropriateness of the annual expenditures for each planned activity.

While this approach has been traditional, its failing is its lack of flexibility. It is true that most malls will amend their calendar and budget plan during the course of the year, but for most malls, the actual will look very similar to the plan. Good retailers have much more flexibility, within their budget constraints. But with measurement and technology, mall owners increasingly have the ability to immediately implement activities to take advantage of strong periods and boost slow ones. An extra dollar of sales per square foot is just as helpful in April as it is in December.

Another trend that is still in its infancy but gaining momentum is to spend far less on media. Astute MDs have discovered more cost effectiveness in getting the shopper who is already at the mall to spend more while they are there, rather than spending substantial media dollars to attract them again. Research shows that shoppers come to a mall every 7 to 10 days without media prompting.

One example of this strategy is the use of a premium with a purchase, a tactic designed to increase the average purchase by giving the customer an incentive to increase his or her spending right now to receive the premium. If the available budget funds are $10,000, often 70% is spent on media to promote the event and 30% to purchase the premiums. By eliminating outside media advertising, 95% can be spent on premiums and 5% on in-mall signage to promote the additional spending.

The result in a shift away from media promotion is that with three times the premiums, both spending and the number of happy customers can be tripled. Some MDs think the key measure of success is the rate at which the premiums are redeemed, but the only important measurement is how many additional sales were generated, which is determined by multiplying the number of premiums given away by the average additional amount spent. (The additional money spent by redeeming customers to get the premiums is determined at redemption.) The math is the same if the premiums go in a day, a week, or a month.

Premium events work well because the merchant doesn't have to advertise or discount—he just rings up the sales. Customers come to know that malls offer value. The mall can control the cost of sales by setting the premium award based on the premium cost ($25 cost of premium with $500 purchase = 5% cost of sales). A premium that cost $25 would retail at $50 to $75, so the perceived value to the redeeming customer is very high.

By allocating more of the budget to immediately implementable activities, the MD can take rapid action when sales are down. If month-to-date (MTD) sales are down 8% on the 10th of the month, the MD can implement programs to spur sales until the MTD is back on the year-to-date sales trend line, exactly as department stores and other entrepreneurial retail managers would do. As this responsive spending becomes more common, a mall's budgeted fixed-date activities and media expenditures will both diminish. In-mall signage expense (point-of-purchase advertising) will increase to promote immediately implementable activities to existing mall customers.

UNIQUE MARKETING OPPORTUNITIES

Grand Openings

A marketing plan for a grand opening has a defined objection: to launch the mall successfully to facilitate the lease-up of the remaining vacant space. Unfortunately, this objective isn't universal because many MDs don't focus on leasing. Nothing hurts a mall retailer more than to be in a poorly leased mall. Successfully implementing a marketing plan to drive sales to drive leasing will enable those merchants who open with the mall to happily get new neighbors. If the marketing plan (not to be confused with the marketing budget) includes strategies for leasing personnel to quickly communicate the new mall's success to prospective retailers, it should be applauded by the existing mall retailers.

There are two objectives for the ribbon-cutting ceremony: to get the press there so you'll be on the evening news and on the front page of the morning paper, and to stage a photo that will get you on the cover of mall trade publications. The speeches are important for the companies involved and local government leaders; the crowd waits for them to finish so they can start shopping. And getting the crowd shopping is really what the retailers and developer want also. The ceremony consists typically of 20 minutes of formality that gives an official opening to the center.

The opening day crowd provides the opportunity, but also the challenge. Making a positive first impression is more than providing a stunning physical product; it also means making sure the visit is comfortable and convenient. The grand opening plan needs to trace the customers' paths from the moment they enter the parking lot until the moment they leave it. The signs and service need to be there to make the visit easy and enjoyable. If they can't find their cars or the restrooms, the opening campaign won't mean much.

There is a natural tendency for the MD to focus on the advertising or the grand opening party on the night before instead of customer convenience. There is also a tendency for marketing to focus on the wrong product: too often the mall is promoted instead of the merchandise. Not only is the budget big enough to do things rights, but the stores are in the mood to participate, offer value, and advertise in a way they only do for grand openings. Promoting the stores, their merchandise, and their values is what will create sales. The desired result should not be great ads, great bags, great parties, or great colors—just great sales!

Having a daily sales measurement tool is never as important as it is at the grand opening. For as long as there have been mall grand openings there has been seat-of-the-pants grand opening sales analysis. Grand opening day sales per square foot can be used to project an accurate estimate of annual mall shop sales. The first two weeks' results can make that estimate very precise. This estimate enables the MD to accelerate or decelerate spending to meet the sales objective. The plan needs to have immediately implementable contingency activities to drive sales, if necessary.

Mall rents are based on sales expectations. The value creation model mentioned earlier quantifies the value of exceeding expectations, but an even greater value reduction effect occurs if sales levels don't support the rent. So the grand opening plan helps to set the objective, measure the results, and adjust the marketing plan as necessary.

Renovations: A Marketing Event

In the shopping center business, the only way to get a second chance to make a good first impression is with a major renovation. The strategy here is very similar to a grand opening marketing plan. In most cases, the renovation is being done to attract more and better tenants and ultimately increase sales. Hopefully the renderings and brochures will get some of that job done concurrently with construction. The message to trade area shoppers will be something like "great new stores and great new look." But unless the mall is being expanded as well as renovated, it is hard to create a powerful grand opening surprise. Regular customers watch the changes occur day-by-day. Most malls remain open for business during the renovation process, and the new stores open when completed, not all on a single day.

The renovated mall provides the opportunity to reach out to the trade area customers who are currently shopping elsewhere. It gives them a reason to reconsider the mall. Unlike grand openings, renovations usually do not have a big budget to launch the new look. In fact, the on-going marketing budget may be negatively impacted by the stores that are closed or relocated during the renovation, so it is important for the landlord to provide funds for marketing as well as construction. After all, the whole purpose of the renovation is to increase sales and enable the mall to better compete in the marketplace. It is important to identify the new customer potential that the renovation and new tenants will bring so that marketing programs can be created to get the customers to see the renovated mall and to return regularly.

One of the most glaring weaknesses of even the better mall shop chains is their inability to change the success of an underperforming store. It is not uncommon to see a chain run a C store in an A mall. Somewhere along the line someone in the company decided it was a C mall, because of the way their store was performing. So the quality of management, the size and quality of inventory, and delayed renovations make it a self-fulfilling prophecy. No amount of evidence from the landlord can easily change the retailer's mind. After all what does a mall landlord know about retail?

This situation creates a big challenge for marketing a renovation. It takes renovated, well-operated stores, not just a renovated mall, to change perceptions. The marketing plan that is established long before construction starts needs to have the upgrading of existing stores as a major objective. The MD's time in working with leasing and management to identify and accomplish the strategies and tactics to achieve this objective can significantly improve the success of the renovation.

Just persuading or offering incentives to a store to upgrade its look will not automatically make it successful unless the store merchandise as well as the store manager and home office attitude toward the mall are remodeled as well. The MD will need to exercise all of the strategies listed earlier in the chapter to influence the stores, the region, and the home office to cause the store to reach its marketing potential. This task needs to be undertaken knowing that the store will probably resist all the way, and that, if successful, the MD's efforts will probably go unrecognized.

Equality is a noble cause but an MD cannot fall into the rut of promoting all stores all the time. A department store doesn't spend an equal amount of money promoting every line it carries, but it certainly considers when it's the best time to promote a certain item. Every item in a department store has a better chance of being sold if the store promotes hot items and gets traffic in the store. So it is with a mall. The best thing a mall can do to help weaker stores is to promote stronger stores, an essential task during a renovation. When the time is right to make a mass appeal to the trade area to come see the renewed mall, promote the new stores, promote the remodeled stores, promote the stores that are coming soon. Promote the new physical mall and list the rest of the stores. Name them. Number them. Brag about them, especially the ones that day in and day out do a lot of business and create a lot of traffic. You will benefit the weaker stores by bringing them traffic instead of ineffective equal exposure.

New Department Stores

MDs can get so busy with their regular efforts to increase traffic and sales that they sometimes get surprised when they come to their center and see considerable additional traffic when they aren't currently running a promotion. They quickly realize the traffic is due to a large new store opening and promotion. Or it may be one of the department stores running a major sale that they weren't aware of and didn't see advertised. These occurrences quickly teach MDs the marketing value of larger promotional stores. These are the kinds of benefits that come to a mall by adding an additional department store. It might be a Nordstrom or a Wal-Mart. The benefits will differ with each, but there will be benefits. It is the MD's opportunity to create a marketing plan to take advantage of them.

A new anchor is a great opportunity to work hand-in-hand with that store. The mall's objective is to get additional customers to the new store and into the mall, for those new customers to come frequently and add the new store's credit card to their wallet. Ideally, other department store customers will walk through the mall to shop the new anchor. Strategies can be coordinated to get the most mileage while avoiding duplication. The rent and tenant mix is much better for a five-department-store mall than for a three-department-store mall, because more and better retailers will want to be at the mall and will spend more because of the sales success they enjoy.

Sales increases are another property's sales decreases. However, the old philosophy that the retail sale pie is only so big is not totally true. A lot of money that could be spent isn't because the sales job doesn't occur. But the old pie theory can affect a mall that adds a department store if it isn't actively promoting itself. With good marketing, the mall shops will get their additional slice from the retail pie across the street or down the road, and the pie will be larger.

Corporate and Joint Mall Campaigns

One of the problems many retailers have with how malls spend their marketing dollars is that malls don't spend as they would. Most retailers would mass produce and mass distribute. However, the developer has usually been so aware of the differences in malls from market to market that each mall is marketed as a unique product. A developer with 30 malls could have 30 different back-to-school and holiday programs, each created by a different advertising agency, with a different theme, and different talent, and produced in relatively small quantity runs. It is as though a department store allowed each store manager to produce their Sunday print ads or supplements for their store alone, a practice that formally existed with department stores.

If an MD can create unique marketing products for a unique mall and justify the expenditure with realistic retail measurements, the MD should continue to do so and operate like those department store managers in the past, with freedom and accountability. No one can escape measurement and accountability in the future. The landlords, retailers, and underwriters will demand it. Corporate programs enable television and radio advertising to be produced with a much larger budget than a mall could afford. A typical spot can be customized for the mall at a fraction of a cost of a lesser quality piece the mall would produce. Print pieces can be printed in large quantities with great graphics, color, and paper, to be overprinted in the local market with the mall's name, event dates, and participating stores.

Corporate programs should be offered to malls as voluntary programs and with a menu of options, ranging from banners, point-of-sale pieces, tent cards for food court tables, free-standing signs, radio and television spots, and full-page print ads, enabling a participating mall to customize the event based on its budget and marketing plan.

In addition to the menu, the corporate program should have an instruction manual of creative promotional strategies to implement and add to the event. This manual can be produced in-house or by marketing consultants. The time the group spends to create it is much less than what all corporate MDs with a large developer would spend working on their own and it yields a creative product superior to what a single MD could create. The MDs can search the manuals for strategies that fit any mall's plan objectives, and the MD can spend his or her time executing tactics instead of creating strategies.

Another type of multicenter program is also possible: the Landlord Network Program. This program links different owners' malls within a metro area in a joint event, with a strong media call to motivate everyone to drive to a participating mall. Something similar has been done in markets where an owner or fee manager controls several malls and several years ago, a number of Canadian centers successfully joined forces to keep Canadians from driving to the United States to shop. The Landlord Network Program should be established with anti-trust considerations in mind.

Developers have been less than enthusiastic about such programs. The traditional thinking has been that the competition is the mall ten miles away instead of the power center across the street, the nearby free-standing big boxes, the catalogs or electronic shopping networks. But when malls get maligned in the media, all malls take the hit. The perception of malls affects capitalization rates and value creation for everyone.

Value Events

Nonmall retail stores and formats have added much more square footage than malls in the last few years, causing market share losses by malls, even though mall sales overall have still grown and were very strong before this massive new competition emerged. Shopping malls do offer value and are enormously competitive environments, but mall shop values are kept secret.

The mall stores do little advertising, but they do mark down prices very regularly to move merchandise and drive sales. They use point-of-purchase promotional pieces and rack top signs to communicate special values. In theory, it is the mall marketing department's responsibility to create enough traffic coming to the mall to discover these values and, of course, the full-priced merchandise as well.

Department stores advertise their values to create traffic. When mandatory advertising existed, this advertising was the mall shop's equivalent to department store advertising though it was conducted much less frequently. Since the elimination of mandatory advertising MDs have created many new types of value events, without requiring advertising expense by the retailer. Some require the participating retailer to discount full-priced merchandise during the event, while others promote the merchandise the retailer has already marked down.

SMALL CENTER MARKETING*

While much of the attention within the shopping center industry is on the regional mall, centers of less than 200,000 square feet represent 63% of the shopping centers in the country. According to the International Council Shopping Centers, 89% of the adult population in the United States shop at small centers. The small center is where a significant amount of shopper patronage is realized. And it can be enhanced through marketing. This section focuses on small centers with traditional small center anchors such as grocery stores, and excludes power centers, outlet centers, or speciality centers.

Small center marketing differs greatly from that of regional malls. Small centers are not recognized as a single unit like a mall. The center is typically known by consumers as the "XYZ grocery store center" rather than "XYZ shopping center." Small center stores are usually service and convenience oriented such as grocery, bank, dry cleaner, card shop, fast food, whereas regional malls focus on fashion merchants and department store anchors. Therefore, sales curves don't play the same role in small centers as they do in regional malls where seasons strongly influence monthly sales.

The trade area is usually small relative to malls, with consumers driving up to 10 minutes to the small center. However, the average number of shopping trips is high: 7.1 visits per month versus 3.9 visits per month for regional malls. As a result of the high shopping frequency and convenience-oriented tenant mix, cross shopping between stores is limited, with consumers usually shopping only one store. Because many landlords don't provide for marketing through a lease clause there are a significant number of small centers in the country with no marketing activity. It is probably safe to say that small center marketing is more the exception than the rule as it relates to small centers.

In those centers that do have marketing programs, the sheer size of the center results in small budgets typically ranging from as little as $5,000 per year to as high as $100,000 per year. Anchor stores

---

* This section was written by Tracey Hall, SCMD, of the Hall Olson Marketing Group which has extensive experience in small center marketing.

are typically very promotional and do not see a need to provide monetary support to center marketing programs. Due to the limited size of the budget, it is difficult for the landlord to provide personnel to administer the program. This task is handled by the center manager, an outside advertising agency, or a marketing professional handling a number of centers for one landlord. While marketing funds are preferred in regional malls, merchants associations are more common in small centers. Through the merchants association structure some of the administrative responsibilities can be assumed by individual merchants.

Because the trade area size is relatively small, media buying is challenging. Direct mail is often the medium of choice. Small budgets limit the quality of advertising production which means the medium actually produces the ads. Often, advertising quality is not consistent with the image of the center. Since many small centers don't provide marketing programs, the store managers in a small center that uses a centerwide marketing program don't know what to expect from such a program, producing expectations that are sometimes greater than what the program can deliver.

With budget and personnel constraints, the use of narrowly focused strategic plans is very important to create a return on investment in small center marketing programs. Objectives and strategies are limited. A typical small center objective focuses on increasing the average number of stores shopped during a visit to the center, supported by a strategy that converts anchor store shoppers to multistore shoppers. Tactics may include items such as bag stuffers, signage outside the center, or a gift with purchase for receipts collected from more than one store in the center. Another objective may focus on increasing penetration from a competitor's trade area. Strategies often include frequent but consistent sales promotion programs such as couponing, a well-proven tactic with small center merchants.

Centers without lease provisions require a time and financial investment on the part of the landlord. If the landlord wants to solely fund the process, the expense is time and money. If the landlord desires merchant financial support, the expense is more time and less money. To obtain merchant support, the landlord needs to invest in the guidance of a marketing professional to develop a proposed marketing plan and merchant contribution guidelines, with contributions typically based on a per square footage basis depending upon the total needs of the center. Simultaneously, the landlord must decide if the marketing program will be administered through a merchants association or marketing fund. A merchants association will require a marketing professional to organize. A marketing fund will require a marketing professional to lead.

Measurement techniques for small centers are similar to those used in regional malls and include sales, traffic counts, research, and merchant evaluations. Sales reporting varies from center to center depending on the landlord's requirements. There are a number of small centers with no sales reporting requirements, thus complicating measurement.

Small center marketing programs are often the most strategic in the industry because they have to be. Small budgets and limited personnel time force the designer and implementor of the program to get the most for their money. Small center marketing programs are typically workhorse kinds of programs simply designed to sell merchandise and increase sales, with simple techniques.

SUMMARY

Mall marketing must constantly adapt not only to consumer behavior, but also to the changes that occur in the retail and mall development business. Mall marketing is affected by department store consolidations, the proliferation of big box users, mall shop store format changes, and changing tenant mixes to name just a few. But the biggest challenge to mall marketing in the next decade will be retail technology's direct and indirect impact. With scanners and UPC codes, retailers have instantaneous access to information that assists them in their profit pursuits.

Information flow may be what it takes to enable the mall shops collectively to compete against the department stores and big boxes who have this information and use it to their advantage daily.

Sixteen

Various Means of Debt Financing for Shopping Centers

Richard B. Jennings

Although several times a year during the 1970s and 1980s a handful of shopping center REITs and developers tapped the debt capital markets with an unsecured debt issue, an offering of convertible debt, or a securitized mortgage issue, conventional lenders were usually the only sources of debt financing for shopping center owners. The debt capital markets now offer shopping center owners an array of new borrowing options, many of which are competitive with conventional lending sources.

CONVENTIONAL FINANCING

Conventional sources of shopping center financing include insurance companies and pension funds as "permanent" lenders, commercial banks as short-term and intermediate-term lenders, and a small number of credit companies that make all types of short-term and medium-term real estate loans. Most of the conventional shopping center lenders, which had retreated from almost all new commercial mortgage lending between 1990 and 1992, returned to the lending market in force in 1993, although using much tighter underwriting standards than previously.

In the late 1980s and early 1990s, mortgage delinquency rates rose sharply. In the case of life insurance companies, delinquency rates in their overall real estate loan portfolios rose from 2.7% in 1988 and peaked at 6.8% in 1992 before falling to 5.8% in 1993. Life insurance company experience with loans on retail properties showed a similar pattern, with the delinquency rate reported at 1.5% in 1988, 5.3% in 1992, and just under 5.0% in 1993. Commercial banks also experienced a rise in their mortgage delinquency rates. Bank loans on commercial real estate experienced higher delinquency rates—8.0% in 1991, 7.7% in 1992, and 5.8% in 1993. Real estate loan defaults became a major problem for leading U.S. financial institutions, threatening the financial integrity of many. In response, banks and insurance companies sought in the early 1990s to reduce their real estate loans outstanding. They did so by both curtailing new lending activity and by demanding repayment of maturing real estate loans.

Commercial Bank Lending

Commercial banks are currently very active in financing new shopping center construction and acquisitions in recovering or growing markets, such as the Southeast, the Southwest, the Northwest, and parts of the Midwest. Most banks are now requiring borrowers to put up 10%, 20%, or 30% cash equity, depending upon the location, the tenants, the level of pre-leasing, the developer's reputation, net worth, and his relationship with the bank. Banks will lend up to a maximum of 75% loan to stabilized value. During the 1980s, many banks made construction or acquisition loans requiring very little cash equity.

Banks are also much more stringent today on the assumptions they will accept in pro formas. For instance, stabilized vacancy is generally 7% to 10%, not 5%. Pre-leasing must be at least 50%, and sometimes 80%, and all anchors must be of high quality and must be signed up prior to beginning construction. Lenders are also paying much more attention to potential environmental problems and are now reading the fine print in all leases. In calculating stabilized debt service coverage, banks are using approximately a 10% debt service rate, not the lower construction loan rate.

On the positive side, the pricing of loans, based on the tougher underwriting assumptions outlined above, has become very competitive again among banks. On regional malls, construction loan rates range from 150 to 250 basis points over the London Interbank

Offered Rate (LIBOR), depending on quality. In October, 1995, LIBOR was quoted at just under 6%. On anchored neighborhood and community centers, construction loan rates range from prime to prime+1%. On all types of shopping centers, banks are trying to hold their construction loans to terms of three years or less. Certain banks also make 3- to 7-year fixed rate loans at rates competitive with insurance companies and pension funds, described below.

Now that so many of the largest shopping center developers have gone public in the form of REITs, banks prefer to lend to REITs or publicly owned corporations that own shopping centers, rather than to privately owned developers. REITs generally have better balance sheets with less than 55% debt and have greater access to additional capital than private developers. Banks' spreads on loans to REITs vary from 125 to 250 basis points over LIBOR. REITs with good track records and debt under 50% loan to value borrow at 125 to 175 basis points over LIBOR, whereas REITs with short or uneven track records or debt over 50% borrow at 200 to 250 basis points over LIBOR. During 1995, banks began making unsecured loans to certain of the better REITs.

Insurance Companies and Pension Funds "Permanent" Loans

Insurance companies and pension funds have resumed making permanent loans on shopping centers, but, like commercial banks, with more conservative underwriting than prior to 1990. Loan to value ratios (LTV) are a maximum of 75% and debt service coverages (DSCs) are generally 1.25 or higher—not too different sounding than pre-1990. However, in arriving at those LTVs and DSCs, the insurance companies are using much tougher assumptions, similar to those of the banks. In addition, only income in place is recognized. Also, permanent lenders do not want borrowers to take money out of the refinancing. Loan maturities are typically 10 years or less, but can be longer on good regional malls and on loans secured by credit leases such as Wal-Mart.

Rates on conventional permanent loans have come down substantially on all types of "A" quality centers and particularly on regional malls, as conventional lenders have been attempting to meet the very strong competition from rated securitized debt issues (discussed later in this chapter). For instance, on regional malls, insurance companies and pension funds are currently quoting fixed rate permanent loans at 110 to 175 basis points over Treasuries, depending upon the loan to value ratio and the mall's age and quality. With respect to

"A" quality community and strip centers, insurance companies' loan rates are currently 125 to 200 basis points over Treasuries, depending on loan to value and quality, and are again very competitive against securitization and conduit rates on "A" quality centers. Insurance companies generally quote their rates, which are payable monthly, as a spread over Treasury rates, which are themselves semi-annual pay rates. Therefore, at current rates, a borrower from an insurance company is paying an additional hidden 15 basis points than on a securitized debt issue, which also pays monthly interest but which adjusts semi-annual Treasury rates downward to reflect monthly payments.

Between 1990 and 1993, rates on securitized debt issues secured by good regional malls with less than 55% loan-to-value ratios (LTVs) were consistently lower than conventional lenders' rates. However, in 1994 and 1995 insurance companies lowered their spreads significantly on "A" quality centers to meet the competition from securitization. Furthermore, conventional lenders offer borrowers several advantages over rated securitized issues. First, conventional lenders close loans in three to four months, whereas securitized issues can take up to five months or longer, to close because of bottlenecks at the rating agencies. Moreover, it is very expensive to lock in an interest rate prior to closing. Second, the total transaction costs of a conventional loan to a borrower, assuming a total of 1% up-front fees to a mortgage broker and/or an insurance company, are 2% to 2.5%, compared to 3% to 3.5% total transaction costs on a securitized debt issue, assuming an underwriter's 1.5% fee. Higher up-front costs of 1%, for example, are equivalent to approximately 30 or 15 basis points, respectively, on a 5-year or 10-year maturity. Third, it is easier to amend an insurance company or pension fund loan agreement than a securitized debt indenture, because a securitized debt issue may be owned by 5 to 20 holders.

Credit Company Loans

As in pre-1990, certain large credit companies will lend on new construction or refinance existing medium-term loans on shopping centers, although there are fewer credit companies in business these days. As in the past, credit companies will lend a higher loan to value than banks or insurance companies and will lend to a DSC as low as 1.10. However, in return, credit companies will charge a floating rate of 300 to 425 basis points over LIBOR and also, depending upon the risk, a participation equal to 50% of cash flow and 50% of the back-end profit on sale or refinancing. Thus, credit companies still offer a tradeoff to borrowers of obtaining more dollars but at a significantly higher cost of funds.

SECURITIZED DEBT

During the early 1990s, as most conventional lenders pulled back from new lending and called in as many commercial real estate loans as possible, shopping centers owners and developers were looking for alternative sources of capital. In response, the capital markets, in various forms of rated debt, surged into the once stable and gentlemanly shopping center lending market, as borrowers refinanced many loans, taking advantage of the significant decline in interest rates in 1992 and 1993. In 1993, most of the traditional shopping center lenders re-entered the lending market. As a result, competition for good shopping center loans from both conventional lenders and the capital markets became intense in 1994 and 1995.

The securitization of commercial mortgages, which started about 10 years ago, has been the single fastest growing source of shopping center debt financing in the early to mid-1990s. This growth has been propelled by (1) the needs of commercial real estate owners for alternative sources of debt financing as a result of the significant pull back in commercial real estate lending by conventional lenders in the early 1990s and (2) the acceptance of securitized commercial mortgages by both bond buyers and the rating agencies, namely Moody's Investors Service, Inc., Standard & Poor's Corporation, Fitch Investors Services, Inc., and Duff & Phelps Credit Rating Co. The rating agencies have become comfortable rating the securitized debt of all of the major types of *anchored* shopping centers, including malls, power centers, and community and neighborhood centers. At the same time, many buyers of corporate bonds, including the bond departments of insurance companies, money managers, mutual funds and pension funds, learned about investing in commercial mortgages by buying the billions of dollars of rated securitized debt sold by the Resolution Trust Corporation in the early 1990s. These same buyers are now buying securitized commercial mortgage debt from private borrowers, principally because of the significantly higher yields on securitized commercial mortgages than yields on comparably rated corporate bonds.

Securitization creates debt instruments, which (1) are rated, (2) can be traded, and (3) evidence ownership of part of an income-producing mortgage asset or pool of assets. In addition to contributing greater liquidity to individual mortgage loans, securitization reduces certain of the risks of owning individual mortgage loans. First, a securitized loan is isolated from the credit risks of the real estate owner by transferring the loan to a special purpose bankruptcy remote entity, which holds the loan and issues one or more classes of rated debt securities. These debt securities are structured with a single class of rated securities or with multiple senior and subordinated classes, with the subordinated classes absorbing the first losses and enhancing the creditworthiness of the senior securities. In addition, if a *pool* of loans is being securitized, the risk of any individual loan going bad is significantly reduced by including a large number of loans in the pool and sometimes also by varying geography and product type.

The rating agencies require that every securitized debt issue be structured so that all of the property cash flow must be used first to pay scheduled debt service on the highest rated class and then, if sufficient, to pay scheduled debt service on the next highest rated class, and so on. Moreover, all early mortgage prepayments must also be used to amortize the principal amount of the highest rated class before amortizing any lower rated class.

The percent of a securitized debt issue that comprises the subordinated classes is typically referred to as the "subordination level(s)," because the lower rated classes protect the higher rated bond classes from default in the event of insufficient cash flow to service all of the debt. The borrower and his advisor or investment banker have a dialogue with the rating agencies regarding the levels of subordination necessary to raise a certain amount of proceeds, attempting to maximize the amount of the least costly higher rated bonds. Investment bankers also attempt to choose among the four rating agencies (normally using two agencies, but in some cases only one) that will allow the lowest subordination levels on a particular securitized debt issue.

The discussion of securitized debt is broken down into single asset financing, mortgage pools, and conduit programs.

Single Asset Securitized Debt

Regional mall mortgages have been the most popular single asset, of all types of real estate, to be securitized, for several reasons. First, the rating agencies and bond buyers like the stability of many regional malls, because of their department store anchors and their usually important position in their market. Second, the desired financing size of many regional malls, of $30 million to $200 million, is the right size for a public or private securitized debt issue. In contrast, the debt on a single community center or apartment building would not be large enough to securitize, unless included in a pool of loans. Securitized issues of less than $75 million are normally sold privately, at a rate of 5 to 15 basis points higher than the rate on a larger publicly offered securitized issue that is registered with the SEC. Issues larger than $75 million are sold either publicly or privately, depending on the availability of a registration statement for a public offering (which can sometimes be "rented" from other issuers for a fee) and of audited financial statements (required for a public issue and sometimes for a private placement).

Most single asset securitized debt issues have been single class AAA or AA rated issues with a loan to value ratio of up to 50% and a DSC of 1.80 or higher. However, a number of single regional mall securitized debt issues have been sold with multiple bond classes ranging from AAA to B, thus raising greater proceeds, up to a 75% loan to value ratio with a DSC as low as 1.30. Furthermore, during 1995 several new mezzanine funds were raised that buy unrated (and unsecured) debt tranches of securitized single assets and mortgage pools at loan to values between 75% and 90%.

Ratings on shopping center debt are highly individualistic and depend upon the same factors and judgments that conventional lenders use in grading shopping center loans, including location, age, demographics, competitive position, the number, quality and sales of the anchors and other tenants, lease terms, operating results, future prospects and management. Before calculating DSCs, the rating agencies will, like conventional lenders, adjust net operating income for an estimate of annual tenant improvements, leasing commissions and capital expenditures. Table 16.1 shows, for regional mall securitized debt, current spreads over 10-year Treasuries (in October 1995), DSCs and loan to value ratios, by rating category.

Securitized debt issues are also sold with floating rate debt, typically floating over LIBOR, usually only for bond classes rated BBB or higher. A securitized debt issue often includes both fixed rate and floating rate bond classes in the same issue and secured by the same mortgage(s).

A positive effect on the market for single asset securitized debt occurred in mid-1995 when the National Association of Insurance Commissioners ruled that insurance companies can book a single asset commercial mortgage securitization as a bond, rather than as a mortgage. Insurance companies' capital reserve requirement for commercial mortgages is 3%, compared to only 0.3% for bonds.

TABLE 16.1

Regional Mall Securitized Debt by Rating Category (10 October 1995)

Rating	Fixed Spread over 10-Year Treasury	DSC	Loan to Value
AAA	75– 90 basis points	2.00x	45%
AA	95– 110	1.80	50
A	115– 150	1.70	60
BBB	165– 215	1.60	65
BB	350– 450	1.40	70
B	600– 700	1.30	75
Unrated	800–1000	1.25 or lower	over 75

Note: These spreads over Treasuries change constantly with changes in market conditions.

Swap Agreements and Interest Rate Caps

Sometimes, as was the case for much of 1994, an issuer that wants to borrow 5- to 7-year fixed-rate debt can obtain a cheaper "execution" by borrowing floating rate debt and simultaneously swapping it into fixed-rate debt with a counterparty (often the same lender or investment banker that makes the floating rate loan). There are always a number of structuring and borrowing options in the worldwide debt capital markets, and the borrower's advisor or investment banker should be attempting to take advantage, for the borrower, of disparities in the different segments of these markets.

The rating agencies will require a rated floating rate issue to have an interest rate cap with a term equal to the life of the bond issue. The cost of a cap varies with its term and the level of LIBOR being capped. Caps are usually purchased separately, the cost payable up front. The issuer amortizes the cost of the cap over the life of the bonds and adds it to the cost of the bonds. Sometimes the interest rate cap is embedded in the bonds themselves, particularly when the maturity of the bonds is longer than 7 years. (Beyond 7 years, interest rate caps are extremely expensive or are unavailable.) If the caps are embedded in the bonds, the bond's spread over LIBOR will be wider, since the additional cost of the embedded caps becomes a part of the pricing of the bonds.

The rating agencies calculate the DSC on a floating rate issue assuming the maximum (worst case) rate under the interest rate cap. For example, if a AA rated-five year floating rate issue is sold at 100 basis points over LIBOR's current 5.875% rate and a cap is purchased capping LIBOR at 8% for five years, the rating agencies will calculate the DSC of the issue using 9% as the interest rate (10.25%, including amortization). Even though the maximum interest rate allowed under the cap is used to calculate the DSC and affects the rating and size of the issue, the borrower on the securitized issue pays only the current floating rate cost plus the amortized cost of the cap.

Pricing of Securitized Debt Affected by Maturities

The maturities of most securitized commercial mortgage issues are 5 to 10 years and use a 20- to 30-year amortization schedule, because rates are lowest and the market is broadest at maturities of 10 years or less. However, fully amortizing 15- to 30-year issues are also sold, and are priced off longer Treasuries, especially if the lease terms of the sole or principal tenant(s) are similarly long. Sometimes, 15- to 30-year securitized issues backed by a *pool* of mortgages are structured to result in estimated average lives of 10 years by using either a faster amortization schedule or justifiable assumptions on early prepayments of mortgages in the pool.

Most securitized debt issues have balloon balances at the typical maturity of 5 to 10 years, but the rating agencies will allow significantly lower subordination levels—and thus more higher rated, lower yielding debt—if an issue fully amortizes my maturity. Therefore, if the major leases in a shopping center are long term, it is worthwhile to compare the cost of selling 20- to 30-year *fully amortizing* securitized debt to the cost of selling 5- to 10-year balloon debt.

In certain cases, the rating agencies will allow scheduled amortization to start after three or five years if the agencies can be convinced that property cash flows will grow more than enough to cover the scheduled amortization when it starts at the later date, and that therefore the required DSC will be maintained or exceeded.

SECURITIZED MORTGAGE POOLS

Securitized mortgage pools have become a very popular and cost effective method of financing all types of anchored shopping centers and have been used by real estate investment trusts (REITs), shopping center owners (one, or several owners, pooling new mortgages in a single securitized issue), owners of net leased properties such as Wal-Marts and Kmarts, and general partners (GPs) aggregating mortgages on properties owned by multiple limited partnerships sponsored by the GP. Securitized mortgage pools are also especially cost effective and efficient in financing individual shopping center mortgages of $1 to $10 million in size. A number of insurance companies and pension funds do not make, or charge higher rates on, mortgages of that size, and certain insurance companies' mortgage departments will not make mortgages secured by multiple assets. The mortgages in securitized pools are sometimes cross collateralized and cross defaulted, and sometimes not, for the reasons discussed below.

Cross-Collateralized Pools

When a single owner, such as a REIT, or sometimes a small group of owners want to finance a group of properties, the lowest cost method of structuring a securitized debt issue is to cross collateralize and cross default the individual mortgages. Cross collateralizing achieves the lowest subordination levels, highest ratings and thus the lowest interest cost for a given size securitized issue. A cross-collateralized structure offers significantly greater protection to bond holders in the event of defaults and losses on individual mortgages in a pool, than if the mortgages are not cross collateralized. On the other hand, certain owners who could cross collateralize their mortgages choose not to do so; they are willing to pay higher interest rates on a non-cross-collateralized pool in order to retain greater refinancing and sales flexibility over individual assets and to avoid subjecting each of their assets to future potential problems of their other assets included in the mortgage pool. The current rate spreads, DSCs and loan to value ratios of cross-collateralized mortgage pools are similar to, and slightly better (for the issuer) across the board, than those shown in Table 16.1 for single asset securitized debt issues, because of the added safety of cross-collateralized pools. Virtually all single asset securitized debt issues since 1990 have been secured by a regional mall, whereas securitized mortgage pool issues have been secured by all types of anchored shopping centers.

Noncross-Collateralized Pools

When multiple owners, such as a group of limited partnerships with different sets of owners, want to securitize a pool of mortgages, the mortgages cannot normally be cross collateralized or cross defaulted, because one set of owners would not want to share in the loss on the mortgage on a property of another set of owners. In this case, each mortgage is secured only by its own property; however, the senior securitized classes can still be enhanced by transferring the "first loss" risk to the subordinated classes.

Mortgage pools that are not cross-collateralized have ratings that are at least one rating category lower, and subordination levels about double, than if the mortgages were cross-collateralized, although it is difficult to generalize. For example, if a cross-collateralized pool of shopping center mortgages has average DSCs on the individual mortgages of 1.40 times, 85% of the securities might receive AA ratings and 15% lower (subordinated) ratings. In contrast, if these same mortgages are not cross-collateralized, only 70% to 75% of the securities might receive AA ratings and 25% to 30% lower (subordinated) ratings. Moreover, if certain shopping centers whose mortgages in a pool have significant weaknesses, such as short-term leases or high vacancies, the rating agencies will overlook the weaknesses of individual shopping centers if the mortgages are cross collateralized and the *overall* pool is strong. In contrast, if the pool is not cross collateralized, the rating agencies will either kick out weak centers or require significantly higher subordination levels.

After asset quality, loan to value ratios and DSCs, the single most important factor to the rating agencies with respect to a noncrosscollateralized securitized mortgage pool is diversification by number of loans and by geography. The rating agencies adjust the subordination levels of securities upwards depending on the "effective" number of loans in a pool, which also takes into account the skewed character of the pool (i.e., the degree to which a pool includes a number of larger loans, as opposed to all similar size smaller loans). The rating agencies first determine the appropriate subordination level for the securities assuming no loan concentration (i.e., 100 loans of the same size). Then the agencies multiply that subordination level by a multiplier corresponding to the pool's effective number of loans (the number of loans weighted by loan size). Each rating agency uses a different multiplier formula.

The geographical spread of the loans in a pool is also important to the rating agencies, which, all other things being equal, will give a higher rating to, or require lower subordination levels of, for example, a pool of loans whose properties are located in five different states than to the same size pool of loans whose properties are located in a single state.

Mortgages Backed by Net Leases

Owners of shopping centers with long-term credit net leases such as to Wal-Mart have made very good use of single asset securitizations or noncross-collateralized mortgage pools. The rates vary depending on the credit, but 100% financing using securitized debt can be sold. For example, a securitized debt issue secured by a 20-year Wal-Mart lease would be priced currently at about 115 basis points over the 10-year Treasury. Securitization is currently the lowest cost execution for financing credit net leased properties for immediate funding. Fortunately, the securitized debt market is so broad that it is not yet saturated with a name like Wal-Mart, whereas certain conventional mortgage lenders are filled up with that name.

Costs of Securitization

The costs of a securitization vary by the size of the offering, the number of loans being securitized, the number and complexity of classes of securities being sold, and the borrower's negotiating skills. Currently, the total transaction costs of securitizing shopping center mortgages are 3% to 3.5% of the issue size. These costs are typically 0.5% to 1% higher than the costs of putting a conventional insurance company loan in place (assuming that total up-front fees of 1% are paid to the insurance company and/or a mortgage broker), but the extra costs of securitization, particularly investment banking and legal fees, should come down in the future due to competition and repetition. Securitizing shopping center mortgages is no longer a pioneering transaction, and most of the documents are now mark-ups of the last 10 transactions.

Investment bankers quote fees that vary significantly, between 1% and 2% of the proceeds. The fee varies with (1) the offering's size and complexity, (2) the investment banker's value added, such as a new structure that saves the borrower a lot of money, (3) the investment banker's risk taking, (i.e., buying the securities before they are pre-sold) and (4) the competition among investment bankers for the business. Investment bankers quote either a single percentage fee for the entire issue or a schedule of fees that vary by rating category, with higher fees on the lower rated classes. A borrower should compare the costs of these two ways of quoting investment banking fees, in order to obtain the lowest overall fee. If the fee quotes are similar in effective cost, the borrower is better off with the single percentage fee for the entire issue, because the securitization structure always changes during the process, and the investment banker should not be motivated toward recommending a securitization structure with more lower rated (higher yielding) classes that pay higher fees to him.

Investment bankers sometimes ask for a higher fee if they commit to *buy* all of the securities before they are presold. This is a complex subject, because investment bankers almost always presell or take indications of interest for all or most of the securities before they commit to buy the securities. Furthermore, if an investment banker commits to buy a complex set of securities before having presold them, there is considerable risk that the investment banker will recommend yields or spreads on those securities that are higher than if the securities had been presold. Also, the securities cannot be bought or sold until after the rating agencies have rated them, which is just before the marketing begins.

Legal fees are the next highest transaction cost of a securitization and vary significantly, by law firm, even on similar sizes and structures of offerings. The borrower's legal fees on a first time offering vary between $150,000 and $400,000 for his own counsel and the same for the investment banker's counsel. The borrower should attempt to fix these legal fees up front, although certain lawyers will not agree to do so. Typically, the borrower on a securitization pays the legal fees of both his own counsel and the investment banker's counsel, although on certain publicly offered debt securitizations the underwriters will pay some or all of their own legal fees. (On public debt offerings by most industrial and financial companies, the underwriters pay their own legal fees, although such legal fees are normally lower than underwriters' legal fees on debt securitizations.)

It is very difficult to compare the legal fees on a mortgage securitization to the legal fees on a conventional mortgage loan because there are so many variables. For instance, the aggregate legal fees to close 25 separate $5 to $10 million conventional loans would be enormous, especially if 25 different lenders were involved (which would probably not be the case).

Other transaction costs that exceed the costs of closing a conventional loan(s) are the due diligence and accounting costs. Certain investment banking firms use outside due diligence or accounting firms to visit the properties and supervise the appraisals, engineering and environmental reports and prepare undated financials on the properties, while other underwriters do their own due diligence or pay for the work done by these due diligence firms. The fees to these outside firms vary from as low as $5,000 per property (e.g., $125,000 on a 25-property pool) to as much as 0.5% of the amount of the offering.

One cost that borrowers should attempt to avoid on a private placement of securitized debt is the cost of an audit of the properties' cash flow. Such special audits are very expensive, unless the borrower is a public company such as a REIT that already has audited numbers. Certain rating agencies require an audit of the latest calendar year or 12 months cash flow, whereas other rating agencies require only an accounting firm's *review* of the latest 12 months numbers. Public offerings, including public securitized debt offerings, always require audited numbers.

Another cost of a debt securitization is rating agency fees, which vary by offering size and by rating agency. For example, the cost of two ratings on a $100 million securitized offering is about $150,000.

A debt securitization will also require a trustee and an independent servicer, which together will cost 15 to 20 basis points annually and about $30,000 up front. In the event that a scheduled payment has not been received by the due date, the rating agencies require that the master servicer advance from its own funds scheduled payments, as well as real estate taxes, insurance premiums and certain other costs, to the extent that they are judged to be recoverable, at the master servicer's discretion.

A debt securitization will also have printing costs, which vary significantly depending on whether the offering memorandum, the pooling and servicing agreement and the bond indenture are printed. On a private placement, printing may not be necessary, whereas printing would be required on a public offering. The other costs to close a debt securitization, including appraisals, engineering and environmental reports and title insurance, are also required, and are similar to the costs, on conventional loans.

Time Schedule of a Securitized Debt Issue

A privately placed securitized debt issue will take five to six months for a first offering (a minimum of seven months for a first time *public* offering), with the major variable being the rating agencies' timing. The rating agencies are sometimes so busy on other ratings that they have taken six months to do their visits and due diligence. The rating agencies act more quickly if there are only a few assets in a pool, for obvious reasons. During all of 1993, certain of the major rating agencies were so overloaded with requests for securitized debt ratings that it generally took six months or more to obtain ratings. In contrast, during most of 1994, as a result of the significant increase in interest rates, securitized debt issue volume fell off markedly, and the rating agencies took only about two months to rate new securitized debt issues.

A public offering would add about two months to the time schedule, on a first time offering, to allow for SEC review and audited financial statements. The time schedule for a repeat offering would be only three or four months, due to major time savings on the documents.

CONDUIT PROGRAMS

Conduits of shopping center mortgages are pools of mortgages that are not cross collateralized or cross defaulted and which are put together by investment bankers, commercial banks and other financial companies. The conduits make or purchase mortgages from many different borrowers (or lenders) and combine them into noncrosscollateralized debt securitizations. By combining large numbers of mortgages together from many sources, the conduits seek to achieve significant diversification in a pool of loans by number and by geography, and thereby receive low subordination levels and high ratings from the rating agencies.

There are several conduits that specialize in buying shopping center loans, and other conduits that purchase all types of commercial real estate loans including shopping center loans. Conduits are especially suitable for (a) mortgages of $1 to $10 million, since insurance companies and pension funds generally charge higher rates and fees on these size loans than on larger loans—although certain conduits will also purchase individual loans of up to $25 million in size, and (b) owners with less than 20 mortgages, since structuring one's own securitization with less than 20 mortgages will result in high subordination levels from the rating agencies.

In order to be accepted by a conduit, the shopping centers must be of good quality with, for example, good anchor tenants with leases longer than 10 years. However, the centers can be older and of "B" or even "C" quality—many of which might be rejected by certain insurance company and pension fund mortgage lenders that lend only on "A" centers. The yields at which conduits will purchase shopping center loans vary significantly from conduit to conduit, and are affected by the quality and number of assets being purchased, the number of loans to be securitized and rated, and the overhead and profit margins of the particular conduit. Conduit sponsors will also come down on rates and fees if quoting on a pool of loans of $25 million or larger, for competitive reasons and because of savings from economies of scale.

The principal advantages of selling a mortgage to a conduit are (1) the convenience of utilizing a canned securitized financing put together by someone else who has prepared all the documentation and negotiated with the rating agencies and (2) the possibility of obtaining better pricing than by doing one's own securitized financing or from conventional financing, as a result of combining one's mortgages into a much larger pool. The principal disadvantages of selling a mortgage to a conduit are (1) the yield and fees that are quoted are sometimes high compared to the cost of conventional financing or of doing one's own securitization (assuming one has sufficient mortgages to do one's own securitization), either because the conduit sponsor is trying to make very large profits or because the conduit's pricing may reflect the inclusion of other lower quality assets for which the rating agencies are requiring higher subordination levels and (2) the conduit may back out of or delay a purchase until other mortgages are also purchased, in order, for example, to put together a large enough securitized pool in order to obtain sufficiently high ratings. The individual conduit's track record is key. The conduit business for shopping center mortgages is in its infancy, and innovations are constantly occurring.

At this time, conduits and other forms of debt securitization are not being used to make forward commitments or for construction lending—still the domains of insurance companies and commercial banks—but securitization is expanding and innovating rapidly and may get into those businesses in the future.

RATED UNSECURED DEBT

A rated unsecured privately placed or publicly offered bond issue (not convertible into common stock) is a financing alternative that has been used sporadically by REITs for more than 20 years—no more than 20 times by all REITs prior to 1992—as an alternative to mortgage financing. However, since 1992, more than 20 REITs have sold more than $3 billion of unsecured bond issues, and more than 25 other REITs have applied to the rating agencies for unsecured bond ratings. Such issues will likely see a lot more use by shopping center REITs in the future, because most of the largest shopping center developers went public as REITs in 1993 and 1994 and most of them would like to sell rated unsecured debt, and many will be able to obtain unsecured "investment grade" bond ratings, that is, ratings of BBB or higher.

Rated unsecured bond issues cost less than securitized or conventional mortgage debt only for issuers that can obtain investment grade bond ratings. Unsecured "junk" bond issues (i.e., those rated BB or lower) will generally be more costly to a borrower than borrowing by using secured mortgage debt.

Rated unsecured bond issues can take a number of different forms. They can be sold publicly (registered with the SEC) or privately to institutions as single large issues or in $5 to $20 million size medium-term note issues. Generally, a borrower will save 5 to 15 basis points in rate by selling a public rather than a private issue. Transaction costs on a Baa2/BBB rated unsecured issue, including a 0.75% underwriter's fee and other up-front offering and closing costs, will total 1.25% to 1.50% of gross proceeds. These up-front costs are 1% to 2% less than the up-front costs of a conventional mortgage or securitized debt issue, because investment grade unsecured corporate bond issues have low investment banking fees and low legal fees and there is no title insurance necessary or other expensive mortgage closing costs.

Maturities of most fixed-rate unsecured bond issues are 5 to 10 years, and maturities of most floating rate issues are 5 to 7 years, because the market is broadest and rates are lowest in those maturities. Most floating rate issues float at a spread over LIBOR. Most issues are "bullet" maturities, with no amortization prior to maturity. Both the base index (Treasuries or LIBOR) over which the unsecured bond issue is priced, and the spread over the index, change daily with general bond market conditions and with the bond market's opinion about shopping center companies.

Bond buyers want stability above all else, and many bond buyers view real estate as cyclical. Even within the same rating category, the name and reputation of a particular borrower significantly affect the pricing of a bond issue. Unfortunately, the names of only a small number of shopping center REITs are recognized by bond buyers, and recognition is worth 25 to 50 basis points in yield over a comparably rated but unknown issuer. These are the reasons why the rated unsecured debt of a shopping center REIT will trade at a 25 to 50 basis points higher yield than the debt of a comparably rated industrial borrower. Said another way, the debt of a BBB rated industrial issue will generally be priced at a lower interest rate than a single-A rated REIT issue. Current spreads over 10-year Treasuries for a 10-year fixed-rate unsecured REIT bond issue are 75 to 90 basis points for a single-A rated issue, 100 to 125 basis points for a Baa1/BBB1 rated issue and 150 to 170 basis points for a Baa3/BBB2 rated issue. Floating rate spreads for a 5-year unsecured REIT bond issue are currently 50 to 60 basis points over LIBOR for a single-A rated issue and 75 to 90 basis points over LIBOR for a BBB-rated issue.

The rating agencies use the following criteria in rating unsecured bond issues of shopping center REITs. First, they want to see a history over a 3- to 5-year period of stable operating income, including during the latest real estate cycle, by a consistent management team. The rating agencies understand the shopping center business and will ask most of the same questions about the properties and the business as banks and insurance companies do. The rating agencies are judging the borrower's historical and prospective earning stability, not growth. For an investment grade rating, the rating agencies will want to see the REIT's total debt equal to less than 50%, and preferably less than 40%, of its total market capitalization (the sum of its debt and the market value of its common stock). Historical and prospective coverage of interest by cash flow from operations after capital expenditures is the most important rating agency criterion, and the likelihood of the issuer's sustaining that ratio over the life of the bond issue. Generally, the rating agencies require that the ratio of operating cash flow to debt service be at least 2.2 times for a BBB rating and at least 5.0 times for a single-A rating, but there are some major differences in such requirements, which depend on quality of assets and stability of cash flow.

A problem for many REITs in obtaining investment grade bond ratings is that almost all of their real estate has been heretofore financed with secured mortgage debt, which by definition has a priority over any unsecured debt. In order to obtain, and maintain, an investment grade unsecured bond rating, an issuer must agree to limit most of its future financing and refinancing to unsecured debt. In general, if a REIT has a significant amount of secured debt, such as more than 30% of total market capitalization, the rating agencies will rate the REIT's senior unsecured debt one full rating category lower (i.e., like subordinated debt) than if the REIT's secured debt were low.

COMMERCIAL PAPER

A small number of shopping center REITs and corporations have been meeting a portion of their short-term borrowing needs, for acquisitions, construction and development, by selling commercial paper, as a cheaper alternative to commercial bank borrowings. Commercial paper is rated unsecured short-term notes sold by highly creditworthy borrowers through dealers to institutional buyers. Commercial paper typically carries maturities of 5 to 90 days and is rolled over continuously. The commercial paper market is huge, with more than $500 billion outstanding. The cost of commercial paper approximates LIBOR rates or 5.75% to 6.00% in October 1995. In addition, the commercial paper dealers charge approximately 10 basis points on an annual basis. An additional cost of commercial paper is the cost of unused back-up bank lines of credit, which an issuer must keep in place in the unlikely event that its commercial paper cannot be rolled over. The cost of such back-up bank lines varies between 10 to 25 basis points per year. The issuer would have to use such lines to refund its maturing commercial paper in the event the issuer lost its credit ratings or in the event of a major negative surprise in the money markets, such as the bankruptcy of Penn Central in the early 1970s.

The key to gaining access to the commercial paper market is to obtain, and maintain, the top commercial paper ratings from two of the major rating agencies. The rating agencies analyze the stability of the borrower's business, as well as the borrower's use of short term borrowings and the availability of liquidity, and like to see conservative leverage (debt less than 50% of total market capitalization).

CONVERTIBLE DEBT AND PREFERRED STOCK

Convertible debt and convertible preferred stock are other forms of unsecured financing being used by shopping center REITs and corporations. In most cases, convertible debt is sold with maturities of 7 to 30 years, is usually subordinated to all other debt, and is regarded by the market as part debt and part equity. Convertible preferred stock is usually sold as "perpetual" with no maturity and in such cases is 100% equity. Convertible debt and convertible preferred stock are convertible into the common stock of the REIT or corporate issuer. The price (the "conversion price") at which convertible debt or convertible preferred stock is convertible into common stock is usually fixed on the date of the offering and is set within a range of 0% to a 20% premium over the market price of the common stock on such date. Convertible securities appeal to institutional investors, such as certain mutual funds and money managers, that specialize in buying convertible securities, as well as to certain equity investors that want to own a more senior equity security.

Existing REITs have been selling convertible debt and convertible preferred stock since the early 1970s, but there have been usually less than five, and often no, such new issues sold in any year by the entire real estate industry. In the future, issues of convertible securities should grow substantially, since more than 100 new REITs, including more than a dozen shopping center REITs, went public between 1992 and 1995. Certain of these REITs will choose to sell convertible securities in the future for the following reasons. First, convertible securities are unsecured, do not tie up collateral, and typically allow for additional senior debt to be put on top of them in the issuer's capital structure. In fact, the proceeds of convertible securities issues are often used to pay down secured debt. Second, convertible securities are used most typically by issuers (excluding the special case of initial public offerings) as a means of selling common stock at a price above the current market price, i.e., at a conversion premium, by offering investors a higher yield on the convertible security than the yield on the common stock. Third, the interest cost of convertible securities is usually less than the cost of secured or unsecured straight debt. However, because most REIT stock prices already sell at relatively high dividend yields, such as 6% to 8.5%, the interest rate put on a REIT convertible security is typically only a small amount above the dividend yield on the common stock, such as 1% to 2%. Consequently, the conversion premiums on REIT convertible securities are also low, such as 5% to 15% (or zero if there is no interest differential over the common stock's dividend yield). For example, during 1993 and 1994, several new REITs on their initial public offerings, in addition to selling common stock, also sold convertible debt that is convertible into common stock at a 0% premium over the common stock price at the date of the offering. These so-called zero premium convertible debt issues carried interest rates of between 0% and 0.5% below the initial dividend yield on the common stock.

Convertible preferred stock is an equity security, especially when sold with no maturity, as is usually the case. If an issuer misses a preferred stock dividend payment, the issuer will, typically after missing six such payments, have to add to its Board one or two new directors who represent the preferred stockholders, but the issue will not be in default and will not be accelerated, as would be the case if the issuer missed a convertible debt (or any debt) interest or principal payment.

Convertible preferred stock of most companies is priced very similarly to convertible debt, but convertible preferred stock of REITs is priced somewhat worse than REIT convertible debt, for the following reason. The preferred stock dividends of REITs do not qualify for the partial dividend exclusion for corporate buyers under the tax code, as do the preferred stock dividends of most corporate issuers. Despite the fact that a new issue of convertible preferred stock will be priced somewhat worse for a REIT than a new issue of convertible debt, a REIT may still choose to sell an issue of perpetual preferred stock because lenders, investors and rating agencies will regard such an issue as 100% equity, whereas convertible debt will be regarded as part debt and part equity.

During 1995, for the first time ever, a half dozen REITs have sold perpetual nonconvertible preferred stock, at dividend rates varying between 8.50% and 9.50%. The buyers have been principally individuals, not institutions. Preferred stocks of most corporations trade at lower yields than debt of the same company because of the partial dividend exclusion received by certain buyers under the tax code, mentioned above. However, because REIT preferred stock dividends do not qualify for such exclusion, the yield on a REIT preferred stock will be higher than the yield on a REIT's unsecured debt, because preferred stock is subordinated to debt.

CONCLUSION

Debt financing for shopping centers underwent rapid change between 1990 and 1995 in response to the needs of shopping center owners for alternative sources of capital, as most conventional sources dried up between 1990 and 1992. Wall Street responded to these needs by designing debt securities that were ratable by the rating agencies and that were attractive to debt buyers. Securitization of shopping center debt became increasingly sophisticated, with offerings of both rated single asset mortgage securities and cross-collateralized and noncross-collateralized mortgage pools.

Reacting to the strong competition from securitization, conventional lenders re-entered the shopping center loan market aggressively in 1993–1995 and significantly reduced their rates and spreads on loans on class A community shopping centers and regional malls, while tightening their underwriting standards. Now that both the capital markets and conventional lenders are competing to make shopping center loans, it is a certainty that innovations in shopping center debt financing will continue at a rapid pace.

Seventeen

Capital for Shopping Centers Through Public and Private Equity Issues

Charles Grossman

E quity financing of shopping centers has changed dramatically in recent years. This chapter reviews the evolution of shopping center ownership and financing practices, highlighting how the securities markets have come to play a significant role as an alternative to investment via privately negotiated arrangements.

TRADITIONAL EQUITY FINANCE FOR DEVELOPMENT: PRIVATE MARKETS

Limited Equity Requirements

During the periods of the shopping center industry's initial development and greatest growth, equity requirements for construction and ownership were easily met by private sources. The level of required equity was relatively modest, and both prospective economic returns and income tax benefits encouraged private investors to supply any necessary capital. A number of factors operated to limit the level of equity needed to build and operate the shopping center:

- The cost of land, the element of a development project that is most difficult to finance on a debt basis, was relatively modest since shopping centers tended to be built in outlying areas where bulk acreage was available at low prices. Moreover, purchase option arrangements often permitted the developer to defer paying for land until institutional debt financing for the project was in place.

- In the case of regional malls, the developer could avoid the cost of constructing facilities for the department stores anchoring the center. Typical arrangements called for the developer to convey portions of the site at modest or no cost to each of the department stores and for the department stores then to construct their own buildings. Similar arrangements have prevailed on occasion in neighborhood and community centers with supermarkets and discount stores.

- Typically, shopping center design and construction is relatively simple and straightforward. Until the second half of the 1980s, small shop space in centers leased promptly once the developer had secured anchor tenants. As a result, delays and unanticipated costs producing unforeseen equity requirements were unusual.

Conventional Debt Finance from Private Markets

Developers were generally able to obtain from mortgage lenders on a debt basis all or substantially all of the cost of constructing a shopping center. The following example illustrates how third-party debt finance might have covered most of the cost of a shopping center development undertaken in the late 1970s or early 1980s. It assumes development of a four department store regional center containing 900,000 square feet of gross leasable area. The department stores occupy a total of 600,000 square feet and build their own stores on land contributed by the developer. Small shops represent 300,000 square feet of space, pay annual fixed rents averaging $15.00 per square foot and reimburse the landlord for common area maintenance and real estate tax expenses. Total project cost is assumed to equal $40 million. With an interest rate of 8½% and amortization over a 30-year period, the lender might have advanced $37.3 million or over 90% of the hypothesized cost of the development. The following table illustrates the analysis that might have led the lender to make such a loan. It assumes full tenant reimbursement of property operating expenses and real estate taxes.

Gross potential income	
Mall space (300,000 s.f. @ $15)	$ 4,500,000
Outparcels (5 @ $25,000)	125,000
Total	$ 4,625,000
Vacancy (5%)	230,000
Gross effective income	$ 4,395,000
Management (5%)	220,000
Capital reserve (300,000 s.f. @ $.15)	45,000
Cash flow before debt service	$ 4,130,000
Debt service coverage factor	÷ 1.2
Maximum debt service	$ 3,442,800
Debt service constant (8.5%, 30 yrs.)	9.23%
Loan amount	$37,300,000

The developer and its partners would thus own the property for a relatively modest capital investment of $2.7 million.

Equity Finance from Private Markets

In cases where equity capital was required, the developer could obtain it without resorting to the public markets. As a result of the success of the shopping center industry, larger shopping center developers became very wealthy, possessing personal resources often sufficient to cover any equity capital required for a particular development. To the extent the developer either did not have adequate personal resources or did not wish to commit them to a given project, the developer could raise the equity required from other private investors. These investors would own a partnership interest in the property and enjoy a share of the property's cash flow. They would, in addition, receive significant income tax benefits, with depreciation deductions sheltering all or at least a significant portion of the property's cash flow from taxation. Coupled with interest deductions on the mortgage loan, depreciation allowances sometimes produced an annual "tax loss," notwithstanding that the property generated a positive cash flow.

The following table illustrates the attractiveness of an investment in a shopping center to a private investor as a result of economic cash flow and tax shelter in the form of depreciation and interest deductions. It continues the prior example, postulating a center with a cost of $40 million, a mortgage loan of $37.3 million and an equity investment of $2.7 million. Straight-line depreciation, permitting deduction in equal annual amounts of the cost of improvements over a 30-year useful life is assumed, with land cost representing 10% of total project cost.

I. *Pre-Tax Analysis*

Cash flow before debt service	$4,130,000
Debt service ($37,300,000 loan @ 9.23% constant)	3,442,800
Cash flow after debt service	$ 687,200
Equity investment	2,700,000
Pre-tax return	25.5%

II. *After-Tax Analysis*

Cash flow after debt service (pre-tax)	687,200
Mortgage amortization (Annual average, yrs. 1–10)	425,200
Depreciation ($40,000,000 × .9 ÷ 30)	(1,200,000)
Taxable income (loss)	$ (87,600)
Income tax (tax loss value) @ 50%	(43,800)
Cash flow after debt service (pre-tax)	687,200
Tax loss value	43,800
Cash flow after tax	731,000
Equity investment	$2,700,000
After tax return	27.1%

In this case, the interest and depreciation deductions not only fully shelter the property's cash flow from taxation but also produce a net loss for taxation purposes. This tax loss was, until the enactment of tax law changes in the mid 1980s, available to protect other income from taxation and was thus valuable to the investor. As indicated in our example which assumed a 50% marginal income tax rate, the tax loss would produce an after-tax return on equity higher than the pre-tax return.

Finally, the availability of financial leverage enhanced the potential for extraordinary capital gains on sale of shopping centers. Sale of the property upon completion and lease-up at a price set by capitalizing cash flow before debt service at a rate of 8.5% would produce:

- An overall profit over total cost of $8.6 million or over 20%.
- A leveraged capital gain on equity of over 300%.

The following table illustrates the computation:

Cash flow before debt service	$ 4,130,000
Capitalization rate	8.5%
Sale price	48,600,000
Mortgage balance	37,300,000
Cash proceeds	11,300,000
Equity investment	2,700,000
Profit to equity owner	8,600,000
Profit as percent of project cost	21.5%
Profit as percent of equity invested	318.5%

Increasing Equity Demands in Recent Years

As the 1980s unfolded, the equity investment required for shopping center development tended to rise, and it became more difficult for the developer to raise substantially all of the cost of a new project from the first mortgage lender. A number of factors contributed to this need for more equity finance by combining to increase development costs and reduce borrowing capacity. First, environmental reviews of proposed developments generally became more exacting and elaborate, necessitating greater preconstruction expenditures on professional assistance and longer, more costly land holding periods. Second, shopping center design became more elaborate and costly, particularly in the area of interior finishes. Third, department stores began to ask for landlord contributions to the costs of constructing, fixturing and sometimes inventorying their stores. Fourth, the rising and fluctuating interest rate environment that generally prevailed in much of the 1980s, as compared to the 1960s and 1970s, reduced the amount that a lender would typically extend on a shopping center development. Difficulties in arranging ample levels of debt finance from traditional lenders foreshadowed the problems that developers would experience at the end of the 1980s when the real estate recession took hold.

During the era of the shopping center industry's greatest growth, developers had little need to resort to the securities markets to obtain equity finance for new projects. They could rely upon direct, private negotiations with institutional investors to arrange debt capital that would supply most, if not all, of the cost of a development and upon individual private investors for any required balance. In so doing, developers avoided the burdens and costs associated with the operation of a public company, including disclosure of operating performance and financial results on a continuing basis and maintenance of relationships with analysts who follow closely public companies. Moreover, by avoiding the public markets, developers did not expose their personal net worths to stock price movements. Developers did not turn to the public markets until the private markets could no longer meet their capital requirements.

TRADITIONAL EQUITY FINANCE FOR INVESTMENT: PRIVATE MARKETS

As the industry matured, an aftermarket in shopping center ownership emerged, with investors acquiring completed and leased properties from developers. Many developers—particularly those specializing in large, regional malls—have traditionally retained ownership in their properties on a long-term basis. But, such long-term holders did, on occasion, sell entire or partial interests in order to raise capital for a new development or for physical refurbishment of an older center. Smaller scale developers were more commonly sellers of shopping centers. Thus, an investment market in shopping centers did develop, beginning in the 1970s. Buyers of operating shopping centers have traditionally been individuals and financial institutions including life insurance companies and pension funds. Until very recently, few buyers were public companies, for reasons discussed next.

Private Individuals

Individual investors often invested in shopping centers through partnerships sponsored and organized by specialist firms. Shopping centers offered these individual investors an attractive, tax-sheltered current return and the potential for capital appreciation as income from minimum and percentage rents rose. These private partnerships became active in the 1970s, and the liberalization of depreciation deductions contained in the tax legislation of 1981 stimulated their growth. Income tax legislation in 1986, however, curtailed their activities by restricting the deductibility of real estate tax losses against other types of income. Significant limits on tax benefits as well as difficulties with existing investments as a result of weakening markets led individual investors to turn away from real estate in the second half of the 1980s.

Institutional investors, motivated not by income tax deductions but by the prospects of attractive economic returns, have made a more enduring commitment to shopping center equity ownership.

Life Insurance Companies

Life insurance companies often coupled equity investing in shopping centers with mortgage lending. In some cases, the life insurance companies would make a conventional mortgage loan on a project with interest on the loan including not only a fixed component but also a contingent participation in gross revenue or net cash flow. Frequently, the contingent return encompassed a share of the property's appreciation in value upon loan maturity. In other cases, lenders would separately acquire an interest in the residual equity in the property. These companies also purchased shopping centers in which they had no involvement as lender. By the 1980s, however, the changing nature of the life insurance industry, particularly the declining importance of whole life coverage, made long-term ownership of an illiquid asset such as real estate less appropriate for these companies. Pension funds have now supplanted life insurance companies as the leading institutional buyers of real estate.

Pension Funds

Pension funds began to acquire real estate in the 1970s, and their commitment to real estate equity investing accelerated in the first half of the 1980s. The long-term nature of their liabilities made real estate ownership, with its promise of long-term rewards, appropriate for pension funds. Whetting their interest were the relatively high returns achieved by real estate investors in the second half of the 1970s and the first half of the 1980s, the low volatility evidenced in the data on real estate returns during that period, and the negative correlation suggested by that data between real estate returns and stock market returns. Real estate thus promised high returns, low risk (as measured by volatility in total return), and a diversifying effect upon a pension fund's overall portfolio. Real estate equity investing unfortunately did not fulfill these expectations. The overbuilding that occurred in all sectors of the real estate industry in the second half of the 1980s produced falling rents and falling returns. It became apparent by 1990 that real estate equity investing was substantially more volatile than had been imagined. Of the three benefits promised by real estate equity—high return, low risk, and diversification—only the last was achieved and that only because the stock market rose as real estate values collapsed.

Pension funds generally ceased making new real estate equity investments by 1990. Acquisition activity fell sharply with the bulk accounted for by pension funds not previously active and seeking to take advantage of market distress. Pension funds remained substantially out of the market for the ensuing three years. Nonetheless, as evidence of a bottoming and in some cases, of improvement in the real estate markets has mounted, renewed interest by pension funds in real estate equity has appeared. Pension funds will probably remain major participants in the real estate equity markets in coming years. Accordingly, it is appropriate to review why and how they invest in real estate equity, the degree to which they have invested in shopping centers and the returns produced by their retail investments in both absolute and comparative terms.

Pension Fund Investment Formats

Pension funds did not initially enter the real estate equity area by buying shares in public real estate companies. In the late 1970s and early 1980s, the public arena did not provide a realistic avenue for pension funds to invest substantial amounts in the ownership of retail properties. Initially, real estate equity investments by most pension funds consisted of the purchase of units in commingled funds in which only pension funds could invest. Managers of these commingled funds included large life insurance companies such as Equitable Life Assurance, John Hancock Life Insurance, Prudential Life Insurance, and private companies specializing in investment management such as Heitman Advisory Corporation, JMB Institutional Realty Corporation, LaSalle Advisors Limited, RREEF Funds, and TCW Realty Advisors. These sponsors have been responsible for:

- Organizing the commingled vehicle;
- Raising capital by marketing units to the pension fund community;

- Investing its capital in suitable properties;

- Managing at the portfolio level the properties acquired;

- Overseeing as asset manager, on-site management, leasing and capital improvement programs and in some cases, carrying out as property manager on-site functions;

- Selling of properties;

- Exercising financial control and reporting to unitholders; and

- Appraising property interests including reviewing appraisals performed by independent firms.

Investing through Separate Accounts

In the early 1980s, a number of larger pension funds began to invest in real estate on a separate account basis; in such cases, the pension fund acquires interests in property directly rather than through a commingled vehicle. The size of large funds permits them to acquire major, top quality assets without fear of making a disproportionate commitment of their total resources. Pension funds investing through separate accounts often have small in-house real estate investment staffs, but generally retain an investment manager to execute an approved investment strategy. In some cases, the investment manager is granted discretion in making acquisitions on behalf of the pension fund client; in others, authority to approve investments is retained by the pension fund. Investment managers active here include those also managing commingled funds (examples being the firms listed earlier) and others specializing in separate account relationships (such as Jones Lang Wootton Realty Advisors and Hart Advisors). Advantages of separate account investing to a pension fund include development and execution of the specific investment strategy appropriate to the pension fund, control over the investment and asset management process, participation in and ultimate control over a decision to sell a property, and customized financial reporting.

The relative importance in the future of separate account as opposed to commingled investing by pension funds is not clear. Disenchantment with commingled arrangements developed during the downturn that began in the late 1980s, as pension funds were severely frustrated by their inability to either liquidate their holdings of units in a particular fund or in the absence of liquidation, to control operating decisions and/or to force sale of designated properties. Uncertainty as to the reliability of appraised values of property assets also contributed to the unhappiness of many pension funds with holdings in commingled funds. Considerable discussion of ways in which to improve the governance of commingled vehicles and to insure their responsiveness to the interests of their investors has ensued. Steps that have been taken include organizing the fund as a corporation (often a real estate investment trust), providing for control over the corporation by an independent Board of Directors and granting the Board or shareholders authority to make important decisions including changes in management. With enhanced accountability, it seems premature to dismiss commingled formats as vehicles for future pension fund investment in real estate equity.

Many observers believe that appropriately structured commingled funds will continue to appeal to smaller pension funds disinclined to commit to a single asset the large sums required to buy major properties. Under this view, larger pension funds will tend to use separate account formats for real estate investing.

Pension Fund Investment Parameters

Pension funds, whether acting through commingled funds or through separate accounts, have acquired and owned properties on both a leveraged and unleveraged basis. Leverage in the form of mortgage borrowings secured by real estate can enhance the returns from properties. Utilizing leverage in equity real estate investing is also consistent with practices in other varieties of institutional equity investing since, for example, pension funds commonly buy shares in corporations having debt in their capital structures. Leverage, on the other hand, increases volatility, and pension fund investors typically seek, at least at the portfolio level, to reduce fluctuations in performance. Moreover, pension funds are generally net lenders on an overall basis, with their portfolios containing debt instruments as well as equity holdings. Utilizing leverage in a real estate portfolio may thus be viewed as inconsistent with a pension fund's overall portfolio position.

Real estate equity investments made by pension funds have typically consisted of completed, income-producing properties requiring only limited leasing and capital improvement programs at the time of purchase. To a lesser extent, pension funds have invested in properties under development or rehabilitation, where higher prospective returns justify increased risks. In the shopping center field, pension funds have focused upon the acquisition of modern, fully competitive operating properties. They have, on occasion, invested in development projects and in centers requiring renovation and remerchandising.

Size of Pension Fund Investment

Pension funds are now major owners of property and as a class, constitute the largest institutional holder of real estate. It is estimated that their real estate equity holdings totaled $120 billion at the end of 1993, about 44% of the $270 billion held by institutions. Real estate equity holdings by insurance companies amounted to an estimated $47 billion at the end of 1993, those by foreign investors to about $35 billion and those by real estate investment trusts to about $20 billion.[1]

In terms of the type of property favored by pension funds, the composition of a leading index of performance of properties owned by pension funds indicates that shopping centers now rank second to office buildings. Pension fund purchases of shopping centers exceed those of industrial buildings, apartments and hotels, as the following Table 17.1 illustrates.

Leading pension funds to invest in shopping centers have been a number of considerations:

- Retail properties have historically performed well. Consumer spending has steadily risen during the post-World War II period, as a result of growth in both population and personal income and wealth. Increasing expenditures have boosted retail sales, retailer demand for additional locations and retail rents.

- The horizontal spread of residential and employment centers into suburban and then exurban locations has created a need for

TABLE 17.1

Pension Fund Investment—1993

Type	Percent of Total
Office	30.6
Retail	28.0
Industrial	23.1
Residential	15.7
Hotel	2.6
Total	100.0

Source: Russell-NCREIF Performance Report, First Quarter 1994.

retail facilities in outlying locations away from the traditional center city. Accommodation of the automobile has been required, and the shopping center has emerged as the appropriate format.

- The presence of anchor tenants in investment grade shopping centers generally provide stability to the income from and value of such properties. These anchor tenants include department stores in regional malls, discount stores in community centers, value (often labeled big box or category-killer) retailers in the power centers appearing in recent years and supermarkets and drug stores in neighborhood centers.

- Retail rents have over time increased as retail sales have risen. The shopping center owner benefits from increases in either or both real unit volume or the nominal value of units sold. There is thus direct linkage between consumer expenditures and/or price inflation and rental income from shopping centers.

- The physical simplicity of shopping center design and construction has permitted the types of retail uses found in particular shopping centers to evolve over time in response to consumer preferences and shopping patterns. Successful regional malls have over the years replaced "hard good" operations such as furniture and hardware stores with smaller "soft good" retailers in the apparel, accessories, and leisure fields. Well-located neighborhood and community centers have typically been able to respond successfully to the desire on the part of supermarkets for larger stores, either by permitting the supermarket to expand or by replacing the supermarket with other retail uses.

Shopping centers have not been perfect investment vehicles, and difficulties have on occasion arisen with certain retail investments. Chief causes have been (1) excessive new construction producing on over-supply of space and falling rents, which has been most common with smaller neighborhood centers; (2) bankruptcy and closure of anchor tenants accompanied by a reduction in customer traffic and a loss of business for smaller retailers; and (3) the emergence of new retail formats that have taken business away from more established retailers, an example being the competition afforded department stores by value retailers in recent years.

Nonetheless, returns achieved by pension funds from retail properties have generally exceeded those produced by other property types. The National Council of Real Estate Investment Fiduciaries and Frank Russell Company have published since 1977 the Russell-NCREIF Real Estate Performance Report (Table 17.2) which presents returns in index form from properties owned by pension funds. The Russell-NCREIF Property Index presents for completed, unleveraged, and nonagricultural properties, income, appreciation and total returns with the market value of properties determined by appraisal. It indicates that total returns from retail properties have generally exceeded those from office, research and development/office and warehouse properties over the past 15 years. Retail property returns have not performed as well as apartment properties since the early 1990s, reflecting the earlier recovery by the residential sector from the real estate downturn occurring in the second half of the 1980s.

Shopping centers have suffered during the real estate downturn that began in the second half of the 1980s to a lesser extent than office buildings and warehouses. Review of the Russell-NCREIF Index suggests that capital values of retail properties nationally have slid by

TABLE 17.2

Russell-NCREIF Property Index
Total Return Summary (%)—March 31, 1994

Period	Apartment	Office	Retail	R&D/Office	Warehouse
Q1 1994	2.82	1.09	1.20	1.97	2.10
Q4 1993	4.48	(4.29)	2.12	(0.01)	(1.20)
1 year	12.59	(5.72)	5.86	2.88	(1.21)
2 years	8.07	(7.35)	2.05	(1.12)	(1.67)
3 years	4.52	(8.57)	0.27	(3.11)	(1.89)
4 years	4.67	(7.51)	1.45	(2.49)	(1.04)
5 years	4.92	(5.48)	3.10	(0.89)	0.95
6 years	5.26	(3.98)	4.78	0.17	2.30
7 years	—	(3.36)	5.75	1.06	3.62
8 years	—	(2.51)	6.45	1.91	4.25
9 years	—	(1.30)	6.97	2.67	5.15
10 years	—	(0.16)	7.75	3.72	5.80
11 years	—	1.06	8.50	5.27	6.33
12 years	—	1.63	8.45	5.86	6.50
13 years	—	2.90	8.66	6.93	7.08
14 years	—	3.90	8.88	7.87	7.64
15 years	—	5.29	9.04	8.31	8.50

Source: Russell-NCREIF Real Estate Performance Report, First Quarter, 1994.

over 20% since the peak achieved in mid-1990. Office building values have fallen by over 50% on a national basis since peaking at the end of 1985. Warehouses have experienced a 30% drop in value since the end of 1989, and apartments fell in value by 16% between mid-1988 and mid-1993, at which time their recovery began.

EMERGENCE OF THE PUBLIC EQUITY MARKETS

Equity investment in shopping centers was substantially a private market activity for many years. Until the beginning years of the 1990s, there were only a small number of publicly owned companies with substantial shopping center portfolios, and large pension funds faced significant difficulties in investing substantial sums in them. Moreover, in many cases, these companies had substantial commitments to property types other than shopping centers, and an investor could not view their shares as offering a focused participation in the shopping center industry. Thus, the public equity markets did not, as recently as the late-1980s, provide large institutional investors with a feasible means of investing in shopping center equity.

By early 1995, or only about nine years later, there were numerous publicly owned companies with substantial shopping center portfolios. The investing public had become a major source of equity finance for the shopping center industry.

Factors Underlying the Appearance of Public Companies

In the late 1980s and early 1990s, the private entrepreneurs who had built and continued to own large shopping center portfolios needed capital to reschedule maturing loans, refurbish older properties, and consummate planned developments for which they had already acquired land. At the same time, life insurance companies and commercial banks were not only unwilling to extend new finance but were seeking reductions in their existing real estate loan portfolios and repayments of outstanding loans.

Regulatory Restraints

Encouraging greater constraint in real estate lending—and seemingly likely to do so for the foreseeable future—are new regulations. New risk-based capital requirements now require banks to reserve capital in the amount of 8% of commercial real estate loans, a significant increase over the 6% previously required. In the case of life insurance companies, the National Association of Insurance Commissioners (NAIC) developed model legislation enacted by a number of states mandating similar risk-weighted capital requirements for real estate investments by life insurance companies. The NAIC model code calls for 3% capital reserves for real estate loans in good standing, rising to 15% for delinquent loans and 20% for loans in foreclosure. This code also calls for 20% capital reserves for partnership interests and 10% for company-owned real estate. The new bank and insurance company regulations make commercial property lending significantly more expensive than single family home lending.

Resulting Liquidity Pressures on Owners

It was not only banks and insurance companies that pulled back from real estate lending and investing. Other established capital sources pulled back as well. Pension funds had generally ceased making new property investments due to the poor returns by real estate. The Tax Reform Act of 1986 discouraged individual investors from committing equity to private real estate ventures.

Shopping center owners did seek private market solutions to their resulting liquidity problems. A number, including some of the largest developer-owners in the country, attempted to sell existing and newly finished holdings to raise the cash required to retire debt. Several sales of prime regional malls did occur in the 1989 to 1992 period. Pension funds, particularly those who were late in entering the real estate equity field, were the principal buyers.

Private market sales, however, were time consuming and arduous, particularly since with the weak markets prevailing, there were few institutions willing to buy real estate. By 1991 and 1992, a number of owners had concluded that only resort to the public equity markets would permit them to satisfy their liquidity needs. Initial public offerings of shares in real estate investment trusts accordingly rose sharply in the early 1990s.

REAL ESTATE INVESTMENT TRUSTS

Basic Characteristics

Real estate investment trusts (REITs) were created by revisions to the Internal Revenue Code enacted by Congress in 1960. The objective of

Congress was to provide a means for small investors to invest in real estate, and Congress sought to achieve this purpose by exempting REITs from federal income tax so long as they meet certain requirements. This pass-through tax status permits REIT shareholders to avoid the effects of double taxation. Requirements that REITs must meet include three income tests, two asset tests and one distribution test. The distribution test requires that a REIT distribute as dividends to shareholders 95% of its taxable income. In addition to these tests, the REIT must meet organizational and other requirements specified by the Internal Revenue Code. It must, for example, have at least 100 shareholders and five or fewer individuals cannot own more than 50% of its shares.

After a rocky experience in the 1970s and early 1980s, REITs began to regain investor interest in the mid-1980s, partly as a result of income tax legislation reducing the tax benefits traditionally extended to individual investors in real estate. The development of the finite life real estate investment trust during this period also contributed to a renewal of investor interest in the REIT format. The introduction of the UPREIT structure (described next) in the 1990s further facilitated the growth of publicly-held REITs as did changes in the tax law permitting pension fund beneficiaries to be counted as shareholders for the purpose of applying the restriction that shareholdings by five or fewer persons not exceed 50% of total shares.

Recent Rapid Growth

Of most relevance to those interested in the shopping center industry are developments during the early years of the 1990s, when publicly-owned REITs with substantial shopping center portfolios appeared. Rapid growth in the REIT industry occurred between 1970 and 1975 and between 1985 and mid-1994. REITs specializing in mortgage lending accounted for most of the 1970–1975 expansion, but those engaged in property ownership produced the growth after 1985. The sharp acceleration in initial public offerings in 1993 and the first half of 1994 is particularly noteworthy. The dollar value of REIT initial public offerings during that 18-month period exceeded the cumulative amount raised in all prior REIT offerings.

As a result of the initial public offering activity and rising share prices, the stock market capitalization of equity REITs has risen rapidly. During 1993, the capitalized value of the shares in all REITs rose by 89% and of those in equity REITs by 119% (Table 17.3). Disregarding any change in share prices since the end of 1993, the $7.1

TABLE 17.3

REIT Market Capitalization (Billions)

Date	All REITs	Equity REITs
12/31/92	$16.7	$11.7
12/31/93	31.6	25.6
Percent change	89.2%	118.8%

Source: Salomon Brothers, "Real Estate Investment Trusts—The 1993 REIT Explosion in Perspective," January 1994.

billion in initial share offerings during the first six months of 1994 produced by itself a total increase in the capitalization of equity REITs since 1991 of 179%.

Not only is the equity REIT industry bigger, the individual companies constituting it are larger. At the end of 1991, the 10 largest equity REITs had an average stock market capitalization of $391 million and the 20 largest an average capitalization of $261 million. Two years later, at the end of 1993, those figures had approximately doubled—to $774 million and $579 million, respectively.

Shopping center owners have played a prominent role in the emergence of the publicly owned REIT as a major actor on the real estate scene. In terms of stock market capitalization, equity REITs specializing in retail properties (including regional, community, neighborhood, power and factory outlet centers) represented 43% of the total equity REIT market. No other single property type accounted for as much as one-half of the proportion represented by retail properties (Table 17.4). REITs specializing in shopping centers thus account for 40 of the 112 equity REITs surveyed.

Reasons for Emergence of REITs as Equity Source

A major contributor to this upsurge in REIT offerings had been the inability of developers and owners to raise capital in the private markets. Indeed, sponsors and ongoing managers of many of these new public REITs include some of the largest real estate development

TABLE 17.4

Stock Market Capitalization at 6/30/94 (Millions)

	Public Prior to 1994	Public Between 1/1/94 and 6/30/94	Total	Percent
Retail				
Regional	4,671	798	5,469	14.3
Shopping center	8,269	1,122	9,391	24.7
Factory outlet	1,329	229	1,558	4.1
Subtotal	14,269	2,149	16,418	43.1
Apartment	6,665	1,498	8,163	21.5
Manufactured home	793		793	2.1
Hotels	1,577	140	1,717	4.5
Diversified	4,072	76	4,148	10.9
Office	684	979	1,663	4.4
Net lease	801	816	1,617	4.2
Industrial	980	962	1,942	5.1
Self-storage	1,146	468	1,614	4.2
Total	30,987	7,088	38,075	100.0

Source: Salomon Brothers, Inc., "REIT 1994 Midyear Review Part 1," July 11, 1994.

firms in the country, with names such as Simon, DeBartolo, CBL, Glimcher, Smith, and Taubman. Another contributing factor has been the impressive performance of equity REIT shares in terms of total return to investors. After a poor 1990, in which publicly owned equity REITs posted a negative total return of 15.4% (much worse than the S&P's return of minus 3.3%), equity REITs posted attractive returns on both an absolute and comparative basis in the years 1991, 1992, and 1993. Table 17.5 compares the equity REIT index published by The National Association of Real Estate Investment Trusts to the S&P 500 and indicates that between 1991 and 1993, equity REITs significantly outperformed the S&P 500.

Changes in the operating and financial characteristics of REITs in recent years have enhanced their appeal to investors and security analysts and facilitated the development of a growing public market

TABLE 17.5

Total Annual Returns

Year	S&P 500 (%)	NAREIT Equity Index (%)
1990	(3.3)	(15.4)
1991	30.4	35.7
1992	4.5	14.6
1993	10.1	19.7
1991–93	15.6	23.0

Source: Salomon Brothers, Inc., "Real Estate Investment Trusts—The 1993 REIT Explosion in Perspective," January 1994. Peter M. Fass, Michale E. Shaff, and Donald B. Zief. "Real Estate Investment Trusts Handbook," 1994 Edition.

for their shares. Three such changes distinguish REITs thought most desirable:

1. REITs now tend to have balanced capital structures, with analysts and underwriters generally discouraging excessive leverage. Typically, debt now represents 30% to 50% of the total capital of a company, as opposed to the 100% to 300% prevailing in the case of the construction and development mortgage REITs of the 1970s.

2. REITs that initially issued shares to the public in the 1990s have usually focused upon a particular type of property and in many cases, have restricted their activities to limited and defined geographic areas. Investors and analysts appear to prefer REITs whose attention is restricted by reference to product type and/or geographic market in the belief that such focus should produce superior operating results. A well-defined investment strategy also enhances the investor's ability to weigh the potential returns and risks of a particular security investment and its place in the investor's portfolio.

3. There is a marked tendency of new REITs to rely upon internal staff for management as opposed to utilizing independent firms providing services on a contractual basis. Use of external

advisors was common for REITs in the 1960s and 1970s. Most newer REITs are integrated real estate organizations, with internal staff competent in finance and capital markets, property management, leasing, construction and development, and shareholder relations. Reliance upon internal staff should lead to avoidance of conflicts of interest often associated with use of external managers and facilitate achieving rising earnings per share through long range planning, intense asset management and intelligent development and acquisition programs. Encouraging this view is management's ownership of shares in the REIT.

A number of the new public REITs have utilized the UPREIT structure, a feature which has attracted much commentary. One of the hurdles facing many property owners wishing to convey their holdings to new REITs has been the income tax liability that might result if they were to receive cash or REIT shares in exchange. An UPREIT is an umbrella partnership REIT, and its utilization permits the property owner sponsoring the REIT to defer such taxation. Under this structure, the sponsor enters into partnership with the REIT for ownership of the properties, and the REIT does not own the properties directly but rather an interest in the partnership owning them. The sponsor has the right usually to convert its partnership interest into shares of the REIT. One possible result of the UPREIT device might be reluctance of the sponsor to sell properties in the future since such sales might produce a tax liability. In this respect, the UPREIT arrangement places the sponsor (who usually constitutes the ongoing management of the REIT) in a position different from that of the public shareholders, raising the risk that less than optimal results might be achieved for those shareholders. On the other hand, the tax advantages produced by the UPREIT structure have facilitated the growth of publicly owned real estate companies since in its absence, substantial tax liabilities might have deterred property owners from tapping the public capital markets.

ASSET PRICING MODELS IN THE PUBLIC AND PRIVATE MARKETS

Ownership of shopping centers by both public companies and private institutional investors raises the possibility of discrepancies in the pricing of a particular asset, depending upon the character of the particular owner. Publicly owned companies have only recently emerged as substantial owners of shopping centers, and experience in this area is too limited to permit the drawing of any firm conclusions. There is, however, some evidence that public and private markets utilize differing pricing models, with the result that pricing discrepancies might occur. It is thus worthwhile to consider how pension funds price properties in their private market purchases and how public shareholders value shares in investing in public equities.

Pension Funds and Private Market Purchases

In valuing retail properties and in deciding the price to be paid for them, pension funds and their advisors place primary reliance upon a discounted cash flow analysis which results in an estimate of a property's net present value or conversely, the internal rate of return (IRR) achieved assuming purchase at that price. Fundamental to this methodology is the preparation of long-term (typically 10-year) cash flow projections for a property with assumptions made as to future rental and occupancy rates, tenant sales, operating expenses and real estate taxes, capital expenditures (including both leasing costs and physical refurbishment and/or expansion programs), and the sale price of the property at the end of the holding period. The value estimate or proposed purchase price hinges upon the assumptions underlying the projections. A number of analysts now regularly poll substantial pension funds and their investment managers to determine prevailing views on such major variables as discount rate, rental growth rate, expense growth rate and the capitalization rate at which sale occurs at the end of the holding period (the "terminal" capitalization rate).

Comparing Initial Return to IRR

Where the long-term cash flow projections assume growth in rental income as a result of either higher market rents that are realized upon re-leasing space or higher occupancy, the internal rate of return from the investment would likely exceed the current annual return at the time of purchase. This spread will be greater as the projected growth in rental income rises, and its magnitude indicates the extent of the buyer's confidence in such rental growth and willingness to recognize it in the purchase price. Regional shopping centers have been regarded by institutional investors as offering both limited risk of decline in current income and strong potential for growth in that income as tenant sales and market rents rise in the future. Investors have been willing to accept in the case of regional malls a relatively low current return at purchase and a relatively high spread between the current return at purchase and the projected internal rate of return. Neighborhood, community, and power centers are generally viewed as offering more limited growth prospects, with the result that typically, their current return at purchase is higher both in absolute terms and in proportion to the internal rate of return projected by the buyer.

High-quality regional malls, for example, were selling at current returns as low as 5% (and in a few cases, reportedly below 5%) at the peak pricing levels experienced in 1987–1988. Investors were, at that time, expecting internal rates of return of 10% to 11%, suggesting a spread between current and discounted long-term returns of 500 to 600 basis points. As the market corrected in the early 1990s, the limited number of regional malls sold produced current returns to the buyer of 7% to 8% and estimated internal rates of return of 11% to 12%, implying a smaller spread of 300 to 400 basis points. Other shopping center formats have consistently offered higher current returns, with investors divided on their long-term prospects.

Pension funds operating in the private markets therefore adopt explicitly a long-term view of a property in reaching a pricing decision. Their analysis requires very detailed information on a property's tenancy, historic financial results, market trends and physical condition. This property-specific information is available to the private market purchaser to a much greater extent than to the public market investor in company shares.

Share Purchasers in Public Markets

Buyers of REIT shares appear to attach primary importance to expected total return in evaluating whether to invest. This total return is a function of the present and likely future dividend paid by the REIT and its estimated future share price. Since REITs must pay out as dividends 95% of their income, the dividend yield forms a substantial portion of the total return.

Importance of Funds from Operations

The principal determinant of a REIT's dividend is its Funds From Operations (FFO) which is approximately equivalent to operating cash flow before capital expenditures. FFO has been defined as:

net income (computed in accordance with GAAP), excluding gains (or losses) from debt restructuring and sales of property, plus depreciation and amortization, and after adjustments for unconsolidated partnerships and joint ventures. Adjustments for unconsolidated partnerships and joint ventures will be calculated to reflect funds from operations on the same basis.[2]

The current dividend yield at which the market will price a particular REIT's shares is substantially affected by the prospects for growth in the dividend. A rising dividend generally requires growth in FFO, and thus the outlook for FFO is critical to the pricing of a REIT's shares.

The stock market's confidence in the ability of a REIT's management team to deliver growth in FFO therefore becomes central to the REIT's share price. Sources of growth that management may exploit include acquisition of properties, development of new projects, and intense management of existing holdings including renovation and re-merchandising where appropriate. Returns from incremental equity capital deployed by management must exceed the current dividend yield in order to achieve dividend growth. Management may also leverage its capital structure and utilize borrowings to enhance growth in FFO.

In assessing the prospects for FFO growth, analysts and investors face limits on available information on the properties owned by a REIT. Unlike the private purchaser of a shopping center, the buyer of REIT shares cannot typically obtain for specific properties owned by the REIT such information as current or past financial results, rent rolls, tenant sales, and future lease expirations. It becomes impossible in the case of a REIT to prepare the 10-year financial projections utilized by pension funds in private market purchases. It is thus not surprising that dividend estimates for public REITs cover much shorter periods than cash flow projections for properties bought in the private market. Financial projections contained in prospectuses for initial public offerings have typically covered only the next one to two years.

Pricing Differences

The need for REIT investors to take a shorter term view of earnings leads to the speculation that the public markets will more fully value properties offering relatively high current returns as opposed to those promising higher long-term rewards. This judgment accords with the importance of dividend yield in the evaluation of REIT shares. Accordingly, it may be expected that as compared to private market buyers, REIT share investors will more fully value shopping centers offering attractive current returns even at the cost of more limited growth prospects. If so, community, neighborhood and power centers may over time prove to be more appropriate for REIT ownership than regional malls, with the latter better suited for private market ownership. It may also be that private ownership is best for development or redevelopment projects where rewards do not come until well into the future.

There are other factors that might produce differences between public market and private market pricing. First, as noted earlier, the public market's opinion of management can substantially influence share price. In the private market, investors rarely reflect management in pricing decisions, focusing instead upon the property's value as an asset. Second, there is evidence that REITs, by utilizing their corporate balance sheets, may be able to borrow more advantageously than private investors. REIT earnings would be favorably affected by lower cost borrowings, and the prospect of such beneficial leverage should enhance share price. Chapter 16 covers thoroughly debt financing by REITs. Third, participation in a portfolio of properties offered by purchase of REIT shares might influence investors to grant higher valuations than would be warranted in the private market purchase of a single asset. Fourth, investors preferring liquidity may be expected to pay more for REIT shares than for private market interests.

For these reasons, differences in pricing between similar assets held in private market and public market formats may persist over time. Shopping center equity investors may find it possible to take advantage of these discrepancies and to exploit interesting arbitrage opportunities.

Treatment of Capital Expenditures

One issue has become of increased concern to both private market and public market investors in shopping centers. During the 1980s, the capital investment required to sustain the performance of established and successful shopping centers rose significantly. Contributing to higher capital expenditures have been a number of factors:

- Owners have found it necessary to modernize the appearance of the common areas and exterior of older centers. Many now believe that enclosed regional malls require major interior refurbishment every 10 to 15 years, and modernization of the exterior of neighborhood and community centers is becoming increasingly common.

- Successful retailers demand significant landlord contribution to space improvement and fixturing costs. The number of retailers able to generate high volumes in the competitive environment that now prevails has shrunk, and those able to do so possess a strong bargaining position with landlords in lease negotiations.

- Realignment of tenant space is now often required in order to accommodate larger formats. Supermarkets, discount stores and other types of promotional retailers have increased in size in recent years, necessitating re-configuration of neighborhood and community centers in order to retain tenants. In regional malls, a number of specialty operators have shifted to larger store sizes, as have certain department store chains.

Private market investors now find it essential to assess and allow for future capital requirements in their financial analysis of a proposed transaction. Insistence that the pricing or valuation of a particular property be reduced to reflect the present value of estimated future capital expenditures has become increasingly widespread. Private market investors are able to handle capital expenditures in a straightforward fashion because of their possession of detailed information on the property under review and its competitors and trade area.

Incorporation of future capital requirements in the evaluation of an investment in the shares of a public REIT is more difficult. Detailed, property-level information of the sort available to a private market investor is not generally available to the investing public, and it is difficult to make specific estimates of future capital expenditures. Exacerbating this difficulty is omission from the settled definition of FFO of any allowance for leasing or other capital costs.[3] Moreover, even if it is possible to identify a particular REIT's future capital needs, the REIT's ability to fund future capital expenditures may be uncertain. Federal tax law requires that REITs pay out as dividends 95% of taxable income. By itself, this requirement permits REITs to accumulate that portion of gross revenue offset by depreciation deductions. However, the need to maintain an attractive dividend yield may require that REITs pay out a higher proportion of their annual operating cash flow than that mandated by the income tax law. The ability of REITs to accumulate liquid resources for future use may thus be limited, and funding capital projects may necessitate repeat visits to the capital markets by REITs, heightening the role of their chief financial officers in their management teams.

CONCLUSION

Over the past 25 years, there has been a remarkable shift in the equity financing of retail properties. Changes in income taxation and mortgage financing practices have reduced the attractiveness of shopping center ownership to individual investors. Pension funds have become increasingly prominent as owners of shopping centers. At the same time, losses incurred during the property market collapse of the late 1980s and new regulatory requirements have led financial institutions to more conservative real estate lending practices. Traditional sources of finance have thus receded. Replacing them to a substantial degree have been buyers of securitized debt instruments produced and sold in the capital markets. Although a degree of uncertainty and pain has accompanied these changes, their occurrence is a tribute to the flexibility of the capital markets.

Looking forward, it seems reasonable to assume that the public and private markets will co-exist as providers of real estate finance. Both public REITs and pension funds seem likely to continue as owners and purchasers of shopping centers. Mortgage loans will be available from both financial institutions holding such debt in their portfolios and from investors acting through securitized vehicles. The relative activity and influence of private and public market participants will probably vary from time, but both seem likely to remain as long term participants.

Underlying the ability and willingness of investors to respond to the needs of the shopping center industry has been the profitability of the industry in general. Confidence in the returns produced by shopping centers has, for example, led the capital markets to embrace REITs as equity owners and securitized pools as debt holders. To continue to attract the capital that it requires, the shopping center industry must allay concerns that have arisen in recent years:

- Investors worry that the perceived over-storing of the United States will depress market rentals, occupancy levels, and operating income of shopping centers in a number of areas.

- Growth in real personal incomes may continue to be sluggish and may reduce long-term retail sales growth. Virtually all recent income growth has been enjoyed by those with higher incomes, a trend which if it continues, might hurt centers in lower and moderate income areas.

- The need for continuing capital expenditures to maintain the value of a property may depress values. Substantial sums are needed, and it is not always clear that the incremental return on such investments is satisfactory.

- Centers unable to accommodate physically the size and configuration requirements of new retail formats may suffer substantial obsolescence.

- Alternative shopping methods, such as catalogues and television, may take sales away from traditional stores and shopping centers.

While each of these concerns is valid, continued investor interest in and support for shopping centers appears likely. Retail properties have demonstrated an ability to respond to evolving consumer preferences and as a result, there is reason to be optimistic about their ongoing performance.

ENDNOTES

1. Black, J. Thomas, "The Restructuring of Commercial Real Estate Finance," Urban Land Institute, May 1994.
2. Salomon Brothers, Inc., "The REIT Reemerges," August 1993.
3. The National Association of Real Estate Investment Trusts is now considering a revision to the definition of FFO to allow for capital expenditures.

Eighteen

How Investors Purchase and Sell Retail Properties

Glenn E. Whitmore

T he maturation of the shopping center development business in the United States combined with the wrenching recapitalization of the industry during 1990–1993 to produce a revolutionary metamorphosis of the shopping center investment and capital markets. New development and financing no longer drive the investment market. Entrepreneurial ownership and investment has been replaced by institutional dominance and the transition of the largely privately owned business to a publicly owned and traded one. Saturated trade areas and new retailing formats are the underlying dynamics steering acquisition investment, debt placement, and selected, niche development and, most significantly, redevelopment. Investment intermediaries are at the heart of new types of equity investment and debt innovation. Indeed, their business is undergoing radical change as downsized clients require greater levels of sophisticated, value-adding consultative services in addition to transactional expertise.

However, out of this crucible of distress, a reinvigorated capital market for shopping centers as the preferred commercial real estate asset has emerged in 1994 with new directions and innovations that should make the rest of the decade one of the most important trend-setting periods in the history of shopping center investment. This chapter will concentrate on the role that investors, developers, and financiers play in making the critical decisions to purchase land for development; to develop; to invest; to renovate and modernize; to finance by mortgage or public issue; and, to value in anticipation of purchase, sale, or financing. The analytic process, previously ad hoc and often intuitive, has become a disciplined pre-requirement for action, either accomplished in-house or through outside consultants.

VALUE-ENHANCEMENT INVESTMENT

The shopping center capital markets and investment value are no longer ones driven by new construction as they have been for the past 40 years. The saturation of markets and the maturation of most areas of the country demographically has changed the industry to value-creation through investment in the three Rs—Renovation/Redevelopment/Remerchandising.

The momentum of this trend is clear from a recent Urban Land Institute (ULI) study of the pace of shopping center renovation: generally one-fifth of the nation's inventory has undergone significant renovation over the last five years while new development has been extremely limited.

The principle motivation for acquisition and investment interest in the three Rs are improving the market share, the sales productivity, the bottom line return, and the long-term residual by:

- Making dated centers contemporary, physically attractive, and shopper friendly.
- Repositioning the center competitively through remerchandising the tenant mix that matches the trade area's changing demographics so that growth and income niches are being addressed.
- Expanding the center and its anchors to increase market penetration.
- Correcting declining occupancy or flat sales due to lifecycle conditions.

- Staying current with fresh retailing concepts, shopper amenities, and design innovations.

ICSC studies reinforce the investment effectiveness of the three Rs. In a 1991 survey of regional malls, 40% of the shoppers sampled had spent more time in renovated malls. In a 1992 survey of strip center shoppers, the survey showed that traffic had increased 20%, while 33% were shopping more as a direct result of the renovation.

Initially, rates of return for renovation or expansion lag those achieved by new construction by roughly 2:1 or 8% vs. 15%. However, the impact of a renovation becomes very significant over time as enhancements in sales productivity and new rollover rents in an upgraded center commence. The long-term residual is unquestionably improved by a successful three-R program. The terminal rate can decline more than 100 basis points (bp) for a repositioned center. For example, taking a tired community center and converting it to a discount power center could easily lower the going-in and terminal rates 100 bp each.

An owner devising the right strategy for a shopping center disposition where the three Rs can enhance return for the next owner must consider how to get a higher price today for this potential. In doing so, an underperforming property or a static one can be positioned in the acquisition market at an above-normative price (and lower yield) than "as is" cash flow to take advantage of this seminal redevelopment trend. While no investor will pay a price today incorporating all the value upside of a major improvement program that will cost additional holding investment, nevertheless, the well-crafted sale of this future value can be realized at a premium above today's conventional value. The keys to this sales tactic are: (1) location and market analysis that, in depth, proves the viability of the property for the three Rs, and (2) a dual financial analysis including not just a current operating pro forma, but a projected pro forma after redevelopment, including the estimated investment for redevelopment, and the returns upon post redevelopment sale or refinance that can be achieved. Both these evaluations must be linked together in the sales offering along with supporting graphics like a redevelopment site plan and a remerchandised mall/lease plan.

Acquisition Benchmarks

As Figure 18.1 shows, shopping center investors, especially institutional ones, evaluate purchases in the context of current entry value

FIGURE 18.1

Acquisition Pyramid

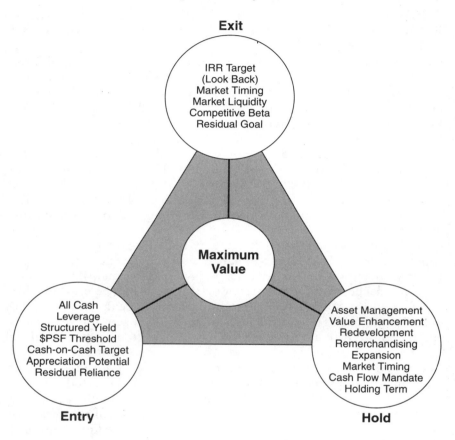

correlated to expected exit strategy and the holding philosophy. The importance of a well-defined exit strategy and asset management program has grown dramatically as the painful commercial real estate depression of the last five years has irrevocably proven the fallacy of exit strategies based on inexorable value appreciation or "futures." For perhaps the first time, real estate capital markets have been sufficiently burned by this down cycle, requiring government-subsidized bailouts, so that exit strategies, especially market timing tactics, reflect the volatility of residual value rather than the assumption of a sure thing. Too often in the 1980s exit strategy IRR projections have been unmasked as ERRs. Nowhere is this new prudence more apparent than in shopping center investment where the ongoing innovations and transformations in retailing and retailer's corporate fortunes continue to be more fast-paced than any other major commercial asset class.

Shopping center investors place different emphasis on the following factors depending on their motivation to achieve a real rate of return hurdle over a defined time of holding:

- Operating cash flow.
- Residual value.
- Value enhancement during hold.
- Return on equity.
- Market timing.

The majority of shopping center investors seek assets that have stable performance rather than major lease-up risk. Risk-oriented investors who buy underperforming centers tend to be very focused on the purchase price per square foot discount from replacement cost and going-in yield rather than IRR targets. They measure by this physical value parameter because their value-enhancement scenario depends on additional capital investment to reposition a shopping center and generate much higher turnaround returns and residual value.

While shopping center purchasers with different investment motivation and orientation will weight return measures differently, investors analyze a standard set of key parameters which the sales agent's analysis for the seller should mirror:

- Initial yield (going-in capitalization rate).*
- Initial cash-on-cash yield.*
- Asset price per rentable square foot (per GLA owned).
- Ratio of asset price to reproduction cost.
- Residual/terminal capitalization rate.

---

* If not stabilized net operating income, additional yields per stabilized pro forma are needed.

- Internal rate of return (IRR) yield.
  - Unleveraged
  - Leveraged
  - Income-stripping returns, such as minimum rent and recoveries (with percentage rent discounted heavily) and differential net present value of tenancy income based on creditworthiness, tenant-by-tenant.
- Ratio of asset price to sales productivity.

REIT INVESTMENT OBJECTIVES

REITs have become a large scale investor in the shopping center industry, mainly but certainly not exclusively, as a result of the sale of the portfolios as Taubman and Simon, to newly formed REITs. A REITs' primary acquisition objective is to maximize current yield at acquisition and over the long-term holding to build cash-flow return in order to grow dividend yield and stock value. Focused on current cash flow, REITs are very sensitive to net operating income in place and purchase price per square foot parameters. IRRs are secondary. They are not risk-averse and have been notable buyers of foreclosed property, but only at values supporting current yield or discounts to reproduction value.

On strip purchases, REIT investors have been very effective in making cosmetic investments, especially to an exterior facade, to storefronts, to identity singage, or to parking fields that immediately make a dated center contemporary. REITs real return targets are simple; they must buy shopping centers whose current yield is sufficiently higher (200–300 bp) than their cost of capital as measured by their dividend yield. For example, a REIT with a 7% yield cannot buy a shopping center with an 8% yield and expect to grow the dividend through operating cash flow improvements.

PENSION FUNDS AND LIFE
INSURANCE COMPANIES

Pension funds and life insurance company general accounts have historically focused more on long-term appreciation and residual value than mandates for year to year net operating income and net cash flow yields. Pension funds fully subscribe to IRR analysis and yield targets. Their holding time frame has been 10 years and it has been indifferent to market timing. The latter psyche has however changed under the impact of the real estate depression between 1990–1993 when the funds clearly missed timing a market in the late 1980s such that their target returns for purchasers then may be impossible to achieve, even if they extend the typical holding time frame. The issue of market timing has also become more influential because: changes in retailing and retailing formats continue to revolutionize the "bricks-and-mortar" business; modern portfolio theory places more emphasis on cyclic, market-timed investment rather than deep pocket staying power; liquidity is more available in the public markets due to REIT growth. Depending on the risk-adjusted perspective on real estate investment in the broad capital markets, all-cash institutional investors have historically sought a 6% real rate of return over the average holding period. The internal rate of return is pegged, on a disinflated basis, against like-term U.S. Treasury bonds which are perceived as the least risky proxies for guaranteed return on and of capital.

THIRD-PARTY ACQUISITION SUPPORT

Paralleling the trend toward institutionalized ownership has been the sophistication and specialization of the acquisition project team. A key component has been the proliferation of third-party consultants, appraisers, environmental and physical/structural experts who provide objective, detached perspective to the investor and to the core acquisition group and its conventional specialists like lawyers and accountants. In fact, most pension fund sponsors mandate that their advisors support their acquisition recommendations with independent, expert analysis by outside consultants. They also retain consultants to develop real estate portfolio strategy and to scrutinize the advisors' acquisitions process and initiatives.

Two important adjuncts to the basic shopping center acquisition team's feasibility study are outside appraisers and market consultants. Appraisers are typically engaged to establish objectively a market comparable investment value independent of the acquisition team's perspective. Market consultants on shopping center acquisitions are particularly important to purchasers whose investment return pivots not just on market dynamics, but on market capture and share potential, especially if value-enhancement through re-merchandising or renovation is the objective. Consultative analysis of the trade area's shopper goods expenditure potential and under-merchandised categories can make the difference between a successful or a costly investment.

Internally, acquisition teams maintain their own capacity for market feasibility, emphasizing field and locational evaluation. Most advisors to pension funds also maintain a market research group detached from the acquisition team, but essential to formulation of acquisition strategies and the internal ratification of recommended acquisitions. This market research group also does independent macroeconomic and econometric studies in order to determine the best areas and assets for target purchasing. As real estate holdings for pension funds have matured as a core business, real estate research has begun to mirror stock research at the portfolio level. Modern portfolio theory (MPT) has increasingly penetrated the real estate pension fund industry. As such, capital markets theory and statistical analysis has become as significant as "bottoms up" market research and property feasibility analysis.

IMPORTANCE OF MARKET FEASIBILITY

One of the most critical studies from consultants retained by the acquisition source is market feasibility. Like the acquisition team, the consultants analyze data collected at the field level as well as demographic data and economic base information pertinent to the shopping center's trade area. This locational analysis focuses on the inherent attributes and limitations of the target shopping center counterpointed to its competitive marketplace. Perhaps the most important keynote of this acquisition approach is the motto: "Acquire the competitive profile, not just the property."

The out-of-house objective study of the acquisition process is one of the most important changes in the investment arena. As the shopping center industry, stimulated by further REIT growth and other public market phenomenon, becomes more like the stock and bond public markets, it is inevitable that the utilization of third-party experts and research services will expand in significance. The REIT industry growth alone necessitates a major surge in research analysis by money managers. Like the stock market, analysts of REITs for Wall Street investment firms and mutual funds conduct property-specific as well as cash flow-specific evaluations to determine underlying REIT asset value and relevant stock price conversion and dividend level.

MANY OTHER SPECIALISTS RETAINED

Ancillary professional specialists are also valuable as purposes of acquisition due diligence becomes ever-more demanding, principally due to environmental, zoning, and governmental regulations that proliferated in the 1980s. No shopping center acquisition or financing is possible today without an independent environmental study, testing for hazardous waste like asbestos or property contamination. When entitlements and zoning allowances became more restrictive in the 1980s as anti-growth sentiments in communities grew, a shopping center's viability for investment appreciation through renovation or expansion mandated specialized political and regulatory land planning counsel. New government mandates for special purposes like handicapped people access or disabled person's accommodations have necessitated special conformity analysts. In some respects, compliance has become as important as verification of property facts during due diligence. Specialized consultants are no longer a "maybe" for acquisition teams, but a "must" from start to finish of a shopping center purchase.

PURCHASING PROPERTIES OUT OF FORECLOSURE

The enormous foreclosure problem for lenders has certainly created an unprecedented acquisition opportunity for the risk-oriented shopping center buyer. Distressed liquidation values have been attractive. Windfall returns are possible. However, the viability of many of these shopping centers was inherently flawed by poor location and poor alignment. Savvy acquisition specialists focused only on distressed shopping centers whose fundamentals and feasibility were sound. These foreclosed situations represented true bargains and are highly sought after either through purchase of the REO equity or, prior to foreclosure, the nonperforming loan.

Because of the nature of the process, the uncertain deliverability of the asset and the destabilized quality, the buyers for these shopping centers were not pension funds or core institutional investors. REITs were selective purchasers, but not bulk buyers. Either entrepreneurial partnerships of high net worth individuals funding an operating group, or large, speculatively oriented hedge funds (like Soros Realty) or a specialized financial services conglomerate (like GE Capital), the foreclosure investors have a totally different investment program. To maximize acquisition cost efficiencies, the typical goal was to buy loans or shopping center equities in bulk where possible at near "salvage value" prices, and always with highly advantageous seller-financing. Indeed, the nature of seller-finance with high leverage and low coupons (often quoted at LIBOR-based interest rates) reflected the lenders' overriding goals to get these REO assets off the balance sheet now and worry later about the quality of the seller-financed loan.

The investment horizon of foreclosure purchasers is short-term (3–5 years): it is based on turnaround in overall real estate market liquidity and value, rather than property-specific enhancement. The philosophy can be summarized: Buy Low, Sell High, Sell Quick. In effect, the exit strategy for most foreclosure investors can be simply called a "short-term flip" with potentially very high returns (greater than 30–50% on leveraged equity) primarily due to the liquidation purchase price that offers nothing but upside when markets turn. Investment returns are not standardized due to the various levels of foreclosure distress. If there is operating income, current yield thresholds rarely fall below 13% cash-on-cash which may approximate a 15% to 20% capitalization rate depending on lease-up costs. The most important criterion is usually price per square foot as a discount ratio to reproduction cost (assuming minimal land value). Typically, foreclosure investors are seeking "bricks-and-mortar" value at 50% to 75% of reproduction cost. Many of these purchases were made between 1990–1993. Already, sales of these foreclosed purchases are occurring because the overall commercial real estate market, especially as measured by capital flows, has turned up from the bottom in the early 1990s.

PARTIAL INTEREST INVESTMENT AND SALES

Disposition of partial interests in shopping centers reached a crescendo between 1991 and 1993. They have been concentrated in regional malls where approximately 32 centers' million square feet valued at over $40 billion represented sales where less than 100% fee transfer occurred. The majority of these malls were dominant regional malls with high sales productivity and strong appreciation potential. The typical interest conveyed by the owners, usually development companies, was 50% to 75%. For example, in 1991, of the 15 major regional mall sales, 9 were partial interest sales including

Paradise Valley (Phoenix), Victor Valley (Victorville, CA), Maine Mall (Portland), The Oaks (Thousand Oaks, CA), and Valley Fair (Santa Clara, CA). Of the 24 major regional mall sales in 1992, half were partial interest transactions.

The genesis of this partial sale pattern was a combination of general market illiquidity, recapitalization among developers, corporate earnings goal among certain partial interest sellers and capital limitations among investors, especially domestic pension funds.

During the 1980s, public and private pension funds (and their advisors) tended to acquire shopping centers wholly and as a single-asset holding. There was no limit or ceiling on equity capital (or hybrid equity through convertible debt) for any one asset. As such, it was common for funds to acquire assets, particularly regional malls, at 100% values in excess of $100 million and frequently in excess of $150 million all cash. Perhaps the high water mark of single asset purchases on an equity basis was the 50% interest acquisition of Woodfield Mall in Schaumberg, IL., in 1988. The sale for one of the truly superior retail centers in the nation approximated $250 million of equity capital invested by a California pension fund for the half interest.

As the real estate market plunged into a recession in 1990, pension funds in reallocating their capital thresholds and strategies, dramatically departed from the megapurchase philosophy of the 1980s. Capital ceilings for single asset purchases were developed: in shopping centers, it was rare to see an equity threshold for a single asset, 100% interest available above $60 million all cash. The single asset purchase by one fund above $100 million became a rarity. This new capital threshold forced an institutional investor shift away from regional malls. However, in 1993, only four regional centers were acquired as a single asset for all cash above $100 million. Eleven regional malls were acquired on a partial interest base with equity capital below $100 million, typically between $60 million and $80 million for a partial interest.

Pension funds began to seriously diversify among retail center asset types. More and more, neighborhood centers with strong grocery anchors became a diversifying favorite: this purchase deployed the same level of equity capital to own 4 to 5 shopping centers in diverse geographic and economic areas for the $60 million available rather than 50% of a regional mall in one area for the same amount of acquisition capital. Similarly, community center-dedicated funds were developed by advisors and sponsors to address the diversification and capital allocation issues among a balanced portfolio that may have been over weighted in regional mall ownership.

Among pension funds still seeking regional malls, the capital thresholds of the early 1990s effectively restricted them to a partial interest to acquire. At the same time, owners, especially developers but also general accounts, seeking liquidity or gain through sale of their desirable regional centers could accomplish this goal through a partial interest sale while retaining a major ownership interest along with asset management fees.

In designing a sales strategy around a partial interest disposition, the seller or sales agent must address issues of control, management fees, financial and return parameters.

When closing of the partial interest sale occurs, the seller's objectives can, at best, be only partially achieved because the retained interest's objectives are yet to be realized. Partial interest dispositions in essence are first and foremost not sales; they are structured and negotiated new partnerships. The sales strategy must have this as its guiding principle if the objectives of the seller and new investor are to be mutually realized.

REO DISPOSITION

Due to the dramatic overbuilding and excessive financing of retail centers, the first half of the 1990s has been characterized by the disposition of non-performing assets. The shopping centers, generally owned and built by developers and syndications, were unable to service their debt obligations as oversupply forced fatal rent reductions and other lease-up concessions while underlying valuations plunged, exacerbated by a national recession from 1989–1992. Loans on improved properties were principally issued by life companies and credit companies in the form of bullet or mini-perm notes. For properties under construction or on land ready for retail development, loans were generally issued by commercial banks and thrifts (savings and loans).

For REO assets held by solvent, stable institutions, the disposition approach depends on the quality of the asset as well as corporate finance issues. If it is income-producing and stabilized or near stabilization, the equity should be marketed in a traditional manner on an asset-by-asset basis through an exclusive offering process to target investors. Pricing of the shopping center would vary according to the degree of stabilization as well as other conventional characteristics. Assuming the REO asset management program has fully stabilized the property, the pricing would reflect normal return thresholds that investors have for that type of center.

CLOSING PROCESS

The difficulty of closing can be greatly diminished by the disposition team's underwriting and analysis during the advisory phase before going to market. A successful disposition program is characterized by this depth of pre-due diligence, buyer-verifiable review by the sales agent which makes the real due diligence process as efficient as possible. The sales agent's quasi-audit of the relevant documents promotes a smooth due diligence. Lease by lease review and abstracting is paramount. For example, an offering preparation process in which the rent roll has been assembled after all leases have been read, abstracted, and compared to the owner's records as opposed to a process where the owner's rent roll has been accepted and reproduced will greatly eliminate lease review problems during due diligence. All operating projections must be tied back to audited actuals. All leasable GLA on the owner's Rent Roll must "foot out" to the actual physical GLA in the mall and outparcels. CAM and other major expense recoveries must be accurate on the books and verified from lease review. In fact, many shopping center purchasers read the CAM clauses and crosscheck the billing records before they read and scrutinize minimum rent. Why? Because experience has shown that many offering memorandum cash flows have been generated without this type of detailed "tieback" to leases and billings. In most of these cases, the seller's agent has underestimated expense recoveries and left significant value out of the offering. An offering memorandum with comprehensive data supported by this pre-marketing due diligence of the seller's agent will give investors support to bid aggressively rather than more conservatively in order to accommodate the risk of discovery in due diligence that will lower the price.

Environmental Review

Any real estate due diligence and closing can become more than difficult and protracted if environmental problems are discovered. All investors today will conduct an independent environmental study to, at least, the Phase One level. For shopping centers, buyers are particularly focused on structural asbestos-containing materials (ACM) and hazardous waste contamination (from storage tanks on site in gas stations and car accessory stores). ACM has also proven to be a problem in older flooring tile. If an environmental hazard is discovered, the closing will be held up until the remediation and cost is determined. Sellers generally have to credit this cost in full against the sales price. Since environmental approval today is mandatory for clearing due diligence, it is more than prudent for sellers to have conducted recent environmental review studies of their property and site *prior* to commencing a disposition process. Sellers should generally not make representations or warranties as to environmental conditions and liability; this is a buyer's contingency and liability to ascertain and waive during due diligence. The agent must inform all buyers in advance that the transaction is "as is" so that negotiating leverage on reps and warrants is established before the fact.

Closing Time Frame

A normative timeline for disposition due diligence correlated to the major types of shopping center would be:

Type of Center	Time (Days)
Neighborhood centers/strips (unanchored)	30
Neighborhood centers anchored (e.g., grocery/drug)	40
Community centers	45
Power centers	45
Specialty, fashion centers	45
Regional mall	50–60

Closing should occur 30 days or less after waiver of due diligence and other contingencies assuming purchase and sale contract has been negotiated and executed. To conduct an efficient "off the market" cycle, it is highly recommended that purchase and sales (P&S) contract milestones parallel due diligence. To facilitate and control the due diligence process on behalf of the seller, the sales agent should establish sign-off milestones for the buyer to meet within due diligence. For instance, in a 45-day due diligence cycle there could be a milestone for completion of all lease and financial document review by 30 days. In so doing, if there are serious issues to negotiate here, there will be ample "rational" time for both parties to do so. If the seller and the agent allow a buyer to raise serious issues only at the end of due diligence, there can be needlessly irrational negotiations and the buyer clearly can enjoy unnecessary leverage. In any case, a disposition agent can not be a passive participant in due diligence. The role is one as an active facilitator pushing seller and buyer to stay on schedule while helping the seller's closing team respond to due diligence information requests and negotiated issues.

POST-CLOSING RESPONSIBILITIES

Experienced sellers and their exclusive agents always present the investors with offering materials that contain an information disclaimer that provides no representations or warranties regarding the accuracy of these materials, especially financial performance projections. Subject to the conditions of the executed purchase and sale contract, it is rare that any liability for the offering, post-closing, remains with the sales agent. The seller retains whatever post-closing liability that the P&S contract stipulates which has been agreed to during contract negotiation prior to closing. Throughout the engagement, the agent must maintain an efficient "record and book" of all pertinent correspondence, information exchange and conversations on behalf of the seller during the marketing process. A copy of these records and books are turned over to the seller after closing.

CURRENT TRENDS

The massive debt restructurings and foreclosures during 1990–1993 concentrated in the developer-owned segment of retailing has redistributed major ownership categories. This is a secular event and not a cyclical trend for the shopping center industry. It represents no less than a "sea change" in the segmentation of shopping center ownership in the United States.

With many areas of the country saturated by retail supply and few capital sources willing to finance new development without substantial equity (20%–25%) and recourse loans, it is improbable that developers will regain their prominence as owners. Moreover, most REITs, especially Unbrella Partnership Real Estate Investment Trust (UPREITS), avoid development given their dividend requirements and charters.

The redistribution of ownership precipitated by the overbuilding and default paroxysm over the last five years ratified further the emergence of institutions as the predominant owner of shopping centers. Institutional dominance extends beyond regional malls to community centers and large neighborhood centers. The REIT conversion of developer-entrepreneur to publicly traded company designed to increase certainty of dividend/cash flow return (as an alternative to utility stocks and dividends) rather than to create value through new development and sale only re-enforces the hegemony of institutional-like ownership.

In retrospect, the heyday of the entrepreneurial developer as the major force in the investment and ownership aspects of the shopping center industry extended from 1950 to approximately 1975.

For the foreseeable future, ownership of the vast majority of retail shopping centers will be concentrated in institutional domestic pension funds and REITs rather than development companies or partnerships. Selectively, life companies will own retail centers for their general account; however, because of limitations on equity ownership imposed by risk-based capital requirements for life companies, this source of acquisition will not be significant.

Domestic pension funds will continue as the dominant equity investor in shopping centers through separate accounts. Despite the market and liquidity trough in 1993, domestic funds, often in club partnerships or co-investing structures, were the major equity investors in the eight regional mall sales of individual assets in excess of $100 million in value. Approximately 80% of the $2 billion in major regional mall sales that occurred in 1993 was funded (both new debt and equity) by domestic pension funds.

The general accounts and pension funds of foreign institutional capital are increasing their ownership ratio in shopping centers stateside. In 1992–1993, a number of institutional Dutch funds and Australian investors were active in acquiring U.S. regional malls such as Garden State Plaza in Paramus, New Jersey, and Mall of Florida in Orlando, Florida. Continental European sources (especially German and Dutch) and Canadian sources are currently seeking major U.S. shopping center acquisitions. New foreign capital sources are emerging from Mexico, Brazil, Argentina and the non-Japanese Pacific Rim (Singapore, Hong Kong, Taiwan, Korea, Indonesia) for community and neighborhood centers in particular.

Over the last five years, neighborhood centers, community centers, and power centers have experienced greater acquisition interest by pension funds due to portfolio diversification and equity thresholds. Major metropolitan area centers in growth markets and strong infill markets with restricted new supply have been priorities. Over the last two years, high-credit regional power centers with four-five "big box" discount anchors of 50,000 to 125,000 square feet have gained major pension fund interest. The competitive viability of the product has become proven as the retailing industry evolves in the direction of large, value-oriented, "category killer" tenants. Whereas historically landlords profited from in-line, satellite space, future profits in discount power alignments are tied to the magnitude of credit anchors and the diminution of shop space. While outparcels sales provide some speculative gain potential, power centers are reflective of an investor preference today for low risk rather than high return which has emerged from the trough of the market cycle. However, by no means, is the dominant regional mall investment preference dying. In fact, due to the renaissance in department store streamlining, remerchandising and sales productivity, it can be argued that strong regional malls are in the best competitive shape in two decades.

A NEW ACQUISITION APPROACH: CLUB INVESTING

In the early 1990s, club investing among a combination of public pension funds on a deal-by-deal basis grew significantly. In fact, club investing through pension fund advisors was the dominant source of regional mall acquisition and recapitalization in 1992–1993. This pooled investment accomplishes a number of investment goals that coincide with modern portfolio theory: First, it allows funds to maximize capital across a diversity of shopping center purchases; this diversity should lower the volatility beta of exposure to large, single, capital-intensive acquisitions like regional malls. Second, it allows smaller pension funds to co-invest, thereby increasing their capacity to bid on larger transactions like regional mall purchases that they would otherwise be precluded from by equity capital ceilings. If ERISA pension fund guidelines can be satisfied, it is probable that two major public market vehicles—REITs and real estate mutual funds—could also pool capital to invest together in a "mega club" format with pension funds. Globalization of real estate capital and money management's constant search for diversification portends co-investing among foreign and onshore funds. International co-investment in U.S. office equities was prominent in the 1980s; offshore investment in U.S. retail centers is, by comparison, underallocated. More importantly, foreign investors have learned that high-quality shopping center assets have a much lower volatility beta than similar office equities which got whipsawed despite their grandeur of construction and tenant roster in the oversupply of the late 1980s.

REITs have been the most dominant buyer of retail properties in the strip to community center categories. To date, dominant regional malls and power centers have entry values that on an asset-by-asset basis are too steep for the existing capitalization level of most REITs given their necessity to grow cash flow and dividend yields. However,

REITs have begun to purchase regional malls in secondary and tertiary markets where going-in yields are significantly higher at lower overall values than dominant regionals. Also, entry values are more reasonable than major, metro area regionals so that they do not overly skew the rest of the asset base valuation and dividend volatility of the REIT.

Ironically, but very powerfully, the REIT IPOs themselves in the 1990s have effectively removed a major amount of shopping center inventory from the potential disposition marketplace. This has created a scarcity of potential assets for sale in the near term which should only stimulate greater competition in pricing among REITs for shopping centers that come to market for sale. Theoretically, there should be reduced sales volume in the capital markets compared to historical norms; the sales activity will be concentrated in non-REIT holdings, often with institutional pension funds selling in a normal hold/gain cycles.

Mutual funds in 1993 began to build their REIT investments aggressively, and expansion in a yield-conscious stock market environment continues. On the horizon of emerging buyers, it is probable that major real estate mutual funds (e.g., Fidelity, Vanguard) will start to make direct, single asset real estate purchases rather than to continue indirectly building a real estate holding through REITs. Such mutual funds could invest in shopping center equities and in rated debt syndications. Different levels of traunched debt, both rated and unrated, could also be purchased by these mutual funds in the real estate capital markets version of high credit corporate debt and junk bonds. Hedge funds like Soros Realty, Odyssey Partners, Steinhardt Partners and Tiger Capital are beginning to selectively bid on shopping centers in 1995. As they become more experienced, expect this Wall Street money fund source to grow significantly.

WHAT THE FUTURE HOLDS

In certain situations, REITs may be sellers rather than long-term holders in order to unlock major appreciation value. Many UPREITs have "hold harmless" sale clauses which prevent the ownership (generally former development companies) from selling until four years from the IPO formation. Therefore, 1996 to 1998 may be a period when "pent up" demand to sell can legally occur within many new REITs. Certain UPREITs have tax considerations affecting the

original developer owners that may motivate sales as soon as the prohibition period against sale expires. A number of established REITs
were able to buy high-quality retail centers during the distress and
dislocation among sellers and REO owners in the early 1990s. These
assets purchased at deep discounts to reproduction cost and at high
going-in yields could have extraordinary appreciation in value that
will not coincide with cash flow value. Asset value and stock appreciation may have to be unlocked by selective disposition. An alternative would be to privatize the public REIT so that appreciated value
could be maximized.

A major source of disposition from 1996 to 2000 should be the
domestic pension funds who purchased the majority of their shopping center holdings, especially regional malls, between 1983 and
1990. A gradual recovery in value should intensify within the last
five years of the decade as excess supply evaporates and new construction remains scarce in a period expected to reflect strong
macroeconomic growth and steady retail sales growth. This trend
will coincide with the typical disposition timeframe of many funds
after a 10-year holding.

CONCLUSION

The 1990s will be historically viewed as the decade when the shopping center investment business went public as part of the ongoing
evolution from a private, entrepreneurial localized business to a
global, institutionalized, mass capital market where small and large,
nonreal estate investors could participate.

The real estate capital markets are nowhere as mature as the
global stock and bond markets. Hopefully, the financial inventive-
ness of the future will not run aground the capital shoals of the past
where tenant-demand as the key criteria for value was badly dis-
placed by excess capital flow or placement demand which spawned
poor asset appraising and underwriting. Simply put, acquisition and
disposition trends of the future must, like a good shopping center,
be well-anchored in the viability of the asset itself, not just the fun-
gibility of the investment or financial trend. Basic shopping center
analysis remains the constant anchor in this sea of change within the
capital markets and the retailing industry.

Nineteen

Sales Agency Marketing of Shopping Centers

Glenn E. Whitmore

T he ever-changing nature of the retail industry and shopping center development has become paralleled by the fast-evolving nature of capital trends in the sale and finance of shopping centers. The sale and financing of major shopping centers has become a highly specialized field for transactional intermediaries. The complexity of the shopping center real asset is compounded by the business complexity of the retail tenancy which occupies it had generates investment value. No other real estate use requires the same sophistication in both investment expertise, user familiarity and operating knowledge by the transactional intermediary. As a result, transactional agents tend to specialize and segment by shopping center types: for example, regional mall intermediaries usually concentrate their activities in that category of retail center. Owners, whether institutional or entrepreneurial, recognize the need for specialists and differentiation amongst these capital market advisors.

PREPARING THE PROPERTY FOR SALE— ENGAGEMENT COMPONENTS

The exclusive sales agent is more than a marketing specialist and a placement expert accessing acquisition capital on a local, regional, national, or international basis depending on the location and calibre of the shopping center. Advisory services delivered objectively and in advance of the disposition decision and agency designation are mandatory attributes of the investment sales firm. In fact, the total sales agency process is best defined as consultative brokerage.[1]

Here local market knowledge, shopping center product knowledge, operating knowledge, and real estate investment banking expertise are combined. The key advisory attributes are market research, financial analysis, valuation underwriting, and strategic planning in synchronization with the client's goals and objectives. The effective synthesis of advisory capacities and marketing capabilities distinguishes the sales agency tone and performance.

There are three components to a disposition engagement. The advisory phase is the premarketing period of analysis, strategy and offering preparation. The agency phase is the marketing period culminating in the closing phase after facilitation of due diligence and negotiation of the purchase/sale contract. The major, linked elements of a shopping center investment marketing are shown in Figure 19.1.

ADVISORY STAGE

The primary goals of the advisory phase of the sales agency are property knowledge; valuation (offering price and trading value range); marketing strategy; and marketing materials.

Figure 19.2 details the principal tasks of the advisory stage.

The spirit of the advisory stage is thorough understanding and underwriting of the asset for sale. Such premarketing due diligence by the agency team is the depth of evaluation necessary to maximize value and credibility of the offering. In essence, the sales agency team performs both a near audit to support financial projections where original records and documents like leases are read (rather than summary statements and records accepted) and a market feasibility review to confirm the long-term viability and competitiveness of the center. A good sales agency team in many ways performs the same project analysis as a good acquisition team with different goals in mind.

FIGURE 19.1

Major, Linked Elements of a Shopping Center

Advisory Phase

Property Analysis
Offering Valuation
Premarketing Due Diligence
Marketing Strategy

Agency Phase

Property Analysis
Offering Valuation
Premarketing Due Diligence
Marketing Strategy

Closing Phase

Monitoring Due Diligence
Negotiation of Purchase/Sale Contract
Negotiation of Due Diligence Discovery
Support of Tenant Estoppel Process
Waiver of Contingencies
Closing Statement
Closing: Passing Title and Funding
Post Closing: Records and Books

CREATING A COMPREHENSIVE OFFERING

Offerings of investment-grade shopping centers require sophisticated production and presentation to capture an investor's focus. Developing the proper sales offering requires the agent to do original document review, research, and distillation. The process is analogous to the level of detail and diligence with which an acquisition team would review an offering to purchase. In fact, the agent's disposition approach must involve a team of multidisciplined specialists, including

FIGURE 19.2

Advisory Stage

Goal	Tasks
Property knowledge	• Site inspection • Building inspection • Market and trade area research (economic base, growth potential, sales potential, competitive position, expansion/redevelopment capacity) • Locational evaluation (access, visibility, traffic counts, new transportation factors, surrounding uses and synergy)
Valuation (through premarketing due diligence)	• Appraisal: current comparable sales • Review audited operating histories • Read/abstract all leases (compare to Rent Roll) • Review budget and management plan • Review pertinent legal documents • Review tenant sales histories • Develop investment pro forma (10-year discounted cash flow) • Establish investor parameters and yield targets • Establish trading values (sensitivity analysis) • Establish offering price (all cash and/or leveraged)
Marketing strategy	• Identification of appropriate investors (preregistration) — Local, regional, national or international • Prequalify target investors' interest — Preview letter and discussion • Determine type of marketing program — Confidential offering to limited investors only (presentations) — Open market registration to investors and outside brokers — Auction — Use of date certain — Use of multimedia (advertising)
Marketing materials	• Determine length of marketing program (establish milestones) • Determine scope and style of offering materials — Executive summary solicitation — Full offering memoranda — Text presentation — Media presentation (VCR, CD-Rom) — Advertising • Prepare offering materials

financial analysts and retail disposition experts, that mirrors the acquisition process but from a seller's perspective and objectives. Creating a comprehensive shopping center offering is no longer a province of investment generalists. The shopping center offering, especially for regional mall sales, is the most complicated type of offering among real estate assets.

PREMARKETING SALES ANALYSIS

To start the offering preparation process, the agency team, at a minimum, brings together the skills of a specialist in market, financial and product feasibilities. Basic research, review and discovery not only allow the agent's team to verify the information on the property; but also to build the marketing and financial case for offering valuation based on a review of property and market facts that will stand the test of buyer scrutiny during the marketing phase and due diligence.

For a shopping center, Figure 19.3 shows the check points of information and documentation requiring analysis and review during the advisory phase by the sales agent.

The product of this analysis is an Offering Memorandum. The organization and key components of these offering materials for a shopping center sale are shown in Figure 19.4 of the contents standard. This standard applies to any shopping center type, though the depth of description varies by the size of the center.

OFFERING PRESENTATION TACTICS

Effective offering memoranda emphasize graphic elements that distill the narrative content and highlight the essential features of the property. Mandatory graphics for an institutional quality-offering are shown in Figure 19.5.

The key parts of the market analysis for all shopping center sales are a convincing evaluation of: economic base analysis of market; locational dynamics; access and visibility (including traffic counts); property identity and consumer image; competition study (strengths and weaknesses compared to sale property); and trade area analysis.

Perhaps the most important component is the trade area analysis where, too commonly, all the sales agent shows are demographic data base runs for rings of distance around the shopping center. This is

FIGURE 19.3

Agent's Punchlist for Shopping Center Offering Memorandum

I. Lease by lease file review and abstracting

II. Income expense histories (3 actual years) and management budget analysis

III. Tenant sales (tenant by tenant) analysis
   — Historical actual sales (gross $ and $/sf) over three years
   — % change, annual over three years
   — YTD actuals

IV. Special rent roll notes
   — Percentage rent
   — Option rents
   — Expense recaptures/offsets
   — Termination rights
   — Purchase rights
   — Kickout clauses
   — Noncompete clauses

V. Physical data
   a. Site plan (including clear demarcation of what is being conveyed; anchor owned; pad owned; outparcels)
   b. Survey of property
   c. Center leasing plan (space ID; tenant; GLA; dimensions)
   d. Zoning designation (description)
   e. Parking capacity and ratio/GLA (cars/1,000 GLA)
   f. Easements
   g. Description of center
      — Existing materials/structural description
      — History of ownership and physical evolution
      — Environmental studies (hazardous waste)
      — Notable capital improvements
   h. Outparcels (including TBAs)
   i. Peripheral land, if any
   j. Expansion potential/cost
   k. Redevelopment potential/cost
   l. Remerchandising potential/cost
      — Description (size, zoning)
      — Development potential
      — Value

(Continued)

FIGURE 19.3 *(Continued)*

VI.   Tenant data

VII.   Legal data
    a.   Declarations affecting real property
    b.   Operating covenants (REA) with reciprocal cross-easements
    c.   Tax assessment procedure (tax ID by parcels)
    d.   Financing documents

VIII.   Market data
    a.   Economic base analysis
    b.   Delineation of total trade area and primary trade area
    c.   Demographics in trade area
    d.   Expenditure ratios in trade area/shopper goods; buying potential
    e.   Traffic counts (transportation improvements; any public transit)
    f.   Competition survey (market share/capture)
    g.   Consumer surveys (by center; by store)
    h.   Growth potential data (demographics and psychographics)
    i.   Impact of proposed new construction or developable sites

not analysis. First, the primary and secondary trade areas, not ring radii, must be determined from historical shopping center sales data (by zip code) and customer surveys (intercept studies); then, the boundaries are drawn in consideration of competitive trade areas and physical, transportation factors. Ideally, computer-generated and color-coded trade area graphics can be shown to illustrate relative demographic performance regarding key measures of income, population growth and population character.

In a credible market chapter, the sales agent should take a retailers' perspective in studying whether to locate at the shopping center. The demographic analysis therefore should be feasibility-oriented to the center's trade area and competitive gravity, not general economic base data. Ideally the market chapter would include historic shopper survey and sales intercept studies; a color-coded analysis of key demographic variables by zip code; a merchandise category capture analysis and a residential housing growth analysis. An objective sales presentation should mirror both an owner's ongoing, in-depth asset analysis and a retailer's standard trade area analysis in the market chapter. In the Offering Memorandum, the highlights must energize investment interest, not merely describe it, if valuation is to be enhanced.

FIGURE 19.4

Shopping Center Offering Memorandum
Table of Contents

I. EXECUTIVE SUMMARY
- Investment Property Highlights
- Key Physical Characteristics
- Site Plan
- Principal Investment Components
- Consolidated Yield Analysis
- Property Photography
- Aerial Photography

II. MARKET ANALYSIS
- Regional Map
- Property Overview
- Access and Visibility
- Surroundings and Identity
- Local Economic Base
- Regional Economic Overview
- Trade Area Analysis
- Trade Area Map
- Trade Area Demographics
- Shoppers Goods Expenditure Potential
- Competition

III. THE PROPERTY
- Location Map
- History
- Description (Building and Design)
- Site Plan
- Covenants

IV. FINANCIAL ANALYSIS
- Assumptions and Methodology
- Cost of Occupancy Analysis
- Project Cash Flow Analysis
- Operating Expense History
- Income History

V. THE TENANTS
- Mall Plan
- Tenant Credit Classification
- Overview of Tenant Productivity
- Merchandise Mix by Category
- Merchandise Mix by Productivity
- Rent Roll
- Notes to The Rent Roll
- Analysis of Comparable Sales by Merchandise Category
- Lease Expiration Schedule
- Annual Space by Space Absorption Schedule

VI. APPENDIX
- Financing Abstract
- Detailed Demographic Tables
- Summary of Covenants
- Sponsorship
- Summary of Anchor Tenants and Parent Chain

MULTIMEDIA PRESENTATION

The ongoing evolution of information technology will have an incrementally radical impact on marketing techniques. In fact, the written Offering Memorandum may become obsolete. Its electronic replacements, already making inroads, could be a combination of: Video and audio tape presentation (VCR format); CD-Rom or digital

FIGURE 19.5

Shopping Center Offering Graphics

Photography — Aerial property view (with major roadways and
surroundings coded)
Exterior perspectives
Interior perspectives, with tenant spaces (if enclosed mall)
— Anchors
— Center court
— Food court
— Special features

Maps   — Location (in region and in local economy)
Trade area
Competition
Demographic trends (colorized computer graphs)

Plans   — Site plan (ownership demarcation; distinction between
anchor-owned stores and parcels; leased vs. owned outparcels)
Lease plan (floor by floor)
Expansion (if any)

Charts   — Sales productivity
— Tenant by tenant
— By merchandise category
Demographic indicators
— Growth trends for population and income
— Comparison to ICSC and ULI benchmarks

cassette presentation; and E-mail or modem PC transmission and presentation.

The vital financial projections as conventionally presented in text and cash flow pro forma tables have become insufficient. PRO-JECT™ or equivalent diskettes accompanying Offering Memorandum (assuming well-qualified interest and confidentiality protection have been achieved by the agent) are now conventional for the sophisticated sale.

It is important to distinguish between presentation and acquisition analysis in terms of the long-term prospects of text: Multimedia presentation may supplant text as the first stage of offering, but text in a detailed Offering Memoranda (whether downloaded or standard brochure) is still a requisite for the most important part of a sale—acquisition analysis by investors which gets them to make a purchase offer.

VALUATION ISSUES

The most critical part of the advisory phase is the valuation. The sales agent needs to develop not only an offering value, but a range of probable trading prices based on current investor parameters, comparable sales benchmarks, and a sensitivity analysis of the projected cash flow baseline. A recent third-party appraisal detailing comparable sales is highly valuable. A cash flow pro forma, whether based on in-place income or projected discounted cash flow, that is used for establishing value without the context of comparable sales is like flying a plane without maintaining ground contact (see Figure 19.6).

Comparable sales analysis is then combined, interactively and synthetically, with the property's cash flow pro forma as projected from the rent roll for the holding period in order to project marketing value. The property pro forma includes assumptions by the seller and

FIGURE 19.6

Comparable Sales Benchmarks for Disposition Value

- Center type
- Occupancy at sale
- Sales productivity (mall "in-line" sales and anchor sales in $ psf with growth trends)
- Ratio of sales price per square foot to mall sales per square foot
- Going-in yield (including any income supports)
- Residual (terminal) capitalization rate
- Market rent/expense growth rate assumptions
- Unique expansion/redevelopment features
- Ratio of national/regional credit tenancy to overall occupancy
- Trade area dynamics and growth prognosis (new competition)
- Holding period internal rate of return (with or without structure like earnout or lookback IRR)
- Debt features (if not all cash)
- Full fee or partial interest transfer

agent of future operating performance and tenant rollover at the shopping center. These assumptions on a line-item basis must be described as part of the offering memoranda if the sale is to galvanize investor's credibility. The offering pro forma and comparable sales insights most crucially intersect in the following parameters of return: capitalization rate, internal rate of return, and residual (terminal) capitalization rate. Establishing both an offering price and a trading price requires the property's cash flow to be calibrated to truly comparable sales, not just aggressive marketing projections.

An offering valuation is priced to anticipate the market in its current and projected dynamics, rather than only reflect historical comparable sales parameters. The cash flow assumptions, unlike an appraiser's discounted cash flow analysis, are based on the broker's and investment banker's awareness of current market and investor thresholds, none of which may have been proven by recent closings and comparables. The sales broker owes it to his client to rationally push where plausible new and higher purchase price points with the latest shopping center offering.

VALUATION TRIPWIRES

The object of any sale is to bring the property to market at the highest, *credible* offering price combining the in-depth, baseline information of the property's current financials with aggressively realistic assumptions and projections about future performance. If the assumptions template governing the projected cash flow is not integrally tied to what is achievable, given verifiable local market standards or to generally-accepted macro assumptions (e.g., rate of expense growth, terminal rate for that age of center), then investors will discount the price, if they bid at all. The art of establishing a selling value is not just an enlightened iteration between what a seller wants and what market comparables signal: the projected discounted cash flow pro forma is the palette, the assumptions are the paint, but if the brush isn't realistic, the sale price portrait will turn heads the wrong way. If an agent convinces a seller to go to market where all income is capitalized (and discounted) at one rate without sensitivity, the agent is just missing the mark in order to simply set the highest value, rather than the best sales value. For example, a sales agent must know from experience that:

- Acquisition experts will not capitalize (discount) uncertain percentage rent at the same rate that they will certain, contractual minimum rent, unless sales productivity is distinctively unique and assured;

- That credit income, especially for anchors and national tenants should not be discounted at the same rate as local/regional credit tenants; rather, through income-stripping and differential discounting (see example) the credit stream of an income flow can be segmented to justifiably add value where, alternatively, making aggressive global assumptions to drive offering price would not be as credible;

- That tenant improvement cost projections need to relate, on a tenant by tenant basis, to history and to special rental opportunities that will require above-average TIs to induce the tenant. Globalizing TIs is the type of crude technique that creates fluff rather than substance behind an aggressive sale price;

- That special tenant rollover assumptions about administrative charges over CAM passthroughs need to be in sync with whether it will be a tenant's or landlord's market at that time;

- That replacement reserves must be correlated to historic experience and life cycle status of the shopping center; and

- That market rent at rollover projections must be in line with standard cost of occupancy tolerances for tenants.

As noted, a pro forma projection requires a detailed assumption template to support its credibility. Cash flow projections in offerings should similarly show more than broad income and expense category estimates. Again, for the purpose of substantively seizing the investor's credibility through sophistication of offering that mirrors their sophistication of acquisition, line-item detail is important.

It is rare that no offering value is set for investors to bid against. Without an asking price, investors usually question the owner's earnestness to sell; they abhor bidding blind with no indication of an owner's motivation or selling threshold. On occasion and usually only for the truly "trophy" retail center, investor interest in a particular asset can be so intense that it may be tactically advantageous for the agent to conduct a premium auction with no sales price. This tactic has been employed successfully during the sale of certain super-regional trophy malls, during the sale of certain single tenant flagship stores, and during the sale of "one-of-a kind" specialty centers in "carriage trade" shopping districts. In all instances, for performing assets, this tactic has been employed only in rapidly peaking markets, not conventional investment climates.

PREMARKETING STRATEGY

Marketing strategy for selling shopping centers pivots on priming the target market in advance of the submission of offering materials, matching the type of center and its performance to the optimum investor universe, and establishing the appropriate time frame for the agency phase when offers will be generated and the property taken off the market into due diligence. The scope of marketing presentation is critical to determine. Will the shopping center sale have more than local/regional appeal? If offshore investors would be interested, how can they be accessed? Should all investors be sent the Offering Memorandum simultaneously; or should investors be ranked and submitted the marketing materials in a hierarchy of most probable buyers and secondary buyers? Are personal presentations necessary to truly maximize value and competitive interest?

Premarketing tactics are designed to "tee up" the target market so that they will prioritize their commitment and resources to respond to the offering. Proven premarketing initiatives include preview or announcement letters of the engagement describing the timing of the submission and goals of the offering process, such as the closing objective of the seller or whether the sale funding should be all-cash. While a full Offering Memorandum is in final preparation, an executive summary can be submitted showing the investment and property highlights (generally in five pages or less). In fact, the executive summary should be used to screen and prequalify investor interest: The agent requires the investor to review it and discuss their interest as a prerequisite to the agent's decision to transmit the full offering. This type of premarketing conforms to the overall goal of the marketing strategy: to get the highest price, the offering should be highly controlled and directed only to the most capable and most interested investors at that time. Less is absolutely more in terms of number of investors targeted for most institutional offerings. As an example, there may be 20 to 25 domestic investors who could acquire a large regional mall sale; but there may be only ten actively in the market and interested in the asset; and only five who have discretionary funding control. By screening the market through experienced knowledge of the buyer base and premarketing qualification, the best marketing strategy may be to present the offer to only the five investors with full discretion. If these investors don't submit a satisfactory offer, then open up the marketing strategy to the nondiscretionary tier of 10. Sequencing investors through an offering ironically appeals to many investors who prefer bidding against a limited set of proven buyers rather than to be caught up in a lengthy, mass marketing process.

AGENCY STAGE

Sophisticated institutional investors engage sales agents exclusively to maximize the control and the confidentiality of the offering. This approach to selling has consistently proven to generate the highest competitive bidding from the most capable investors.

Institutional sellers expect an exclusive sales agent to execute the marketing program and place the equity to a targeted, limited marketplace that will compete actively against each other in a controlled bid environment. These sellers are not hiring agents simply to list the property as outside brokers are registering buyers in an uncontrolled manner. Such an approach simply diminishes value potential and is little better than posting a sales ad. Most importantly, confidentiality (particularly financial performance and rent rolls) is badly breached. The experienced agent's value-added benefit comes from knowing target buyers, their investment criteria and, from experience, their motivation and orientation. By exclusively orchestrating a controlled marketing program, the sales agent presenting the offering directly to principals establishes a consistent playing field for all investors, while assuring financial confidentiality.

In an open, nonexclusive agency, no investor can be sure of the accuracy of the information received on the property, of the owner's objectives, and, most importantly, of the owner's earnestness. Since the owner in an open agency has empowered no single agent to coherently and authoritatively represent its interest, the marketplace is forced to respond to information that is frequently disparately disseminated and filtered, often through intermediaries whose interests are uncertain and without fiduciary responsibility. An open agency can on occasion undermine the basic credibility of an offering.

Target marketing, in itself, means that the sales agent is expected to perform more than a property listing function. A confidential offering process demands that the sales agent be hired on the basis of their track record in execution and placement. Experienced sellers recognize the value of target marketing and confidentiality. They understand that broad marketing exposure does not produce optimum valuation.

The owner's concern about precision marketing and confidentiality dictates the co-operating brokerage process. A co-brokerage process should be initiated solely to broaden the marketability of a shopping center asset if the target market of the most proven and probable investors does not respond to the sale offering.

Institutional investors must act efficiently in acquisitions because they can not maintain the overhead, especially representing separate account pension funds, to "chase" every deal. Rationing and common sense dictate that most investors spend their diligent acquisition hours pursuing exclusively marketed public sales (or private purchases directly with the owner in which no agents are involved). An open agency not only may maximize confusion about the offering, it may also turn off investors who must use acquisition resources productively. Investors prioritize exclusive controlled offerings.

IDENTIFYING AND REACHING LIKELY BUYERS

Sales agents are active placement experts, not just a listing source. Identifying traditional and emerging buyers for the particular shopping center asset is the touchstone of the marketing magic. Agents must be constantly in touch with likely investors, based on past preference and performance on shopping center acquisitions. This contact must be maintained currently at local, regional, national, and international levels.

Geographic and product targets among investors change at least annually and often more frequently in a transitional market. Risk orientation is a key criterion in such a rapidly evolving business as retailing and shopping center ownership. For example, certain pension fund investors prefer stabilized assets only, while others are focused on higher risk, higher return redevelopment strategies. Many investment advisors today do not have discretion over the capital. Thus, in an often nondiscretionary separate account world of capital, it is vital for the sales agent to know the process of approval each nondiscretionary advisor must go through. The agent must know what source(s) of funds they represent. The agent must know the advisors' closing "track record" in general and with the represented fund(s) in particular. Since multiple advisors often represent the same pension fund, the agent must know which advisor is not appropriate or most experienced with the sponsor vis-à-vis the asset type. An advisor specializing in regional malls for a fund is not the one to whom to present a community center. Offshore buyers have different investment criteria, including tax motivation and currency issues, than domestic capital sources. Changes in ERISA legislation and tax regulation (UBTI) can govern how investors financially structure an acquisition.

New public market vehicles like REITs and real estate mutual funds can change the investment market. It is the most critical responsibility of the sales agent to know the investor's individual acquisition profiles and the changing context of any macroeconomic issues that would affect their investment motivation.

A DISTINCT SHIFT IN BUYING STRATEGIES

During the late 1980s, funding sources (and their advisors) moved toward highly segmented buying strategies. First, based on product type and geography, the capital sources sought further diversity (adding yield or trading down risk) by seeking value-enhancement opportunities through redevelopment, through expansion and most significantly, through remerchandising. Second, as certain asset types became overly favored such as regional malls, certain buyers who had historically focused on this shopping center type only, repositioned themselves (and had their funds reallocate) into community or neighborhood centers or, unconventionally, into new directions like power centers or factory outlet malls. Investors who had traditionally sought stabilized "core" holdings with high asset-quality and low operating risk shifted gears to value-enhancement funding where redevelopment and risk were assumed, sometimes with contrarian investment logic, in order to generate higher yields. Certain factory outlet mall buyers (like New Plan Realty Trust) diversified further by buying the factory outlet company as well as their real estate and operating centers. The stratification and evolving specialization of funding sources mirrors the transitions and segmentation of the retailers. Effective disposition strategy must not lag the knowledge of these ever changing funding niches.

THE EQUITY INVESTOR CLASSIFICATION CHART

The equity investor classification chart in Figure 19.7 reflects the key issues that segment buyers and allow sales agents to properly target offerings. From a seller's perspective, the most important criteria are performance issues and closing track record. Performance is not simply a matter of track record or access to capital, ideally discretionary funding: the sales agent's knowledge of the individuals spearheading the acquisitions and the organizational decision-making process are vital. The real estate equity markets for acquisition vary

FIGURE 19.7

Equity Investor Classification

- Shopping center type preferences
- Geographic preferences (region, area, market, submarket)
  — Recent acquisitions (comparable sales)
  — Recent offers
  — Buying philosophy/acquisition style
- Purchasing power
  — All cash (discretionary and/or non-discretionary funds; which funds advised)
  — Leverage (including hybrid debt)
  — Structured ventures
  — Target yield requirements (capitalization rate; IRR; $PSF)
- Holding strategy (length of holding; reliance on cash flow return or residual premium)
  — Institutional 10 year cycle
  — Entrepreneurial 3–7 year cycle
- Capital capacity (minimum and maximum capital investment)
- Operating capacity
  — Asset management
- Special investment characteristics
  — Value-enhancement orientation (redevelopment; expansion; major remerchandising)
  — Price $ psf sensitivity
  — Tolerance for releasing risk
  — Partnership or venture capacity (partial interest)
  — Capacity for hybrid equity/debt engineering
- Closing track record
  — Due diligence style
  — Purchase/Sale contract "hot buttons"
  — Fund approval process (discretionary; nondiscretionary)
  — Offshore buyer issues

among investors by the efficiency and efficiency with which people and organizations get things done. As sophisticated as the capital market instruments have become, a key variable is still "people skills" and performance.

THE AGENT'S RELATIONSHIP WITH INSTITUTIONAL CAPITAL

In the institutional capital market, for both onshore and offshore funding, it is important for the agent to stay in touch with the plan sponsors directly as well as their advisors. Certain funds (Ohio State Teachers Retirement System, Stat of Wisconsin Investment Board) will invest directly without a pre-requisite to present the offering through an advisor. As the pension fund real estate business evolves, this direct pattern may grow significantly. Also, it is vital that the sales agent know from advisors what each fund or group of funds that they represent is seeking. Too often, advisors describe acquisition programs without discussing the sponsor represented and their specific goals.

TIMING THE SALE

Ideally, sellers can time the sale of an asset to maximize its value, given real estate capital market conditions and the overall viability of the macro investment climate. However, selling when demand is strong and supply is tight has historically proven an art, rather than a science. Unfortunately, real estate values have been cyclically prone with deep troughs if over-building is extreme. Ironically, new construction activity often continues to reinforce value expectation, while disguising an overheated market, because new reproduction values are set.

To maximize market timing, the sales agent's knowledge of current comparable sales and capital flows by major shopping center type is vital. Comparing "comps" quarter to quarter and then market to market can alert sellers to, say, decreasing cap rate trends which is always a "sell alert" signal. In addition to actual trades, the agent's awareness of shopping centers on the market for sale and their asking price parameters will show a pattern of a changing investment climate. In addition to transactional knowledge, a quarterly survey sampling representative investor categories per different shopping center types is a very proactive and reliable indicator of how investors' criteria are changing.

On an asset specific timing basis, the optimum value for a center's sale residual is the peak of its competitive lifecycle. This is not simply a function of age since contemporary renovation can always extend a center's physical lifecycle. Judging the center's competitive position is the key. Selling a center before new competition that will erode performance comes on-line is an obvious timing trigger. Optimum value is usually achieved when centers are stabilized and a consistent sales productivity record has been established. A strongly aligned and located center requiring renovation and expansion may ironically generate more value on sale prior to the major capital improvement if there is pent up demand, as ascertained by the agent in its knowledge of shopping center capital flows for these types of acquisition.

THE "DATE CERTAIN" TACTIC

While investors may prefer an open bid marketing process, the best way an agent can help the seller to control the timing variable is to conduct a date certain marketing program. This approach insures that interested investors will prioritize their analysis and response given the target date by which all offers must be in. Date certain marketing generally motivates investors to make stronger initial offers. This tactic also allows for an orchestrated "best-and-final" bid process thereafter.

SERVICE FEES

Engagement fees for brokers and investment bankers typically vary by the purchase price or loan value. Generally speaking, equity dispositions of shopping centers between $10 to $25 million have a commission fee of 2% to 2.5% between $25 to $50 million, a fee of 1.25% to 2% and over $50 million a fee of 1% or less. All success fees are supplemented typically by cost reimbursement for marketing expense. Conventional debt placements typically cost 1% of the loan value placed; rated debt and securitized debt costs vary by the degree of complexity and number of loans involved.

CONCLUSION

The trend toward the new technology in marketing shopping center sales and the impact of the conversion of a privately traded asset class to a public one are surely profound for the future. An intermediary's style, if not role, may be radically changed. The benchmarks of client representation during dispositions of shopping centers should remain a constant.

ENDNOTE

1. For a detailed discussion of the contractual obligations of the seller and its sales agent, see White, John R. The Office Building: From Concept to Investment Reality, Chapter 21, published by Counselors of Real Estate, Appraisal Foundation, and the Society of Office & Industrial Realtors, 1993.

Twenty

Appraising Retail Properties

Peter F. Korpacz

The reasons for appraising retail properties are as extensive and as varied as the questions that can be asked about their value. Market valuations are prepared for financing, purchase, disposition, expansion, and renovation. A common need for an appraisal of retail property is to set an asking price for sale of a shopping center and/or outlying land parcels. Appraisals are also ordered by owners in tax appeals and by assessors for verification of property value. Institutional investors need periodic appraisals for documentation of real estate value as part of total portfolio valuation. Additionally, appraisals are important in litigation and arbitration matters.

Retail property interests appraised range from fee simple to partnership interests and include leased fee estate, leasehold estate, ground lease, and mortgage interests. A single appraisal may involve valuation of one or more property interests. The purpose of most retail appraisals is to estimate current market value, "the most probable price, as of a specified date, in cash or in terms equivalent to cash, or in other precisely revealed terms, for which the specified property rights should sell after reasonable exposure in a competitive market under all conditions requisite to fair sale, with the buyer and seller each acting prudently, knowledgeably, and for self-interest, and assuming that neither is under undue duress."[1] The "specified date" may be a date prior to or after the date of the appraisal in which case the estimated market value is retrospective or prospective. A client who needs to know the value of a shopping center after expansion or renovation, for example, may request an estimate of prospective market value, based on carefully defined conditions.

Unlike market value, which is based on objective analyses of a property in the context of market conditions and the collective actions of buyers and sellers, investment value satisfies a specific investor's investment criteria.

In addition to appraisals for market value and investment value, appraisals are performed to estimate use value, going concern value, assessed value, and insurable value. The careful definition of the purpose and type of value to be estimated is essential to the appraisal's credibility.

RELATIONSHIP OF VALUE APPROACHES TO INVESTOR BEHAVIOR

All three approaches to value may be used in valuation of retail properties: Income, Sales Comparison, and Cost. Since retail properties are income producing, the income capitalization approach is generally considered to render the value indication that is most representative of market behavior, and hence market value.

The sales comparison approach is less reliable than the income capitalization approach as a value indicator of major shopping centers and regional malls. One significant deterrent is the difficulty of quantitative measurement of property differences. The approach is more applicable in the valuation of smaller retail properties because of their greater similarity to each other. It may also be useful as a test of the value indication derived from the income capitalization approach. Comparable sales are analyzed to derive discount and capitalization rates and price-per-square-foot indications.

For the most part, the cost approach is used only in appraisals of proposed or new retail properties or as an indication of prospective value of properties undergoing expansion or substantial renovation. Because of the complexity of the process of estimating depreciation, which requires numerous subjective adjustments, the cost approach is seldom a reliable indicator of market value. The required addition of an amount over development costs for entrepreneurial profit is subjective since there is little empirical evidence of how much the appropriate profit percentage should be. Without an estimate of accurate entrepreneurial profit, the cost approach does not produce an authentic indication of total value.

RETAIL MARKET ANALYSIS

The goal of market (trade area) analysis in a retail property appraisal is to evaluate the demand for retail goods and services in the subject property's trade area, the buying power that may be attracted to the property, and the impact of competition. The trade area analysis provides a general representation of the future financial performance of the property in relation to competition in the trade area and national averages. The specific result is an estimate of retail sales that the property will likely generate during the investment forecast period. Thus, the analysis provides necessary guidance to determine the forecast assumptions in the income capitalization approach.

A forecast of the subject's potential sales as a portion of total market share is based on retail sales forecast for the trade area and the market share forecast for the property. For an existing property, historical data for the trade area and the subject are used to derive an estimate of the subject's market share. For a proposed retail facility, market share can be estimated through analysis of sales per square foot of retail space in the trade area and an analysis of the competition. The sales analysis generally is based on a study of trends and projections prepared by a demographic research firm.

CREDIT QUALITY

The owner of retail property often shares directly in the success of the tenants. Many retail space leases provide for rent that is a combination of base rent (minimum fixed, or guaranteed, rent) and percentage rent (a stipulated percentage of the gross dollar volume of the tenant's sales). Therefore, the credit quality of the tenants is a significant factor in the value of a retail center. A reasonable credit rating is necessary to ensure the quantity, quality, and durability of the income. In regional malls, power centers, and some community shopping centers, most tenants are "credit" tenants, that is, national public corporations with adequate credit standing. In most strip centers, the anchor is usually a credit tenant and most, if not all, of the others are not. They are more likely to be regional or local businesses.

In addition to affecting income, the creditworthiness of retail tenants affects discount and capitalization rates. In analyzing a center that contains credit tenants, appraisers may apply lower discount and equity capitalization rates. Where the credit standing of tenants is less favorable, the risk is higher and therefore appraisers are likely to add a premium to the rates to compensate for the risk level.

ENVIRONMENTAL, TRAFFIC, AND ZONING ISSUES

The presence of hazardous substances on a site or in the improvements as well as other environmental conditions may affect the value of a property. However, appraisers are generally not qualified to test for such substances or conditions and must depend on property owners, managers, or other experts for information related to the presence of hazardous substances or conditions. The Uniform Standards of Professional Practice require that an appraiser indicate the inability to detect or measure environmental substances. Therefore, appraisals generally contain a statement disclaiming responsibility for any such conditions and for expertise or engineering knowledge required to discover them.

Traffic issues are noted in the report of accessibility of the site. In an appraisal of a regional mall, accessibility includes identification, location, and description of interstate routes in relation to the site.

Zoning issues identified and reported in a retail property appraisal include zoning district, permitted uses, minimum lot size, maximum lot coverage, maximum building height, parking requirements, any likely zoning change, and the property's legal conformance with zoning regulations.

INCOME CAPITALIZATION APPROACH

Yield Capitalization Method

Purchasers of retail properties typically forecast net operating income (NOI) and cash flow over a period of time and then determine a purchase price that will justify the degree of risk inherent in the proposed investment by discounting the cash flows and reversion at an appropriate discount rate. This process is known as discounted cash flow (DCF) analysis.

It is essential that the application of the yield capitalization method reflect the thinking and actions of market participants. These are discernible through examination of the forecast assumptions used in connection with sales of comparable properties and surveys of investors who buy property similar to the subject property. Although founded on such hard data, forecast assumptions and the cash flow projection in the discounted cash flow analysis are the appraiser's best judgment of how a typical investor would analyze the subject property as of the date of value. Some appraisers are reluctant to look beyond the last sale and occasionally miss trends in their disposition to be historical rather than anticipatory.

Forecast Period

The forecast period in DCF analysis for retail properties is typically 10 years, although specific circumstances may point to the advisability of using shorter or longer forecast periods. An additional one-year forecast is common to estimate a sale price at the end of the forecast period.

GLA

In addition to the items that are typically described for any property type, description of shopping center improvements includes identification of anchor stores and a breakdown of gross leasable area (GLA) for anchors, in-line mall stores, kiosks, food court tenants, and freestanding buildings if any. In appraisals of properties in which a portion of the GLA is owned by the anchors, this is noted and only the owned GLA is reflected in the valuation analysis.

Revenue

The revenue estimate for the forecast period is developed through lease-by-lease analysis to determine current and projected revenue from all sources. Revenue derives from base and percentage rent, indexed rent or graduations, as well as reimbursements, or recoveries, for tenant portions of expenses such as real estate taxes, common area maintenance (CAM), HVAC, sprinkler, and insurance.

A forecast of percentage rent is based on analyses of lease provisions and the forecast retail sales developed in the retail market analysis. The reasonableness of the retail sales estimate may be tested against the experience of the subject and comparable properties. For vacant space, percentage rent may be estimated on the basis of market analysis or analysis of the sales levels of the existing tenants. Recent leasing activity ordinarily identifies typical percentage rental rates and retail sale break points.

Projections of the components of the retail market analysis that support the retail sales forecast—population, households, household income, percent of income spent in shopping centers, and so forth— are estimates of future possibilities based on current trends. To hedge the risk inherent in reliance on such estimates, investors typically forecast retail sales increases at a rate somewhat less than that indicated by the market analysis.

In addition, appraisers, like investors, give careful consideration to an indicated sales growth rate that is above and below the projected CPI over the forecast period. Most appraisers are predisposed to accept a retail sales growth commensurate with the CPI on most properties. However, when market analysis indicates a sales growth rate significantly higher than the CPI, an appraiser or investor will examine the conditions that support the divergence. Even when extraordinary conditions justify it, the analyst may use the high sales forecast for a few years and, at some point in the analysis, reduce it to the CPI. Conversely, if market analysis indicates a retail sales growth less than the CPI, the appraiser must factor this added risk into the valuation of the center and adjust the discount rate to accommodate the risk.

The risk in shopping center investments increases when the cost of occupancy—base rent plus percentage rent plus recovered expenses— rises to above-market levels. Most regional mall investors perform a cost-of-occupancy analysis, which may include examination of the cost of occupancy in the property overall as well as by merchandise type or on a detailed tenant-by-tenant basis. A reasonable cost of occupancy is within the range of 10% to 15%. When retail sales growth is very high, a cost of occupancy above 15% may not be a problem, but if retail sales slow for any extensive period, such a high cost of occupancy can become a serious risk factor. Percentage rent, which is the most variable component of the income forecast, may be analyzed as a factor in risk measurement.

The net operating income and cash flow forecast is reflected in the selected overall rate of return, the internal rate of return (IRR), and the equity capitalization rate (if the property is purchased subject to debt). The greater the anticipation of growth in income and appreciation over time, the greater the spread between the NOI and the IRR. The lower the anticipated growth, the closer these rates are.

Absorption of Vacant Space

Assumptions for the absorption of the vacant space—number of square feet of vacant space and the projected date on which the property will be fully leased—are based on the market and marketability analyses in the appraisal. The absorption assumption is based on factors such as recent leasing activity, current leasing strategy, and trade area trends.

Vacancy

An allowance for vacancy and collection losses is often provided in two ways:

1. The appraiser assumes a weighted average vacancy of a certain number of months as leases expire (lag vacancy) based on the property's experience and current and forecast market conditions. This vacancy assumption is expressed by eliminating minimum rent, percentage rent, and all expense recovery items during the downtime period.

2. An allowance of a percentage of total revenue is provided to reflect the underlying vacancy and possibility of collection losses inherent in a multitenant retail property. The allowance assumption is often based on typical market assumptions and the appraiser's review of the accounts receivable and understanding of a center's competitiveness in attracting tenants.

Re-Leasing Assumptions

Generally, all space in a multitenant retail center is assumed to be released in accordance with the center's standard lease. At lease expiration, minimum rent is often forecast at the greater of (1) the sum of minimum and percentage rent in the last lease year, or (2) market rent. If the tenant is forecast to remain and minimum rent is forecast as the sum of minimum and percentage rent in the last lease year, the tenant is usually assumed to receive the tenant improvement allowance specified for a renewal tenant and the landlord is charged a commission at the renewal rate. If minimum rent is set to market, the tenant is assumed to receive a tenant improvement allowance consistent with that for a new tenant and the landlord pays a full commission. These assumptions typically apply for a shopping center in a balanced market.

In a market where rents are decreasing and contract minimum rents exceed market minimum rents, a different assumption is typically used. At lease expiration, all space within the regional mall is assumed to be re-leased at market rent, with tenants usually assumed to receive a weighted average tenant improvement allowance based on a tenant retention percentage. This is also the assumption typically used for community and neighborhood shopping centers in both balanced and deteriorating markets.

Re-leasing assumptions can be derived from analysis of the center's recent leasing activity and comparative analysis of recent leases at competitive properties. For tenants assumed to re-lease at the last year's minimum plus percentage rent, retail sales are assumed to change according to the retail sales change rate assumption. For tenants re-leasing at market rent, retail sales may be reset at the level that will reach a natural breakpoint after a specified period, say five years or at some market or average change rate.

Operating Expenses

Forecast operating expenses are based on analysis of actual operating expense history for a number of years and the owner's budget. Comparison of the subject's estimated operating expense with the operating expense history of competitive centers is beneficial as a test of reasonableness. These analyses are the basis for the property expense forecast, which may or may not mirror the property owner's budget. For example, the appraiser may stipulate that to increase retail sales and maintain tenant viability, the marketing expense item should be increased. Expenses are ordinarily projected throughout the forecast period at a percent increase based on operating expense analyses and market research. If revenues are based on a major rehabilitation, the appraiser subtracts this capital cost from the value, based on the presumably increased net operating income.

Management Fee/Leasing Commissions

The existing management and leasing agreements and comparison with agreements of similar properties are used to derive appropriate market assumptions. These agreements may be based on tenants' effective gross revenue or base and percentage rent, sometimes less recoveries. Often, and especially in regional malls, management and leasing agreements are combined into a single agreement with one firm.

Replacement Reserve

The assumed replacement reserve for capital expenditures is based on typical market replacement reserves and specific anticipated capital expenditures.

Tenant Improvements

When real estate markets deteriorate and retail sales slow down, shopping center owners find it necessary to offer more generous tenant improvement allowances (TIs) to attract tenants. Usually TIs are at market, that is, the level that is typical in the area. In some markets, TIs vary by tenant classification, so there may be different TI allowances for new tenants and renewal tenants, or for new (never built out) space and used (previously built out) space. The dollar amount of TIs typically is far lower than for office space, because retail space is not extensively subdivided.

TIs represent an important capital demand consideration in department store leasing, particularly in forecasting re-leasing or in a case where a center has a "dark" anchor store. Department stores typically receive significant allowances. A national anchor tenant with high-end price points may receive an allowance in the $5 million to $10 million range, while a regional department store allowance is more likely to be in the $1.5 to $2 million range.

RATE COMPARISONS

The part of the analysis that drives value in retail property is the analysis of yield rates and capitalization rates compared with those of other property types. Therefore, rate analysis is significant in an appraisal.

Regional mall rates reflect generally constant investor demand for this property type due to its historically superior performance compared with other property types. To illustrate the movement of rates and the relative strength and weakness of retail properties compared with other property types, trends in free and clear equity IRRs and free and clear equity capitalization rates are presented in Table 20.1.

The rates shown are used in analyzing *institutional-grade* property in the following national markets: regional mall, strip shopping center, office, industrial, and multifamily. Institutional-grade real estate is defined as real property investments that are sought out by

TABLE 20.1

A. Average Free and Clear Equity IRRs[a]

		Regional Mall (%)	Strip Center (%)[b]	Office (%)	Industrial (%)	Multifamily (%)
1991	4Q	11.34	12.25	12.24	11.64	11.59
1992	1Q	11.38	12.18	12.33	11.71	11.63
	2Q	11.42	12.21	12.33	11.72	12.06
	3Q	11.42	12.36	12.26	11.72	11.94
	4Q	11.42	12.36	12.26	11.83	11.78
1993	1Q	11.47	12.36	12.28	11.83	11.72
	2Q	11.47	12.22	12.20	11.83	11.64
	3Q	11.65	12.16	12.45	11.88	11.43
	4Q	11.65	12.17	12.56	11.95	11.56
1994	1Q	11.65	12.17	12.53	11.82	11.68
	2Q	11.65	12.14	12.49[c]	11.70	11.57
	3Q	11.60	11.92	12.50	11.60	11.73
	4Q	11.60	11.97	12.37	11.44	11.70

B. Average Free and Clear Equity Cap Rates[d]

1991	4Q	7.41	9.54	8.75	9.25	9.06
1992	1Q	7.36	9.75	9.01	9.39	8.94
	2Q	7.45	9.86	9.08	9.44	9.13
	3Q	7.50	9.93	9.23	9.19	9.19
	4Q	7.52	9.98	9.25	9.22	9.05
1993	1Q	7.61	10.02	9.36	9.28	8.94
	2Q	7.64	9.97	9.52	9.31	8.98
	3Q	7.70	9.86	9.67	9.56	9.07
	4Q	7.70	9.86	9.77	9.55	9.04
1994	1Q	7.70	9.86	9.77	9.45	9.06
	2Q	7.70	9.85	9.73[c]	9.39	9.06
	3Q	7.73	9.79	9.60	9.35	8.88
	4Q	7.73	9.77	9.56	9.29	8.86

[a] Internal rate of return on equity, based on annual end-of-year compounding, unencumbered by financing (all cash).
[b] Neighborhood, power, or community center.
[c] In Second Quarter 1994, the national office market report in the Korpacz Survey was separated into two segments: the national CBD office market and the national suburban office market. Second, third, and fourth quarter 1994 rates in this table are national CBD office market rates.
[d] Initial cash-on-cash return on the equity investment unencumbered by financing (all cash, overall capitalization rate).

Source: Korpacz Real Estate Investor Survey, © 1994 Peter F. Korpacz & Associates, Inc.

institutional buyers and have the capacity to meet generally prevalent institutional investment criteria.[2]

Comparison of rate changes in retail markets shows that they are more frequent and often greater in the national strip shopping center market than in the national regional mall market. In the recent past, declines in both average IRRs and average equity capitalization rates coincide with the beginning of significant REIT acquisitions of strip shopping centers in 1993.

Both IRRs and equity cap rates reflect a premium for the added risk associated with strip shopping centers compared with regional malls. Among the risks are (1) weaker regional and local tenants, (2) the consequent greater vulnerability of this property type to downturns in the economy, and (3) difficulty in managing strip centers effectively and economically.

Property Reversion

An appropriate range of residual capitalization rates may be developed from examination of comparable properties and from in-house or published surveys of investors who buy similar properties. The rate applied for the subject property from within the developed range is based on analysis of demographic and economic trends in the trade area and the forecast performance of the subject. A sale price is usually estimated by capitalizing the forecast NOI in the year following the forecast period, year 11, in the case of a 10-year projection. An allowance for selling expense expressed as a percent of the residual sale price is deducted.

Discount Rate

In developing the discount rate or IRR, an appropriate range of discount rates may be developed from examination of comparable properties and surveys of investors who buy similar properties. The rate applied for the subject property from within or, on occasion, outside the developed range is based on analysis of its competitive position.

A complete discounted cash flow analysis for a regional mall is shown in Table 20.2 on pp. 438–439.

Direct Capitalization Method

In the direct capitalization method, net operating income is converted into value through application of an overall capitalization rate derived from comparable sales and other market evidence and used as a divisor. While the typical buyer reviews and analyzes historical revenue and expense information, the major focus is on the future and, in particular, the first year of ownership.

Overall Capitalization Rate Selection

The overall capitalization rate (OAR) expresses the relationship between the forecast first-year NOI and the sale price. In all-cash or nearly all-cash transactions, NOI and pretax cash flow are identical and the OAR and the cash-on-cash rate are the same. The rates derived from comparables sales reflect the buyer's anticipation of increase, stability, or decline in annual income, and the expectation of appreciation or depreciation of the original investment over the ownership period.

Comparable sales and other market evidence, such as investor surveys, are used to develop a range of overall rates. Sales at the low end of the range reflect investment in properties that are expected to provide above-average growth of annual cash flow, near-term refinancing benefits, or unusually good prospects for continuing above-average growth. Sales at the high end of the range reflect investment in properties that are not expected to provide significant income growth increases or value appreciation in the near future. The subject's income growth and value appreciation potential suggest the appropriate rate from within the range.

COST APPROACH

The inherent difficulty in estimating the value of land under existing retail centers, particularly malls, is a strong reason not to use the cost approach in the valuation of retail properties. The most common approach for estimating land value, sales comparison, and the allocation and extraction procedures, are seldom applicable due to the lack of comparable sales.

Typically, a major retail center site is an assemblage of parcels of raw land purchased from 5 to 10 years in advance of development. Before construction begins, the developer must obtain commercial zoning and other approvals, improve the land to ready it for use, and contract with key tenants. If a land sale were to occur at this point, the price would be considerably higher than the developer's original price. Such a sale, however, is extremely infrequent, and the search for comparable sales is limited to the rare sites that may be close to their ultimate use for a regional mall.

TABLE 20.2

Fiscal Year Cash Flow Forecast
Regional Mall

Years Ending April 30th	1996	1997	1998	1999	2000
Revenue:					
Minimum rent	$6,396,325	$ 6,872,152	$ 7,112,911	$ 7,190,896	$ 7,488,954
CAM	1,777,614	1,991,473	2,123,621	2,178,642	2,360,079
Percentage rent	370,776	373,744	405,083	403,873	380,421
Temporary tenants	300,000	302,500	310,063	317,814	325,759
Property taxes	320,219	358,960	383,882	397,389	425,812
Insurance	165,377	185,440	199,100	205,859	221,693
Sprinkler	23,338	23,574	22,306	22,052	21,614
Other recoveries	11,157	10,265	10,021	9,870	6,627
Service charges	10,133	10,539	10,960	11,399	11,855
Other revenue	7,093	7,377	7,672	7,979	8,298
Total revenue	$9,382,032	$10,136,024	$10,585,619	$10,745,773	$11,251,112
Less: vacancy	271,943	294,468	307,708	312,258	327,156
Effective Gross Revenue	$9,110,089	$ 9,841,556	$10,277,911	$10,433,515	$10,923,956
Effective occupancy (%)**	88.48	93.80	96.41	95.82	93.84
Property Expenses:					
Real estate taxes	$ 255,202	$ 265,410	$ 276,026	$ 287,067	$ 298,550
Operating expenses	891,733	927,403	964,499	1,003,079	1,043,202
Insurance	109,440	113,818	118,370	123,105	128,029
Professional fees	76,000	79,040	82,202	85,490	88,909
Advertising & promotion	70,933	73,771	76,721	79,790	82,982
Management	250,526	270,642	282,642	286,922	300,409
Replacement reserve	413,417	429,954	447,152	465,038	483,640
Total Property Expense	$2,067,251	$ 2,160,038	$ 2,247,612	$ 2,330,491	$ 2,425,721
Net Operating Income	$7,042,838	$ 7,681,518	$ 8,030,299	$ 8,103,024	$ 8,498,235
NOI per sq. ft.	17.47	19.05	19.92	20.10	21.08
Cash on cash rate (%)	8.19	8.93	9.34	9.42	9.88
Other Deductions:					
Leasing commissions	71,477	101,077	22,179	52,360	135,567
Capital improvements	0	0	0	0	2,500,000
Tenant improvements	156,839	236,971	78,458	183,521	490,646
Total Deductions	$ 228,316	$ 338,048	$ 100,637	$ 235,881	$ 3,126,213
Cash from Operations	$6,814,522	$ 7,343,470	$ 7,929,662	$ 7,867,143	$ 5,372,022
Equity Reversion:					
Overall capitalization rate					
Sale price					
Selling expenses @ 1.50%					
Net Equity Reversion					
Present Values:					
Present value factor					
@ 12.00%	0.892857	0.797194	0.711780	0.635518	0.567427
Equity cash flow	$6,814,522	$ 7,343,470	$ 7,929,662	$ 7,867,143	$ 5,372,022
Present value	6,084,395	5,854,169	5,644,177	4,999,712	3,048,230
Cumulative Present Value	6,084,395	11,938,564	17,582,741	22,582,452	25,630,682
Equity Reversion					
Present Value					
Total Equity Value					
Rounded at (Say)					

* For calculation of sale price in 2002 only.
** Excludes department stores

2001	2002	2003	2004	2005	2006*
$ 8,005,688	$ 8,226,668	$ 8,414,200	$ 8,422,320	$ 8,797,704	$ 9,000,844
2,566,217	2,687,419	2,800,993	2,867,231	3,055,656	3,202,663
382,956	446,053	555,702	664,056	717,244	847,111
335,559	348,981	362,941	377,458	392,557	408,259
456,784	482,328	505,194	520,535	551,762	571,218
240,744	254,924	266,249	272,520	289,841	302,167
19,245	16,360	14,342	13,478	11,580	10,213
5,067	3,683	2,707	1,256	587	397
12,329	12,822	13,335	13,868	14,423	15,000
8,630	8,975	9,334	9,708	10,096	10,500
$12,033,219	$12,488,213	$12,944,997	$13,162,430	$ 13,841,450	$14,368,372
350,301	363,523	376,782	382,841	402,731	418,039
$11,682,918	$12,124,690	$12,568,215	$12,779,589	$ 13,438,719	$13,950,333
94.36	96.13	96.45	95.89	95.01	95.00
$ 310,492	$ 322,912	$ 335,828	$ 349,261	$ 363,232	$ 377,761
1,084,930	1,128,327	1,173,460	1,220,398	1,269,214	1,319,983
133,150	138,476	144,016	149,776	155,767	161,998
92,466	96,164	100,011	104,011	108,172	112,499
86,301	89,753	93,343	97,077	100,960	104,999
321,281	333,429	345,627	351,439	369,566	383,634
502,985	523,105	544,029	565,790	588,421	611,958
$ 2,531,605	$ 2,632,166	$ 2,736,314	$ 2,837,752	2,955,332	$ 3,072,832
$ 9,151,313	$ 9,492,524	$ 9,831,901	$ 9,941,837	$ 10,483,387	$10,877,501
22.70	23.54	24.38	24.66	26.00	26.98
10.64	11.04	11.43	11.56	12.19	12.65
85,306	45,471	15,140	30,312	82,405	
0	0	0	0	0	
213,409	162,421	48,935	100,160	251,079	
$ 298,715	$ 207,892	64,075	$ 130,472	$ 333,484	
$ 8,852,598	$ 9,284,632	$ 9,767,826	$ 9,811,365	$ 10,149,903	
				8.50%	
				$127,970,600	
				1,919,559	
				$126,051,041	
0.506631	0.452349	0.403883	0.360610	0.321973	% of
$ 8,852,598	$ 9,284,632	$ 9,767,826	$ 9,811,365	$ 10,149,903	Total
4,485,002	4,199,896	3,945,061	3,538,077	3,267,997	
30,115,684	34,315,580	38,260,641	41,798,717	45,066,714	52.62
				$126,051,041	
				40,585,062	47.38
				$ 85,651,776	100.00
				86,000,000	

Land residual techniques often are most appropriate for valuing the land component. Using the stabilized annual NOI estimate, the appraiser calculates how much of the income is attributable to the improvements and subtracts this amount from the total NOI. The remainder is the residual income to the land, which is capitalized at a market-derived capitalization rate to provide an estimate of land value. Alternatively, the appraiser may value the property as improved and deduct the cost of the improvements and any profit. The remainder is the residual value of the land.[3]

SALES COMPARISON APPROACH

The units of comparison most often analyzed in application of the sales comparison approach to value retail properties are the price per square foot of GLA and the effective gross revenue multiplier. The latter is used for properties that are at stabilized occupancy on the date of value. Another technique that has recently surfaced with support from some investors involves the analysis of the relationship of retail sales to price. The formula of price divided by retail sales achievable at the property is applied to the comparable sales and the results are compared to the subject with appropriate consideration of the property's physical attributes, reimbursable expenses, operating cost ratio, and its competitive position.

A major factor in deciding where a center places within the range of comparable sales is the inclusion of anchors in the sale. Usually most of the anchors are included in sales at the low end; none are included at the high end. Because department stores generate low rents compared with in-line mall stores, their inclusion in the sale greatly affects the price per square foot.

Statistical analysis of comparable sales often shows high correlation between NOI per square foot and sale price per square foot. Typically, the higher the NOI per square foot of GLA, the higher the sale price per square foot.

DISTINCTIVE ASPECTS OF REGIONAL MALL AND LARGE RETAIL PROPERTY APPRAISALS

Appreciation

The growth potential of a regional mall is a function of estimated annual increases in income as well as an estimated price for a hypothetical sale at the end of a holding period. The sale price is usually based on the income for the year following the last year of the holding period, that is, the 11th year if the holding period is 10 years as is typical in the current investment marketplace. Depending on the volatility of the individual factors in the analysis, the appraiser may develop a residual value estimate using a holding period either longer or shorter than 10 years. Alternatively, multiple holding periods may be analyzed.

The difference between the initial capitalization and discount rates is an indication of the growth potential of the investment. A significant difference indicates greater growth potential.

The residual capitalization rate is derived from market evidence illustrated in sales of comparable properties and the rates applied by investors in similar properties. The residual capitalization rate should reasonably be expected to be higher than the going-in rate which represents the anticipated value of future returns and the risk involved in holding the investment for a number of years. Occasionally, there are circumstances that require a rate equal to or less than the going-in rate.

Estimating the Value of Contiguous Excess Land

Developers of regional malls often purchase more acreage than needed for a shopping center to allow for future expansion. Especially in trade areas that demonstrate substantial growth potential, a judicious developer will acquire excess land at the predevelopment price to provide for additional facilities at a later date, such as fast food restaurants, gas stations, and branch banks. Consequently, a regional mall appraisal may include valuation of contiguous excess land, either for establishing an asking price for an anticipated sale of the mall or the land parcel. When the land is to be sold, the appraiser generally includes an analysis to determine the most probable use of the land, identification of a most probable buyer, and most probable price.

APPRAISING COMPONENTS OF RETAIL PROPERTIES

The value of a component of a shopping center—for example, an anchor pad, department store, or in-line mall store—is based on the income generated by the component. Mall stores usually generate the greatest portion of total center income and anchor pads the least.

When valuation of the component is part of a full shopping center appraisal, income may be divided into pro rata shares for the components and valued on that basis.

The market rent study for department stores is based on analysis of comparable rentals as well as research instruments such as surveys and interviews. Typically, department stores at the low end of the rental range are national chains and stores at the high end of the range are regional or local. To develop a range of estimated market rent for a department store, the appraiser estimates a level of retail sales for the typical department store that could be attracted to the site; estimates a reasonable range of occupancy cost for a department store at the site; and allocates the estimated occupancy cost to minimum rent, percentage rent, and CAM.

NEIGHBORHOOD AND COMMUNITY CENTER APPRAISALS

As a property type, neighborhood and community centers are more susceptible to overbuilding. This is due in part to new construction following population shifts. In addition, their tenancy makes them more vulnerable than other types of shopping centers to fluctuations in economic conditions. Downswings in the economy can cause rapid increases in vacancies, which tend to be relatively long lasting. Consequently, appraisers tend to consider primarily income from tenants in place. In an overbuilt market, they do not allow for rent that is contingent on leasing vacant space.

In neighborhood and community centers, the only national credit tenants are likely to be the anchors, and in-line store tenants tend to be regional or local businesses. Supermarket anchor leases generally provide for base plus percentage rent. However, most other tenants pay fixed rents with periodic increases that may be fixed amounts or tied to the CPI. Leases tend to be shorter term than in other retail centers.

FREESTANDING AND NET LEASE APPRAISALS

The market value of freestanding net leased retail properties is a direct corollary of the creditworthiness of the tenant in place. Freestanding net lease retail uses represent a wide range that encompasses department store anchors in regional malls, supermarket, or drug store anchors in strip centers, single-tenant power centers, and service businesses such as banks and restaurants on outparcels. The owner's risk increases in direct relationship to the tenant's credit standing, with local businesses often representing the highest risk.

The single tenant's lease may provide for base rent that is below market and when the lease includes percentage rent, the breakpoint may be higher than the market standard for the amount of retail sales the tenant is expected to achieve. This is a result of the advantages to the landlord of a long-term commitment and factors such as the additional diversity, product, or service that they bring to an adjacent shopping center or cluster of freestanding stores.

Unlike shopping centers where the number and mix of tenants spread the income risk, the focus on a single tenant's ability to pay rent is critical in the valuation of these properties. Hence, the level of analysis of the quality, quantity, and durability of the income stream may be greater to assess the potential additional risk. Freestanding net lease retail properties are bought and sold on the credit of the tenant, a factor in the rates applied by the appraiser to the tenant's income stream.

CURRENT ISSUES

Business Enterprise Value

A matter of substantial debate related to the appraisal of regional malls is the possible existence of business enterprise value and the increment, if any, that it might add to real property value. Business enterprise value is broadly defined as "intangible asset value that is not attributable to the site and structure."[4] The intangibles referred to include business organization, management, workforce, skills, working capital, and legal rights such as trade names, franchises, patents, trademarks, contracts, leases, and operating agreements.[5] Business enterprise value theorists contend that the value of these intangibles is embodied in entrepreneurship, which implies a measurable and transferable differential between market value with normal management and market value with superlative management.[6]

Management is the crux of most of the current research exploring business enterprise value in regional malls. Some researchers cite the acceptance of business value in management-intensive properties such as hotels and nursing homes and extend it to relate to regional malls. This is considered a highly subjective concept, and there is no consensus that the degree of management required for regional malls is in itself evidence of superlative, or supernormal, management. It may be simply the typical level of management defined by the market for this property type.[7] Although business expertise and management skills are required in the operation of a shopping center, this requirement applies to any large income-producing property. Certainly the financial institutions that became office building owners through the widespread foreclosures of the late 1980s and early 1990s would acknowledge that the owner must be able to "work the property."

Measuring business enterprise value is beyond the scope of this chapter. However, theorists who contend that a sale price of a mall in excess of market value through the cost approach supports the notion of business enterprise value, suggest that an appropriate measure of business enterprise value is the excess value over depreciated cost new. Their reliance on the use of the cost approach presents significant difficulty in acceptance of the concept in the marketplace, since the cost approach is seldom applicable in valuation of regional malls.

A particularly contentious point in the controversy surrounding business enterprise value as separate and distinct from real property value in regional malls is the fact that attempts to apply it have been confined primarily to appealing real estate tax assessments on mall properties. In real estate tax matters, the conclusive opinion depends on the local jurisdiction, and business enterprise value may be separated from real estate value for assessment purposes. However, the concept has not been accepted in the transaction marketplace. Mall businesses have not been sold, exchanged, or valued outside of tax appeal assignments. Typical regional mall investors— the presumed prudent buyers and sellers in the hypothetical sale of the market value definition—do not buy on the basis of business enterprise value.

Functional and Economic Obsolescence

Shopping centers experience a very high rate of obsolescence. Although appraisers may rate the construction quality of a shopping center "superior," "average," or "below average," superior construction is not necessarily a particularly critical component of a shopping center's value. It is not even always a determining factor in the equation. The most significant aspect of regional mall construction is that the design and quality be suitable for the market—that is, appealing to the customers who are the ultimate dictators of the center's success. Remodeling is a frequent and continual fact of shopping center life.

Rapidly emerging innovations in retailing cause functional obsolescence in shopping centers long before they deteriorate physically. For example, the emphasis in the early 1990s on cost cutting and efficiency in manufacturing, retailing, and distribution favors methods such as just-in-time inventory management. Daily analysis of point-of-purchase information makes it possible to have exactly the required merchandise at the correct store in a matter of days. Such operational efficiencies have changed the optimum size and depth of stores. The amount of required storage space has diminished, and selling space has increased even as store depth and total area have been reduced.

The difficulty of putting a dollar value on the many and varied exhibitions of obsolescence in shopping centers is another argument against using the cost approach in their valuation.

The Relationship of Equity Value after Debt to Market Value

In a financial environment in which interest rates are low and the availability of credit is limited, buyers who have access to credit may have an advantage in a tight bidding situation.[8] With cheap money available to a select few, potential buyers can finance a portion of the sale price, offer slightly more for a property than the all-cash buyer, and win the bid. The effect of leverage on market value in such a situation can be controversial because of varied definitions and interpretations of market value.

Even in a case in which a leveraged purchase is at the same price as an all-cash price, the equity yield will be higher than in an all-cash transaction if the interest rate on the mortgage is less than the property IRR. The effect is positive leverage. If the interest rate on the mortgage is higher than the property IRR, negative leverage occurs and the equity IRR will be lower. The ability to bring positive leverage to the negotiation permits a potential buyer to raise the offer somewhat, still getting a better yield than the indicated property yield and, most importantly, to successfully outbid the all-cash competition.

When confronted with similarly financed competition for a deal, most leverage buyers are willing to bid up the price above the all-cash price because (1) they can increase their equity IRR above the property IRR and thus do better than in an all-cash deal, and (2) they perceive only minimal additional risk, assuming that the leverage is only 50%+/−. In effect, they can "afford" to win the purchase.

Some appraisers might protest that the higher price paid by the leverage buyer does not represent market value. If, for example, a leverage buyer is successful at a purchase price of $18.5 million, and the highest bid from an all-cash buyer was $17.6, which should be the appraised value of the property? Is it $17.6 million or $18.5 million? Should the sales financed at market terms with slightly higher prices prevail, or should the all-cash pricing assumptions set market value?

Usual market value definitions provide for the payment assumption to be cash or in "terms of financial arrangements comparable thereto."[9] If the sellers in the leveraged transactions receive cash and the financing is at market terms, such leveraged transactions qualify without adjustment for financing as evidence of market value.

The appraisal decision as to which sales to rely on most heavily should rest on the most likely purchaser of the property and the most likely purchase terms (all-cash or financed at market terms). On that basis, in the example above, a market value estimate of $18.6 million is valid. Alternatively, the appraiser could value the property on both an all-cash and leveraged basis and report both values in the appraisal report. Depending on the nature of the assignment, this could be useful to the client.

The economics at work in a distressed market affect the valuation of an income-producing property. Assumptions related to income, absorption, and vacancy (including months vacant, tenant retention percentage, and underlying vacancy and credit loss) in the cash flow forecast analysis indicate the level and anticipated duration of the overbuilt conditions. Appropriate discount and capitalization rates are likely to be relatively high, reflecting the added risk of investing in overbuilt markets.

If all available comparable sales, which are used to derive discount and capitalization rates, are distressed sales (sales involving a seller acting under duress), can they be used for indications of market value, or are they only indicative of liquidation value? The market value of a distressed property is negatively impacted by the vacancy level. However, if the vacancies are due to conditions that could be remedied—for example, by improved management, more effective marketing, or refurbishment—the negative effect on value may not be substantial.

While some theorists suggest that different valuation models are required for appraising in distressed markets, the key to a credible appraisal in overbuilt markets is no different from appraising in balanced markets. Thorough and meticulous analyses of property and market conditions will furnish the appropriate data to develop a value estimate. The numbers and rates will differ from those obtained from a balanced market, but the methods and techniques of the appraisal need not.

Concurrence in Current Value Appraisals

Concurrence is a method in which the in-house staff of a publicly traded real estate development company performs a current value appraisal, which is reviewed by an outside appraiser and an outside auditor and on which they approve and express agreement with the staff's valuation processes and conclusions. The value estimate, which is an aggregate estimate of the company's real property, is reported on the company's balance sheet as part of the annual report.

The purpose of concurrence is to provide shareholders with a better understanding of the intrinsic value of the company's real estate assets than is evident from either an analysis of the profit and loss statement or the traditional balance sheet. Although land and construction in progress are included "at cost" in the traditional balance sheet, the book values of the completed projects do not include appreciation in value due to entrepreneurial efforts, inflation, and management achievements in the operating properties. The investing public may not fully comprehend the intrinsic strength of a company's real estate operations.

Concurrence was developed in the mid-1970s by Landauer Associates, a real estate consulting firm, with a shopping center-owner-developer client that engaged in a high rate of development activity annually, held land for future development, and owned and managed completed projects built by the company. Current value is a term created by the accounting profession. Its definition stems from a 1984 AICPA study and mirrors the Appraisal Institute definition of market value. The SEC approved the concurrence method in principle, although they had previously prohibited the inclusion of current value estimate in any annual report submitted to public shareholders.

In the concurrence method, the outside appraisal firm reviews the client's annual in-house appraisal and provides a letter of concurrence, affirming that the owner's aggregate current (market) value of the completed projects estimated is within 10% of the aggregate value the appraisal firm might estimate in a full and complete appraisal of the individual properties. The appraisals of the properties must follow an approved valuation process using acceptable appraisal methodology. All revenue forecasts are to be based on, and consistent with, current market studies performed by the owner's experts in that field.

Further, the appraisal firm has the right, after review of the value estimates, to return individual property appraisals for discussion, modification, or revision in instances in which the values appear to be out of line with the market. Although the aggregate value is the primary issue, the appraisal firm would likely question individual values that are at significant variance with its professional judgment.

A 10% variance is a generally-accepted standard used by review appraisers in the industry. A review appraiser will generally approve an appraisal that is within 10% of the reviewer's own opinion of value. An additional theory of the concurrence method is that in the aggregate value of multiple properties, plus and minus variances tend to average out and produce an aggregate variance within the 10% standard. As a precaution, however, the reviewing firm must be careful to make sure the pattern of variances is neither consistently high or consistently low, to assure that the aggregate value is well within the certified aggregate margin.

It is essential that the auditor be totally involved in the process and participate in the property inspections and in the reviews of the client's value estimates. The appraisal firm needs to be made aware of the accounting profession rules on the use of outside experts since a significant function of the concurrence letter is to give support to the auditor, who ultimately must certify the financial content of the annual report.

Are Shopping Centers Fairly Appraised?

The "fairness" with which shopping centers, like other property types, are appraised is a corollary of the capability of the appraiser. Special knowledge, skills, and experience are involved in appraising shopping centers. Among other capabilities, the shopping center appraiser needs proficiency in interpreting particular demographic indicators as well as a relatively thorough familiarity with the retail industry.

As well as keeping abreast of the real estate industry, the shopping center appraiser needs to be aware of advances and trends in the highly dynamic retail industry. New retailing formats and retailers emerge in response to a continuously evolving retail environment and changing customer preferences. The regularly changing tenant mix in a shopping center presents a challenge in identifying appropriate inputs for the analyses in the appraisal.

The major stipulation in obtaining a fair appraisal is awareness on the part of the client of the particular competencies required to complete a valid retail property appraisal. As with any appraisal of any property type, the buyer's risk for the quality of the product may be more or less, depending on the appraiser selection decision.

ENDNOTES

1. Appraisal Institute, *The Appraisal of Real Estate*, 10th ed. (Chicago: Appraisal Institute, 1992), p. 20. This definition of market value is widely accepted. Other similar definitions may be required in particular legal jurisdictions or by individual clients. Appraisals for financial institutions subject to the provisions of the Financial Institutions Reform, Recovery and Enforcement Act of 1989 (FIRREA) are required to use the market value definition specified in the Act.

2. Peter F. Korpacz and Karla L. Heuer, "Institutional-Grade Real Estate," *The Appraisal Journal*, vol. LXII, no. 4 (October 1994): 618.

3. Appraisal Institute, *The Appraisal of Real Estate*, pp. 307–308.

4. Mark J. Eppli and John D. Benjamin, "The Evolution of Shopping Center Research: A Review and Analysis," *The Journal of Real Estate Research*, vol. 9, no. 1 (Winter 1994): 21.

5. Jeffrey D. Fisher and William N. Kinnard, Jr., "The Business Enterprise Value Compoennt of Operating Properties: The Example of Shopping Malls," *Journal of Property Taxation*, vol. 2, no. 1 (1990).

6. Appraisal Institute, Memorandum to Appraisal Standards Council of the Appraisal Institute from Subcommittee Studying Business Enterprise Value, July 13, 1994, p. 2.

7. *Ibid.*, p. 5.

8. "Leverage, Price, and Market Value," *Korpacz Real Estate Investor Survey*, vol. 6, no. 4 (1993): 5–8.

9. Uniform Standards of Professional Appraisal Practice (USPAP), Appraisal Foundation, Appraisal Standards Board, 1992 edition.

Twenty-One

Accounting Aspects of Retail Properties

Richard W. Lowe

Although some principles and applications of principles have been developed which are relatively unique to retail properties, they are based on the underlying premises of the accounting model. Accordingly, many accounting concepts have a broad application beyond retail real estate.

GENERALLY ACCEPTED ACCOUNTING PRINCIPLES

"The term generally accepted accounting principles is a technical accounting term that encompasses the conventions, rules and procedures necessary to define accepted accounting practice at a particular time."[1] It is important to understand that GAAPs are evolutionary in nature. Therefore, the principles and procedures that constitute GAAP will not always be the same as they are today and changes, sometimes radical changes, can be expected to occur. At any time, those charged with the responsibility for promulgating accounting standards are considering numerous changes in existing standards, establishment of new standards, or interpretations to clarify existing standards.

450

Accounting standards are generally promulgated within the private sector in the United States. Although the U.S. Securities and Exchange Commission has the authority to set accounting standards for publicly held companies, it very rarely has exercised its authority to do so. The SEC has, however, established extensive rules and regulations governing financial statement and other financial matters disclosures for such companies. Within the private sector, accounting standards are set by the Financial Accounting Standards Board, the American Institute of Certified Public Accountants and, for state and local government entities, the Governmental Accounting Standards Board. Pronouncements of the standard setters may be very broad in scope or of limited application. Although the collective body of literature is very extensive and voluminous, the diversity and complexity of American business makes it impossible for every situation to be covered by official and unofficial pronouncements, either directly or by analogy. In the absence of any such guidance, accountants rely on guidance contained in other literature, such as accounting textbooks or handbooks and published articles or on customary practices relevant to specific industries or forms of doing business.

Notwithstanding the large volume of accounting literature, preparers of financial statements need to deal with numerous decisions and judgments. In many cases, alternative accounting principles or methods of applying them exist and many aspects of accounting involve judgments and estimates relating to future economic consequences of current business decisions. Consequently, accounting is more of an art than a science. Financial statements, which can be viewed as one end product of accounting, do not attempt to provide the "correct answers" in the sense that $2 + 2$ will always equal 4. The objective of financial statements is to fairly present the financial position, results of operations and cash flows of the reporting entity within the context of GAAP.

Underlying basic accounting concepts exert a powerful influence on financial reporting because they affect what is considered to be "fair" within the context of GAAP. A fundamental concept of conservatism is always a principal consideration. This concept causes reporting entities to use a historical cost accounting model under which all probable losses are recognized currently and no gains are recognized until realized in the form of cash or other assets whose value is determinable and realizable. The application of this concept is illustrated by a situation where the reporting entity has entered into a firm contract to sell a real estate project at a future date. To the extent that the sale will result in a loss to the seller, the loss is immediately recognized, whereas, if there will be a gain, the gain is not recognizable until the sale is consummated, which is unlikely to be prior to the date of closing.[2]

Another fundamental concept is that transactions are accounted for based on their economic substance as compared with their legal form. At times, this concept is particularly difficult to apply in practice and a considerable portion of the body of accounting literature ultimately deals with this issue.

An illustration of this is the issue of whether a legal sale of a retail property is, in substance, merely a deposit because the seller economically retains substantially all of the risk of future losses. For instance, if a buyer purchased undeveloped land for an insignificant down payment and gave the seller a nonrecourse mortgage note for the balance of the sales price, with interest and principal payments to be deferred until the occurrence of a future event, the seller would be required to account for the cash received as a deposit. The seller would continue to account for the real estate as if it continued to legally own it until such time as it disposed of the purchase money mortgage note, the future event had occurred, or sufficient payments by the buyer on the mortgage note had been received to demonstrate the buyer's commitment.[3] Outside of the United States, accounting principles used in various countries are promulgated in manners similar to the United States, prescribed by governmental bodies (sometimes referred to as statutory accounting) or a combination of the two. As a result, accounting standards vary considerably among countries, both in respect to the accounting methods used and in the nature and extent of financial statement disclosures. The need for a higher degree of standardization in what is quickly becoming a global economy is being addressed by a continuing series of accounting standards promulgated by the International Accounting Standards Committee. Adoption of these standards is, however, entirely voluntary. In the United States, the IASC standards are not considered to be GAAP. Financial standards which have been prepared based on these standards are considered to be prepared under an "Other Comprehensive Basis of Accounting."

Accounting and financial reporting is a very technical and complex function in the modern business world. Appropriately educated and trained accountants, be they internal or external, are essential to the management of an enterprise. This is true not only in respect of "keeping score" and communicating with parties in interest through financial statements, but also in assisting management in understanding the financial reporting consequences of proposed transactions and assisting in structuring the transactions so as to avoid unintended financial reporting consequences.

ACCOUNTING MODELS

In the United States, there are two accounting models that are considered to be in accordance with GAAP. These two models are, however, not interchangeable as only one of them would be GAAP in a particular situation. The most common model is the historical cost model (sometimes referred to as the accrual method) which is applicable to all business enterprises, except for those using special accounting principles. These include entities who hold securities as their principal assets, entities in voluntary or involuntary liquidation and employee benefit plans, or entities owned principally by such plans. Accordingly, real estate enterprises that are not in liquidation are required to use the historical cost model, except for real estate funds, partnerships, and so on, whose principal owners are private employee benefit plans. These entities are required to use the current value model as GAAP. Substantially all authoritative accounting literature deals principally with the historical cost model.

The fundamental difference between the historical cost model and the current value model is that the current value model permits assets owned by an entity to be "written up" to amounts above their historical cost in order to reflect their current values. The historical cost model contemplates the possibility of writing down the historical cost of owned assets but does not permit write-ups, irrespective of the degree of evidence that an asset has appreciated in value.

The historical cost model has certain limiting characteristics that are particularly important for those real estate entities who are required to use it. One of these limitations is that while the value of a property may be clearly increasing, absent any property additions, the financial statements will be portraying a declining asset carrying amount as a result of the requirement to depreciate the improvements over their estimated useful lives. Another result of depreciation is that a nonrecourse financing or refinancing of appreciated real estate may result in reporting a negative owner's equity in the property because the carrying amount of the debt exceeds the depreciated carrying amount of the property. Management intentions with respect to a property have an influence on the maximum allowable carrying amount of a property for financial reporting purposes under the historical cost model. This occurs because different accounting standards may apply. For example, a developer simultaneously builds two adjacent strip centers whose current appraised values are exactly the same. The historical cost of each of the properties is identical and is greater than its current appraised value. The developer intends to sell one strip center over the coming year and intends to (and has the financial ability to) hold the other strip center as a long-term asset. The historical cost carrying amount of the strip center held for sale must be written down to its net realizable value (expected sales proceeds less the cost to dispose of the strip center and the estimated net cost, if any, to hold the strip center until the estimated sale date). The strip center to be held as an investment would continue to be carried at its historical cost, provided that such carrying amount is not permanently impaired.

One method used by the management of some real estate enterprises to overcome these limitations is to provide current value financial statements as a supplement to the primary historical cost model financial statements. While this usually entails incurring significant additional costs, it has the advantage of informing the user of the financial statements as to what the enterprise's management (and possibly outside real estate professionals) think the net equity value of the enterprise's real estate holdings really is.

Some real estate enterprises who are required to use the historical cost model by GAAP, but are not publicly held companies, hold the view that historical cost model financial statements are not meaningful to their investors. These enterprises may prepare financial statements on a basis of accounting which is not GAAP but is considered to be an other comprehensive basis of accounting or OCBOA. An OCBOA must be a comprehensive set of principles that is applied to all significant items in the financial statements and cannot represent a mixture of what a preparer thinks are the "best" principles for each financial statement item.

The most common OCBOA in use is the federal income tax basis of accounting. This is commonly used by privately owned partnerships and has the advantage of presenting financial statements which can be directly related to the partnership's federal income tax information return. This reporting method eliminates the confusion among investors which may result from them receiving two sets of very different numbers since there are often major differences from GAAP and income tax reporting. The disadvantage is that the accounting must conform with the provisions of the Internal Revenue Code and the intricate and voluminous regulations promulgated by the Department of the Treasury under that Code. Also, this financial statement presentation does nothing to inform the reader as to the value of the properties owned.

Other types of OCBOAs include the cash receipts and cash disbursements method (usually modified so as to record depreciation and/or accrual of income tax liabilities), the use of International Accounting Standards and financial reporting on a basis of accounting used by the entity to comply with reporting provisions of a governmental regulatory agency to whose jurisdiction the entity is subject, such as the Department of Housing and Urban Development.[4]

There is some debate among professional accountants as to whether the current value model can be considered to be an OCBOA for an enterprise for which the historical cost model is GAAP. Most of them, however, agree that since the current value model is GAAP for certain entities, it can never be an OCBOA, by definition.

ACQUISITION ACCOUNTING

There are two ways to acquire retail properties. The first is to acquire a finished project which is ready for occupancy or is already occupied and the second is to develop and construct the project. The basic accounting principles relating to acquisition are that all costs relating to acquisition are considered to be assets (i.e., capitalized) and no gain or loss is recognized upon acquisition. This applies under either of the two accounting models.

When a turnkey project is acquired, the costs of acquisition include the purchase price and all other costs incurred by the buyer, such as brokerage commissions, title insurance, real estate transfer taxes, costs of acquisition due diligence, legal fees, and so on. Closing prorations, such as those for real estate taxes, unpaid rent, etc., are recorded by the purchaser as various prepaid assets, accounts payable, or accrued liabilities.

When the seller, as a part of the settlement of the purchase price, accepts a non-recourse mortgage note at a below market interest rate, the recorded purchase price is adjusted downward to reflect the equivalent of an all cash transaction. This is accomplished by discounting the required mortgage principal and interest payments to their present value at the current market rate for mortgage notes with similar characteristics. The resulting debt discount is amortized over the term of the mortgage on the interest method. The interest method amortizes debt discount over the life of the mortgage note in "such a way as to result in a constant rate of interest when applied to the amount outstanding at the beginning of any given accounting period."[5]

The costs associated with originating a third party mortgage note in connection with the acquisition of the project, such as legal fees, are capitalized as a separate asset and are amortized over the term of the note, generally using the straight-line method. The straight-line method apportions expense ratably over each accounting period (i.e., monthly, quarterly, or annually).

At acquisition, it is important to determine the amount of the acquisition cost which is to be assigned to land and the amounts to be assigned to the improvements and other assets such as personal property, if significant. Land will not be subject to depreciation under the historical cost model or for income tax purposes. Personal property is depreciated more quickly for accounting purposes and income tax purposes than are improvements. To the extent that the current value model is applicable, it is still desirable for this allocation to be made inasmuch as there may come a time when the land or improvements, but not both, are sold. At that time, a determination of the amount of realized gain will need to be made that will require a determination of the historical cost basis for the land and improvements. Personal property is usually not separately valued during the process of arriving at current values and is accounted for at depreciated historical cost.

The two most common methods of allocation between land and building are basing the allocation on appraisal amounts and basing the allocation on assessed valuations for ad valorem tax purposes. An appraisal performed in connection with the purchaser's due diligence should be requested to include a separate value for the land. Since the total cost of acquisition will normally exceed the appraised value due to brokerage commissions and other closing costs, the total acquisition costs are allocated to land in the same proportion that the land value appraisal bears to the total appraised value. The assessed value method is applied in the same manner, but can only be used if the taxing authority separately assesses land. Where personal property is significant, the seller's historical carrying amount or a separate value estimate should be deducted from acquisition costs in making the land/building allocation. Other methods of allocation, such as rules of thumb and allocation percentages applicable to other properties acquired in the past, are also used but, for taxable owners, this results in a higher level of risk of challenge from income tax examiners as to the amount of depreciation claimed on the entity's tax returns.

When a retail property is constructed, costs to be capitalized include the cost of land acquisition, all direct construction costs and certain indirect construction costs. Land acquisition costs include the same types of costs as those applicable to turn key projects. They also may include costs incurred to effect zoning changes and those relating to the process of determining the suitability of the land for the intended construction.

Many of the costs relating to land acquisition are incurred during the period in which the potential purchaser holds an option to acquire the land and is completing its evaluation of suitability. The price paid to acquire the option is recorded as an asset. Other costs are also classified as an asset, typically called pre-development costs. To the extent that the option is exercised, such costs and the option cost are reclassified to the land account. If the option is not exercised, these costs are written off. In some cases, options may be obtained on multiple land parcels while the developer determines which one is the most suitable for development. Only those costs that relate to the parcel actually acquired are eligible to be transferred to the land account and the costs relating to the other parcels are required to be written off.

The land acquisition process may add value to the land in excess of total costs incurred. In theory, entities who are required to use the current value model would recognize that increment, however, in practice such recognition is rare if construction is contemplated by the owner. This is because the incremental value is usually not significant in relation to the ultimate costs of building a retail facility and because the risks inherent in the construction process suggest that recognition of the incremental value is premature. Costs incurred to hold the acquired land prior to commencement of physical construction are generally capitalizable to the land account or to another asset account typically called construction-in-progress, provided that "activities necessary to get the property ready for its intended use are in process."[6] These costs would typically include real estate taxes and insurance and will include interest costs if interest is being incurred by the owner. Any incidental income from holding the land (such as rental receipts in excess of related costs from an existing structure which will be razed) are offset against such holding costs.

Interest costs are capitalized when interest costs are directly or indirectly being incurred during the land acquisition/pre-development process. "The amount of interest cost to be capitalized for qualifying assets is intended to be that portion of the interest cost incurred during the asset's acquisition periods that theoretically could have been avoided (for example, by avoiding additional borrowings or by using the funds, expended for the assets to repay existing borrowings) if expenditures for the assets had not been made."[7] To the extent that the owner's only interest-bearing debt is that associated with the acquired land, this would normally be the total interest cost incurred. If, however, the owner has multiple properties and has debt which is not secured by specific properties, this becomes a more complex issue which is beyond the scope of this chapter. The absolute limitation in capitalizing interest cost is the actual amount of interest incurred by the owner.

The costs of physically constructing the retail facility, including site improvements and tenant improvements are capitalized to the construction-in-progress account as they are incurred. These costs include demolishing existing structures, architectural costs, legal fees, permits, etc., and direct project supervision costs. These costs also include allocated indirect costs of the owner, except for costs which do not clearly relate to the construction process.[8] Interest cost is also required to be capitalized, to the extent it is incurred, on the basis previously discussed, as are real estate taxes and insurance costs. To the extent that costs have been incurred but not fully paid for, the difference between the amount incurred and the amount paid is recognized as a liability usually categorized as accounts payable or accrued expense. Retainage amounts are usually recorded as a separate liability categorized as retainage payable.

The capitalization period for all costs which would not be capitalized during the operating phase of the project (such as interest, real estate taxes, insurance, payroll costs and certain other overhead, etc.) ceases when the retail facility is ready for its intended use. This is the time at which the facility is substantially completed and held available for occupancy that is defined, for accounting purposes, as "upon completion of tenant improvements by the developer but no later than one year from cessation of major construction activity (as distinguished from activities such as routine maintenance and clean-up)."[9] When a significant distinguishable portion of a retail facility meets the criteria of ready for its intended use but the remainder does not, the ready for use portion is accounted for as if it were a separate project and proportionate amounts of eligible costs are continued to be capitalized in respect to the remainder of the facility.

The point at which a retail facility is substantially complete is also the point at which those who are required to use the current value model will usually first value the project and recognize any unrealized appreciation. Under both the current value and/or under the historical cost models, if at any time during the development or construction period the costs incurred to date have accumulated to a point where the carrying amount, after considering costs to complete, has become permanently impaired for projects to be held and operated, such diminution must be recognized as a loss as soon as the determination is made. If the project is to be sold, the diminution is measured by the excess of costs incurred over the net realizable value of the project. The concepts of permanent impairment and net realizable value are discussed in more detail later in this chapter.

During the construction period, it is not unusual for disputes with contractors to arise, particularly in connection with change orders. Disputed costs are currently capitalized and recorded as a liability to the extent that it is probable that the owner will eventually pay them. If it is probable that the owner will pay a portion, but not all, of the disputed costs, the amount expected to be paid is recorded currently. Amounts in dispute for which it is not possible to determine the probability of payment are not currently recorded, however, the amounts in question are required to be disclosed in the owner's financial statements, if significant. If the probability of the owner paying amounts in dispute is remote, no recordation or disclosure is required.[10]

Irrespective of manner of acquisition, it is advisable for owners to segregate as many of the costs between various categories as is practical. Appropriate segregation is particularly important for entities required to use the historical cost method as this will form the basis for calculating an appropriate amount of depreciation.

At a minimum, entities who are subject to income taxation or "pass through" entities whose owners are subject to such taxation should specifically identify land, land improvements, buildings and personal property, as different cost recovery (depreciation) periods will apply to each of these categories. In practice, particularly when a turn-key retail facility is acquired, costs are only segregated between land and buildings. Personal property (i.e., furniture and furnishings, motor vehicles) are often not separately identified because their value is usually not significant to the total acquisition cost. It is, however, possible to appropriately assign costs to major building components and personal property of turn-key properties acquired by retaining the services of experts in doing what is known as cost segregation studies. The concept of depreciation and amortization is discussed further in a separate section of this chapter.

OPERATIONS ACCOUNTING

Revenues from operations of retail facilities are recognized as income as they are earned. Differences between cash actually collected and amounts earned are recorded as assets or liabilities. Expenses of operating retail facilities are recognized as they are incurred. Differences between cash actually paid and amounts incurred are also recognized as assets or liabilities. Certain costs incurred represent capital assets or deferred charges which are not immediately recognized as expenses, but are charged to expense over future periods through depreciation or amortization charges. While this may seem to be very simple, the application of these principles is often more complex and requires many judgments and estimates.

Leasing Costs

Costs associated with obtaining tenants are capitalized as assets under the generic term of deferred charges and are amortized over the term of the lease, normally using the straight-line method. These costs will include legal costs associated with negotiating and drafting the lease, brokerage commissions, and finder's fees. Advertising costs are, however, charged to expense as they are incurred. Costs associated with "buying out" tenant leases are capitalized and amortized over the term of the lease of the replacement tenant. Costs related to tenant improvements that are paid for by the owner are capitalized and depreciated over the lesser of the term of the lease or the estimated useful life of the improvements. To the extent that leasing costs for tenants are not significant, it is acceptable to charge the costs directly to operating expenses.

When a lease has a fixed term with no renewal options, determining the term of the lease is a simple matter. When a month-to-month lease is involved, an estimate will need to be made as to the expected term that the tenant will occupy the premises. One manner in which such an estimate can be made is by analyzing the owner's experience with other month-to-month tenants, ideally those in the same or similar types of businesses. When a lease contains renewal options, the amortization period would be the primary lease term unless the renewal conditions and/or other factors are such that it is a virtual certainty, at the inception of the lease, that the option will be exercised. In such a rare case, the amortization period would extend over all renewal option periods for which renewal options are virtually certain to be exercised.

Lease Incentives

Lease incentives may take various forms. The general rule is that the lessor's cost of such incentives are capitalized and amortized or depreciated over the term of the lease for which the incentives are granted on the straight-line method.

One very common lease incentive is granting a "rent holiday" for the initial portion of the lease term. GAAP requires that minimum base rental income be recognized at a level amount during each period of the lease term. The amount to be recognized during each accounting period is simply the total minimum base rent for the term of the lease divided by the number of accounting periods included in the lease term. This results in the owner initially recognizing income during periods in which no cash rental income is received and recording an asset for such amount. In later periods, the cash rental income received will exceed the amount of rental income recorded by the owner, the difference being applied to amortize the previously recorded asset. The recorded asset is sometimes included in the caption "rent receivable" or "accrued rental income," but it is technically a deferred charge. This deferred charge is reflected under various titles, however, a suggested heading is "rental income recorded in advance of billing." To illustrate deferred changes, assume that a five-year lease is entered into with an aggregate minimum base rent of $25 per year with the first year constituting a rent holiday, resulting in the following accounting:

Year	Income Recognized	Amounts Billed	Deferred Charge Increase (Decrease)	Deferred Charge Balance
1	$ 20	$ 0	$20	$20
2	20	25	(5)	15
3	20	25	(5)	10
4	20	25	(5)	5
5	20	25	(5)	0
	$100	$100	$ 0	$55

Another common lease incentive is a lower minimum base rent in the initial years of the lease with a predetermined dollar amount of increases or fixed percentage increases at various times during the remainder of the lease term. As a result of the requirement to recognize minimum base rents at a level amount, such incentives have a similar effect to that of "rent holidays." To illustrate, again assume that a five year lease is entered into with an aggregate base rent of $100. The rent is payable at the rate of $10 for the first year, $15 per year for the second and third years, and $30 per year for the last two years. The accounting would be as follows:

Year	Income Recognized	Amounts Billed	Deferred Charge Increase (Decrease)	Balance
1	$ 20	$ 10	$ 10	$10
2	20	15	5	15
3	20	15	5	20
4	20	30	(10)	10
5	20	30	(10)	0
	$100	$100	$ 0	$55

Another form of lease incentive is for the owner to provide "above standard" tenant improvements to the lessee. The cost of such improvements is accounted for in the same manner as "standard" tenant improvements, as discussed under the caption leasing costs.

Another form of incentive is for the owner to assume the tenant's obligations in respect to its current lease at another property in order to attract the tenant to relocate to the owner's project. If the space assumed by the owner cannot be subleased, the estimated amount of all future payments to be made by the owner is estimated and recorded as a deferred charge offset by a liability. The deferred charge is amortized over the term of the new tenant's lease. The liability is satisfied as payments are made to the owner of the space previously occupied by the new tenant. If it is feasible to sublease the space, only the amount of the estimated sublease loss is recorded as a deferred charge and a liability. It is acceptable to record sublease losses at either the total (i.e., future value) amount or at the present value of the future payments. The recording of the incentive at the future value of the payments will result in a level amount of amortization in each accounting period.

Yet another form of lease incentive is to pay the lessee a non-accountable "allowance." The amount paid is capitalized as a deferred charge and amortized on the straight-line method. If, however, such allowance is to be used only for improvements to the leased space and the tenant is accountable to the owner for such use, the amount paid would be accounted for as a tenant improvement.

Financial statements prepared under the current value accounting model do not recognize, as separate assets, the deferred charges resulting from accounting for leasing costs and lease incentives because they have no value, separate and apart from the value of the real estate. Accordingly, such charges are added to the historical cost of the real estate, including tenant improvements, which is compared with the property's current value in determining the amount of unrealized appreciation or depreciation of the property at any point in time.

Recognition of Percentage Rents

In theory, percentage rents are recognized in income as they are earned. The practical issues in recognizing percentage rents are the timing of recognition and the amount to be recognized. The timing issue and amount issues are inter-related and are difficult because retail sales tend to be so heavily skewed around the winter holiday season. In addition, retailers may have accounting periods which are not synchronized with that of the owner or the lease year.

Some owners take the approach that tenant sales should be estimated for the entire lease year and any resulting estimated percentage rent recognized on a level basis for each reporting period of that year. Differences between estimated and actual percentage rents are adjusted for when the actual amount becomes known. This approach is supported in accounting theory by the "matching principle" under which income and expenses should be recorded on a matching basis. Those who support this approach argue that inasmuch as expenses are incurred on a more or less level basis throughout the year for retail properties, percentage rents should also be recognized on a level basis. Others take the approach that percentage rents should not be recorded until the tenant's sales exceed the breakpoint. They support their position with the "realization principle" under which income should not be recorded before its realization is reasonably assured. At the present time, either approach is acceptable under GAAP.

The two approaches may result in substantially different timing of the amounts of revenue being recognized, as shown in the table below. This illustration assumes that the tenant's fiscal year, the lease year and the owner's fiscal year are all the calendar year. Tenant sales are $15,000 for each of the first three quarters and $25,000 for the last quarter. The breakpoint is $50,000 and the owner is entitled to additional rent equal to 5% of sales in excess of the breakpoint. Total percentage rent is $1,000 ($15,000 × 3 + $25,000 =

$70,000 − $50,000 = $20,000 × 5%). The owner's recognition of percentage rent income would be as follows under the two approaches:

Quarter	Matching Approach	Realization Approach
1st	$ 250	$ 0
2nd	250	0
3rd	250	0
4th	250	1,000
	$1,000	$1,000

Another approach to this is to periodically recognize percentage rents in proportion to estimated tenant sales. Using the above illustration, this approach would result in the owner recognizing $214 of percentage rent income in each of the first three quarters ($15,000/$70,000 = 21.4% × $1,000) and $358 in the fourth quarter ($25,000/$70,000 = 35.8% × $1,000).

Recognition of percentage rent on the basis of anything other than actual information provided by the tenant requires that the owner be in a position to reasonably estimate tenant sales amounts. The ability to do so is facilitated if the lease requires the tenant to periodically (monthly or quarterly) report actual sales to the owner. This information can be used to compare to the information for the same period in the prior year to estimate sales growth in the current year as a basis for estimating tenant sales for the year. Alternate means may also be available, such as referring to various overall statistical measures to estimate tenant sales. Such means would, of course, be most relevant when a new tenant has no sales history at the owner's project.

Common Area Maintenance Charges

Revenues from reimbursements of common area maintenance costs which are chargeable to tenants should be recognized as the common area costs are incurred by the owner, irrespective to the timing of billing to the tenants. To the extent that certain tenants pay fixed amounts to the owner as CAM contributions, such contributions should also be recognized throughout the year, irrespective of timing of payment.

Where levels of CAM expenses have significant peaks and valleys during the year, for instance as a result of seasonality, recognition of reimbursements ideally should be recognized during the year in proportion to the costs incurred. As a practical matter, however, such reimbursements are often recognized as a level monthly or quarterly amount.

Many owners have adopted a practice of billing tenants for CAM charges monthly based on an estimate of the total of such charges for the entire year. If the owner recognizes CAM reimbursement income monthly or quarterly on the basis of the proportion of expenses incurred relative to total costs expected for the year, but bills a level amount each month or quarter, then an asset or liability, as appropriate, will be recognized for the difference between the billed amount and the income recognized. To illustrate, assume that the owner's estimated CAM costs, net of anchor tenant contributions, is $4,000 expected to be incurred at the rate of $1,200 in each of the first and fourth quarters and $800 in each of the second and third quarters. Also assume that the entire $4,000 can be passed through to the tenants and that the owner bills each tenant a level amount quarterly for CAM contributions. The following accounting would apply:

Quarter	Revenue Recognized	CAM Billed	Excess (Deficit) of Revenue Over Billing	Accrued Rent Receivable (Prepaid Rent Liability)
1	$1,200	$1,000	$200	$200
2	800	1,000	(200)	0
3	800	1,000	(200)	(200)
4	1,200	1,000	200	0
	$4,000	$4,000	$ 0	$ 0

Operating Expenses

Operating expenses are recognized as they are incurred under GAAP, irrespective of the timing of actual payment. To the extent that expenses have been incurred but not paid for, the amount due is recognized as accounts payable (if supported by an invoice) or accrued expenses (if an estimate based on something other than an invoice). For instance, an electric bill received which covers a period through mid-month but not paid as of the end of the month is an accounts payable. The estimated cost of electricity from mid-month to the end of the month is an accrued expense. Normally, accounts payable and accrued expenses are reported as a single line item on the balance sheet.

Payments of expense items that are made in one accounting period which will benefit future accounting periods are capitalized and amortized over all of the periods which benefit from the cost incurred. As an example, insurance is normally paid for at one time but covers an entire year. When payment is made, a prepaid asset is recognized for the amount paid and $\frac{1}{12}$ of the amount paid is amortized to insurance expense each month.

A critical issue is the determination of whether certain costs related to the operation of a retail property are repair and maintenance costs or are capital improvements. This determination affects financial reporting and tax reporting as well as the determination of the amount of costs to be included in the CAM pool eligible to be billed to tenants. Repair and maintenance costs are those expenses which are incurred to keep an asset in proper working order or remediate ordinary wear and tear from the use of the asset. Capital improvement costs are those incurred to acquire new capital assets, replace existing capital assets or for renewals of and betterments to such assets. A renewal is a cost incurred to extend the useful life of an asset beyond its reasonably expected useful life at the time it was acquired and a betterment is a cost incurred to improve in some manner an existing capital asset without replacing it.

The following list illustrates the distinctions:

- Repainting parking lot strips is a repair and maintenance cost because it remediates ordinary wear and tear, whereas resurfacing the parking lot is a capital improvement because it replaces an existing capital asset.

- Upgrading life safety systems is a capital improvement because it is a betterment of the existing system, whereas correcting malfunctions of the existing system is a repair and maintenance cost because the expense was incurred to keep the system in proper working order.

- The cost of overhauling an escalator which is approaching the end of its estimated useful life is a capital improvement because it is a renewal of a capital asset whereas the replacement of a moving handrail that has become worn is a repair and maintenance cost incurred to keep the escalator in proper working order.

This area can become highly debatable, particularly where renewals are involved, because estimates of useful lives are judgments which may not be supportable by empirical evidence. Also, certain capital assets contain various components which may have useful lives which are less than the system as a whole. As a result, pro and con arguments as to the nature of the cost can be made when a component of a system is replaced. For example: if a blower motor (with a 10-year life) which is a component of the HVAC system (which has a 30-year estimated useful life) needs to be replaced, is that replacement a repair of the HVAC system or a new capital asset? Accounting literature will not answer the question, however, to the extent that it can be shown that the blower motor was not recorded as a separate capital asset and/or that its more limited useful life was not a significant consideration in estimating the overall useful life of the HVAC system, the argument that it is a repair and not a capital asset is much enhanced.

Costs incurred to treat environmental contamination (asbestos removal/encapsulation, replacement of lead pipes, etc.) generally should be accounted for as an expense. However, such costs should be treated as capital improvements when the treatment extends the life of or improves the safety and efficiency of an asset relative to conditions at the time the asset was acquired, or mitigates or prevents potential future contamination or when the treatment is made to prepare the property for sale.[11]

Costs which are repair and maintenance costs are treated as capital expenditures when they are components of a project which is a capital item, such as a total renovation of all or a significant portion of common areas.

In order to simplify capitalization vs. expense accounting, owners will generally establish a dollar threshold below which all items are treated as if they were expenses. This threshold will vary depending on the magnitude of costs expected to be incurred but generally ranges from $1,000 to $25,000. In establishing a threshold, owners should be particularly sensitive to the potential for challenges to CAM billing amounts that may arise from tenants, as discussed later in this chapter.

Depreciation and Amortization

Although the terms depreciation and amortization are often used in combination with one another, they represent different things. Depreciation is associated with tangible assets, such as buildings, tenant improvements, machinery, and equipment vehicles. Amortization is associated with intangible assets, deferred charges and credits and financing costs, such as deferred leasing commissions, debt discount or premium, prepaid insurance deferred financing costs. Depreciation and amortization both serve to allocate capital expenditures over the accounting periods benefited by the costs incurred, pursuant to the matching principle previously discussed.

Depreciation for accounting purposes is fundamentally different than the appraiser's or economist's concept because the accounting views depreciation as an allocation of capital asset costs incurred to accounting periods to which such costs benefit, which may have little, if anything, to do with physical deterioration or the various forms of obsolescence.

There are three principal factors which drive the determination of periodic depreciation charges. These are:

- The cost amount to be depreciated.
- The estimated useful life of the asset.
- The method to be used.

A fourth factor, the estimated salvage value at the expiration of the asset's useful life, is generally not used in practice by real estate owners because it is not significant. The cost amount to be depreciated is the acquisition cost of the assets acquired by purchase or construction, including all capitalized amounts such as interest, real estate taxes, and so on, but excluding all amounts assigned to land. The land cost is not depreciated since land has an indefinite life. Once an asset has become fully depreciated, depreciation of that asset ceases.

The useful life of retail real estate properties is inherently an imprecise measurement. Among other things, technology and demographic shifts may render a property noneconomic or functionally obsolete long before its physical viability comes into question. On the other hand, the ability to adapt physical configurations to meet changing demand patterns may partially or completely offset other factors.

A retail facility has many components within it, the useful life of which may vary considerably. For example: the building shell may have a useful life in excess of 100 years while the escalators may have a useful life of 15 years. In theory, each major component should be assigned a reasonable useful life and its cost should be specifically identified to permit the calculation of depreciation. In practice, however, owners tend to use composite depreciation method which is intended to represent a weighted average life for groups of components. Such groups may, for instance, be land improvements, buildings, machinery and equipment, or vehicles. Additions to each group are typically categorized by year to permit identification of fully depreciated asset pools.

The process of assigning useful lives to asset groups or individual assets will normally consider questions such as:

Were the assets acquired "new" or "used"?

What lives were assigned to similar assets in the past?

What has the owner's experience been with respect to longevity of assets?

What period does the tax code permit for depreciation deductions?

There are two basic depreciation methods available. The straight-line method, which apportions depreciation at a level amount over each accounting period of the useful life of an asset, and accelerated methods which record higher depreciation amounts in the accounting periods during the early part of an asset's useful life and lesser amounts during the later periods of its useful life. Accelerated methods are most appropriate for assets whose values decline rapidly when placed in service and later decline less rapidly, such as motor vehicles. In practice, the straight-line method is nearly always used for real estate structures and components.

Tenant improvements which are paid for by the owner are depreciated, usually using the straight-line method, over the lesser of the useful life of the improvements or the term of the lease.

Where the current value model is appropriate, no depreciation charges are recognized, except with respect to any significant personal property which is not included within the current value determination. These assets are usually depreciated in the same manner as the historical cost model. The depreciated net carrying amount of the asset thus becomes a surrogate for its fair value. While this is not the theoretically "correct" approach, personal property is almost never a significant portion of a retail property owner's assets.

Amortization charges are normally determined on the straight-line method unless some other method is more representative of the "consumption" of the assets or liabilities being amortized. However, amortization or accretion of receivable or debt discounts and premiums is always determined on the interest method explained earlier in this chapter.

Unlike depreciation, amortization charges are not necessarily classified as a single line item in financial statements. Such charges are classified based on the nature of the activity which caused the asset or liability to be recorded. Therefore, amortization of prepaid insurance is recorded as insurance expense, accretion of debt discounts and amortization of debt premium are recorded as interest expense or reductions in interest expense. Also, amortization of deferred charges relating to lease incentives such as rent holidays and scheduled base rent increases are recorded as rental revenues or reductions thereof.

Owners who use current value accounting should record amortization charges in the same way as those who use historical cost accounting. In view of the effects of recording unrealized appreciation or depreciation in asset values under current value accounting, the "bottom line" should be the same with or without amortization. However, the classification of income as that from operations and that from realized and unrealized gains will be different because unamortized deferred charges must be added to the historical cost of property when determining unrealized appreciation or depreciation of the property. The lower the balance of deferred charges, the greater the unrealized appreciation or lesser the unrealized depreciation. The differential is recorded in net investment income. To illustrate, assume that an owner's retail property is appraised for $5,000 and has a historical cost basis of $3,000. Gross deferred leasing costs are $2,000 for which the amortization period is five years. The calculations underlying the statement of changes in net assets, under the current value accounting model would be as follows:

	Amortization Not Recorded	Amortization Recorded
Leasing expenses (Amortization of $400 ($2,000 ÷ 5 years))	<u>$0</u>	<u>$ 400</u>
Net investment income	0	$(400)
Increase in unrealized appreciation		
Appraised value	$5,000	
Less: Historical cost	(3,000)	
Unamortized deferred leasing costs	(2,000)	0
Appraised value	$5,000	
Less: Historical cost	(3,000)	
Unamortized deferred leasing costs	(1,600)	400
Net increase in net assets	<u>$0</u>	<u>$ 0</u>

DISPOSITION ACCOUNTING

Accounting for the disposition of real estate is the most complex accounting area affecting real estate owners. The appropriate accounting for sales of real estate, as well as for other transactions, has always had as its premise "economic substance over legal form." Nevertheless, the accounting profession has had difficulty in reaching the same conclusions on different transactions that involve similar circumstances. As a result, the authoritative literature, primarily Statement of Financial Accounting Standards (SFAS) No. 66, "Accounting for Sales of Real Estate," prescribes detailed rules aimed at narrowing significantly the opportunity to reach different conclusions in similar fact circumstances by striving to clarify the meaning of "economic substance." These rules often create a sense of arbitrariness and, in fact, some of them may, in certain circumstances, appear harsh. For example:

- Certain types of real estate sales must have a minimum cash down payment of 20% if all of the profit on the sale is to be recognized immediately. This does not mean approximately 20%. No materiality judgment is permitted.

- Cash down payment means cash. It does not mean marketable securities. It does not mean a note receivable, backed by the full faith and credit of a significant creditworthy entity.

- Cash used to effect a down payment cannot be borrowed money which is collaterized by the property sold if the seller is accepting a subordinated mortgage note as part of the settlement of the sales price.

- A transaction in which the buyer has the right to compel the seller to repurchase the property is not a sale for accounting purposes. Such a transaction is accounted for as a financing. In addition, a transaction in which the seller has any option to repurchase the property, even at fair market value, is also deemed not to be a sale.

The rules, which developed over many years and were codified in SFAS No. 66, are in some respects a reaction by the accounting profession and the U.S. Securities and Exchange Commission to abuses in accounting for real estate transactions during the late 1960s. The rules have two primary aims: first, to recognize profit on a sale only to the extent there is a high probability that a profit has been realized from a completed sale and, second, to the extent the seller remains involved with a property after the sale, to defer profit in proportion to the seller's continuing risks and involvement.

The determination of the appropriate accounting for the sale of real estate begins with the determination as to whether a sale has been consummated. A sale is not consummated until all of the following conditions have been met:

- The parties are bound by the terms of a contract.
- All consideration has been exchanged.
- Any permanent financing for which the seller is responsible has been arranged.
- All conditions precedent to closing (except for completion of construction of structures) have been performed.[12]

If a sale has not been consummated, any monies received from the buyer are accounted for by the seller as a deposit. A deposit represents a liability of the seller, and the seller continues to account for the real estate as if the seller continued to own the property. However, if the terms of the sale agreement indicate that the seller has incurred a loss, the seller must recognize the loss and reduce the balance sheet carrying amount of the property to the all cash equivalent of the sales consideration. If a sale has been consummated, a further determination must be made as to whether the transaction is a sale for accounting purposes. Conditions which would disqualify the transaction from sale treatment include:

- When the seller agrees to subordinate a mortgage note received from the buyer at any time subsequent to the closing date where the proceeds from the new first mortgage loan are not applied to reduce the principal balance of the newly subordinated note.
- The seller has an obligation to repurchase the property at some future time or the seller has an option to repurchase the property, irrespective of the method by which the repurchase price is determined.
- The seller is a general partner in a limited partnership acquiring the property sold and the seller holds a receivable from the buyer for a significant part of the sales price.
- The seller guarantees the return of the buyer's investment or a return on that investment for an extended period without a maximum dollar amount of such guarantee.

- The seller is required to support the operations of the property or continue to operate the property at its own risk for an extended period of time.

If any of these conditions exist, the seller is required to account for the transaction as a deposit, a financing arrangement (i.e., any cash proceeds are accounted for by the seller as if they were a loan) or a profit sharing arrangement.

If none of these conditions are present, the transaction will generally be treated as a sale for accounting purposes, however, additional tests must be applied in order to determine the method by which any profit may be recognized. These tests involve the amount of money initially paid by the buyer and the terms of any purchase money mortgage taken back by the seller. SFAS No. 66 prescribes specific methods of calculation and minimum down payment percentages for various types of properties and conditions and minimum acceptable payment terms for purchase money mortgages taken back by the seller.

If the buyer's initial payment is adequate and the purchase money mortgage terms are within the guidelines, the entire gain on sale will generally be recognizable currently. Exceptions to this occur when the seller has continuing involvement with the property sold. For example:

- If the seller sells an uncompleted project on a "turnkey" basis, the seller must recognize the gain on a percentage of completion basis.
- If the seller has made guarantees to the buyer up to a fixed dollar amount or has agreed to support the property's operations only to the extent of a fixed dollar amount, that amount must be deducted from the sales value in determining the amount of gain currently recognizable.
- If the property is sold to a limited partnership in which the seller is a limited partner, with no control over the partnership's affairs, the amount of gain currently recognizable is limited to the percentage of the gain which is equal to the percentage interests of the other partners of the partnership.

If the buyer's initial investment is less than the specified criteria of SFAS No. 66, the sale must be accounted for by the cost recovery method or, if the recovery of the carrying amount of the property is reasonably assured if the buyer defaults on any purchase money mortgage given to the seller, by the installment method. The cost recovery method requires that all payments received from the borrower be applied to reduce the balance of the seller's receivable (initially, the carrying amount of the property on the seller's balance sheet which has been reclassified to a receivable) from the buyer until such time that it has been reduced to zero. Thereafter, all payments received are recorded as income. The installment method of accounting prorates the total gain to be recognized to current and future accounting periods on the basis of current down payment and/or principal payments received in relation to the total sales value. If the initial investment of the buyer is so small as to raise a question as to the buyer's commitment to the project, the initial investment is considered to be a deposit.

If the buyer's initial down payment qualifies but the terms of the purchase money mortgage taken back by the seller are not within the guidelines, any "excess" down payment may be applied to "cure" the "deficiency." If the deficiency cannot be cured, SFAS No. 66 prescribes a method of recognizing a reduced amount of gain on the transaction.

Further complications in recognizing profit may exist in certain circumstances, such as:

- The seller sells property improvements and leases the underlying land to the buyer.

- The seller has made guarantees to the buyer or has agreed to support the property's operations, either of which only apply for a limited period of time with no maximum fixed dollar amount involved.

- The seller "master net leases" back from the buyer the property sold.

- A transaction does not initially qualify as a sale or does not qualify for full profit recognition but, at a later date, does qualify.

SFAS No. 66 and other accounting pronouncements provide specific guidance as to the appropriate accounting in such circumstances.

Although the above discussion of disposition accounting may seem very detailed, it is merely an overview. Since the ability to recognize gain on a real estate sale and/or the ability to remove the property from "the books" is often a key objective of the seller, it is critical to seek the advice of a qualified accountant early on in the sale negotiations. Once the deal has been "inked," there is generally little which can be done to avoid an unintended accounting consequence.

The profit recognition accounting rules are applicable to both the historical cost and current value accounting models. In the case of the current value model, however, in theory, the principal effect is in the classification of gains as realized or unrealized.

TENANT AND LANDLORD ISSUES

Contentious issues often arise between owners and tenants. Two issues in which accounting becomes particularly relevant to retail properties are the determination of percentage rents and the determination of the CAM pool eligible to be passed on to tenants.

Percentage Rents

Percentage rent arrangements introduce the prospect of conflict because the interests of the owner and tenant are mutually exclusive.

The underreporting of tenant sales is less likely when a tenant is operated by major national or regional retail chains. The owner's risk is reduced because the store's management is usually held accountable to the retailer for meeting sales goals which are rewarded based on sales performance. Also, the tenant may be subject to audits performed by the retailer's internal audit department and/or its external auditors. Consequently, if the owner has access to the sales reports used by the tenant to report results to the chain retailer, verification is a simple matter. It is important for the percentage rent clause in leases with such tenants to give the owner access to such reports, ideally by reference to the nomenclature of specific report(s) used by the tenant.

Tenants which are operated by sole proprietors or small partnerships are far more likely to underreport sales to the owner because of limited, if any, accountability to others. Also, to the extent that cash sales are a significant aspect of the tenant's business, the underreporting of sales is more difficult to detect.

The most effective protection an owner has against underreported sales is a regular program of lease audits. Such audits may be conducted by the owner's internal audit department, others within the owner's organization who have appropriate skills or independent contractors. Some accounting firms specialize in this type of auditing. A prerequisite to the ability to audit tenant sales is a properly drafted lease clause permitting the owner or its representatives to conduct sales audits and requiring the tenant to make available all relevant books and records, including, among other things, bank statements, inventory records, and purchase journals.

Some owners prefer to audit sales periodically of all tenants in order to send them a message about the risks of underreporting sales. Others employ a screening process in order to identify those tenants for which an audit is most likely to reveal underreported sales.

Typical screening techniques include:

- Comparison of trends of tenant sales to published industry information.
- Comparison of trends of tenant sales to that of other mall tenants.
- Alertness to changes in owners and/or managers of outlets accompanied by large changes in reported sales levels.
- Alertness to significant increases in mall traffic not accompanied by increases in a tenant's reported sales.
- Assessing the proximity of reported tenant sales to the breakpoint level.

When other than minor underreporting of sales is encountered and sufficient evidence has been accumulated to prove the case, it is often advisable to take advantage of all remedies available under the terms of the lease in order to make an example of the errant tenant to other tenants.

CAM Charges

CAM charges are also a prime source of owner and tenant conflict, again because their economic interests are not mutual. Tenants, in attempts to control and/or reduce their operating costs, are increasingly paying close attention to the CAM billings rendered to them by owners. With increasing frequency, tenants are using their internal audit departments or external accountants to audit the CAM cost pool and percentage allocations on which the tenant's billing is based.

External accountants hired by tenants are commonly compensated on a contingent basis based upon the savings achieved for the tenant. This compensation arrangement provides a powerful incentive for such accountants to challenge anything and everything which is included in CAM costs by the owner, but not specifically identified as a part of the CAM pool by the language used in the lease. Owners, in far too many circumstances, inadvertently assist accountants in challenging CAM billings in a number of ways. This form of "assistance" begins at the time that the CAM clauses in leases are drafted.

CAM lease clauses are generally drafted from a conceptual point of view which is seldom coordinated with the owner's or property manager's accounting systems. As a result, the accounting system may not be readily able to provide accurately the amount which is intended to be included in the CAM pool. For example, the lease may state that the cost of all of the owner's *on-site* personnel, except for the property manager and leasing personnel, are to be included in the CAM pool. However, the accounting system is only capable of capturing the total payroll cost.

Such clauses also may use terms which have no commonly understood definition. For example, a lease may state that capital expenditures, as determined in accordance with generally accepted accounting principles applicable to retail property owners, are to be excluded from the CAM pool. The issue is simply that no one really knows what those principles may happen to be. Where terms that are commonly understood are used, they are often still inadequately defined in the lease. For example, a lease may require that repair and maintenance costs, determined under generally accepted accounting principles, are to be included in the CAM pool. As discussed at the beginning of this chapter, GAAP is subject to changes from time to time. The lease clause thus leaves open the issue of whether GAAP means GAAP applicable at the date of the lease or as of the date the CAM pool is determined for any given year.

Compounding these types of issues is the problem of departures from the owner's standard CAM lease clause in order to accommodate prospective tenants. These special clauses may result in the need to separately calculate the appropriate CAM pool applicable to a number of different tenants. The amount of time and effort involved in doing this may be beyond the capabilities of the accounting function with the result that only one or two calculations are actually made resulting in a CAM billing to a number of tenants which is clearly not in accordance with the lease terms.

Many of these problems may be avoided by involving a qualified accountant as part of the leasing function. In addition to reviewing standard CAM lease terms for compatibility to the accounting system's ability to capture information and definitional clarity, an accountant should review all CAM lease clauses which depart from the standard language for these issues as well as the feasibility of creating multiple CAM pool calculations.

Other forms of "assistance" provided by the owner often include the use of persons with inadequate accounting training and/or experience preparing CAM billings without substantive review and supervision by qualified accountants; inconsistent calculations of proportionate shares applicable to individual tenants; and inadvertent failure to apply the CAM contributions of major or anchor to reduce the CAM cost pool.

A very common area of contention involves the delineation between repair and maintenance costs and capital improvements. This situation occurs because there are borderline cases and because the words "capital improvements" may not be adequately defined in the lease. The lease should define capital improvements in a manner consistent with GAAP, i.e., new capital assets, replacements of existing capital assets, renewals, and betterments. Where borderline cases are involved, it is advisable at the same time to document the reasons for concluding that the costs involved were determined to be repair and maintenance costs.

ENDNOTES

1. Statement on Auditing Standards (SAS) No. 69, "The Meaning of Present Fairly in Conformity with Generally Accepted Accounting Principles in the Independent Auditor's Report," the American Institute of Certified Accountants, Inc. (AICPA), 1992 (Paragraph 2).
2. Statement of Financial Accounting Standard (SFAS) No. 66, "Accounting for Sales of Real Estate," Financial Accounting Standards Board (FASB), 1982 (Paragraph 6).
3. SFAS No. 66, FASB, 1982 (Paragraphs 31 and 65).
4. Codification of Statements on Auditing Standards Nos. 1 to 64, (CSAS), AICPA, 1991 (Section 623.04).
5. Accounting Principles Board Opinion (APBO) No. 21 "Interest on Receivables and Payables," AICPA, 1971 (Paragraph 15).
6. SFAS No. 67, "Accounting for Costs and Initial Rental Operations of Real Estate Projects," FASB, 1982 (Paragraph 6).
7. SFAS No. 34, "Capitalization of Interest Cost," FASB, 1979 (Paragraph 12).
8. SFAS No. 67, FASB, 1982 (Paragraph 7).
9. SFAS No. 67, FASB, 1982 (Paragraph 22).
10. SFAS No. 5, "Accounting for Contingencies," FASB, 1975 (Paragraphs 8–12).
11. Emerging Issue Task Force Issue No. 90-8, "Capitalization of Costs to Treat Environmental Contamination," FASB, 1990.
12. SFAS No. 66, FASB, 1982 (Paragraph 6).

Twenty-Two

Counseling for Retail Properties and Performance Measures

Richard Marchitelli and
John Melaniphy

R eal estate counseling requires a firm grasp of the physical and financial operation of shopping centers. Leasing plans, tenant synergies, market segmentation, penetration rates, sources of revenue and reimbursements, and operating expenses must be properly understood. The actual performance of a property as well as its competitive position vis-à-vis others in its trade area are measured in terms of various units of comparison. Effective rent per square foot, contract rent vs. market rent, retail sales per square foot, and occupancy costs are useful analytical tools. In addition, counselors consider the physical condition, layout, adequacy of the capital-improvement program, and overall appeal of a shopping center as well as similar attributes of competitive properties. This and other information is useful if the counselor is required to assist in an attempt to reposition a property; to identify reasons for disappointing performance; to develop a new marketing plan; to evaluate an opportunity for acquisition, sale, expansion, or renovation; or to help in a myriad of other situations in which the insights of an expert are sought.

With the chronic overbuilding in the industry and the contraction of real estate lending, documentation has become the rule rather than the exception. As a result, small and large development projects are being heavily scrutinized. The role of the counselor in assisting the developer or landlord has become more important. The success or failure of any investment strategy is also tied to performance measurement, which is discussed in the second half of this chapter.

Shopping Center Services Provided by the Counselor

Counseling activities for neighborhood, community, and regional shopping centers are discussed next.

Location Identification

The role of the counselor in selecting locations requires investigating the overall market, locational alternatives, land costs, comparable values accessibility, curb cuts, location of utilities, zoning, governmental requirements, the approval process, community reaction, and timing of the development. Many companies use counselors as an impartial check and balance in auditing the results of their internal real estate people or real estate brokers. Moreover, the counselor can continue to assist the developer through the planning, zoning, building, financing, leasing, construction, and development processes.

Counselors are aware that locational needs vary greatly depending upon the type of retailer. However, there are several locational needs that many retailers have in common. First, most retailers need to be near activity. Even the largest retailers such as discounters and "big box" users, tend to locate many units in proximity to major malls. Smaller retailers, restaurants, automobile dealers, auto after-market facilities, supermarkets, drugstores, hardware stores, and many others locate in proximity to these generators. The second common element is the need to locate within the existing shopping pattern. By being in the pattern, a retailer can both be generative and parasitical, intercepting customers traveling to and from a primary destination. Today, we find most successful retailers located on primary traffic arteries and in proximity to a major mall, power center, or retail concentration.

Market Feasibility

A market study should not be undertaken until a specific set of objectives has been established. The study would normally include the following:

The delineated retail area.
An inventory of competing centers including strengths and weaknesses.
Present and future demographics.
An evaluation of accessibility and possible changes.
A study of income and expenditure patterns.
An analysis of area dynamics.
A review of existing shopping habits and buying patterns.
An analysis of employment dynamics.
A determination of resident's personal consumption expenditures.
An estimate of potential sales for the project.
Recommended placement of the retailers.
A determination of supportable square footage.
Parking spaces required.

The market is constantly changing. During the later 1980s and certainly through mid-1990s, the consumer turned frugal. The word sale has been replaced by the reality of price/value.

One of the most important study elements often overlooked is interviewing the customers within the shopping center at strategically selected stations. By interviewing at the stations, the counselor can tabulate the data by individual station, as well as by all of the stations collectively. The stations are important, because they provide an indication of trade area variations in proximity to certain store positions, and further indicate store interchange (or the lack of) for individual stations. They also provide additional data for shopping center segments which may have varying performances.

The next step includes computing the shopping center's market penetration or market share by retail categories. Through an evaluation of sales performance in relation to potential within the trading area, one can identify strengths and weaknesses by individual retail categories. This is helpful in sorting out alternative strategies and the likelihood of accomplishing the same.

The individual store performances are evaluated in terms of sales, sales per square foot, base rentals, overages, lease length, merchandise mix, tenant strength financially, placement, and other considerations. The objective is to determine the contributing nature of each store and each retail category to the shopping center, including their individual and collective placement in the shopping center. Through this type of analysis, the counselor can gain insight into the stores that should be replaced, weaknesses within the shopping center that need to be changed, and the financial ramifications of any and all actions.

For many of the retailers, it has been very difficult to forecast consumer demands. Faddishness certainly continues to exist and dictate fashion and style. The counselor can advise the owner or developer on the impact that these changes may have over time, or how he or she may capitalize upon them.

Investment Analysis

Financial analysis is a critical element in the counselor's experience that can assist the developer. By identifying alternative developmental scenarios and their costs, the counselor can determine which scenarios will offer the greatest return on investment and create the greatest amount of value over time, including consideration of varying rents, percentage rental overages, operating expenses, and real estate taxes.

Architectural Considerations

Counselors are often asked to comment on architectural design, store placement, parking layout, position of curb cuts, and other pertinent elements. The counselor can assist the architect in providing a "reality" check. Architects have wonderful concepts that appear exciting and unusual in drawings or renderings. However, they occasionally do not work as planned from a marketability viewpoint.

Obviously, the first objective is to get the customer in the door, while the second objective is to encourage the customer to peruse the entire store, thereby increasing the opportunity for larger sales. Through this process, the counselor can assist the retailer in determining the optimum store size for specific sized markets as well as the optimum layout. The "ring" or "race track" store layout is popular in encouraging the customer to go around the store. Here the store is often carpeted except for the track that "leads" the consumer around the store past all of the displays and departments.

Governmental Issues

Planning, zoning, building, and environmental approval is necessary for the project to proceed. The counselor can play a very pivotal role in this segment by meeting with the planners to discuss the project, its market support, its positive impact on the community, its fiscal impact, job generation, traffic, and other important issues.

The counselor may meet with community residents to alleviate concerns. Additionally, the counselor can testify before planning and zoning boards regarding each of these issues and can provide answers to questions that may be raised.

Construction and Development

There are times when the developer needs someone to offer assistance in dealing with the general contractor. The counselor can assist in selecting the general contractor and in monitoring the job. He or she might also review the billing and the draw or payments.

Value Estimation

Many counselors have appraisers on their staff or are accredited appraisers themselves and have the capability of determining current market value. The techniques of real estate valuation are fully set forth in Chapter 20 and should be read in conjunction with this chapter on counseling and property performance.

Land and Free-Standing Property Issues

For single-user, free-standing retail properties, the demand for consulting assistance varies considerably. Small retail site or property users include most types of retailers, restaurants, fast-food facilities, automobile after-market shops, tire dealers, theaters, service stores, banks, health clubs, and numerous others. Many, at most times use the services of an outside counselor.

Most free-standing oriented retailers or food service operators prefer to acquire land and build their buildings or have them built for them. Naturally, there are others who prefer to find existing buildings that apparently did not work for the previous occupant. These types of situations are generally more difficult as a consistent strategy for a major retailer because of the varying sizes of available buildings or lack of them. As a counselor, it is important to know changes taking place in the market and to be aware of the availability of vacant anchor retail stores that a particular retailer might utilize.

The largest single small user of free-standing land is the restaurant and fast-food industry. In John Melaniphy's book, *Restaurant and Fast-Food Site Selection* (John Wiley & Sons), he points out the importance of a free-standing location versus shopping centers or mall locations, especially for most restaurants. Perhaps the two most important benefits are visibility and lower occupancy costs. Others include: freedom of hours, control of maintenance costs and real estate taxes, lower or no overage percentage rentals, and the ability to generate similar or higher sales levels than those in a shopping center. In contrast, shopping center locations usually have higher common area charges, including a merchants association contribution. When combined, the costs usually are higher and the additional anticipated sales often do not materialize. One of the real advantages of a shopping center location is usually availability of parking and a concentration of consumers.

The areas where most free-standing retailers or food service people seek guidance include site selection, what they should pay for the land, and the amount of sales that they can capture. In considering land values, the counselor will address not only the total cost of the land, but also the cost per square foot and the cost per front foot. In the retail and food service business, frontage on the main or primary traffic artery is critical.

Transaction Advisory Services

Through experiences and current research, the counselor can advise the shopping center developer on the purchase price of the property and the conditions that must be met for the deal to close. In the case of existing malls, the counselor can advise the potential buyer or seller on the structure of the transaction, either assisting the buyer in acquiring the property at a fair price or directing the seller to either maximize the selling price or to reduce the price to shorten the marketing time.

The counselor can evaluate an existing shopping center's tenant rent roll, cash flow, rent structure, percentage rental overages, occupancy, vacancy, expandability, parking ratio, and potential tenant additions. He or she can then forecast revenues, expenses, and cash flow by making some assumptions regarding new tenants and sales potential. Additionally, the counselor can prepare net present value discount analyses of the shopping center under alternative redevelopment or releasing schemes. Thus, alternative values, both present and future, can be tested to eliminate the uncertainty of the future value of the transaction.

From the seller's perspective, a counselor can help to structure the deal to make it as appealing as possible, while at the same time, maximizing the selling price. This includes identifying expansion possibilities; future rent increases; changes in the market area that will create stronger percentage lease overages; potential solutions or additions of retailers to further enhance the mall; and other appealing and informative issues that broaden the salability of the property.

Financing

Counseling assistance in the financing of regional shopping centers came to the forefront after 1988, when the real estate balloon burst and so many properties were taken over by lenders. Prior to that time, most shopping center developers either negotiated directly with major insurance companies or operated through mortgage bankers who negotiated and obtained the required financing.

The counselor's role in financing can be multidimensional. It can begin by assisting in the preparation of the necessary documentation to encourage lender participation. This might include pro formas, descriptions, brochures, prospective tenancy, rental and overage forecasting, estimated land and construction costs, site improvement charges, leasing expenses, loan fees, and the like. Next, the counselor can assist the developer in identifying potential lenders who might be interested in a particular project. Rather than shopping the market, the experienced counselor would assist in negotiating financing size and terms. Often, this does not represent front-line negotiation, but rather reaction-response. The counselor provides advice regarding what to accept, what not to accept, what the parameters might be, how far the lender might be willing to go, what conditions the developer should stand fast on, and so forth.

On the opposite side, many counselors represent lenders. In that capacity, the counselor can provide advice on various types of commercial developments. The role of the counselor is to protect the lender. He or she will evaluate all of the documentation, visit the location, inspect the site and its environs, drive the market area, visit and shop competitive facilities, test accessibility, review zoning approvals, consider prospective retailers, check local retailer performance, and study other pertinent factors. The counselor might then evaluate the loan application, supporting financial data, shopping center leases, the shopping center pro forma financial analysis, any appraisals that have been provided to support land value, and other necessary documentation. In some cases, the counselor might also be asked to service the loan after the deal is completed.

Joint Venture Analysis

Joint venture analysis requires understanding the benefits that might accrue to joint venture partners. Often, counselors are employed by one partner seeking another joint venture partner. In that case, the counselor's role involves identifying who a suitable joint venture partner might be. He or she might then assist in the introduction, negotiation, and agreement. In other instances, the role is more preparatory. In order to prepare for joint venture discussions, it is necessary to prepare the required documentation and supporting materials to encourage joint venture participation. In yet other instances, counselors are brought in as the objective third party to assess a prospective joint venture where certain aspects of the agreement are disputed.

Lease Negotiations

The role of the counselor in lease negotiation is usually more on the retailer side than on the developer side. In that role, a counselor might be described as "the person behind the person." Retailers come to counselors because they are experienced, fully understand the business, know what the developers or landlords will accept, understand the trade-offs, and can assist in establishing a better deal than they can make by themselves.

Sometimes counselors do become involved with developers and landlords in adding a new major tenant. The landlord may be a small player in the shopping center field and may require assistance to be sure that the ultimate deal is realistic. In those cases, the counselor works with the landlord in identifying potential tenants, in establishing the parameters for negotiation, and usually in negotiating in the background through the landlord. In several cases, however, the counselor might negotiate directly with major tenants or landlords.

One of the benefits of such a negotiation strategy is role playing, permitting the counselor to avoid making a decision because he or she must take the offer back to management to see how they react.

Mall Management Issues

The counselor may see from his or her evaluation that management changes can have a significant impact upon both performance and net income of a shopping center. Moreover, he or she may see that a major change in promotional activities, advertising agency, marketing aggressiveness, and creativity might have a very positive impact upon future sales. The evaluation of the security team may indicate strength or weakness in the program.

Counseling for the Merchants Association

Merchants' associations often make marketing, promotion, and advertising decisions based upon opinion and supposition. Major landlords interview customers in their mall at least every other year to determine the customer profile, the actual trade area, customer likes and dislikes, and other important merchandising data. This information, along with sales performance, is used to develop a marketing and promotional plan. An overlooked part of this process is to develop the shopping center's market share or market penetration by submarket within the trade area. As counselors, we can provide a better service by going this extra step. Analyzing market ratio by smaller submeters indicates the areas of strength and weakness of an existing mall more specifically than simply analyzing the overall trading area, which enables the Merchants Association by advertising or direct mail specifically to direct funds to areas from which the shopping center should be attracting more customer's. It is the counselors role to assist management in developing the necessary decision data and in advising the Merchants Association regarding the best way to spend their funds to derive the biggest impact.

Shopping Center Remodeling and Renovation Issues

In recent years, shopping center renovation and remodeling has become more important to the shopping center industry than building new facilities. Numerous malls and shopping centers throughout the United States and Canada have experienced the sudden loss of a major anchor because of department store failure, sale, or consolidation.

This necessitates not only attempting to find a new anchor, but addressing the entire issue of repositioning the shopping center within its trade area.

The need for remodeling and renovation covers all shopping centers and malls. They are not always inspired by the loss of a major tenant, however, that certainly is a major reason for making changes. There was a time when renovation was a function of refinancing that naturally occurred because of fast depreciation write-offs. With the tax law of 1986, all of that has changed, as did interest rates and the availability of capital for refinancing. The popularity of REITs (Real Estate Investment Trusts) and the sale of stock in the capital markets has once again provided liquidity to major shopping center landlords for improvements and renovation.

Counselors can play a very important role in helping the landlord to decide exactly what remodeling and renovation is required, generally what the costs may be, issues of expansion such as additional parking needs, prospective tenants, design, engineering alternatives, construction, financing, and numerous others. Defining the objectives is extremely important.

Each shopping center has its own physical limitations. Sometimes the limitations can be overcome through the development of parking decks, the acquisition of adjacent property, or by some other means. The counselor can be of assistance in defining the physical alternatives for improvement or simply for remodeling. Sometimes the limitations relate to store sizes and their proximity to one another. With the demand for larger, big box users, sometimes it is appropriate to consider eliminating a number of smaller stores (usually vacant ones or those on short-term leases) in order to provide an adequate site.

Redevelopment scenarios define or identify the realistic redevelopment or renovation alternatives that might be undertaken and that need to be examined. These can range from selling the property or doing nothing to a maximum endeavor including the addition of other major department stores and major anchors, along with significant new construction and remodeling. It is important to define each of the scenarios, considering the magnitude of each, the costs related to each, the likelihood of accomplishing the defined scenario, a financial analysis of the present and long-term return from the actions defined, the value that might be created, the debt that will be required, and the financing mechanisms and sources that may be available.

Experienced counselors can be of assistance to the landlord in the re-leasing process. In some cases, existing tenants will have to be relocated within the shopping center. It is necessary to convince them of the benefits, especially if they are not required to move. Often, an outside counselor can be very beneficial to the landlord in approaching the tenants, explaining the situation objectively, allaying their fears, and reflecting upon the potential available to them in the relocation process. Such a strategy does not always work, but it works more often than not with a lot fewer problems. It also still permits the landlord to come forward and adjust anything that the counselor might offer. The counselor should also be of help in the entire leasing process, in identifying the largest retailers, in their placement, and in negotiating rental deals, the percentage leases, the lease terms, and other clauses.

Almost any physical change in a shopping center requires varying levels of governmental approvals. Obviously, the more extensive, the greater the number of approvals. Counselors can be of assistance to the landlord in discussing the approval process, determining the critical path, the prospective stumbling blocks or delay areas, and the actions which should be taken in advance to ameliorate the problem. Moreover, the counselor can often meet with the architects and contractor as well as with the landlord to discuss the entire process, making sure that each major player understands his or her role and the coordination required to make it happen within a reasonable time frame. Furthermore, the counselors can meet with the important governmental officials to discuss the project and the changes which the owner will be seeking. The team then can discuss how to address the potential road blocks, either through compromise, redesign, replacement, or lobbying.

Often in major renovation of a shopping center, some changes must occur in either the parking ratio or parking placement. The counselor can assist the landlord or management in the preparation of a viable parking plan for a renovated shopping center. Sometimes, this involves consideration of costly parking decks as a solution. Nevertheless, the cost of the parking can be included in the financial analyses in order to weigh the risks and returns.

Major anchor negotiations are always complicated. Unless the shopping center is a major mall, today more of the anchors are being forced to pay their fair share. Unfortunately that is not always the case. The counselor can play a vital role in listening to both sides and in attempting to come to some compromises that will be acceptable to both parties. Such a role gives the counselor clear insight into the type of store the anchor is planning in relation to what the mall has planned. Thus, it may be necessary to refine the sales and rental estimates and reprocess the financial analyses.

The counselor's role is to bring a total understanding of retailing and shopping center merchandising to the table. In reviewing the plans, the counselor should be able to identify problem areas before they are constructed. By doing so, alternative solutions can be determined. A counselor can assist greatly in making sure that all of the components interact, that pedestrian traffic flow is uninhibited, and that the components work together toward a common goal of maximum sales per square foot toward landlord profitability.

MEASURES OF PERFORMANCE

Counseling is a value-added activity which leads to the all important issue of performance measurement. In order to be meaningful, measures of performance must be understood in relative as opposed to absolute terms. Such measures have little or no meaning in the abstract. Instead, they must be benchmarked to some other standard. For example, equity return as a measure of performance is meaningful only if it is compared to another standard such as the returns obtainable from similar types of equity investments in real estate or from alternate forms of investment. Useful measures of performance are always gauged in relation to a specified standard.

Net Present Value

Advances in computer technology and the influence of the discipline of finance were largely responsible for the development of the net present value and internal rate of return methodologies used by the real estate industry beginning in the mid-1970s. Such methodologies have become widespread. The appeal of the net present value and internal rate of return concepts is that they enable market and portfolio strategists to compare readily real estate to alternate forms of investment. In addition, they permit the counselor to measure more accurately the effects of the time value of money, contract rent, lease rollovers, and other property-specific characteristics of a real estate asset.

The net present value (NPV) reflects the present worth of the cash flows of an investment to the extent that it exceeds the equity investment. If the present value is positive, then the investment was profitable. If it is negative, a loss was incurred. For purposes of illustration, assume that a shopping center was purchased for $9 million and that it was resold 5 years later for $12 million. Further

assume that the investment generated the following cash flows which
were received at the end of each year.

Year	Cash Flow	
0	($ 9,000,000)	Equity
1	700,000	
2	757,000	
3	825,000	
4	750,000	
5	835,000	
5	$12,000,000	Resale

The cash flows consist of rent received in each year of the holding
period and the proceeds from resale in the fifth year. Discounting
this income stream at 11% indicates that its present value is
$9,959,258 from which the equity investment of $9 million must be
deducted. The difference between the present value of the cash flows
and the original or equity investment is the net present value or
$959,258 as illustrated below:

Present value of cash flows	$9,959,258
Less equity investment	($9,000,000)
Net present value	$ 959,258

Internal Rate of Return

The internal rate of return (IRR) is another measure of profit or loss.
"It is that discount rate which discounts all returns to equal the original investment. Put another way, it is that discount rate which equates
the present value of the benefits to the present value of the capital out-
lays."[1] The internal rate of return not only measures the profitability
of a particular property but also permits comparison of that property
to other investment opportunities whether real estate or otherwise.

Theoretically, the IRR analysis assumes the investment has already been terminated. In actual practice, however, it can also be
used prospectively in projecting the likely or anticipated performance of a property in the future. Based on the previous example in
the discussion of NPV, use of a hand-held financial calculator indicates that the IRR of that investment is 13.60%

Internal rates of return are important analytical tools in real
estate investment decisions, since they standardize the evaluation

process. The difficulty with IRRs is not in their derivation, which is purely mechanical but rather in development of the projected cash flows, a requisite step. Because spreadsheets can produce widely divergent results depending on the utilized assumptions, the reliability of any IRR analysis depends on the reasonableness of the assumptions made in developing the cash flow model.

The IRR can also be analyzed on a retrospective basis by looking back at a property's performance over a specified period and calculating the profitability of a presumed current sale, based on a transaction that has actually occurred.

Measures Per Square Foot

In operational terms, some of the more important performance measures include retail sales, rental income, occupancy costs, expenses, capture rates, overall capitalization rates, and sale prices on a "per square foot" basis. To have any significance, these measures should be compared with data from similar properties.

Retail Sales

Retail sales per square foot is a significant statistical measure, because it demonstrates the appeal of a particular tenant and the overall competitive strength of the property. It is also illustrative of the spending patterns and affluence of residents of the trade area. Retail sales per square represents the total gross receipts of a particular store divided by its leasable area. It can be calculated on an individual basis whether the property is a single free-standing building or a store in a shopping center or enclosed mall. Widely used sources of sales comparisons include *Dollars and Cents of Shopping Centers*, which is published by the Urban Land Institute, and the *ICSC Retail Barometer*, published by the International Council of Shopping Centers. Retail sales per square foot are also measured as the aggregate volume of retail sales of all stores in a particular shopping center, sales of stores in a smaller portion of the mall, or sales by tenant category. Comparisons can be made to other stores in the trade area as well as to retail sales on a regional and national basis.

There can be considerable differences in retail sales depending on the industry category of the tenant. For example, *Dollars and Cents of Shopping Centers: 1993* indicates that jewelry stores in regional shopping centers achieved median sales of $499.30 per square foot, while median sales in stationery stores were $172.73 per square foot.

Market Rent

Market rent per square foot is another unit of comparison. Market rent is measured on the basis of what competing space commands in the trade area or larger real estate market, as well as on the rents commanded by similar space in the subject property. It is useful in forecasting the upside potential of a property when contract rent is below market levels, and it can demonstrate whether actual rents are above the market and are likely to decline as existing leases expire.

Occupancy Costs

Occupancy costs per square foot are the total cost (i.e., base and percentage rents, CAM charges and expense recoveries, and all other charges) incurred by a tenant to occupy its space. They are used as a measure of affordability to determine if a tenant can afford to pay a particular rent. Industry standards hold that most retailers can pay between 10% and 15% of gross sales in the form of occupancy costs. Thus, assuming gross receipts of $300 per square foot, the tenant could afford to pay occupancy costs equivalent to $30.00 per square foot if 10% were used or $45.00 per square foot if 15% were applied.

Because a tenant can afford to pay a specific rent does not mean that the tenant is willing to pay such rent. Rent is determined by market forces such as supply, demand, location, and physical condition, and is also a product of negotiation. Market rent and tenant affordability are distinct concepts. Nevertheless, they are often misapplied as being synonymous. As a practical matter, such confusion can lead to grossly distorted (i.e., higher) projections of potential revenue and value when market rent is less than what an affordability analysis indicates.

Another problem is that occupancy costs tend to be industry specific. Differences in sales volumes can be vast. If this information is not used judiciously and correctly, significant miscalculations can result.

Retail Sales

The U.S. Department of Commerce provides extensive data on overall retail sales, GAFO, General Apparel, Furniture and retail, and department store sales in selected states and MSAs. This information offers monthly comparisons of the various regions that can be used to benchmark a property strength and weakness in relation to other areas and national averages.

Geographic Information Systems (GIS)

Military and government planners developed Geographic Information Systems (GIS) to provide information on the demographic and economic characteristics of the residents of a defined area. Use of GIS for real estate analysis is important to retailers, developers, analysts, and others interested in detailed information on a particular area. The area under study can be expanded or contracted literally to the nearest street or property. Studies are limited only by the type of information that is data-based by the existing vendors and can provide detailed insights into the affluence, spending patterns, age, and shopping habits of people residing in the control area. Counselors interpret this data to compare the characteristics of a specific market area or property to other trade areas and to shopping centers individually or collectively. Road layouts and physical geography influence the effective use of these systems.

Russell-NCREIF Property Index

The Russell-NCREIF index had measured the historical performance of investment-grade real estate (including retail properties) owned by co-mingled funds on behalf of tax-exempt pension trusts, on an all-cash basis, since 1978. Individual returns are measured on the basis of appraised market value. As of March 1994, there were 1,568 properties with an aggregate appraised value of $22.38 billion in the index.

Total Return includes net income as well as any changes in the asset's value (appreciation or depreciation). It is computed by adding the income return to the capital appreciation return on a quarterly basis.[2] The methodology assumes that the property is purchased at the beginning of the period and that it can be sold at the end of the same period at its appraised value.

$$\text{Total return} = \frac{\text{NOI} + (\text{Sale price} - \text{Purchase price})}{\text{Purchase price}}$$

In calculating Total Return, the actual index also reflects capital improvements as well as sales of partial property interests, which have been ignored here for purposes of simplicity. The actual survey also includes hotel, warehouse, and R & D properties.

The total return for retail properties only were around 3% per quarter (about 12% per year) until the downturn in the real estate market in the early 1990s. At the present time, returns for retail property appear to have peaked for the current cycle.

Income Return measures the portion of total return attributable to each property's net operating income. Because of certain adjustments, this is not precisely the same capitalization rate that an appraiser might use. Nevertheless, if tracked over time, it could indicate trends in capitalization rates. In simplified terms, the Income Return is calculated as follows:

$$\text{Income return} = \frac{\text{NOI}}{\text{Purchase price}}$$

Capital Appreciation Return measures changes in a property's appraised market value, adjusted for any capital improvements or partial sales for the quarter:

$$\text{Capital appreciation return} = \frac{\text{Sale price} - \text{Purchase price}}{\text{Purchase price}}$$

This methodology assumes that any gain or loss (appreciation or depreciation) in appraised value is recognized in each period. Figure 22.1 illustrates the contribution of both income return and capital appreciation to the IRR of retail properties in the survey. It is interesting to note that the income return was almost a flat 2% per quarter (8% per year) since mid-1981 despite fluctuating property values.

The most serious deficiency of The Russell-NCREIF Property Index is that it is based on appraised values and does not reflect actual recorded sales. Assumptions relative to rents, growth rates, expense and occupancy levels, capital appreciation or depreciation, and other major factors are generally based on historical data. Because much of the data lags the market, particularly in times of accelerated change, appraised values sometimes fail to reflect the volatility of existing market conditions. However unintentional, appraisal indices tend to overstate value in the declining phase of a cycle and understate value in a rising phase. Nevertheless, independent studies tend to suggest that the Russell-NCREIF Property Index is useful in demonstrating long-term cyclical trends with a reasonable degree of accuracy.[3]

FIGURE 22.1

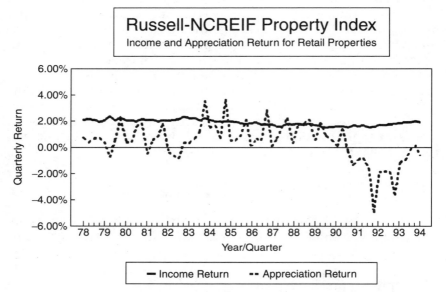

Russell-NCREIF Property Index

Income and Appreciation Return for Retail Properties

— Income Return   ▪▪ Appreciation Return

Source: Jeffrey D. Fisher, Director, Center for Real Estate Studies, Indiana University School of Business.

Psychographics

In order to maximize performance, property managers are continually re-evaluating tenant synergies and leasing strategies. The objective is a tenant mix that is optimally compatible and results in the highest retail sales per square foot. The presumption is that such a balance will produce the greatest rental rates, and, therefore, the highest property value. To achieve this objective, it is necessary to develop an economic and demographic profile of market area residents. Among other things, it is necessary to identify income levels, age distribution, and spending patterns. This process is known as psychographics. It can be as basic or as sophisticated as the needs of the client.

The use of psychographics is likely to increase and grow more refined in the years ahead as the quality and quantity of data sources improves, in tandem with GIS.

Actual Net Operating Results

A performance measure in widespread use is the comparison of actual shopping center operating results against the budgeted numbers, usually on both a quarterly and annual basis. The concept is to analyze how well a given property is operating per line item as a means of determining the relative performance of the property against the benchmark budget. In many instances, such an analysis can assist in spotlighting management weaknesses, or in sensing market trends that affect line item costs.

The obvious drawback of actual against budget analysis is the absolute rather than the relative nature of the comparison, which in many instances can be overcome if there are comparable properties in a given portfolio. Also, various industry sources publish statistics on operating costs per square foot for all property types which provide the investor with a basis on which to judge the operating results of shopping centers by specific type. A widely used source of operating figures is *Dollars & Cents of Shopping Centers*, published every two years by the Urban Land Institute.

There are occasions where this comparative technique may show that management has miscalculated the original annual budget estimate. One common illustration relates to the turnover rate in mall stores in regional malls. Those responsible for budget preparation must base their estimates not only on operating history but also on market trends.

Public Ownership

Due to the increased activity of REITs, other measures of performance have gained in importance. They include dividends, share price, funds from operations (FFO), and funds available for distribution (FAD). The success of REITs is largely attributable to the positive spread between their cost of capital and the total returns on property. The criticism of REIT managers has been their focus on share price, other short-term measures of performance, and their failure to understand that real estate by its nature is more of a long-term investment. In addition to the risk of interest rate swings, some REITs appear to have an inner conflict that results in postponement of needed capital expenditures and other fundamental needs in favor of maintaining a positive image of performance for the benefit of investors, market analysts, and the rating agencies. On the other hand, many REITs maintain a low dividend payout ratio to FFO, in order to use depreciation allowances for major capital improvements, thus assuming competitive parity at a high level. The discerning investor is aware of this.

For some time there has been debate over the use of funds from operations (FFO) as a measure of performance. Although this term is the REIT industry's equivalent of earnings, it has not been adopted as an accounting standard. Neither generally accepted accounting nor the Securities and Exchange Commission recognize the term. Momentum has been growing to use funds available for distribution (FAD) as the formal measure of performance, because it is a better indication of the dividend-paying ability of a REIT. Most analysts calculate FAD by adjusting FFO so that amortization is not deducted and by adjusting FFO further to reflect non-revenue-generating capital expenditures such as roof and HVAC replacement. Thus, the actual revenue generated by a real estate asset, which typically fluctuates, can be more realistically reflected in the REIT's cash flow.[4]

The increasing activity of REITs has also resulted in the heightened awareness of real estate professionals of the importance of the rating agencies, their market analysts and the influence they exert on the securitization process. Analysts have enormous power because of their direct and indirect influence on investors. Because rating agencies determine the cost, and ultimately the success of a public offering, a favorable rating is critical.

Comparative measures of performance between private and public real estate markets are difficult, because participants in each market have distinctly different objectives. REITs tend to be more concerned with growth. Private market participants, however, have longer investment horizons and a greater tolerance for the cyclical nature of real estate returns.

CONCLUSION

Real estate counseling consists of providing advice to assist in the resolution of a particular problem or to achieve a specific objective. Real estate counselors typically receive training in one or more technical areas, such as brokerage, management, underwriting, finance, or appraisal. The counselor builds from a base of formal education and acquired experience to develop multidisciplinary skill sets that are applied in situations requiring special expertise. Such services provide value-added benefits to the client and affect the decision-making process. These services can be in the form of recommending a particular course of action, presenting a series of more or less acceptable options, developing and executing a particular strategy, or otherwise influencing an outcome. In simplest terms, the real estate counselor is an experienced and visionary problem solver.

One of the defining characteristics of real estate counseling is its relationalism. Architects have elevated maintenance of the client relationship to an art form, probably because they are involved in a project from its inception to completion and interact frequently, sometimes daily, with the client. Counselors also recognize the importance of such relationships and that the need for counseling services is continually shaped and defined, indeed justified, by the client. Counselors additionally recognize that communication is the cornerstone of any successful relationship, and that they can be effective only to the extent that they fully understand a client's needs. From this perspective, counselors draw on their advisory skills and practical backgrounds to recommend an appropriate action or attempt to achieve a positive result. Such advice is not merely used to validate a decision that has already been reached. Rather, it is used throughout the decision-making process and often influences a client's behavior. Understandably, the extent to which a client is satisfied determines the strength of the relationship. Success in the form of positive results will serve as the foundation of long-term business relationships.

ENDNOTES

1. The Counselors and the American Institute of Real Estate Appraisers, *The Internal Rate of Return in Real Estate Investments*, (Chicago: American Institute of Real Estate Appraisers, 1988), 1.

2. *The Russell-NCREIF Property Index*, Statistical Appendix, National Council of Real Estate Investment Fiduciaries and Frank Russell Company.

3. "On Reliability of Commercial Appraisals: An Analysis of Properties Sold from the Russell-NCREIF Index (1978–1992)," R. Brian Webb, *Real Estate Finance* (Volume II, Number 1), Spring 1994.

4. "When Are Earnings Not Earnings? When They're FFO, or Is That Just an Accounting FAD?" Barry Vinocur, *Barrons*, October 17, 1994, 30–31.

Epilogue

Melvin Simon

An Epilogue suggests writing about something that is finished; a shopping center is never finished, from the moment of conception through construction, grand opening, and a dozen face lifts or more extensive plastic surgery, unless we have sold it at its prime, or at least before it fades into oblivion.

My brother Herb and I were fortunate to have started our development activities when the shopping center industry was in its infancy. We made mistakes, but no one knew they were mistakes at the time. Interest rates were low and often we were able to borrow out, that is, get enough financing to cover all our costs. Occasionally, we were able to borrow even more than our costs, what the Texans describe as "now-now money."

The attitude of the department store representatives was dramatically different then. I can recall going back to the anchors' real estate representatives and telling them that I had made a mistake by giving such a low rent that I was unable to meet our mortgage obligations. I would then share all our figures and ask for a modest increase. I was never refused. They trusted us and knew that we would be working together and getting them new locations for years to come. That kind of informal personal relationship has largely disappeared.

500

In its place is respect for our size and expertise. We recognized early the need for geographic diversification so that we would not be dependent on local or regional economies. We also realized that the major chains and financing sources—banks, insurance companies, and pension funds—felt more comfortable dealing with larger, more established developers.

That is how we grew to a company with 130 properties containing regional malls, community centers, specialty centers, and mixed-use projects. In addition, we have interests in 14 properties to be developed. The existing centers contain approximately 62 million square feet of gross leasable area (GLA) and are located in 28 states. Recently, we issued $840 million through an initial public offering and are now one of the largest United States' real estate investment trusts (REITs). This process is known as "economic concentration." Today, for example, the ten largest developers own over 418 million square feet or about 8.7% of all shopping center GLA.

It is important to combine education with field experience to become a "situational thinker." Start with a clearly defined objective. Assuming that you want to ultimately become a developer, begin in the leasing or management end of the business. In either of these two fields, you will be exposed to the crucially important elements of retailing, which embrace everything from the evaluation of the suitability of tenants for your centers to their potential for overage rents and their financeability. You will also be exposed to all the operational considerations that determine the financial success of a shopping center. If you approach leasing and/or management with an open mind and questing curiosity, you will build the foundation for a successful career.

When you understand the full implications of a "use" clause or a "relocation" provision, you will have achieved a major goal—thinking like a professional developer. If the construction or accounting aspects of development interest you, once again you can take an entry-level or mid-level job, but adopt the attitude of the developer, approaching every issue and problem not only from the perspective of your job responsibilities, but also from the developer's viewpoint. You will understand the implications for him and the center's success, regardless of size.

Look at each aspect of every problem, keeping in mind that each situation, its characteristics, and the personalities involved are unique.

I wish I could prepare you for the future by forecasting the changes that are likely to take place. You are already familiar with the demographic trends, that is, the graying of America, the growth of ethnic groups, and the likely effect these will have on merchandise mix and retailing.

Here is my view of what is likely to happen during your active period in the shopping center field. First, department stores will continue their mergers and acquisitions at a declining rate until there are only a small number of players in the field. This consolidation will give the dominant chains the negotiating strength to exact even more subsidies from the mall developers. Most of their new locations will be in existing dominant centers. From a retailing standpoint, department stores will remain the main outlet for adult apparel, even though the number of shopping trips to department stores will continue to decline.

B and C quality centers will be redeveloped and strengthened into different uses. Some will become more value-oriented and others more entertainment-driven. Larger space users offering more-for-less will become dominant players in enclosed malls.

Power centers will continue to multiply except at a decreasing rate with the inevitable overbuilding problem by the year 2000. Once again, merger and acquisition mania will lead to the elimination of many competitors in each category. The resulting vacancies will have to be devoted to other services, special interest, nonretail, and even light industrial uses.

Outlet centers will grow both in size and number at an accelerating pace for the next few years and, in the process, will move closer and closer to their department store customers—despite their protests. This process will dramatically undermine the value of outlying suburban locations, which currently characterize this form of retailing. Once again, mergers and acquisitions will reduce the field to a few dominant players.

With ever-increasing frequency, there will be a significant movement of chain retailers to neighborhood and community shopping center locations, where convenience for the customer, which contiguous parking can satisfy, will be a primary consideration. Recreation units—themed and otherwise—will proliferate as a device to attract families to shopping centers.

Perhaps the most significant changes will occur as a direct result of the information highway technical revolution. Customers will be able to step in front of a preprogrammed electronic mirror, punch in an identification number for a particular style, and will be able to see on screen exactly how the finished, altered product will look on them. There will be a rapid growth in home interactive shopping technology.

The shopper also will be able to order a variety of merchandise, not in stock, via in-store computers, with the items being delivered either to their homes or the store where they were purchased. There will be other manifestations of this trend to target special groups with definable tastes and adequate disposable income.

The merger and acquisition trends of category killers will also affect the three dominant warehouse chains. At one point, Price Club was averaging $166 million annually per unit. That average has dropped by 33% in the last few years. The trend will continue and force warehouse chains to increase the number of items they carry, thus, placing greater pressure on profits or forcing higher prices. There also will be an explosion of novel retailing concepts stimulated by technological developments, but also by new trends in health, environment, and fashion.

If I could ask my crystal ball where the funding would be found for these new manifestations, I feel certain I would get a one-word answer—securitization.

Mortgage financing will take the form of mortgage bonds and centers will be acquired through additional public offerings of REITs, who with all this surplus cash will establish the market for shopping centers. Developers will get their centers evaluated by rating agencies and then sell bonds to the corporate bond departments of insurance companies as a substitute for conventional mortgages.

For other questions, my crystal ball remains, in all candor, quite murky. Some turns that our society and government took over the last 25 years were foreseen by few if any observers. Many of us were surprised by oil crises, wage and price controls, a war in the Persian Gulf, and the savings and loan fiasco. As I write this, nobody is quite sure about the final shape of health care legislation and its impact on operations. Other issues that nobody can see on the horizon now may eventually have an incalculable effect on business.

But from this cloud of uncertainty, I can see one clear image, I see you and other newcomers to our industry as paratroopers, grabbing the nearest parachute and preparing to jump into an uncharted future. All your preparations can assist you as you descend through the turbulence, but the winds of change may blow you far off course. What you learned from this book, a little luck, and a lot of your own shrewdness can help you survive in this unfamiliar territory.

Index